Higher Education Developments:
The Technological Universities 1956–1976

SOCIETY TODAY AND TOMORROW
General Editor: A. H. Halsey

CONSTITUENCY POLITICS: *A Study of Newcastle-under-Lyme*
   by Frank Bealey, J. Blondel and W. P. McCann
MODERN BRITISH POLITICS
   by Samuel Beer
WINCHESTER AND THE PUBLIC SCHOOL ELITE
   by T. J. H. Bishop and Rupert Wilkinson
TELEVISION IN POLITICS
   by Jay G. Blumler and Denis McQuail
LSD, MAN AND SOCIETY
   by Richard C. DeBold and Russell C. Leaf
PEOPLE AND PLANNING: *The Sociology of Housing in Sunderland*
   by Norman Dennis
PUBLIC PARTICIPATION AND PLANNERS' BLIGHT
   by Norman Dennis
THE FAWLEY PRODUCTIVITY AGREEMENTS
   by Allan Flanders
IS SCIENTIFIC MANAGEMENT POSSIBLE?
   by Joe Kelly
ART STUDENTS OBSERVED
   by Charles Madge and Barbara Weinberger
POLITICAL MOBILIZATION
   by J. P. Nettl
THE YOUNG WORKER AT COLLEGE: *A Study of a Local Tech.*
   by Ethel Venables
APPRENTICES OUT OF THEIR TIME: *A Follow-up Study*
   by Ethel Venables

PETER VENABLES

Higher Education Developments: The Technological Universities 1956–1976

FABER AND FABER
LONDON · BOSTON

First published in 1978
by Faber and Faber Limited
3 Queen Square London WC1
Printed in Great Britain by
Latimer Trend & Company Ltd
All rights reserved

British Library Cataloguing in Publication Data

Venables, *Sir* Peter
  Higher education developments. –
  (Society today and tomorrow).
  1. Technical education – Great Britain – History,
  20th century
  2. Universities and colleges – Great Britain –
  History, 20th century
  I. Title II. Series
  378.41   T107

ISBN 0–571–10283–2

Contents

Preface

THE changes in higher education in the 1950s and 1960s, accelerated by the publication of the Robbins Committee Report in 1963, were substantial and far-reaching. Of these, the designation of the Colleges of Advanced Technology (CATs) from 1956 onwards, their attainment of independent status as direct grant institutions in 1962, and of University status with Royal Charters in 1966–67, constituted an unprecedented sequence of institutional transformations. Having played a continuing part in the developments over the period 1956–69, I had it in mind that on retirement I might make a study of the institutional changes involved. This I was encouraged to do by Sir Keith (now Lord) Murray, Director of the Leverhulme Trust, which subsequently made a grant for the project of up to £7,800 over three years to the University of Aston for the appointment of a graduate secretary and to cover travel and other expenses. This was for my proposal for 'A study of *British Technological Universities* i.e. more particularly a study of the transition to University status of the former Colleges of Advanced Technology'.

The onlooker may see most of the game but the insider is more apt to feel the stresses and strains, the uncertainties, hopes and fears of so strenuous a period of development. However, as observing participant, he must be prepared to minimise the predilections and shortcomings inherent in his experience within only one institution. Sustained visits to each institution, and the recording of many individual interviews and of small discussion groups, were therefore essential. So also were the specific enquiries made of academic staff at all levels as well as of Members of Council and of the members of the Academic Advisory Committees. In addition, a wide range of publications and statistical material was collected with the generous help of the Vice-Chancellors and Principals concerned, as well as their senior

7

staff, particularly the Registrars. To those involved in these various ways, I was and remain greatly indebted for all their invaluable help, and for the many courtesies so readily extended to me.

The total sample of institutions comprised ten former CATs in England and Heriot-Watt University in Scotland. As the study progressed, however, it was concentrated to some degree on the eight independent Technological Universities in England. Two aspects which affected the time-scale of the study became increasingly important. First of all, it became clear that the Technological Universities would have to establish themselves in a world very different from that envisaged in 1963 when the Robbins Committee reported. For example, they would have to contend with the competition for diminishing resources (including students) arising not least from the emergence of the Polytechnics. The programme of study was therefore extended to include a sample of Polytechnics – time and resources simply did not permit a detailed study of them all. Visits were arranged, and published material including statistics was gathered with the generous help of their Directors, as well as from P. L. Flowerday, Secretary of the Committee of Directors of Polytechnics (CDP).

The second aspect of the time-scale of the study was the question of the minimum period of years which would provide a reasonable basis for comparison of the functions and work of the CATs with those of the Technological Universities they became. Had they in fact held to their ideas and practices in a new context, or had they merely provided a study in conforming influences on joining 'the University club', and simply become neo-civic in character? In the circumstances it became clear that a period of ten years before and after the granting of the Charters in 1966 was a minimum basis for comparison of their progress and of changes within them, i.e. the total period 1956 to 1976.

The Leverhulme Trust appreciated the necessities of widening the scope of the study and of the consequential increase of time, but of course there was no increase of grant. I remain most grateful to the Trust for their support, and particularly in being able to appoint Mrs J. B. Dixon BA, as secretary (and *de facto* research assistant) from June 1970. Her work was excellent in every respect, and her ability, competence and tolerant resilience were altogether exceptional. In September 1969 the University of Aston appointed me to a University Fellowship, held until August 1972, with accommodation and other facilities provided, which were also enjoyed by my wife as a former Senior Research Fellow. The University also generously continued Mrs Dixon's appointment until April 1976, when she left for family reasons. Accommodation and facilities have continued to be available, and my wife and I have thus been very fortunate in being able to continue our work in retirement up to the present in very congenial conditions; we are very grateful indeed to the Vice-Chancellor, Dr J. A. Pope, and to the Senate, for making this possible. My thanks are due also to Mr Douglas Porter, University Planning Officer, for much practical help.

Help is also gratefully acknowledged from sources other than those already mentioned, namely, Sir William Pile, former Permanent Secretary, and Mr K. G. Forecast, Director of Statistics at the Department of Education and Science; Sir Frederick Dainton FRS, Chairman of the University Grants Committee; Mr R. St. J. Walker CBE, Secretary of the Science Research Council; the Office of the Committee of Vice-Chancellors and Principals (CVCP), and particularly Mr Brian Taylor, the Executive Secretary; and to Dr Edwin Kerr, Chief Officer, CNAA. Responses to enquiries from individuals, too numerous to list, are warmly acknowledged. As for stimulating comparative studies, I have been indebted to Dr Clark Kerr, Chairman of the Carnegie Commission on Higher Education in the USA, for the receipt of many of the volumes sponsored and published by the Commission in their monumental series. The text makes very evident my indebtedness to many published sources, especially those of HMSO, as well as to *The Times Higher Educational Supplement* for its excellent coverage of the contemporary scene. Thanks are due to the following for the use of quotations in the text: Sir John Hunter, Professor Mary Douglas, Dr Clark Kerr, Penguin Books Ltd. The opportunity to quote freely from the work, *The British Academics*, by A. H. Halsey and Martin Trow (with Oliver Fulton's assistance), particularly for comparative purposes, and to use items from their questionnaires, is gladly acknowledged. However, responsibility for the interpretation and use of statistical and other material from all the foregoing sources is of course entirely mine.

Looking back over the eventful years, I feel I must take the opportunity to pay tribute to the lay members of Governing Bodies, Councils and Committees for their indispensable contributions to the well-being and effectiveness of our institutions. In general they are exemplified by those whose names are recorded in the Brief Histories but, as author, I have particular pleasure in recording my great indebtedness to three chairmen with whom I was closely associated: Alderman John Brentnall at the Royal Technical College, Salford, where I was Principal 1947–56; Dr J. J. Gracie CBE, at the Birmingham College of Advanced Technology, 1956–62; and Sir Joseph Hunt MBE, at the College 1962–66, who then became Pro-Chancellor and Chairman of Council of the University of Aston in Birmingham.

Finally, to all these proper and cordial acknowledgements, I cannot fail to add a very personal note. For forty-five years my wife, Ethel Venables, and I have shared and discussed our academic and professional interests, to our mutual advantage; and to mine certainly, most of all, in the making of this study and the writing of this book. More particularly, she designed the statistical enquiries as recorded by her in Appendix IV. These have been very busy years for both of us, and for all such sharing over so long a period of time I naturally am profoundly grateful.

PETER VENABLES

1

From Technical School to Technological University

LIKE all other educational institutions, technological ones are both the products and the causes of change in society. They cannot be protected from the stresses and strains involved in such change, nor isolated from a wide range of influences, including those of a conforming character. Institutions of higher education have sustained and increased the rate of scientific discovery and its application in the emergence of modern technological nations, and have themselves changed accordingly. Such developments have also profoundly affected the structure of society, the range and kind of employment available, the standard of living and the use of leisure, and indeed the economic and political relationships between nations.

These institutions also ensure the continuity of modern civilisations by preserving and extending culture, science and the arts, and by providing vocational, professional and adult education. In recent times, however, the basis of society has been threatened increasingly by the impact of technological innovation, and this has emphasised the importance of fostering the biological and the social sciences alongside the physical ones.

In the last decade, the purposes and functions of higher educational institutions throughout the world have thus been increasingly the subject of sceptical enquiry, even of hostile attack from without, and of anxious concern and radically divisive philosophies and responses from within. 'Men make institutions, institutions mould men', said Winston Churchill, but it is important to note that the men and women who are thus moulded by institutions are mostly those who did not make them. Moulding constraints are of course indispensable to the continuity of civilised society, but its institutions and their moulding purposes need to be understood and modified in response to the changing needs and aspirations of mankind.

11

In former times the slow rate of change enabled the moulds to be turned to developing needs at a reasonably commensurate rate. Now the pace and character of change, induced by science and technology, produce problems which cannot be contained or solved within the traditional moulds, and the resulting stresses and strains put a premium on understanding and reasonable action. Men and women are less and less inclined to acquiesce quietly to the institutional moulds designed by their forefathers, as these are keenly felt to embody irritating, not to say highly abrasive, outmoded values and practices. They thus feel compelled to remould their existing institutions – whether they be educational or social, political or religious – to redesign them, and to establish entirely new ones: to require institutions, indeed, that will secure humane objectives and desirable social advances within their own lifetime, and not in some distant future period.

There is one further consideration which underlies this sense of urgency. Education is perforce the basis of a technological society, but it is now beginning to be understood that it is no less an indispensable defence against its abuses if that society is to become truly democratic, and to remain so. 'Without education, human opportunities and lasting satisfactions and the citizen's rights are apt to wither away, a fact not overlooked by dictators. "Power always tends to corrupt, absolute power corrupts absolutely", said Acton. Technological power can all too readily become an absolutely corrupting power, as the last three decades right up to the present bear frequent and terrible witness. Access to education is therefore increasingly felt to be of paramount importance, and it should not be subject to arbitrary, unreasonable or removable barriers on the part of the institutions which provide it.'[1]

This study is concerned with the development of technological institutions in this country during two decades. The first, starting in 1956, when the Colleges of Advanced Technology were designated, covers their progress until 1966 when they became Universities. The second ten years sees them establishing themselves as a definitive section of the University system, both nationally and internationally. This period also saw the designation of the Polytechnics and other major developments in Further Education. The changing character of all these institutions must be seen in relation to the changing nature of the society of which they are a part.

The evolution of human society has taken place sequentially in

12

four main phases: the nomadic, the agrarian, the industrial and, most recently, the technological. Profound changes in economic and social structure, combined with an accelerating rate of change, have characterised the last two phases so that the word 'revolution' rather than 'evolution' comes more readily to mind. The inescapable stresses and strains involved, the adjustments, transformations and innovations of economic, political and social structures to meet changing needs, bear most hardly where the rate of change is fastest and is seemingly compelled from without. This is most evident with the underdeveloped countries in a world increasingly dominated by modern technological societies and systems, mainly those of Europe, Russia and the United States.

The four phases of development are characterised by an increasing withdrawal of labour from the land to towns of increasing size and complexity, which require ever-growing complex services to sustain them. A second characteristic is increasing horsepower/wattage per worker in productive industry with increasing productivity. In turn this leads to a diminution in the proportion of workers in productive industry relative to those in secondary and tertiary occupations as, for example, in engineering and coalmining compared with those employed in commerce and the distributive trades, and in social, governmental and other service occupations and professions. Primary industries become increasingly capital-intensive, agriculture included, while the secondary and tertiary sectors remain labour-intensive.

Such characteristics and trends might indicate an incipient transition from the technological to a sociological phase, a transition towards greater and not less complexity, because of the greater indeterminacy of the sociological problems as compared with the technological ones. In relation to this, we may note that the industrial phase grew out of a scientific empiricism and pragmatism, whereas rigorous scientific research and application is indispensable to the technological phase. By contrast, research, for the incipient psycho-sociological phase has scarcely begun, and is certainly not commensurate with present, let alone future, needs – as witness, for example, the founding of the Department of Scientific and Industrial Research (DSIR) in 1916 (now the Science Research Council – SRC), and the Social Science Research Council (SSRC) as late as 1965.

As expanding cities have coalesced into conurbations, states and nations have combined into supranational groups, almost coincident

13

with continents and with ever-increasing economic power, for which the furtherance of science and technology is vital. In this context science and technology know no frontiers, with the creation perforce of international cartels to exploit them to the full. For all the debate about other aspects, this is the scientific-technological, and therefore economic, reality of being in the Common Market.

The inherent educational implications and consequences have yet to be worked out, though innovations have already begun in British tertiary institutions. Indeed, educational changes are the concomitants of social, political and economic changes. They may frequently be delayed, through unawareness or inertia in institutions, and even through active hostility on the part of their members. The slow, reluctant introduction of science and technology into British Universities, as recounted by Eric Ashby,[2] fully exemplifies such reactions.

Because of their major commitment to technology, the Technological Universities and Polytechnics are open to particularly searching questions, the answers to which are among the close concerns of this book. For example, are Technological Universities, and Polytechnics also, simply service-stations for a technological society, the values of which are beyond question? What are and what should be the relationships of higher educational institutions to society at large, to government, industry, commerce and the professions? What should be the nature of their governance to relate them responsibly to the needs of society and no less to protect their autonomy against undue political and economic pressures? What should be the breadth, specialisation and relevance of their studies, and what is the significance and feasibility of general studies? How far should admission procedures and range of courses take account of the special needs of disadvantaged groups in society?

These questions have acquired a sharper cutting edge because of the changing social conditions and human expectations of the last decade. The attempt to answer some of these questions has led to the emergence of new institutions and the substantial modification or change of direction of others,[3] and calls for comment on related educational terminology.

Long-term pressures, exerted against widespread inertia if not active professional resistance, have impelled us towards the belated recognition of the underlying unity of 'higher education' and 'Further Education' which also includes 'Teacher Education' (formerly 'Teacher Training'), professional education, adult education and leisure activities (in Evening Institutes). All these must be considered as integral parts of the last of the three major phases of the educational system – primary, secondary, tertiary. Tertiary education covers the whole range of educational provision for adult citizens.

Raising of the school-leaving age has always been followed over the years by increased enrolments in Further and higher education. So we may expect that the proportion staying on at school will continue to increase, and that day release will be increasingly supplemented by block release and sandwich courses in schools and Junior Colleges which will share the same educational aims and provide similar social and counselling services for adolescent students. The present overlap between secondary schools and Technical Colleges is likely to be a transient problem and there are sound psychological considerations for marking the attainment of adult citizenship at eighteen in an unambiguous educational way, that is by eligibility for entry to tertiary institutions.

With the exception of Brunel, which began as Acton Technical College in 1928, the Technological Universities stem from part-time classes which started in the nineteenth century, and the earliest of the technological institutions derive from Mechanics' Institutes originating in the period 1820–35. The best history of the origins of the further education colleges is *Mechanics' Institutes of Lancashire and Yorkshire before 1851* by Mabel Tylecote.[4] The Mechanics' Institutes are indeed the spiritual ancestors not only of the Technological Universities but of some Civic Universities as well.[5]

Impetus for change came with the 1851 Exhibition, made more urgent with the unfavourable comparisons in the 1862 Exhibition of British products with those of Continental manufacturers, and strengthened by Lyon Playfair's advocacy of the need to develop technical education. The establishment of the Department of Science and Art in 1853 and of the Education Department, into which it was incorporated, in 1857, were indispensable steps forward.[6] Their examinations proved a positive catalyst of change – an early adumbration of 'the importance of being qualified'[7] – and the same was true of those of the Society of Arts from 1856 and, later still, of the examinations of the City and Guilds of London Institute, founded in 1881. In the north, the Union of Lancashire and Cheshire Institutes, founded in 1839, pioneered examinations from 1847 onwards.

W. H. G. Armytage, commenting on the Paris Exhibition of 1867, writes, 'When English industrialists heard that their exhibits . . . were characterised as "slovenly intruded heaps of raw material mingled with pieces of rusty iron", intimations of their mortality began to dawn on them.'[8] Progress was slow, intermittent and unpredictable, and between 1902 and 1918 no more than ten technical schools were built. The 1914–18 war produced another fitful spurt, but the impulse to establish compulsory part-time day education under the Fisher Acts of 1917 and 1919 petered out except at Rugby.[9]

The ardent advocacy of Lord Eustace Percy over several years raised hopes of substantial progress and in 1929 he felt that 'there were signs that during the next ten years there would be a national development in technical education as broad and far-reaching as that seen during the last twenty years in secondary education.'[10] The world economic blizzard of 1929–30 blighted all such hopes, and developments began again only in the late 1930s, and then on a scale totally inadequate for the enormous load of work so soon to fall upon the Technical Colleges in World War II. The Colleges responded magnificently to wartime tasks, by acquiring and making use of whatever buildings were available, however unsuitable and inadequate for the purpose. 'Make do and mend', a wartime necessity, was highly detrimental to technical education, but the policy continued into the 1950s.

Day courses were soon added to evening classes in arts, crafts and domestic science, but they remained a small proportion of the total enrolments. Secondly, advanced work grew slowly, but derived strength from the London University external degree system. For the then Polytechnics in London, a definitive stage was reached with the University of London Act in 1898, which led to the system of having some of their teachers recognised by the University, enabling their matriculated students to take internal degrees of the University.

Nationally from 1921 onwards part-time day advanced work grew under the National Certificate schemes, with 'endorsements' thereon which exempted holders from the requirements for professional examinations. In due time, however, courses for Ordinary National Certificate were transferred to other local institutions of less standing, while Higher National Certificate courses, and subsequently Higher National Diplomas also, were concentrated in the major technological institutions. Such changes and reorganisations were a normal feature of growth, varying only in detail in the particular institution. It is therefore totally misleading to represent the shedding of courses by the Colleges of Advanced Technology on becoming Universities as a quite novel and unjustifiable aspect of their evolution.

General education and social activities were included from the earliest days. However, with notable exceptions such as the Regent Street Polytechnic, the provision was voluntary and very limited. Official policy changed slowly, but with enlightened developments in various Local Authorities, such as the Essex Technical Colleges under Sir John Sargent's leadership, so that such work and activities became more widely recognised as an integral part of the educational work of a Technical College.

Technical education became a duty of the Local authorities only with the passing of the 1944 Education Act, but it remained a loosely knit system responding variously to the needs of the times under the guidance of the Regional Advisory Councils (RACs). These were established as a result of the Percy Committee Report on Higher Technological Education, which was the first of many post-war reports[11] stressing the increased need for scientists and technologists, especially in industry. The nine RACs had the National Advisory Committee for Industry and Commerce (NACEIC) at the apex. This Council raised the question of creating a central awarding body many times and eventually, in July 1955 the Government established the National Council for Technological Awards (NCTA) under the chairmanship of Lord Hives for the award of the Diploma in Technology (Dip.Tech.). This was not a degree but was to be regarded as a degree equivalent, a limitation which was removed when its successor, the Council for National Academic Awards (CNAA), was established with a Royal Charter in 1964.

1956 White Paper on Technical Education

The Ministry of Education Pamphlet No. 8, *Further Education*, published in 1946, envisaged a new structure for Local Colleges of Further Education and Regional Colleges, with new roles and defined catchment areas, but this did not become official planning policy until the publication of a White Paper ten years later in February 1956*. This set out a plan for the Technical Colleges of England and Wales, based on a five-year capital development pro-

* *Technical Education* (Cmnd. 9703, HMSO 1956).

gramme of £70m, with a rapid increase in the capacity of advanced courses from 9,500 to about 15,000. Students in these courses became eligible for State Scholarships.

The Government strongly endorsed a report on sandwich courses by NACEIC[12] which recommended that expansion was to be mainly in courses leading to the award of the Dip.Tech. and that the bulk of full-time or sandwich courses should be carried on in Colleges which concentrated on advanced courses at technological (as distinct from technician) level. The 1956 White Paper listed in para. 68 twenty-four colleges in receipt of 75 per cent grant for certain parts of their advanced work, and the Government confirmed its wish to see 'the proportion of advanced work at these Colleges vigorously increased, so that as many of them as possible may develop speedily into Colleges of Advanced Technology'. Strong governing bodies were essential, with power to spend within the heads of annual estimates approved by the Local Authority. The scale and standard of staffing were to be improved, and the academic staff were to be given 'appropriate freedom to plan their courses'.

The building-up of the Advanced Colleges was not intended to prevent development of advanced courses elsewhere, especially the part-time ones, and the White Paper noted that some 150 Colleges already provided Higher National Certificate and other advanced part-time courses. In retrospect, this can be seen as a serious failure to grasp the nettle of concentration, the lack of which has plagued the development of advanced work ever since. Circular 305 which followed[13] delineated a structure of Local Colleges, Area Colleges, Regional Colleges and, at the apex, the Colleges of Advanced Technology. More specifically, the last group were 'to provide a broad range and substantial volume of work exclusively at advanced level (whether in full-time, sandwich or part-time courses), including postgraduate and research work', and which satisfied conditions set out in the Appendix to the Circular. The Minister considered it important that 'a small number of Colleges should develop as speedily as possible into Colleges of Advanced Technology concentrating entirely on advanced studies and providing a broad range of work of the highest quality . . . such Colleges will be required to comply with certain conditions in respect of administration, finance, staffing and accommodation.' The Minister proposed 'to announce a provisional list of Colleges of Advanced Technology . . . (which) will be formally designated as soon as the Minister is able to satisfy himself the

College already fulfils the conditions or will be able to do so in the near future'.

In the event eight were provisionally designated[14] and later confirmed by the Minister:

Birmingham College of Technology
Bradford Technical College
Cardiff College of Technology and Commerce
Loughborough College of Technology
Royal Technical College, Salford
and in London, *Battersea*, *Chelsea* and *Northampton Polytechnics*.

Two others were considered: *Bristol College of Technology*, which was later confirmed; and *Rutherford College, Newcastle upon Tyne*, which was not, and which eventually became a Polytechnic. *Brunel College of Technology* was added to this list in 1962. The remainder of the twenty-four institutions in receipt of 75 per cent grant became the nucleus of some twenty-five institutions subsequently recognised as Regional Colleges. The foregoing basic structure is set out in Diagram 1.1, and it remained broadly the same until after the Robbins Report in 1963. In due course the Regional Colleges named in Diagram 1.1 became the Polytechnics.*

Technical education had evolved differently in Scotland, with a strong group of central institutions and a less adequate system of Local Colleges compared with England and Wales. The continuance of this structure was accepted in the White Paper, but reinforcement was considered essential especially at local level. A capital grant of £10m was allocated for this purpose. Seven of the central institutions were technical in character, the leading ones being the Royal Technical College, Glasgow, and the Heriot-Watt College, Edinburgh.

The change of status requiring exclusive concentration on advanced work speeded the process of shedding craft, technician and similar courses which was already under way. This in turn meant an increased intake for the Local Colleges, and in some cases the creation of new ones. At Birmingham, for example, it meant the creation of two separate Colleges in 1957–58.

The academic situation in the Colleges up to 1955 had been one of almost total dependence on approval of courses by external bodies. This meant that academic boards, wherever and in whatever form they existed, were largely formal in character. The main examining bodies were London University concerning both external and in-

* See Table AIIIf for details.

Diagram 1.1 Structure of technical education at the time of publication of the Robbins Committee Report

Qualifications		Present number	Likely future number	Types of courses	Courses for
Dip.Tech., BSc. London; professional qualifications; postgraduate diplomas; higher degrees & diplomas	Colleges of Advanced Technology	10——→?		PT +FT	University level only TGT +P + research + postgraduate
Some Dip.Tech. & BSc. London; professional qualifications; Higher National Diplomas & Certificates; City & Guilds Final examinations	?. Regional Colleges	25——→30?		PT +FT	Superior TN + C + some TGT +P +some postgraduate + research
Some Higher and Ordinary National Certificates; some City & Guilds Final and Inter examinations; general education e.g. GCE O- and A-level; domestic and catering courses (a)	? Area Colleges	155 (b)→210 (b)		PT +FT	TN +C + some P
Ordinary National Certificates; City and Guilds Inter and some Final examinations; general education e.g. GCE O-level and some A-level; full-time domestic and catering courses, etc. (a)	? Local Colleges of Further Education	275? (b)→?(b)		PT +FT	TN +C + general education

Note (a): commercial courses not indicated, though many Technical Colleges have commerce departments and courses; the same is true for art courses and schools within Technical Colleges

Four-tier structure – see White Paper on Technical Education (Cmd 9703) and Ministry of Education Circular 305

Note (b): no official numbers yet stated

PT = Part-time courses
FT = Full-time courses including sandwich courses

TGT = technologists
TN = technicians
C = craftsmen
P = courses to graduateship of professional institutions

Colleges of Advanced Technology: Battersea (London); Birmingham; Bradford; Bristol; Brunel (Middlesex); Chelsea (London); Loughborough; Northampton (London); Salford; Welsh (Cardiff)

Regional Colleges: Borough (London); Brighton; Brixton (London); Hatfield College of Technology; Huddersfield; Kingston-upon-Thames; Lanchester College of Technology; Coventry; Leeds College of Technology; Leicester; Liverpool (Building); Liverpool (Technology); North Staffordshire; Northern (London); Nottingham; Plymouth and Devonport; Portsmouth; Rugby; Rutherford College of Technology (Newcastle-upon-Tyne); Sir John Cass (London); South East Essex Technical College, School of Art (Dagenham); Sunderland; The Polytechnic (London); Treforest; West Ham; Woolwich (London)

Note: The diagram oversimplifies somewhat by omitting specific reference to separate Colleges of Art, Colleges of Commerce, National Colleges and their various relationships with Technical Colleges, quite a number of which themselves contained Schools of Art and Departments of Commerce and, in a few cases, National Colleges as well.

ternal degree courses, and the Ministry of Education joint committees with professional institutions concerning courses for Higher National Certificates and Diplomas. In a relatively few instances College Associateship courses were recognised by the respective professional institutions for full or partial exemption from their own final examinations.

In this respect the National Council for Technological Awards exercised a very powerful and beneficial influence, by making it possible for the Colleges to develop and administer their own Dip.Tech. courses. These were designed by academic staff according to principles generally applicable to whole groups of courses, instead of isolated ones, thus requiring the kind of joint discussion and decision-making appropriate to academic boards. Though the system appeared in some ways to be similar to that used for approving National Diploma courses, in reality contact and fruitful discussion took place directly with the visiting boards appointed by NCTA. Most important of all were the External Examiners, recommended by the College and approved by NCTA.

Unlike the remote, anonymous Assessors of the National Certificate and Diploma system, they worked closely with academic staff in general support of the courses, and specifically in the moderation of examinations set by the College staff. Their appointments were generally for three years but renewable, and this continuity of influence was important. The approval of courses following visitation by NCTA boards was for five years, and this again was another important factor in the growth of confidence and independence within the colleges. Criteria for approval by NCTA related to the suitability of the curriculum, the qualifications of the staff, the facilities and accommodation within the particular college, and the proportion of advanced work in them. These were applied rigorously but not punitively, and were powerful levers in moving governing bodies and LEAs to improve standards accordingly. After the Robbins Report, the NCTA was replaced by the CNAA, which operates an essentially similar system.

The standard of the Dip.Tech. was set at the level of an honours degree of a British University, and this later came under criticism as being too exclusive. It was generally supposed that Dip.Tech. would be awarded almost wholly for sandwich courses, but in practice over the years the proportion of traditional three-year full-time courses increased, a continuing trend under the CNAA which has been heavily criticised as weakening the commitment of institutions to sandwich courses.

A third substantial criticism was that Dip.Tech. courses too closely resembled University degree courses in content and method. This ignored the fact that within sandwich courses the aim is to make the link between the training for industry and the academic study periods as close and mutually supportive as possible. This unawareness revealed the inertia of past practice but also suggested some sensitivity about the implied criticism of traditional practice. It could also be held to exemplify a quite normal academic (not to say wholly human) feeling when facing change, that any change from the traditional is bound to be a change for the worse; which is perhaps akin to the reaction of administrators that nothing should ever be tried for the first time, especially if it is original.

Before the designation of the Colleges as CATs, their governing bodies (apart from those in the London Polytechnics and Loughborough) shared responsibility with the LEAs who tended to be the dominating partner. The College office was an outpost of the LEA office, and the office staff were responsible ultimately to the Chief Education Officer and not to the Principal. The establishment of posts not only needed approval by the Education Committee but also by the Establishment Committee of the Council.

The consequent rigorous application of existing criteria was felt, for example, very severely in the lack of clerical posts and in the limitation of laboratory technicians. The College was apt to be treated simply as one of many under the LEA and its proposals were subject always to the first consideration in mind: 'If we do it for you, we will have to do it for the others.' Even after achieving special status there was still the external control of establishment, especially of grading and salaries of posts, the control of furniture, apparatus and equipment by the LEA's Sites and Buildings Sub-Committee, and the delay of final approval of expenditure above certain meagre limits (such as £50–£100) until passed by the Further Education Sub-Committee, the Education Committee and the Council. With all this, the frustrations of having a governing body (*sic*) which was simply a sub-committee of a sub-committee of the Education Committee of the Council[15] remained real enough.

The Regional Advisory Councils existed for the approval of courses in the colleges of the particular region and the prevention of wasteful duplication among them. Prior to designation the Advanced Colleges were subject to these procedures and each was treated as one among many, i.e. many institutions with supposedly similar claims; inevitably thereafter they found the regional supervision increasingly irksome. While they endeavoured to assume their special position by informing the Regional Councils of their plans rather than asking for approval, it was not until after independence in 1962 that the Ministry dealt with this problem in their favour. The Advanced Colleges then began to approach the position of the Universities by simply informing the respective Councils of their proposed developments. This has brought the criticism that the Advanced Colleges 'had simply opted for regional irresponsibility',[16] but it was a nonsense to treat the apex in the same way as the rest of the complex pyramid of institutions (as the Polytechnics were themselves later to discover).

Another problem was that of employer-employee relationships, as between LEA-governing body and academic staff. The Principal was the focal point of functioning between these two spheres, passing down policies and instructions from on high and, much less frequently, perhaps even rarely, passing views and recommendations upwards from the staff. Not surprisingly, similar authoritarian relationships were apt to obtain from the Heads of Departments downwards; and the roles and relationships of Principal and Heads especially suffered sharp reorientation, which engendered quite severe strains in the changes of 1962 and 1966–67.

Accommodation problems were acute. Where courses were shed, the workshops and other rooms vacated were seldom appropriate to the new demands. Building plans thus became an early and persistent preoccupation. At Bradford and Birmingham the eventual result was a very substantial expansion of city centre sites despite existing land values,[17] but the far more costly London sites posed altogether more formidable problems of expansion.

Committee of Principals

From 1956 onwards the Colleges of Advanced Technology felt the need to establish a common understanding as a basis for joint action where this seemed desirable. The Principals were loyal members of the Association of Principals of Technical Institutions and were reluctant at first to form their own group lest they appear to be separatist and divisive.

23

However, their common needs prevailed, and the Principals first met together on 6th June 1957.* Lack of a voice to represent their interests led them to make a formal announcement of the establishment of their Committee in June 1959. Fifty-four meetings were held, the last being on 13th January 1965, just before the Principals became members of the Committee of Vice-Chancellors and Principals of the Universities of the United Kingdom (CVCP). The Principals' Committee could not make decisions which were binding on their institutions, but there was a great deal of agreement which resulted in similar action within them, to a far greater degree than they later experienced or witnessed within the admittedly much larger VC's Committee. That was not merely a question of size, but one especially of the rigour of institutional autonomy, whereby the prospect of common action was apt to fade away through a timeless series of interdependent bottlenecks; and the case for the Universities thus went by default.

On a regular basis and additionally as necessity required, the Principals' Committee had invited senior officers of the Ministry to their meetings and this proved invaluable for clarifying if not always resolving common problems. This again was in sharp contrast to the relationship which obtained between the VC's Committee and the UGC at the time the Principals of the Colleges became Vice-Chancellors.

Among the many concerns of the Principals' Committee the lack of higher academic awards was one of the most urgent. Advice was taken as to whether there was any legal barrier to the Colleges awarding their own higher degrees of M Tech. and D Tech., and finding none, they informed the Ministry accordingly. The reaction was very sharp to the effect that, 'if the Governors, in spite of the advice of the Ministry of Education, decided to support the staff in instituting higher awards carrying the titles suggested, the Ministry would withdraw the financial grant to the College.' This was in May 1961, almost coincident with the founding of the first of the new Universities (Sussex), which were given the right to award degrees before either staff were appointed or students enrolled. In no time at all after this, owing to the impetus of the Robbins Report, degree-granting powers were given to a body which was never to have

* The author served as Chairman, and Dr (later Sir) James Tait as Hon. Secretary of the Committee throughout the whole of its existence. Secretarial services were provided throughout by Miss G. M. Needham MBE.

teaching staff or students of its own – the Council for National Academic Awards. It is arguable that the same impetus was necessary to enable the Colleges to break out of the academic frustration created by the entrenched power of the traditional Universities. There was also a strong disinclination in powerful academic circles to recognise the importance of technology,[18] which increased the resistance against giving University status to technological institutions.

Independent status 1962

Paragraph 71 of the 1956 White Paper reads: 'There are those who argue that a College of Advanced Technology cannot be successfully administered within the framework of local government. The Government do not accept this. Local Authorities take great pride in such Colleges and often have been willing to find more money for them than the pressure on national resources has allowed them to spend. To remove these Colleges from local control against the wishes of the Authorities could be justified neither by past experience nor by the hope of better results from a more central control. This statement is, however, subject to one qualification: the Government rely on the Local Authorities to work effectively together in planning the provision of courses and – just as important – in making it possible for students to attend courses which best suit their needs, whether these courses are in their own or another Authority's area.'

Within a brief five years, however, on 22nd June 1961, Sir David Eccles, Minister of Education, announced in a Parliamentary answer the intention to transfer control of the Colleges to independent governing bodies which would receive a direct grant from the Ministry of Education.* He reported this diplomatically to the Annual Conference of the Association of Education Committees the following day:[19] 'Since they were designated, these nine Colleges – and the Local Authorities have been responsible for eight of them – have made remarkable progress . . . All these good results have made me feel that I was justified in taking the decision that I did, against some very influential opposition, to rely on the Local Authorities to shape the first years of the Colleges of Advanced Technology. Now the very success of the CATs has faced us with new problems. In terms of the areas from which they draw their students they have

---

* With the exception, already noted, of Loughborough, which gained direct grant status in 1952.

become national institutions.' This action was 'not intended to prejudice any long-term solution. It may be the Robbins Committee will want to go further.' Meanwhile, he proposed to designate one more CAT: Brunel College of Technology.

There was in fact no mention in the 1956 White Paper of the LEAs shaping only the first years, but a brief six years had sufficed to nullify the apparently very strong assertion of confidence in governance by the Local Authorities. The Minister gave the major reason for the change, but there were other powerful factors that it would have been less polite to mention. There was, for example, the dependence on the Local Authority office and their procedures, and the consequent difficulties of initiating developments and of making progress quickly. Good professional and personal relationships, which generally obtained (as, for example, one is glad to record, during this period with Sir Lionel Russell CBE, Chief Education Officer, City of Birmingham Education Committee, in his unqualified support of the emergence of the College of Advanced Technology) helped to surmount the difficulties and frustrations inherent in inadequate and inappropriate procedures and requirements, but that was no reason for continuing them.

The Minister referred to the national catchment of the colleges for students, but did not draw out the consequence that this meant that the Colleges were financed increasingly from the 'Pool'. This was finance contributed to by all LEAs whether they had students on advanced courses or not, which in effect meant that rural areas were paying for technological education in industrial conurbations. Thus one of the major LEAs involved contributed from its own rates less than 3 per cent of the net cost of the College while retaining 100 per cent governance of it. There was considerable ambivalence about these Colleges within the LEAs: pride in their growing achievements mixed with concern about their increasing demands for resources (despite the 'Pool') in comparison with the needs of the growing number of Technical Colleges for which they were also responsible. 'If anyone thinks they're going to take away our Colleges, he can have another think coming', asserted a representative governor at a meeting of the Association of Technical Institutions in the early 1960s, and there was evidence of similar confusion at national level.

A pertinent question, now probably indeterminate, is whether and to what extent problems would have been eased had the Government not insisted on several bites at the one cherry – from College of

Technology to College of Advanced Technology to direct-grant-independent-status to University status – but had granted the final stage at the outset. Despite the granting of full University status and commensurate sites to the 'new' Universities, this was never contemplated for the CATs.

The piecemeal approach affected not only sites but the planning and use of the buildings to be set on them. For example, at Birmingham the LEA had planned a site and buildings 'to bring the Colleges of Technology, Art and Commerce into relationship with each other as institutions of comparable standing with promising prospects of interrelating their work.' Work on the building, planned in pre-war days, was started after the war on this policy, but was overtaken by events. The designation of the College of Technology entailed a reallocation of space for its expansion, the consequent transference of the College of Art to separate buildings on the same site, and of the College of Commerce to a building attached as a large wing to the original rectangular building, while another wing was added to the opposite side of the main building.

Architecturally the result was – to say the least – unfortunate, and would hardly have been contemplated had there been the slightest glimmer of the eventual move to University status, whereby the city centre site was expanded from some 1·8 hectares to about 14 hectares. However for some years the Colleges all remained on the same site and some progress was made in establishing interrelationships. These included, for example, a joint Guild of Students and Students' Union for the University and the two Colleges, and courses in architecture and planning of the College of Art leading to degrees of Aston University under a scheme of affiliation – but these relationships were severed by the later rigours of the binary policy.

Another notable instance was that of the Colleges at Loughborough, where a strong attempt was made in 1972–74 to set the binary policy aside and bring the Colleges into relationship as was once the case.*

In concluding this account of the period of the CATs, including the difficulties and stresses of the penultimate phase, the impression must not be left that relationships between the Colleges and the Ministry were unsatisfactory. Quite the contrary – working relationships became increasingly close and effective over the years, especially between the senior officials concerned and the Principals' Com-

* This was partly achieved in 1976. See Brief Histories, App. II.

Table 1.1 Colleges of Advanced Technology: enrolments before and after designation as CATs

Types of course	Session 1955–56 Lower level	University	Session 1958–59 Lower level	University	Session 1959–60 Lower level	University	Session 1960–61 Lower level	University
Full-time	2,212	3,745 (916)	669	5,154 (1,513)	641	5,804 (1,867)	275	5,347 (1,588)
Sandwich: Dip.Tech.	—	191	—	1,907	—	2,882	—	3,595
Sandwich: professional	172	397	—	713	—	706	—	632
TOTAL: full-time and sandwich	2,384	4,333	669	7,774	641	9,392	275	9,574
Part-time day	10,950	4,896 (201)	3,916	6,528 (566)	3,871	6,935 (585)	412	7,969 (1,839)
Evenings only	13,423 (76)	9,677 (3,811)	5,407 (53)	10,493 (4,097)	5,153 (55)	11,972 (5,910)	2,335 (51)	10,732 (5,188)

Note: Submitted by the Principals' Committee in their evidence to the Robbins Committee. Figures in brackets indicate numbers on short courses included in the totals.

mittee from 1961 to 1964; and a warm tribute is due to Sir Antony Part for his support during the period of transition.

The Robbins Committee

The Committee publicly invited both written and oral evidence, and heard evidence from ninety organisations and thirty-one individual witnesses,[20] and its work of sifting and assessing this cannot of course be repeated here. Only a very short summary of the evidence submitted by the Principals' Committee will be attempted. (Evidence was submitted separately by some of the governing bodies and, not surprisingly, there was a considerable degree of congruence with that of the Principals' Committee.[21])

Table 1.2 Colleges of Advanced Technology: proposed balance of studies

Study	Percentage of total enrolments
Engineering and Applied sciences	*65*
Pure sciences	*15*
Social sciences	*10*
Other studies	*10*

The statistical picture they presented of changing enrolments is given in Table 1.1, and their proposals for the balance of studies are shown in Table 1.2.

It was considered that 'a fully fledged Faculty of Social Sciences is indispensable as a basis for professional studies, industrial administration and management studies. It should probably include Departments of Economics, History, Industrial Sociology, Industrial Psychology, Industrial Administration, and a residential Centre for Management Studies . . . It would also have its own undergraduate full-time and/or sandwich courses in Social Science with increasing specialisation after the first year in Economics, Industrial Sociology and Industrial Psychology. Instead of economists, sociologists and psychologists being trained mainly within Arts Faculties as at present, there would be evident advantage in having some at least of them trained within a predominantly technological institution.'

A proposal to use the terminology 'Royal Colleges' was first bruited in the Percy Committee report and the Principals endorsed this suggestion in their concluding paragraph: 'There is almost a natural inclination on the part of new institutions to strive to become part of the established order. Many would, therefore, urge that we should develop into technological Universities, styled as such. However, we believe in a diversity of institutions, and we are concerned to establish a route in higher education parallel to that of the traditional Universities. We think this would be best secured by fully implementing a suggestion of the Percy Committee Report in the light of modern requirements, namely, that the Colleges should become chartered Royal Colleges of Technology.'

The Robbins Report was published on 23rd October 1963[22] and accepted by the Government in a White Paper.[23]

The Committee stated its conclusions in forthright fashion, as the following key passages in paras. 390 to 395[24] demonstrate:

390. We consider that the present powers and status of the Colleges are not commensurate with the work they are doing.

391. It is anomalous that such colleges should not have the power to grant their own degrees.

392. We recommend that in future these Colleges should in general become Technological Universities, and that this should be recognised in their titles if they so wish.

393. We recommend that the Colleges should have the power to award both first and higher degrees.

394. It also follows that these institutions should have the forms of government appropriate to University status.

395. We recommend that immediate steps be taken to grant charters and to transfer responsibility for finance to the body responsible for University finance.

To those who had tried overseas to explain that a Dip.Tech. was of honours degree standard and therefore equivalent to a degree of a British University (so why not call it a degree?) – or who had striven conscientiously but in vain to establish the MCT, the award at doctorate level of the College of Technologists* (that ill-starred offspring of the NCTA) – to all of these the recognition of the

* The illogicality of nomenclature for a higher award beyond Dip.Tech. was recognised – it could hardly be Dippier Tech: nor was the continental solution of Dr.Ing. available in the British context.

anomaly in para. 391, and the resulting recommendation in para. 393, came as balm to the troubled spirit. However much this may be attributed merely to academic snobbishness, nothing could sell an alternative to the traditional degree pattern to any influential group within the Colleges. This was simply because of the need to ensure the necessary supply of able staff and students vital to development. So ARCT, MRCT and FRCT vanished totally, and BTech. etc., hardly survived at all, against the pressures for BSc., MSc. and above all Ph.D.

The reservation that 'the Colleges should *in general* become Technological Universities' in the event covered the cases of Chelsea and Cardiff. Chelsea was an anomalous choice for a College of Advanced *Technology*, having no such courses at all. It was included by virtue of the high standard of its scientific work, but it had long looked in the direction of London University for incorporation as a constituent College. It had no sandwich courses, and made a small attempt to establish them, but soon abandoned it, partly as a result of difficulties arising from the requirements of the Senate of London University. Thus, Chelsea did not gain its Charter of Incorporation within the University until December 1971.

The reasons why the Cardiff College did not become independent were essentially political, inherent in the context of Wales and Welsh nationalism. It is curious that whereas University expansion in Scotland (population 5,223,600) increased the number of Universities from four to eight, Wales (population 2,724,275) retained a single University. The attempt to found a separate Technological University in Cardiff was stillborn. A further proposal in the Robbins Report for five Special Institutions for Scientific and Technological Education and Research (SISTERS)[25] was not implemented, though three potential candidates* were assisted by special grants in the succeeding years.†

It would be misleadingly inadequate to record the final stages of transition to University status without recalling the sense of exhilaration and deep satisfaction felt at the time by most staff and students, and by members of Council, Court and Convocation. For many these feelings received adequate even moving expression in the traditional ceremonies, variously modified to reflect their own particular histories and locations, which were arranged to celebrate

* Strathclyde, Imperial College and UMIST.
† See Table AIIIc.

the granting of the Royal Charters to them. To these celebrations each new University invited other British Universities to send representatives to support them at this definitive, indeed momentous, stage of their development. Despite so many occasions in so short a period of time – unprecedented in the history of British Universities – the response was high, sustaining visually and unequivocally their entry into the wider academic community. The worldwide significance of attaining University status became evident with the attendance of representatives at the Tenth Quinquennial Congress of Commonwealth Universities in Sydney, Australia in August 1968,[26] preceded by the meeting of their Executive Heads in Melbourne.

Some there are who do not value the inner significance of such occasions, and indeed even of customary congregations for the conferment of degrees, and who disparage them on grounds of cost, or of being outmoded and superfluous. To concede such a stance about public ceremonies would entail an aesthetic and emotional impoverishment of our lives. Critics there are also of the holding of quinquennial congresses for similar reasons, but also alleging that they make no impact, commensurate with the time, effort and cost involved, on the political scene or in contributing to the social and educational well-being of the community. This latter image persists probably because it serves ulterior purposes, since the stereotype is in fact quite obsolete. For instance, the ACU Congress, held in Edinburgh in August 1973, concentrated its discussions on five topics: the problems of the environment and the Universities; contemporary culture and the Universities; resources for higher education; co-operation between Universities; and the government of Universities.[27]

The sense of exhilaration, amounting almost to euphoria, did not last (a quite normal phenomenon) and was soon affected by uncertainties, not least as to how the institutions would fare under the UGC – perhaps very much at the lower end of the traditional list, instead of at the head of the Ministry/DES list as direct grant institutions. Such fears concerned the expansion of and therefore the particular role of the Technological Universities in higher education but in the event, their development was complicated by different factors, most of all by the seriously diminishing response among students to courses in science and technology.*

* However, changes apparent in 1976 may once again prove that a short-term judgement is not necessarily a sound long-term guide.

Chapter 1: Sources

1. Peter Venables, 'Conflicting patterns and purposes in higher education': The Foundation Oration delivered at Birkbeck College, London, on 20th January 1970; *Universities Quarterly*, Autumn 1970.
2. Eric Ashby, *Technology and the Academics* (Macmillan, London 1958).
3. See Peter Venables, *The Changing Pattern of Technical and Higher Education* (BACIE Golden Jubilee Publications, 1970).
4. (Manchester University Press, 1957.)
5. See W. H. G. Armytage, *Civic Universities* (Ernest Benn, London 1955).
6. For the history of this period concerning technical education see Michael Argles, *South Kensington to Robbins* (Longmans, London 1964), Chapter 2.
7. *15 to 18*, Crowther Report (HMSO, 1959), Chapter 47 and Part VI.
8. *As 5*, Chapter 10.
9. P. I. Kitchen, *From Learning to Earning: Birth and Growth of a Young People's College* (Faber & Faber, London 1944).
10. Reported *TES*, 2nd January 1929.
11. For a detailed appraisal of these see Peter Venables, *Technical Education* (G. Bell & Sons, 1956), Chapter XV, pp. 468–77.
12. *Report on Sandwich Training and Education* (NACEIC, February 1956).
13. Circular 305, *The Organisation of Technical Colleges*, 21st June 1956.
14. *Hansard* (House of Commons), 21st June 1956.
15. *As 11*, p. 486.
16. Tyrrell Burgess and John Pratt, *Policy and Practice: The Colleges of Advanced Technology* (Allen Lane Penguin Press, 1970), p. 136.
17. K. L. Stretch, 'Academic Ecology: On the Location of Institutions of Higher Education', *Minerva*, Vol. II, 1963–64, pp. 320–35.
18. Eric (Lord) Ashby, *Adapting Universities to a Technological Society* (Jossey-Bass, London 1974).
19. *Education*, 30th June 1961, p. 1450.
20. Robbins Report, 'Higher Education' (*as 22*), pp. 303–12.
21. This version was itself based substantially on that originally submitted by the present author when interviewed by the Robbins Committee in May 1961 (Report Annex, para. 17). See also Peter Venables, 'The Colleges of Advanced Technology', *Chemistry and Industry*, 8th September 1962.
22. Cmnd. 2154, HMSO, 1963, with volumes of Appendices.
23. Higher Education: Government Statement (HMSO, 1963).
24. *Ibid.*, p. 131.

25. *Ibid.*, paras. 383–87.
26. *Tenth Congress of the Universities of the Commonwealth 1968 Report of Proceedings, Sydney, August 17–23* (Association of Commonwealth Universities, London 1969).
27. *Report of the Proceedings, Commonwealth Universities and Society* (Association of Commonwealth Universities, 1974).

2

Institutional Change: Internal Stresses and Strains

WITH University status came the full realisation of President Truman's quip, 'The buck stops here.' No longer was it possible to blame 'them' – the NCTA, the Joint Committees, the LEA – and the UGC was no substitute. Institutionally, there is no more salutary lesson to be learnt. Changing and growing responsibilities were reflected in changing roles – the professoriate, Deans and other officers, and not least the sharp, though in some respects, subtle change of role from Technical College principal to that of Vice-Chancellor.

Externally there had to be a sequence of reorientations to the Local Education Authority, to the Ministry of Education (later the Department of Education and Science), and to the particular Regional Advisory Council in respect of finance and/or the approval of courses. Relationships with other educational institutions, e.g. Technical Colleges, schools and other Universities, underwent substantial change. With the termination of technician and craft courses, and with the severance of certain sections of work, e.g. catering and domestic science,* the working relationships with industry and commerce were reoriented significantly, strengthened by the growth of sandwich courses, the increase in project work and by industrially sponsored contract research.

Internally relationships were also changed, especially with the emergence of new 'interest-groups' which were liable to conflict in a period of financial stringency. Resources certainly did not grow at a rate commensurate with increasing needs, nor with the aspirations and evident opportunities of the new phase of development. A static presentation of structure and relationships gives an altogether in-

* These were the usual craft-oriented courses, in contrast with the Department of Hotel and Catering Management at Surrey University, which now functions as a business management school for the hotel and catering industry.

adequate picture of the dynamic institution which is a University.[1]

One of the most evident sources of polarisation and stress was the establishment of 'the administration' i.e. a bureaucracy adequate to sustain the University's academic purposes. To understand the need for a more adequate bureaucracy is not the same thing as allocating to it resources that might otherwise be used to provide, for example, more academic or research staff. Thus academics could create their own headaches – *'too much staff effort spent on admin. chores'* – and still reserve the right to complain. Another source of stress was the changing balance of academic studies, particularly by the inclusion of the social sciences in institutions long devoted solely to, or dominated by – according to viewpoint – engineering and applied science. In this polarisation the concept and practice of general studies was powerfully affected.

We are today much preoccupied with the direction and consequences of change, almost as if change itself were the only reality and all else illusory. But for significant periods of time complex social organisations, like living organisms, display equilibrium conditions variously described as stability or consolidation. The articulated structure and the complex of interdependent relationships tend to act as a shock-absorber diminishing the impact of change – whether from internal or external forces. There appears a 'tendency to the norm', a self-adjusting equilibrium reminiscent of le Chatelier's Theorem whereby the equilibrium adjusts itself primarily to nullify or absorb the effects of the changes.

One aspect of this is that in social structures – in this case, either in the structure of governance of the University or in its administration, or yet again in its academic relationships – there may be the persistence of a momentum from the past in the emergence of special power groups or 'oligarchs' – not formally organised as such but nonetheless powerful. The persistence of such groups within an institution from one phase of development to another is a matter of some importance in determining both policy and social custom. This was shown, for example, in the degree of common membership in successive bodies. When the Colleges became Universities the main committee of the Academic Staff Association was replaced by committees of the Senior Common Room and the Academic Assembly respectively; or again the Senate replaced the Academic Board. *'The old hands are still there'* was a comment made quite often during interviews.

36

The internal dynamics of an institution tend, inevitably and necessarily, to favour stability – a self-perpetuating equilibrium – as against change and any pressure for innovation from an 'out' group (e.g. new staff) is likely to be met with some resistance. The particular transformation with which we are concerned was a complex one and 'conforming influences' operated in opposing directions.

At the conscious level most members of staff welcomed the change of status (though for some it was a threat) but various aspects of the change provoked resistances, rational and irrational. Incoming staff were in many cases experienced in the ways of the traditional Universities but office-holders – the 'old hands' – hoping to retain their power displayed no great enthusiasm for making use of that experience. At a more important level there was the understandable and conscious fear that the institutions would become indistinguishable – organisationally and academically – from the civic Universities under the conforming influences of their new colleagues.

Another possible influence in this direction was the schoolteacher reluctant to encourage pupils to try new courses (e.g. sandwich courses). The image of the traditional degree course persisted and inhibited the perception of such new developments. External accrediting agencies such as professional institutions act likewise with tardy recognition of new curricula and teaching methods. The energetics of such equilibria ensure that no institutions will be exempt from such stresses. Furthermore, to ensure successful innovation over a substantial period of time requires a large input of creative energy, which is the prime necessity for securing a significant change of policy: only thus will the tendency to the fashionable or to the established norm be kept in check.

The changes within these technological institutions, examined and considered in this study, were ascertained in the following main ways: (1) from published material; (2) by visits to the institutions to obtain recordings of semi-structured interviews with a sample of staff; (3) by a questionnaire directed likewise to a sample of academic staff; (4) through an enquiry made of members of the Academic Advisory Committees; and (5) through an enquiry similarly of the views of lay members of the governing bodies who were engaged in industry and commerce.

The methodology of these enquiries is given in Appendix IV and the results, analyses and discussion are distributed variously in the ensuing chapters. Wherever applicable, analysis is related to four main periods:

Period O: prior to 1956 and designation as a College of Advanced Technology.

Period I: from late 1956 to 1962 and independence under a trust deed.

Period II: from 1962 to the publication of the Robbins Report in October 1963, with the assurance of Charters and through to receiving them in 1966–67.

Period III: the period since 1966–67 as fully established University institutions, which covered most of the first quinquennium 1967–72 (and of the five-year period of office of the Academic Advisory Committees) and some of the planning of the second quinquennium 1972–77.

These four periods can only be broadly characterised as there is no step function, but each period bears diminishingly some effects of the preceding one, and intelligent anticipation often induced some changes before its termination.

Discussions were recorded with staff of various levels, disciplines and periods of service, and each was asked to speak about the problems of transition to University status out of his or her own personal experience. Length of service is not the only factor involved, and the responses to enquiries about these problems are bound to be subject to hindsight of a varying emotive quality. This will largely depend on whether the individual has had a successful career during this period of fifteen years. Recollection is apt to be very different for one who was initially and still is a lecturer, from that of another who has become a reader or a professor. The difference is not related simply to ability, but can involve a complex of personal attitudes and values, which may surface as a defensive rationalisation about what actually happened at the time. Nevertheless, a persistent core of complaint does indicate something of the nature and scale of the original trouble on which a judgement has to be made, and also as to whether the trouble was inherent or avoidable. In making a generalised appraisal across the twenty-year period, the changed and changing composition of the staff must be borne in mind.

It is more significant in many instances to compare periods O and I with periods II and III, i.e. before and after the attainment of independent status. This was the 'great divide', for example in recruiting staff; for with the Robbins Committee sitting and with independence assured, most staff recruited in period II expected full University autonomy and in period III it became an established fact.

As regards the complexity of the changes which took place, no standard pattern emerged during the discussions. Many aspects were common to all the institutions, and variously recurrent throughout the period, some predominant for a while and a few distressingly persistent for some institutions over the whole period. Of the latter, site and accommodation problems were particularly onerous. The move from Battersea to the site of the University of Surrey at Guildford took two long years. For the Bristol College there was the abortive plan to move from Ashley Down to King's Weston in Bristol, partially begun in 1960, but abandoned after an invitation had been received to become the University of Bath, a move which was finally completed in 1975 with the transference there of management studies. Brunel's move from Acton to Uxbridge/Hillingdon took three years, having been extended distressingly by bitter labour disputes.

Each of these transpositions entailed acute practical problems of operating work on distant sites, and incurred serious risks of loss of identity, purpose and momentum. In each case, the completion of the move was felt as the lifting of an immense burden, and as the long-sought opportunity for constructive consolidation of the work of the University as a basis for further development. Heriot-Watt is still in process of moving from its long-established city site to an entirely new one at Riccarton just outside the boundary of Edinburgh.

Operating on two widely separated sites was an extension of the customary position of Colleges of Technology of having many dispersed sites within a city, but the practical problems were disproportionately greater. A separation of technological subjects from social sciences and the arts meant that the former site probably had no women students, and an imbalance is also inevitable while one site is devoid of social facilities: to maintain even the semblance of a corporate life requires a most determined effort. At some point the new site becomes the main administrative centre and the growing nucleus of the new institution, and the morale of the distant 'out-group' declines as its members feel increasingly isolated, seeming to lack adequate consultation and the opportunity to influence *their* future. There was also the uncertainty as to whether the new site would come to house an entirely new institution or would prove merely to be part of the former one writ large. An inescapable and urgent preoccupation with the severely practical problems of developing a new site makes it difficult for the harassed administrator to pay proper attention to the needs of those left behind. Bearing in mind the nature and range of problems discussed in evidence, the generally successful translocation of these Universities was a remarkable achievement and one that is apt to be underestimated by those who did not carry the major responsibility.

Chelsea and UWIST still remain on their original sites, having endured acute, and seemingly insoluble problems. 1975 saw positive plans for moving to new sites and those for Chelsea have gone ahead, though slowly. In the case of UWIST, plans were finally cancelled and, as far as can be seen, it will remain in Cardiff. One inescapable consequence which followed from the economic circumstances, was that the UGC requested University College, Cardiff, UWIST and the Welsh National School of Medicine to submit proposals for their joint development.[2]

The remaining five Universities: Aston, Bradford, City, Loughborough and Salford, were committed to their original sites as Colleges of Advanced Technology, and have added to them as opportunity and resources made possible. While subject to the common problem of change of scale, they were spared the exacting ones of substantial change of location. They were, moreover, able to build upon their local relationships, whereas the others perforce had to start anew.

This relates closely to a question which was raised frequently in discussion, as to whether it is better to convert an existing institution into a University or to start afresh. The Robbins Report recommended 'the foundation of six* new Universities in addition to those . . . in process of formation' (para. 476), and the giving of 'University status, either by separate Charter or by combination with an existing institution, to some (ten) of the (existing) Regional Colleges, Central Institutions and Colleges of Education' (para. 477). These recommendations were not accepted, the addition of more Universities was put into cold storage by the Government, and the granting of University status to any more existing institutions was rejected in the adoption of the binary policy and the subsequent designation of the Polytechnics. However, over the years there has been recurrent pressure in support of both recommendations, for

* In addition to the technological ones.

example, with advocacy for a new University on Teesside, and with the apparent emergence of certain Polytechnics as 'crypto-Universities'.

The question is many-sided: 'better' in what respect? For the system of higher education in serving the needs of the community, industry or commerce; or for rapidity of development; or better for the students and staff and for the general academic well-being and effectiveness of the institution as such? Various aspects are discussed later, but the adverse effects of the strenuous upheaval from one site to another were generally and not surprisingly felt in retrospect to be an acceptable price to pay for the amplitude of opportunity afforded by the new site.

Nevertheless, reservations were sharply expressed by some staff as to the nature of the change from a College of Advanced Technology to a University, regardless of any change of site, allegedly on the grounds of past tradition retarding the emergence of a University as such, and also on the retarding effect of a continuing core of academic staff appointed for different objectives and from a different academic market. Each effect was felt to be the cause of serious strain, particularly in the period from 1962 onwards, first in the raising of standards and the redesign of courses, and secondly in the polarisation already noted of old *v.* new staff, *'the old gang' v. 'the newcomers who haven't been through it all'*.

The degree to which polarisation obtained in the different institutions depended largely on their particular history, and was affected by the composition of the staff and their length of service. Up till 1966 it had often been assumed in University circles that the problems of transforming an institution were greater than those of starting with a clean slate. In making the comparison, the worst features of transformations are apt to be compared with the best aspects of a new creation, a common mode of argument obviously not unknown even in academic circles. But the comparison was readjusted somewhat after the 'new' Universities, Essex et al., experienced their severe problems of student and staff relationships from the mid-1960s onwards.

The recorded discussions* were semi-structured in order to ensure that the same range of questions was posed in each institution. The taped records were converted to typescript and assembled according to institution and the nature of each staff group (e.g. rank and/or

* See Appendix IV.

subject). Responses to each topic were then extracted and combined. Quantification of staff reactions was not attempted but a reading through of the scripts does convey a sense of the main conflicting issues and of opposing options. In the following pages quotations are printed in italics under each topic. Some written submissions from Governors and Advisory Committee members (Questionnaires 1 and 2) where pertinent are also included. The general comments interspersed between the quotations are intended to convey some idea of the nature of the discussions.

i. The purposes or objects of the institution

The objects of any institution or University need to be clarified, amplified and widely discussed from time to time because an understanding of them by the staff cannot be assumed. This is a continuing necessity but it was considered especially important during the transition. A Technological University is inherently preoccupied with solving scientific and technological problems and its objectives and methods must necessarily be responsive to change: '*A Technological University is there mainly to prepare people to live and work in a technological society, but not necessarily just to fill the slots within it – but to be able to criticise it, to cause it to adapt and to change . . . We thus need historians, philosophers and political scientists and so on to serve a central purpose – but I find it worrying that there is no central policy or purpose to which you can turn to decide whether something is appropriate or not . . .*'

On the other hand there were remarkable instances of complete lack of any concern for the objects of the University on the part of some senior staff (including professors) beyond securing the continuance of teaching and especially research in their particular specialism.

ii. Functional changes

The onset of University status induced a compelling urge towards 'charterdom', which meant conversion of College governing body to University Council, and of academic board to Senate; the introduction of Faculty Boards or Schools above the Departments; and the setting up of the administration. There was also the question of setting up a Court and/or a Convocation and in all this decision-making there was concern to lean on tradition – 'what do other Universities do?'. Innovations were judged according to whether they were likely to be accepted by the Privy Council. Understandably there was *'the problem of learning to use the new structure, and there was a good deal of posturing'*. Misunderstandings and friction came from exploring the limits and interstices of the new structure in an undeveloped and rapidly changing situation, but the most frequent source of difficulty was in the changing roles through which the structure became effective. Such difficulties were not widespread but they were not insignificant, especially in personal terms. Where former bodies such as 'the Heads' Meeting', continued and new bodies like the 'Vice-Chancellor and Deans' Committee' were invented – neither being expressly authorised in the Charter – there was cause for concern.

iii. Changing roles

These were many and important: from chairman of College governing body with an academic board of limited powers to Chairman of Council alongside a powerful Senate which had more representatives on the Council; the change of role from Principal to Vice-Chancellor – an uncertain exchange of a loss of power for a gain in influence. The change from College Head of Department to that of Professor and Head of Department was no less significant: *'In the old days it was easier in some ways, one wasn't in a democracy, one* WAS *the Head of Department, and what one said, went . . . .'*, in contrast with *'A Head now has a lot of responsibilities without concomitant authority and this can put him in a very difficult position.'* The further change from Headship of a Department to a Chairmanship was seen by some if not by most long-established heads as a potentially serious deterioration of their position. The Vice-Chancellor was expected by the heads to be democratic and consultative, whereas the relationships of some Heads with their own staff did not undergo change of a similar kind but remained essentially authoritarian. Thus the expectations upwards differed from actual practice downwards: *'Handing down ex-cathedra doesn't work any more and some Heads find this very difficult to learn.'* Assistant Heads of Departments in Colleges became Senior Tutors in Departments of a University and many were uneasy about *'the comparative vagueness of their role'* if not actively dissatisfied by the apparent loss of status. In this changing context Deans of Faculties and even Pro-Vice-Chancellors had carefully to feel their way, reassured perhaps by the thought of a limited term of office. Some polarisation of interests and representations resulted from the new structure as between the professoriate and the non-professorial staff, amounting in some instances to overt partisanship. *'It was quite evident that a cohesive group of profs in the University had been encouraged to press for the kind of autocracy they have or are believed to have, in other Universities, and this campaign has been pursued quite vigorously.'*

iv. Faculties, Schools Departments

This can be regarded as a subsection of para. ii above, but is separated because this nomenclature received a great deal of attention when charters were drafted, and much concern was subsequently expressed about it in discussion. Although the words are very much part of the everyday academic world, at the working face there is an evident gap between the intentions behind the structure and the way in which procedures and relationships actually obtain in practice.

Faculties are 'in between' – not terminal in any respect – in between a powerful Senate and a collection of determined, self-contained Departments. In this situation there was increasing unease about the problem of balancing the relative size of Faculties, of how to facilitate and secure the establishment of new disciplines and of inter-disciplinary courses. *'What really should rule is the discipline, not whether it is in this or that section, and those concerned should be willing to contribute to it wherever necessary'* ... *'The potentialities of Faculties as intermediate levels in University government have been under-utilised'* ... *'There is no present likelihood of having Schools instead of Faculties – the Heads of Departments are far too rigid in wanting their own number of students and student hours, and this will be reinforced by formula financing.'* Nevertheless, there are growing pressures for revision of Charters for a variety of reasons, but particularly to secure more delegation from Senate to Faculty boards, to reverse the elective process where it obtains, as for example to make all Heads of Department Members of Senate, and perhaps to maintain the proportion of non-professorial staff.

v. Academic staff

Aspects and issues raised in discussion included the following: conditions of service; expectations as to teaching and research – frequently *versus* research; the relevance and necessity of industrial experience; attitudes to 'service-teaching', and to part-time students. Discussion returned repeatedly, like a tongue to a sore tooth, to the contribution and competence of *'the older staff'* with the new conditions and tasks of a University, but some in authority saw *'the problem of the vestigial remains'* (as some described the older staff) as mainly one of leadership and encouragement. *'It's not the age structure that matters, it's the experience structure'* ... *'People recruited from Universities disliked or did not warm to the part-time student and this teaching was increasingly allocated to the older staff'* ... *'the older staff are very good at service classes, the younger subject-oriented staff are less so or not so'* ... *'Too many staff are at the top of the scale and this affects recruitment, promotions and the allocation of duties'* ... *'Certainly the voice of the old stagers is still the predominant voice here. The imports haven't found a collective voice'* ... *'The old brigade has suffered badly here. Justice has not been done to the people who have done a lot of work in this place. The accolades have gone to the new staff.'*

vi. *'Academic v. admin.'*

Antipathy between academics and 'the administration' would appear to be mildly endemic, but it is apt to surface sharply during the planning and allocation of resources. Resource problems are peculiarly difficult for an emergent institution, quite apart from the financial stringency which has increasingly harassed all Universities: *'It's a love-hate relationship ... and in this place the additional problem has been the scramble for space: anything the admin. asks for is jumped on by the academics immediately'* ... *'It is a very difficult situation. They want administration in each Department –* (the academic staff think) *"they can do all we can do" in each Department – and just report to higher authority'* ... *'Because we had so many academic staff in post, the University's charter is biased in favour of the academics as compared with the Charters of Universities starting de novo ... It is a constraint on the evolution of the University'* ... *'In recent years there has been an insistence that all the people coming into the academic admin. side should have qualifications equivalent to their academic colleagues'* ... *and this has helped the academics to respect the administration and eased things, and there is a much better relationship developing'* ... *'filing cabinets were badly wanted in departments. They couldn't get them, but there were plenty in the admin. ... trivial perhaps but very annoying.'* But a disproportionate response to a trivial instance betrays an underlying tension.

vii. Teaching v. research

Universities have the primary tasks of the transmission and the extension of knowledge, i.e. teaching *and* research: but the early history of the Colleges of Advanced Technology shows a generally adverse imbalance of conditions and effort against research. Not that the setting for teaching was perfect, for often it took place despite the conditions, but the long hours of teaching, and the lack of resources, frequently made research virtually impossible. In the period 1956–66 progress was uneven, so that many problems of resources and attitudes came up for discussion. *'It's unfortunate that research has become almost the only criterion for major promotion. It's not only in teaching that there is no incentive really for people to improve their teaching methods, it's also in the organisation and administration of teaching'* . . . *'If the Universities as a whole throughout the country had attached importance to teaching, as they do to research, they would by now have found a way of assessing it'* . . . *'Sensitiveness about teaching v. research – or rather research v. teaching – is inevitable, now that for the first time we can give higher degrees, but it is a simple problem of making a new philosophy active'* . . . *'With four hundred posts here there should be room for some who do nothing but research and some who are excellent teachers'* . . . *'New people from Universities brought expectations of research and of promotion resulting from it: the older members could not follow and so were denied the hitherto well-tried route to promotion of good teaching plus admin. experience.'*

viii. Undergraduate courses

There were two main aspects – first of being weaned from dependence on recognition by external professional and other bodies, and without doubt the experience gained under NCTA, in establishing the Dip.Tech., was very helpful. Secondly, there was an opportunity to design and establish new courses. After so long a period of dependence, there was no instant innovation, no simple solution as the following points raised in discussion made evident enough: *'The most formidable part of the transition was the difficulty of shaking off the London University régime, not from any fact that London University was tending to impose it, but we were tending to impose (their patterns) on ourselves and we had long and bitter discussions in setting up our own degree courses. There was a very strong tendency to have the mixture as before'* ... *'We have been in a constant state of flux – no two years alike; there is a real problem as to what is a tolerable rate of change, and now we are faced with more interdisciplinary courses'* ... *'It was touch and go whether Biology would go (to the new site) and it seemed probable that it would only go if it could establish a sandwich course – there was great stress at the time, and it was especially difficult to convince people to take biology students for the practical, industrial out-of-College periods – a bigger traumatic experience than in establishing engineering sandwich courses'* ... *'University status ended the requirement for general studies. The staff felt themselves to be second-class citizens without their own undergraduate course, etc., and the University needed social sciences anyway. Then the Engineering Departments asked for service-teaching to be cut down* .... *while the Social Science Department developed a lot of new courses, but not general studies'* ... *'The Mechanical Engineering course here has been dramatically altered* ... *to meet the requirements of the profession, rather than what is being done in other institutions'* ... *'In teaching to an external exam, in a sense it is quite legitimate to teach to the exam and to take part in question-spotting: but when you are setting your own exams it isn't. But I have noticed that it persists* ... *and is not confined to former CATs.'*

One consequence of developing full-time courses (including sand-wich courses) was the shedding of part-time courses and this did not go unremarked: *'We had expensive heavy machinery for part-time professional classes* ... *and were obliged to drop these because they were the dreaded evening classes – the dropping was a particular kind of admin, lunacy'* ... *'There is the Marxist view of cumulative small changes suddenly becoming a major one – we suddenly became a CAT and within a year any course which could not be described as of degree standard was gone – not merely re-classified, but sunk without trace. Most were hived off to local Technical Colleges who were glad to have them in a number of cases.'*

ix. Postgraduate courses and Research

The power to grant higher degrees having been gained, there was little discussion about it beyond drawing attention to what had been established in the brief time available. The whole preoccupation was to explore the situation in the endeavour to establish postgraduate work as a proportion of the total academic effort not less than that of other Universities, but with a growing awareness that the national

47

financial situation would make this increasingly difficult.* The same apprehension was felt about developing post-experience courses on a self-financing basis, and about the financial and practical problems of establishing sandwich course arrangements – not only for under-graduate courses but for research at Ph.D level.

x. Students

No clear picture emerged from discussion of the qualities and atti-tudes of students; reactions in the same institution, even department were often totally contradictory. *'Staff have been much surprised by the questioning nature of new full-time students as compared with former older part-time students'* . . . *'Students in the old days were highly resistant to what was not in the syllabus . . . but latterly this attitude has vanished completely, and the students are seizing on any modern knowledge they can get, the more modern the better and this is a pressure on us to keep up to date'* . . . *'I don't see much difference, only that I can talk more to them individually as sandwich students than part-time, but they do not seem to have altered their attitudes in any significant way'* . . . *'Very little change in students – the mean calibre has dropped a bit but we get very good ones'* . . . *'A big change here in buildings but the biggest change has been in attitudes of staff and students – speaking as a former student . . . there was a sense of dedication in both, but I don't see this any more'* . . . *'The numbers in sandwich courses are tending to fall compared with full-time – and is encouraged by the new attitude of students, who wish to look around and not to be totally committed'* . . . *'Others want a degree in three, not four, years and some come in without any real motivation for sandwich courses and transfer to full-time.'*

Student representation and involvement seemed to be highly variable: *'There are still people who don't realise we have got these representatives'* . . . *'Suddenly there were the representation issues which, being won, produced frustration and a sense of anticlimax – there was nothing more to get. It's all there, it's on a plate'* . . . *'It is very difficult to find sufficient student representatives – they have too much to do – and there are too few candidates for the presidency'* . . . *'There is a suspicion of top admin., an overall "them and us" attitude, an overriding thing about bureaucracy and not wanting to be part of it.'*

* But note the figures for 1975–76 (Table 4.1).

xi. External relationships

In the nature of things these are not in the control of the particular institution. In a period of rapid change the problem was not so much active opposition as inertia and confusion: *'Many careers masters in schools viewed sandwich courses simply as an apprenticeship and not as a University education and this tended to cut off our supply'* ... *'We haven't been able to attract large sums from industry, which by and large, as in the Technical College days, still wants things done as a favour or for a very nominal sum'* ... *'The engineering professional institutions played a large part, indirectly or not, in forming the nature and character of the technological institutions, but this needed to change so that as Universities they were free to innovate'* ... *'We are now in a highly conformist situation under UGC control; with the severe first quinquennium and a freeze to follow, innovation is the first casualty.'*

There may be a danger of over-emphasis in quoting so many expressions of dissatisfaction but, however transient some may be, the stresses and strains were real enough at the time. The impression gained from the interviews was that in quite a number of instances, discussions and consultations with staff had not been adequate to give them any real say in policy-making. Generally speaking however, the transition seemed to have been completed without any very serious difficulty or confrontation.

xii. The preparation of Charters

The average time taken to prepare and gain a Royal Charter for each of the Technological Universities was about two years. This length of time was due not to novelty of structure or presentation, but to the desirability, indeed the necessity, of substantial discussions with the large number of staff already in post who were most concerned about future changes. Recorded discussions made it evident that there was ever present the inhibiting thought *'of not stepping too far out of line, and wondering what the UGC and the Privy Council would say'*. *'What has generally been sound for so many will surely be good or safe enough for us, provided the specific technological objectives are made quite clear in the charter.'* After all, the Privy Council had circulated in 1962 a Draft Model Charter and Statutes for Universities. *'We regarded the charter as a traditional thing, almost in the class of heraldry, and when we drew it up there were various little*

49

things we did to make it our own . . . but there was no real attempt to analyse what a University was in this day and age.' In some instances vigorous discussions were remembered with interest: *'The debate itself was a major means of changing people's attitudes.'* However, looking back it is clear that there was little wish to contemplate – let alone try to implement – any substantial change from the traditional Charters. The major upheavals in the University world took place later, but even in the 1970s, when Birmingham University decided to revise its early charter, radical changes were resisted.[3]

xiii. Transition from College governing body to University Council

In recorded discussion the view was common that the transition *'from College governing body to University Council has been a continuing process without abrupt change'*, and the importance of the role of the lay chairman in facilitating this was strongly emphasised. Moreover, the absence of a lay *v.* academic alignment or antipathy was remarked with warm appreciation – *'almost a complete story of betterment and of lay and academic coming closer together – we have had disputes and difficult discussions, but none a simple orientation of lay v. academic – a pretty good consensus really.'* Nevertheless care had to be taken by academics, as they gained representation and power, not to alienate the lay members: *'As compared with the former governing body, members of our new council have not got terribly involved as a general rule'* . . . *'the loss of College advisory committees caused some bitterness for their chairmen were ex-officio members of the governing body – despite putting them on convocation. But that met only once a year and had no responsibilities, and their expert knowledge wasn't needed'* . . . *'Academics going on to the governing body in 1962 meant a definite shift of power and the beginning of a declining interest among lay governors . . . they are now less called upon and are consequently less interested, particularly if they are not really asked to make decisions . . . and this follows partly from the academics discussing things together outside committee and partly from the Vice-Chancellor's own role in these matters.'* Appreciation was expressed that *'. . . it is important to have lay members – staff cannot be judging their own cause all the time and in finance and on conditions of service we have had very useful service and advice.'*

xiv. Structure of Senate and its relationship with Council

Universities are becoming large organisations. There is indeed a peculiar piquancy in that, in the last two decades, many Universities have established departments and schools of management studies, business administration and the like, for the benefit of industry and commerce, but only latterly have begun to put commensurate thought and effort into studying and modernising their own governance and administration.[4] Present trends indicate that the direction of change is towards a unified form of governance at top level, realigning some of the functions of Court, Council and Senate, rather than total change throughout. It has been remarked that ' *"a University is a loose coalition of freeholders"*, and rightly so, for it is in that way that such freedom as we have in research and teaching is guaranteed.'[5] With a modified top structure, under academic control the substructure of Faculties, Schools and Departments could continue as at present, but with more democratic involvement of the freeholders.

The Technological Universities follow a traditional pattern but with some important differences nevertheless. The ex-officio right of professors to Membership of Senate is set aside in nine cases and, above certain minimal figures to cover the early years, all places for professors are held by election for periods normally of three years' duration. Professors who are Heads of Departments or Schools are ex-officio Members of Senate in six institutions, and this has led to mounting pressure from Heads not so placed to be granted this right; or at least until the Charter can be revised, to be allowed to attend Senate and to speak whenever their departmental interests are involved. *'At the time I was one who supported that Heads should not be ex-officio Members of Senate . . . I was wrong because . . . when you get Senate minutes it is sometimes very difficult to understand what Senate is saying . . . To try and run a Department from a back seat is in fact pretty impossible . . . and I think we should have Heads there as observers at least'* . . . but *'the non-professorial staff feel strongly that the present proportions should be retained, otherwise we would have to increase the size of Senate'* . . . *'Senate executive has now been en-larged to include all Heads of Departments, and is not an elected body any more'* . . . *'Senate is too democratic – people have strong opinions about things for which they are not responsible and the hard fact is that they do not understand the problem because they have not borne the responsibility . . . We have more trouble with people of this kind on Senate than with anyone else.'*

One persistent concern was about the existence of allegedly in-formal bodies not specified in the charter, such as the continuance of the Heads' meeting, or the establishment without the formal approval of Senate of a 'Principal and Deans' meeting' or a professorial board *'which bypass Senate or its sub-committee'* . . . *'where the real power lies'* . . . *'If the Deans' committee were very much against something it would be difficult for Senate to put it through.'* *'The Principal and Deans' committee is the focal operating committee between Senate and Court/Council'* and is a device to ensure *'that finance, or allocations to particular sections, e.g. the library, are never discussed on Senate'*. To be executive is clearly felt to be undemocratic, and this confusion is widespread to the point, in one instance at least, that *'the Vice-Chancellor was firmly regarded simply as a creature of Senate . . . and not a person of a great deal of executive power in his own right'*. However, his successor *'has been more accustomed to having an executive role, and this is how he is operating and (it) is causing him some difficulty'*.

In Chapter 15 of the Robbins Report, which deals with internal government, it is recommended (para. 676) that serious attention be given to improving the support services at top level: 'No other enterprise would impose on its chairman the variety and burden of work that the modern University requires of its Vice-Chancellor.' In common with others, the Technological Universities accordingly made senior appointments to this end, such as Pro-Vice-Chancellorships, mostly on short-term periods of three to five years. In addition there has been a great improvement in the provision of statistical data needed by the Senior officers who have to assess proposals for development and the allocation of resource.[6]

The ten former CAT Principals became members of the Committee of Vice-Chancellors and Principals (CVCP) in April 1964, but those of Chelsea and UWIST remained only until the future of their colleges as constituent parts of existing Universities had been determined. The Vice-Chancellor's Committee had emerged in 1912–13 as 'another of those phantom British organisations with neither constitution (until 1930) nor formal power to commit the represented institutions (yet) it nevertheless provided a means of drawing them closer together'.[7] The structure and procedures still belonged to a less urgent age.

As a result the members were presented with matters for comment, or even decision, with insufficient time and without sufficient specialist support, so that the case for the Universities was apt to go by default. The Committee could not speak for the Universities in any constitutional sense of acting collectively on their behalf without prior approval from each and every institution in membership. Great caution amounting to distinguished inertia was always inherently probable. The CAT Principals felt the inertial load at first hand, but the shortcomings were well enough recognised for the Robbins Committee to devote paras. 692–700 of its Report to the future organisation and strengthening of the work of the Committee. Since then the pressure of events and the resilience and collective wisdom of its members have produced big changes, in its own substructure and services, and in its external relationships.

Whereas not all Heads of Departments in the CATs were appointed to Professorships, the transposition from Principal to Vice-Chancellor was automatic. Though it is difficult to imagine it otherwise, it is not unthinkable. Appointments to the Directorships of Polytechnics have not all been so automatic because in some cases several institutions were merged on their inception.

Whatever the experimental errors or maladjustments involved, the flux of time had, by 1st October 1975, brought about replacements of all but one of the former ten Principals, a rate of change far higher than that of the academic staff since University status was gained. Of the seven new Vice-Chancellors, three came direct from important positions in industry, one from a Civil Service research establishment and three from University professorships (one of them after an interlude as Director of a foundation for research grants). Altogether six had worked in industry at some time, and of those who came direct from industry, one had been a University professor beforehand. None of these appointments has been made by internal promotion. The Robbins Committee commented that 'The selection of a Vice-Chancellor or Principal is perhaps the most important single decision that the governing body of a University is called upon to make':[8] it will be of especial interest to see how closely, under the influence of these new appointments, the Technological Universities hold to their original philosophy over the next decade.

Up to the mid-1960s the literature relating to the role of the Vice-Chancellor was meagre[9] but with the subsequent democratising of the governance of Universities[10] and the expansion of higher education generally – particularly in the social sciences – has come a dramatic increase in the output of books, papers and reports dealing with the problems of higher education.[11]

In bringing this chapter on the transition of the CATs to University status to an end it remains to record the responses to four statements on the questionnaire (and to consider the role and effectiveness of the Academic Advisory Committee). The responses relate to topics which were considered at length during the recorded discussions. Results from the two sources proved to be congruent, so the statistical data only is presented here.

Statements 16 and 26* were concerned with departmental structures and the results are shown in Table 2.1.

The 11 per cent of staff who were recruited in Period O were more conservative in attitude than the rest, particularly to statement 16. Permanent headships at the top of a hierarchy, with set relationships and firmly set expectations were precisely what they had long experienced. 'Better the devil you know' . . . and there was little or no practical experience of circulating chairmanships. The other respondents were constant at 55 per cent, which gave an overall value of 54 per cent – no mass of opinion here to demand change, rather a state of contradictory assertions as exemplified in the recorded discussions. The Halsey and Trow sample provided a similar result and analysis by subjects taught showed only 45 per cent of the Technology staff agreeing with statement 16 as against 70 per cent of the social scientists.[12]

The difference between the two samples was greater on statement 26 – 77 per cent agreement compared with 53 per cent – and could not be accounted for by subject differences.[13] Indeed less than half the newly appointed staff agreed and many of them had had recent experience in Redbrick Universities. Halsey and Trow's survey was carried out in 1964 and this one nearly seven years later. Perhaps professorial objectives were less in evidence in the 1970s.

Responses to statements 4 and 17 dealing with status differences between staff are analysed in Table 2.2.

The responses to statements 4 and 17 show negligible differences between the periods. Less than half (45 per cent) considered the status differences outmoded (statement 4), and nearly two thirds (65 per cent) considered the use of the American pattern in Britain would be a retrograde step. In period III 69 per cent agreed with statement 17, and among professors only 73 per cent felt the same. The comparable result in the Halsey and Trow study was 71 per cent.[14]

* See the Academic Staff Questionnaire, p. 357.

Table 2.1 Departmental structure/circulating chairmanship/professorial oligarchy: percentages agreeing with each statement, by period of appointment

| | Period of appointment | | | | | | | | All respondents | | Halsey & Trow* | |
| | O | | I | | II | | III | | | | | |
	%	N	%	N	%	N	%	N	%	N	%	N approx.
16. Most British University departments would be better run by the method of circulating chairmanship than by a permanent Head of Department	25	39	55	89	55	79	55	148	54	355	57	1,367
26. A serious disadvantage of Redbrick Universities is that they are all too often run by a professorial oligarchy	46	39	62	87	55	79	47	145	53	350	77	1,367

Note: * All types of University represented, and percentages varied from 53 to 64 on Q.16, and from 75 to 82 on Q.26.

Table 2.2 Professorships: British/USA pattern:
percentages agreeing with each statement, by period of appointment

| | Period of appointment | | | | | | | | All respondents | |
| | O | | I | | II | | III | | | |
	%	N	%	N	%	N	%	N	%	N
4. The status differences in Britain between professors, lecturers and teachers are outmoded	41	39	48	86	45	79	43	147	45	351
17. The use in Britain of the title 'Professor' for most University teachers, as is done in America, would be a retrograde step	67	39	62	89	61	79	69	147	65	354

Academic Advisory Committees

Institutions have gained University status by a variety of routes, but the most important has been by proven standards through the gaining of London University external degrees.[15] The 1949 charter and statutes of the University College at Keele provided for the granting of first degrees only, under the supervision of an Academic Council composed of the Principal, two members each appointed by the Universities of Oxford, Birmingham and Manchester, three members of and appointed by the Senate, and one member of staff, not a Professor or Head of Department.[16] Each route had drawbacks, and a major step was taken by the UGC in 1961 with the innovation of an Academic Advisory Committee in establishing the University of Sussex. Under its general guidance the University had powers to grant first and higher degrees from the outset. This model was followed with succeeding Charters; including those of the technological universities. Their Academic Advisory Committees (AACS) were established by close consultation between the UGC and the Colleges, and warm tribute is due to the Chairman of the UGC, Sir John Wolfenden, for his help and advice during the whole period of transition.

The constitution, terms of reference, procedures of each Advisory Committee were prescribed in a statute for the particular University, but in view of the way in which they were established, there were surprising variations about the terms of the draft. In one instance, the Committee was required to approve the institution of all degrees other than honorary ones; in another of degrees other than first degrees and honorary degrees; and in another there was no such requirement. The membership varied from five to eight, and there was the requirement that of these 'members of high academic standing' at least one 'shall be actively associated with industry'. In seven cases out of nine – excluding UWIST and Chelsea – there was a requirement to make an annual report to Council, and in two only was there a specific requirement to keep matriculation standards under review.

The powers and functions laid down in the following abstract were – in essence – part of the terms of reference of all the AACs.

'The Academic Advisory Committee shall in addition to all other powers vested in it by the Charter and Statutes have the following powers and functions:

1. To advise the Council and Senate on academic matters.

2. To approve the institution of degrees other than honorary degrees and the degree of Bachelor.

3. To keep under review and to certify annually to the Council that it has satisfied itself about the procedure for the appointment of academic members of staff and the organisation and conduct of examinations including the conditions of appointment and service of external examiners.'

A questionnaire (Appendix IV) was put to the 62 members of the Academic Advisory Committees of the eight Technological Universities: 56 responded and one made a separate statement. Of the 56, all but two (96 per cent) agreed that the terms of reference were reasonably adequate for the work, and also that the number of members was satisfactory. The balance of the membership was agreed by 87·5 per cent to be satisfactory, 7·2 per cent were doubtful and 5·3 per cent disagreed. From their experience no members regarded the appointment of an AAC as unnecessary: on the contrary, 70 per cent thought it desirable (quite a number inserted *very*), and 30 per cent considered it indispensable. No precise time was fixed in the Charters for the period of service of the Committees, and in the event advice was received from the Privy Council via the UGC that it would be about five years. Of the 93 per cent of the respondents who answered this part, 42 per cent thought the period too long, 50 per cent about right and 8 per cent too short.

AAC members were each asked to list the three matters that their particular Committee found most difficult out of all they had had to deal with. Altogether 25 different topics were mentioned, but if those mentioned only once or twice are omitted, nine subjects were mainly in mind, which fell about equally into two main areas. The first concerns the quality of staff as affecting the transference or otherwise from grades of posts in the colleges to University grades of posts. The most important issue was that of the recognition or otherwise of Heads of Departments as University Professors. The Academic Advisory Committees clearly regarded this as of prime importance and gave it a great deal of attention, but of 23 mentions of this subject, 17 were made by members of four AACs.

The other main area concerned the drafting of the Charter and various matters arising from it, which varied with the institution. Student representation was mentioned only three times. Other subjects not in the two main groups were quite diverse, such as the expansion of the social sciences, whether 'technology' should be in the title of the University, the introduction of arts subjects, transformation of attitudes to a University standpoint, the removal to a new site, and unrealistic proposals for new postgraduate courses.

In the recorded discussions with staff frequent and warm tribute was paid to the work and influence of these committees, especially in the early stages in drafting the charter and ordinances, in assessing the structure of courses, particularly postgraduate ones, and especially in acting *'as a longstop on difficult issues'*. They were generally felt to be strong defenders of sandwich courses, though not of general studies. All was not contentment, however: for example, there was a grudging ambivalence about the procedures for considering Heads for Professorships, and the desirability of having Chairmen of Departments rather than Headships with life tenure, which was very upsetting for those directly concerned, still generating heat years later. Some resentment and resistance was shown about the choice of Senate sub-structure and especially about having to accept Faculties rather than schools; and the position was, in one or two cases, complicated by personality problems. However, it would be quite wrong to give the impression that the foregoing difficulties were substantial and widespread: quite the contrary, the operation as a whole was singularly constructive and congenial, well beyond the customary run of committee work.

Though advisory in name, it was implicit in the whole operation that the advice of the Committees would generally be accepted. The sanctions behind the Committees in their work were powerful: delay in the establishment of new courses and degrees, pressure from the UGC following information from the AAC chairman and, in the ultimate, delay in gaining the Charter. Such considerations scarcely surfaced in any strength for the determining influences were quite other – the Colleges were highly motivated to make a success of the venture, and enjoyed the support of the Committee members and the feeling of partnership with them. One other tribute must be paid to the Committee members, for it was not generally realised that they gave their invaluable services out of busy lives without financial reward.

One final point, as to the period of service. Quite a number of Committees were of opinion that they had completed their work well before the end of the five-year period, and when the request to finish was refused, attendances declined accordingly: *'Isn't it time we wound*

up, we've done our job' ... 'We can't be got together for trivia.'
(What a splendid Occam's Razor for a committee-ridden age.)

Chapter 2: Sources

1. See Graeme Moodie and Rowland Eustace, *Power and Authority in British Universities* (Allen & Unwin, 1974).

   J. V. Baldridge, *Power and Conflict in the University: Research in the Sociology of Complex Organisations* (John Wiley & Sons Inc., New York 1971).

   Sir Sydney Caine, *British Universities: Purpose and Prospects* (Bodley Head, 1969).

   F. G. Bailey, *Morality and Expediency: The Folklore of Academic Politics* (Basil Blackwell, Oxford, 1977).

2. *THES*, 10th June 1977 and 29th July 1977.

3. See the Report (September 1972) of the Review Body of the University of Birmingham (Chairman, Jo Grimond MP), of which the present author was a member, and compare the subsequent Report of the University Council arising therefrom *The Governance of The University of Birmingham*, presented to the Court of Governors, 22nd February 1973. The revised Charter was completed in September 1975.

4. e.g. O. R. Marshall / Sir Roy Marshall (Secretary-General of the Committee of Vice-Chancellors and Principals), 'The University as a limited liability company', *THES*, 24th August 1973.

5. The remark is by Elliott Jaques, the quotation from John Vaizey's article 'A loose coalition of freeholders', *THES*, 23rd February 1973.

6. *As 1*, Chapter VIII: 'Budgeting and the allocation of resources'.

7. R. O. Berdahl, *British Universities and the State* (Cambridge University Press, 1959), p. 47.

8. See R. Streter, 'An Academic Patriciate – Vice-Chancellors 1966–67'. *Universities Quarterly*, Winter 1968.

   Peter Collison and James Miller, 'University Chancellors, Vice-Chancellors and College Principals: a social profile', *Sociology*, Vol. 3 No. 1, 1969.

   As 1, Chapters VI: 'The Vice-Chancellor' and VII: 'The bureaucracy'.

9. Two examples being:

   F. M. Cornford, *Microcosmographia Academica* (Bowes & Bowes, Cambridge 1908).

   James Dundonald, *Letters to a Vice-Chancellor* (Edward Arnold, London 1962).

10. See A. H. Halsey & Martin Trow, *The British Academics* (Faber & Faber, London 1971). Table 2.1 calculated from Tables 14.5 and 14.6 of this work, p. 379.

11. e.g. David Martin (ed.), *Anarchy and Culture: The Problem of the Contemporary University* (Routledge & Kegan Paul, London 1969) – in particular, chapter by Rowland Eustace, 'The Government of Scholars' – and James A. Perkins, *The University in Transition* (Princeton University Press, 1966). The author discusses a third 'mission' for the universities beyond those of teaching and research, namely that of public service.

12. *As 10*, Table 14.27, p. 525.

13. *Ibid.*, Table 14.28, p. 525.

14. *Ibid.*, p. 381, where in Table 14.12 only 29 per cent of professors thought that the title of 'Professor' should be a normal expectation.

15. W. H. G. Armytage, *Civic Universities* (Ernest Benn, London 1955). Sir Sydney Caine, *British Universities* (Bodley Head, London 1969).

16. W. B. Gallie, *A New University: A. D. Lindsay and the Keele Experiment* (Chatto & Windus, London 1960).

Sir James Mountford, *Keele. An Historical Critique* (Routledge & Kegan Paul, London 1972).

Drusilla Scott, *A. D. Lindsay – A Biography* (Blackwell, Oxford, 1971).

3

Philosophy and Practice

INSTITUTIONS of higher education do not grow *in vacuo*: they evolve in response to the practical needs of man and society, and to philosophical reflection on their nature as embodied in the curricula and activities provided. Since mediaeval times Universities have interacted with contemporary society in their search for knowledge and in their commitment to teaching – not only in order to preserve the scholarly tradition but also to meet the needs of the law, the Church, medicine and the State. In later times the first became dominant, to the detriment of professional training, which in essence is to the application of knowledge. The uneasy interplay of the commitment to scholarly knowledge and to professional training respectively has been profoundly affected in the last century, increasingly by scientific knowledge and advances in technology, and their economic potential. Not the least consequence has been that education itself, especially higher education, has increasingly engendered and preserved powerful élitist groups in societies seemingly intent on egalitarian objectives. Far from being ivory towers – in the world but not of it – Universities are political institutions (though not overtly party-political). This fact has imperilled two related aspects of Universities: their corporate autonomy and their academic freedom.

The intellectual commitment is fourfold: knowledge is to be preserved, disseminated, extended and applied. Confusion has arisen because of the varying significance attributed to these four aspects at particular times in the history of Universities. These aspects, and their variance, are indicated in Table 3.1.

The Table is subjective and can only be considered to be broadly indicative. For example the prototype mediaeval University was firmly based in scholarship, and teaching was an integral function. When the technological means of printing became available, publication of their scholarly work was a substantial concomitant, and

62

University presses have a long and honourable history. However, the number of publishing houses outside the University has vastly increased so that, relatively, University presses have declined in importance. Where they still obtain it is mostly by special arrangement with an external publisher. The extension of knowledge in earlier

Table 3.1 Fourfold intellectual commitment of Universities to knowledge

Commitment	Mediaeval or prototype University	Civic University	Modern University	Technological University
Preservation: i.e. scholarship	xxx	xx	x	x
Dissemination: i.e. teaching and publication	xxx	xxx	xxx	xxx
Extension: i.e. fundamental research	x	xxx	xxx	xx
Application: i.e. project/applied research		xx	x	xxx
professional education and training	xx	xxx	x	xxx
social involvement and responsibility	x	x	xx	xx

Note: x indicates some commitment, xx substantial and xxx very substantial commitment. They are not intended to imply a simple 1:2:3 ratio of increase.

times was almost wholly by scholarly study of established sources and publications, as distinct from the radical innovatory processes of modern science, which is the mark of later Universities. To establish science and technology in traditional universities was not so much a hardly-won battle as a long-sustained campaign.[1]

Of all four commitments, that to 'application' has constituted the

63

greatest change in orientation of Universities in recent decades, and is apt to be the most contentious. It is one thing to teach traditional University disciplines as ends in themselves, it is quite another deliberately to seek to apply knowledge in such ways as to change, for example, the practical procedures and relationships of industry and commerce; much more to engender a critical constructive scepticism towards their structure and management processes: and still more contentious is it to incur social involvement and responsibility by serious incisive examination of the values and practices of contemporary society. All three are interrelated aspects of professional education and training, and of lifelong education, not only in respect of industry and commerce, but of the professions generally. If Universities are to be concerned with the application of knowledge, as for the well-being of humanity they must be, then professional education and training is of central importance alike to the Universities and society at large.

Successful 'application' involves a continuing concern with the intellectual processes of applying knowledge, and a commitment also to securing certain material results and objectives, including financial rewards. If the latter predominate, however, the University could become increasingly subject to external values and controls, and in the last resort endanger its academic freedom and corporate autonomy.[2] It is quite proper therefore that warning notes should be sounded on the dangers of such involvements. The degree of involvement varies widely, for example, from the simplest externally sponsored project, with no strings attached, through those in which there is the definite consideration of continuing confidential access to work in progress with publication of the results delayed for a period, to the extreme case of classified research for a government which entails the total prohibition of publication and discussion of results with colleagues.

Belatedly, but encouragingly, there has been a growing worldwide concern about the acceptance of classified research by Universities and pressures have mounted for the separation of such work into other establishments. This questioning stems primarily from the alien intrusion of secrecy into Universities, the very negation of 'the open society' for knowledge, with no feedback into teaching internally, or through publication externally. Added to which there is a very proper apprehension also about the subtle untoward effects on the governance and administration of Universities. University sponsorship is a profoundly different matter in scale and significance from the action of individual staff who may participate in classified research in non-University establishments on a personal basis, though here again, the University would be unwise by its conditions of service to encourage a strong commitment in that direction, to the detriment of its own work and objectives.

Apprehension about social involvement and responsibility through application of knowledge may induce a longing for the traditional ivory tower. For better or worse, a return to this is no longer possible. However, the symbiosis of University and society at large is inextricably complex, and though vital to the well-being of both, it will not happen 'naturally' without sustained effort.

Revisions of Charters become necessary as changes in the climate of opinion make 'repugnant' practices which were once acceptable. Discriminations of various kinds are already expressly prevented by statutes, for example:

'Words (in the Charter and Statutes) importing the masculine shall include the feminine . . .'

'Men and women shall be equally eligible for any office or appointment in the University and for membership of the University or any of its constituent bodies and all Degrees and courses of study in the University shall be open to men and women alike.'

'No religious, racial or political test shall be imposed upon any person in order to entitle him or her to be admitted as a member of the University or hold office therein or to graduate thereat or to hold any advantage or privilege thereof.'

Such statutes are now regarded as self-evident propositions, and although some unrevised charters of civic Universities do not expressly include them all, there is everywhere in British Universities the intent to observe them. Such statutes, moreover, constitute a declaration by the Privy Council as well as by the University of an egalitarian, moral and political stance. The question now is not whether the Universities should declare such a stance, but rather whether there are other issues which should be actively considered as possible extensions of or additions to their statutes. How far is it incumbent on a University to endeavour to offset or prevent inegalitarian trends in society, either by active policy or efforts on its own part, or by stimulating, or otherwise engendering, positive action in society?

Statistics show that women, compared with men, have very

unequal opportunities in higher education, both as students and as academic staff. Careful analysis and searching enquiry may show or ensure that this is due to no defect in University procedures, and that the main responsibilities lie in the home and the school, and in their attitudes and lack of facilities. What should or could the Universities do about *that*? – apart from being vigilantly fair about their own procedures and attitudes? The question of stance is central to this also.

In the modern world, a University cannot stand aside from the moral issues and problems of society. Moreover it cannot justifiably pursue a line of conduct or policy, either by definitive action or by apathy, which conflicts with its primary duty as an institution of higher learning.* In some modern Charters the objects commit the University to aim to benefit the community generally, and not only industry and commerce. The objects of the Open University express this more broadly still: 'to promote the educational well-being of the community generally',[3] and this may now be taken as a broad function of Universities. Indeed, the University Extension movement began about 1850[4] but the rub really comes when the need to change society becomes pressing: how best can we expedite change? The contribution of the University to the general and educational well-being of society is not to be determined merely in material and physical needs or in immediacy of needs, but should have regard to long-term interests. To respond fully, imaginatively and creatively to this concept will entail involvement in philosophical, religious, social and political issues.

Acceptance of this stance as basic to a University in the modern world requires that its concern should be evident in its persistent enlightened intellectual exploration of problems for the common good. It is impossible to provide a blueprint for all time, and the onerous responsibility for defining issues in the light of the foregoing general considerations must lie with the Council and Senate of each University in each succeeding generation. This obligation to serve the community and its citizens does not require that the University itself become the special and direct instrument of particular social action. Rather should it help to provide leadership for

---

* This and following paragraphs follow closely some passages which the author had already drafted for this chapter, which were approved with some modification for inclusion in the University of Birmingham Review Body Report, pp. 4–6.

such action and help to engender such conditions in the community that appropriate beneficial social action will be forthcoming and that, if need be, new institutions and agencies will be established accordingly.

Without doubt the adoption of such a stance by a University renders it more vulnerable to external influences. To offset this, special efforts must be made to explain to the body politic the vital importance of University autonomy and academic freedom: that far from merely being concerned with petty academic privileges, their maintenance is essential to securing the widest range of benefits and freedoms – material, social, political, philosophic and religious – in an open democracy.

To turn now from these general considerations to a particular academic aspect, we may note that in the period prior to the publication of the Robbins Report, the comment was frequently made that the range of studies in the Colleges of Advanced Technology was too narrowly restricted to technology and ancillary subjects. In short, they were not characterised by that universality of knowledge assumed to be inherent in Universities as traditionally understood. All knowledge was supposed to be their province, which tended to confuse the wholeness of the body of scholars and students with the whole body of knowledge.

Such has been the vast increase of knowledge that no single institution can comprehend every subject from philosophy to technology, either in its teaching or its researches. With this increase has come an ever-growing demand on scarce resources of manpower, equipment and services, and it is simply not possible for all Universities to be equipped equally, for example, with major nuclear reactors or the most powerful computers. In this situation the particular parts of the spectrum of knowledge in which an institution specialises will arise from its history in the first place, and secondly from the personal intellectual interests of its academic staff. The new Universities, from Sussex onwards, were based mainly on the arts and sciences and the Technological Universities on science and technology. Both are part of the same spectrum of knowledge: there is no fundamental difference between them, only a difference of orientation and specialisation.

To consider the matter solely in terms of the range of subjects covered is misleading: for the quality of an institution resides in the devotion of its staff to the pursuit of truth, and in the rigour of their methods of enquiry and of self-criticism, on which their intellectual standards and academic integrity must perforce be based. These criteria and ideals are not the prerogative of those pursuing any one branch of knowledge. The acceptance of the physical sciences as academically respectable was one of the major factors contributing to the creation and rapid growth of the Provincial or Civic Universities. It was necessary to establish this yet again in evidence to the Robbins Committee in relation to the Colleges of Advanced Technology. Intellectual standards and academic integrity were not precluded by the specialised functions of the Colleges for professional education for industry and commerce, any more than they are for medicine and law in traditional Universities.

Table 3.2 Objects stated in Charters of Technological Universities

Specific commitments	*Number of times included*
to advance learning and knowledge by teaching and research	10
in science and technology/applied science/application of knowledge	9
to meet the needs of/collaboration with industry and commerce	8
extramural periods of training in industry and commerce	2
the professions/professional competence and training	4
human welfare/benefit of community generally, etc.	3
wisdom and understanding	3
education and humanities	1
students to gain (advantages of) a University education	4
corporate life and character of students	4

A minimum coverage is of course essential if it is to justify the name. An institute of ceramics, or of production engineering, or again of plastics or computer technology, however high its standards of teaching and research, is too specialised to be a University. This is now true of an institution devoted wholly to humanistic studies, even though traditional attitudes were against this. All the former Colleges of Advanced Technology have widened to some extent the range of their studies on becoming Universities.

The Robbins Report (para. 392) considered that the title of 'Technological University' would be entirely appropriate for those advanced Colleges which became independent Universities, but in the event only two included 'technology' in their titles, namely Bath and Loughborough. However, they did not choose the titles 'The Technological University of . . .' which would presumably mean a University with a strong technological orientation, that is, primarily a University. These two were each styled a 'University of Technology', which is a complete misnomer, a contradiction in terms, for the lesser cannot contain or confine the greater concept. Bath abandoned the title in 1971 with the approval of the Privy Council, but Loughborough persists in using it, and may perhaps pride itself on being illogically unique.

Table 3.2 conveys a general picture of the objects of the Technological Universities by linking together similar objects and intentions, even though they may be differently expressed.

The four types of commitment to knowledge (Table 3.1) are not all treated alike: preservation is not specifically mentioned, but rather assumed, since no advance is possible except on a basis of preservation; dissemination/teaching and extension/research are explicit in all cases but one; and application is variously mentioned and implied in all but two: social involvement and responsibility are recognised in several statements, as are professions and their needs. The balance has altered with time, and six questions were put to members of the Academic Advisory Committees of the Universities to ascertain their reactions to these changes. Their responses are analysed in Table 3.3.

The response rates to individual questions of the 49 members of the Academic Advisory Committees who replied varied from 88 per cent down to 59 per cent. Understandably column B questions had fewer respondents than column A since these involved judgements about the direction of change in the institutions they had served, rather than an assessment of their own attitudes to possible changes in them. There were differences between institutions in percentage terms, but as the number of potential respondents per institution was a mere 5, 6 or 7, no significance can be attached to a detailed analysis. However, at the individual level voting did tend to follow the trends – traditional *v.* 'CAT man' – within the institution served. This is perhaps not altogether surprising, since in the preliminary discussions about establishing each committee, the UGC and the University concerned each suggested a list of names of suitable

Table 3.3 Technological Universities: changes of emphasis in academic provision: response by members of the Academic Advisory Committees

Possible changes of emphasis	Column A — My attitude to this change is one of:								Column B — My institution has changed in the traditional direction:											
	Approval		Uncertainty		Disapproval		No answer		Very much		Considerably		Not certain		Hardly at all		Not at all		No answer	
	N	%	N	%	N	%	N	%	N	%	N	%	N	%	N	%	N	%	N	%
Fewer part-time courses	21	43	7	14	14	29	7	14	3	6	19	39	5	10	5	10	1	2	16	33
Fewer sandwich courses	4	8	5	10	26	53	14	29	nil	nil	3	6	6	12	14	29	8	16	18	37
An increase in social sciences and arts courses with a consequent decrease in the proportion of science and technology	27	55	5	10	11	23	6	12	3	6	19	39	2	4	10	20	1	2	14	29
A greater emphasis on research	33	67+	7	14+	3	6	6	12	3	6	26	53	5	10	1	2	nil	nil	13	27
The addition of an arts faculty	18	37	10	20	15	31	6	12	3	6	9	18+	4	8	7	14+	9	18	17	35
Reduced interest in applied courses designed to meet the needs of industry and/or commerce	5	10	1	2	34	69+	9	18+	1	2	1	2	3	6	6	12	18	37	20	41

Table 3.4 Technological Universities: changes of emphasis in academic provision: response by members of their Councils engaged in industry and commerce

	Column A								Column B											
	My attitude to this change is one of:								My institution has changed in the traditional direction:											
	1 Approval		2 Un-certainty		3 Dis-approval		4 No answer		1 Very much		2 Con-siderably		3 Not certain		4 Hardly at all		5 Not at all		6 No answer	
Possible changes of emphasis	N	%	N	%	N	%	N	%	N	%	N	%	N	%	N	%	N	%	N	%
Fewer part-time courses	33	51	8	12	18	28	6	9	3	5—	18	28	12	18+	15	23	6	9	11	17
Fewer sandwich courses	2	3	5	8	49	75	9	14	nil	*nil*	14	21+	10	15+	14	21+	14	21+	13	20
An increase in social sciences and arts courses with a consequent decrease in the proportion of science and technology	18	28	8	12	30	46	8	12	nil	*nil*	23	35	12	18+	12	18+	3	5—	15	23
A greater emphasis on research	41	63	12	18+	1	1+	11	17	9	14	24	37	10	15	4	6	nil	*nil*	18	28
The addition of an arts faculty	17	26	14	21+	23	35+	11	17	nil	*nil*	9	14	8	12	15	23	12	18+	21	32
Reduced interest in applied courses designed to meet the needs of industry and/or commerce	nil	*nil*	6	9	50	77	9	14	nil	*nil*	5	8	13	20	11	17	21	32	15	23

persons, from which the UGC made the final choice. It would be improbable that among the persons suggested there would be many opponents of sandwich courses, but nevertheless in order to reach a positive and agreed outcome, traditional academics had to reach a clear understanding of the purpose of sandwich courses. Industrialists on the other hand, needed to be clear about the academic requirements for the establishment of a University.

The 'No answer' columns reach over 25 per cent in seven out of twelve cases and the recurrent phrase 'I am not competent to answer this question' seems to indicate that the role was often played with considerable personal detachment. They were not dictating the future of the institution, but simply holding a watching brief – for what? Academic standards? University norms? The spectrum of studies? Professional education and training? In only one case was there evidence of a serious clash between the recipients and their advisers but, as is not uncommon, its impact declined with the passage of time.

The same range of questions was put to members of council of the Technological Universities who were engaged in industry and commerce, and the results are set out in Table 3.4.

Of 92 forms that were posted, 65 (71 per cent) were completed and returned. Institutions fell into two groups: responses from four – Aston, Bradford, Brunel and Surrey – ranged from 74 to 100 per cent, with a combined response of 81 per cent. The remaining four – Bath, City, Loughborough and Salford – ranged from 56 to 70 per cent, combining to give 61 per cent. The analysis is based on the 65 respondents, not all of whom answered every question.

This particular group of Council members expressed itself in favour of fewer part-time courses and of a greater emphasis on research, and strongly disapproved of any reduction in sandwich courses and in applied courses. Consistently they were lukewarm about a reduction in science and technology courses as a result of increasing the social sciences. The weight of their opinion favoured the retention of the academic structure and range of studies associated with the Colleges of Advanced Technology. Their views may be compared with the views of academic staff discussed in Chapter 8, and with the changes in the academic programme of studies discussed in the next chapter.

Chapter 3: Sources

1. This is shown very clearly in Eric Ashby, *Technology and the Academics* (Macmillan, London 1958).
2. Alan Montefiore (ed.) *Neutrality and Impartiality: the University and Political Commitment* (Cambridge University Press, 1975); but note review by Antony Flew, 'Sitting on the fence', *THES*, 28th Febuary 1975.

   M. D. Stephens and G. W. Roderick (eds), *Universities for a Changing World* (David and Charles, London 1975).
3. For the detailed consideration of which, see the Report *On Continuing Education* of the Open University Committee (Chairman the present author), December 1976.
4. Thomas Kelly, *A History of Adult Education* (Liverpool University Press, 1970), Chapter 14.

4

The Academic Programme

TECHNICAL education has expanded largely in response to industrial changes. The main specialist subjects within engineering – civil, mechanical, electrical, structural – became increasingly dependent on a knowledge of the sciences, and thus mathematics, physics and chemistry became indispensable 'service' subjects. With the growth of modern science-based industries, these subjects had to be developed in their own right, leading to a substantial increase in undergraduate courses. Postgraduate work developed, as did courses for various technologies and applied sciences such as metallurgy, plastics and chemical technology. Over the years, the balance of work moved from part-time to full-time and sandwich courses, the greater amplitude of which encouraged and made feasible an increasingly scientific curriculum for the technologies.

From 1956 to 1963 and the Robbins Report, the pattern of academic commitment to the physical sciences and technology remained substantially unchanged. Some trends, however, were accelerated under the influence of the National Council for Technological Awards (NCTA). For example general or liberal studies were introduced into all Dip.Tech. courses (though seldom in courses for London University degrees). The pattern of undergraduate sandwich courses in the CATs[1] was as follows:

1. *basic sciences,* or other basic disciplines.
2. *technological subjects,* analytically treated, and not merely or mainly descriptively as hitherto, and with a special project in the final year.
3. *introductory professional subjects.*
4. *professional training* not simulated *in academia,* but provided extra-murally in the workaday world as an integral part of the overall period of study.
5. *general studies.*

74

6. *social education* through the activities of the guild of students, the students' union and University residence.*

The educational commitment to the *physical* sciences, pure and applied, was almost total: biology and the life sciences generally, as well as the social sciences, were established with difficulty. Here too, it was occupational needs which provided the initial justification, for example for biology in relation to pharmacy, and for social sciences (economics, sociology, applied psychology, etc.) in relation to industrial administration and management studies. In due course the life sciences and the social sciences also became justified in their own terms. University subjects, not necessarily occupationally justified, thus became available, and indeed fashionable, in the Colleges, widening the choice open to students in a period when the number of student places in Universities was low.

The Council's interest in sandwich courses did not exclude three-year full-time courses, which almost compelled a close identification with traditional University courses. This in turn affected the pattern of sandwich courses. Later, the proportion of full-time courses increased, owing to the introduction of courses in the social sciences and the humanities, including languages. Efforts to develop postgraduate courses and research were largely frustrated because of the lack of higher degrees in the Colleges other than those with recognnition of staff by London University.

The changes in the academic programmes of the CATs as they moved towards Charter day can be summarised broadly in relation to the fourfold aspects of University objectives: the preservation, dissemination, application and extension of knowledge.

Preservation had not been rated of primary importance in the College days and the coming of University status brought a sharper realisation of how seriously ill-equipped they were as Universities to fulfil this obligation. The new modern Universities were given substantial initial capital grants to establish their libraries, but no such consideration obtained with the erstwhile Colleges – perhaps because the UGC assumed that they already had adequate libraries. But the Ministry of Education and the DES never had been convinced of the primary importance of libraries in the Colleges, and the lack of substantial funding grants for them has been a continuing sore point with these institutions under the UGC.

* See Chapter 9.

However, by the end of 1974 the UGC had come to the conclusion that they were not going to have resources to build new libraries at all Universities on the scale to match an indefinitely growing number of books. In April 1976 the UGC published the Report of a Working Party (Chairman: Professor Richard Atkinson) on *Capital Provision for University Libraries*. This recommends the adoption of the principle of a 'self-renewing library of limited growth'.

Dissemination of knowledge through teaching had gained in interest and importance through new developments in teaching methods and resources, e.g. programmed learning, audio-visual aids and computers. With the consequent need for new technical skills in teaching, these innovations became a focal point of demands for training of the academic staff (or 'staff development' as it is now apt to be called).

The teaching aspect is not determined primarily by methodology, important though such innovations are, but by the emergence of new concepts, the impact of new ideas, the cumulative effect of massive discoveries and the radically changed social context which together compel a redrawing of the map of knowledge.[2] But this idea of re-drawing the map has raised urgent questions of the directions to be taken in higher education: whose view of knowledge? Who decides – Senate, Council, Science Research Council, Government, industry – what to transmit, extend and apply? To whom or to what organisation, and for what purposes? Such questions challenge the assumptions underlying the object of enabling 'a student to obtain the advantage of a University education'. What is this 'advantage' – economic? cultural? political? philosophic? – meritocratic to the core? or what? What indeed are the purposes of a University, the values it accepts and is prepared to defend; and how should these relate to the student's life and well-being beyond graduation day? It was a signal service of University students in the 1960s to raise such questions of relevance, the value of which is not to be disposed of merely in narrow practical terms. On the other hand immediate relevance must not be pressed to the detriment of intellectual coherence and long-term perspectives.[3]

Since 1966 there have been some significant changes. First the range of specialist honours degree has been widened considerably beyond the College patterns of mathematics, physics, chemistry, biology and the main branches of engineering, as the following list exemplifies: systems analysis; computer science; statistics; communication science and linguistics; environmental health/science/

76

engineering; ergonomics; biomedical engineering/electronics; materials science/technology; business administration. A traditional course in a physical science such as chemistry, formerly involving subsidiary physics and mathematics as separate disciplines, can be transformed by their interpenetration. So most of the foregoing honours courses are essentially eclectic, based on a variety of subjects, skills and resources.

Demarcation disputes between disciplines are unprofitable, and there has been a strong move towards what are variously described as 'combined honours', 'inter-disciplinary' or 'integrated' courses. At best disciplines are chosen which can be related significantly to changes in society. Examples include a choice of French, German, Spanish, Italian or Russian courses plus one of engineering, transportation engineering, materials science or technology. The language is studied as a means of communication, both oral and written, and to gain an understanding of its everyday socio-cultural context.[4] The simple addition of a year abroad intercalated into a three-year full-time course does not *ensure* that these objectives will be gained,[5] and there are strong arguments for teaching languages on a sandwich course pattern which allows for some supervision during the periods of study abroad.[6]

Economics has proved to be one of the most popular of the social sciences, and it features in many inter-disciplinary courses variously combined with engineering options and the physical sciences; with history, politics, law or management studies.

Significant innovations in combined courses are occurring throughout the University world including for example the 'Liberal Studies in Science' course at Manchester,[7]* the 'History and Social Studies of Science' courses at Sussex, and the 'Science Studies' course at Edinburgh. Following a conference on Combined Studies in Science at Leeds in March 1972, a group of interested teachers from eight Universities and one Polytechnic† was established to develop such courses with a grant of £21,000 from the Nuffield Foundation. This grant was to help the 'Science in a Social Context' (SISCON) Group‡ 'to meet the cost of a three-year project of producing

* Or the 'Science Greats Course', as it quickly came to be known.

† Universities of Aston, Edinburgh, Leeds, Leicester, Manchester, Stirling, Surrey and Sussex, and the Middlesex Polytechnic.

‡ Co-ordinator, Dr W. F. Williams, Director of Combined Studies, Leeds University.

materials to be tried and tested in real teaching/learning situations in their own courses, and then to be published in a form which could be used in any first degree course in science, helping students and teachers to relate their subject to its social context'.[8] One such course in Integrated Science Studies was set up '. . . because many industrial, social and economic problems will not fit into the mould of a single discipline' '. . . and a course may thus be designed' '. . . to explore the intricate relationships between science, technology and society, and to relate scientific activity to its wide social impact'.[9]

Such considerations lead at once to a concern with communication gaps, not only between disciplines but between the generations. Some of the Technological Universities now have courses which combine educational studies with a scientific subject – physical, technological, social or human. To ensure a continuing supply of teachers for the Schools, who have been educated in Technological Universities, may very properly lead in later years to better informed attitudes towards careers in industry, commerce and the professions. Philosophy has also appeared in combination with mathematics and physics, but its writ should run far wider than the physical sciences, into the life sciences and the social sciences, for example about the stance of Universities in relation to values and social obligations in an industrial society. For similar reasons the study of history industrial, economic and social is essential to give perspective to the academic spectrum of a Technological University.

It was perhaps a natural sequel to its very substantial projects for science education in the schools that the Nuffield Foundation should concern itself with teaching in the Universities. The Inter-University Biology Teaching Project, involving four Universities and two University colleges,* started in October 1969 with a supporting grant of £80,000 from the Foundation. Objectives include widening the range of materials available to students and staff, and their methods of presentation, and a special feature is the combining of biological expertise with educational technology.[10] Such innovations relate to establishing common first-year courses and a modular approach, and perhaps then to 'credits' for courses which would facilitate the movement of students between Universities, in contrast with the present high particularity of syllabuses and courses.

* Universities of Bath, Birmingham, Glasgow, London (Queen Elizabeth and Chelsea Colleges) and Sussex.

The extension of knowledge: types of postgraduate study

The scope and scale of postgraduate courses in the Technological Universities have changed very substantially since 1966, the power to award higher degrees being one of the important consequences of Privy Council recognition. The development of research facilities and the recruitment of students for Master's and Doctorate degrees has been rapid and by 1974 the proportion of postgraduate students matched the average within the UK Universities as a whole. The figures for 1975–76 are given in Table 4.1.[11]

The balance of effort between research and study has been altered somewhat in the direction of the American pattern by the inclusion of 'taught courses' as a requirement for the completion of some of the higher degrees. Indeed there are many MSc. courses where 'taught courses' are a major component alongside a research 'project' where the emphasis is likely to be on the extension of the student's knowledge of research methods. These are postgraduate in time but not necessarily entirely so in standard and are planned to facilitate transfer either to another discipline or to the world of work.

Post-experience courses form a second group of postgraduate 'taught courses', and are taken, as the name implies, after a period of practical experience following graduation. Two main needs are met – first, to offset the obsolescence of knowledge produced by recent discoveries; and second, the need to acquire new knowledge and skill to facilitate changes in employment. Such courses are generally part-time and are much more specific in nature and of shorter duration than the Masters' degree courses. They have so far been self-sufficient in their objectives but recently moves have been made to relate them as credits towards the completion of MSc. courses. Whilst such progression could be a valuable incentive to further study, there is always the danger that the more immediate purposes of post-experience courses may be frustrated by more traditional objectives being imposed upon them.

As regards changes in undergraduate studies, extreme disciplinary specialisation is giving way to more generalised courses, and the more specialised professional or vocational aspects are being deferred to the later years. At the same time, as an integral part of the same progression, one-year postgraduate courses have begun to be established, specifically to orientate the student towards a pro-

Table 4.1 Percentage undergraduate and postgraduate enrolments in UK Universities 1975–76

	Technological Universities						All UK Universities					
	Under-graduate	Col. %	Post-graduate	Col. %	TOTALS	Col. %	Under-graduate	Col. %	Post-graduate	Col. %	TOTALS	Col. %
Full-time	22,772	99·4	4,282	57·7	27,054	89·2	218,088	98·3	50,626	69·2	268,714	91·1
Row %	84·2		15·8		100·0		81·2		18·8		100·0	
Part-time	133	0·6	3,133	42·3	3,266	10·8	3,815*	1·7	22,502	30·8	26,317	8·9
Row %	4·1		95·9		100·0		14·5		85·5		100·0	
TOTALS All individual students	22,905	100·0	7,415	100·0		100·0	221,903	100·0	73,128	100·0	295,031	100·0
Row %	75·5		24·5		100·0		75·2		24·8		100·0	

Notes: * The proportion of undergraduates among part-time students ranged from 20 per cent to over 40 per cent in the following Universities and University groups: London, Scotland, Wales, N. Ireland, Bristol, Hull and Newcastle.

fession. Such changes are responses to 'push-pull' factors: the 'push' from student applicants for broader courses, and the 'pull' into employment, the latter varying with the changing structure and economic conditions of industry and commerce.[12]

The application of knowledge: professional education

In mediaeval times European Universities were concerned with education and training for the law, the Church and the State.[13] 'In sociological terms' says Hugh Kearney, 'the Universities between 1500 and 1600 underwent a change of social functions. They were transformed from being institutions geared to training for a particular profession into institutions which acted as instruments of social control.'[14] In some this involved complete separation of academic study from professional training, for example as with medicine and the law at Oxford and Cambridge. At the former the trend was later reversed by the Oxford Commissioners. Developments in engineering were more rapid at Cambridge[15]* and while the Civic Universities emphasised professional education from the outset,[16] the new Universities from Sussex onwards were not so strongly committed.[17] The Technological Universities are perhaps the most strongly committed of all to professional education and training.[18]

In 1958 Sir Eric Ashby asserted that 'the attitude of Universities toward technology is still ambiguous: until the ambiguity is resolved the Universities will not have adapted themselves to one of the major consequences of the scientific revolution'.[19] Even as late as 1967, D. G. Christopherson,[20]† in his book *The Engineer in the University,* devoted his introduction to 'The University and the Professions' as if he felt it necessary to justify the relationship in general, as well as for engineering in particular. It is indeed remarkable how many books on British higher education have been written in recent years showing little awareness of the growing social significance of professionalisation.[21] The recognition by British Universities of the requirements of other professions in, for example, the social services, accountancy, management and administration,[22] has only in the last decade begun to be commensurate with the need. Some still maintain

* The relative development gave rise to the post-war quip from Oxford about 'The Fenland Polytechnic', and the retort courteous from Cambridge about the 'Latin Quarter of Cowley'.

† Now Sir Derman Christopherson FRS.

that professional education and training is no proper concern of Universities, and should be left to the Polytechnics – for otherwise 'the Universities will continue to grow into vast training camps for the professions'.[23]

Over fifty years ago R. H. Tawney questioned 'how industry can be organised to express most perfectly the principle of social purpose. The application to industry of the principle of purpose is simple, however difficult it may be to give effect to it. It is to turn it into a Profession. A Profession may be defined most simply as a trade which is organised, incompletely, no doubt, but genuinely, for the performance of function. It is not simply a collection of individuals who get a living for themselves by the same kind of work. Nor is it merely a group which is organised exclusively for the economic protection of its members, though that is normally among its purposes. It is a body of men who carry on their work in accordance with rules designed to enforce certain standards both for the protection of its members and for the better service of the public.'[24]

It is one of the most challenging tasks of the Technological Universities to accelerate and deepen this process. The whole context has, however, become increasingly complex with, for example, the growth of international companies and the increase in size and influence of the European Economic Community, the full effects of which have yet to be appreciated. The development of management education within British Universities has been a considerable success, and has been recorded by the UGC.[25] Among the many developments have been those at the Technological Universities at Bath, City, Loughborough, Bradford and Aston, as an integral part of their close relationships with industry.

The sociological study of the professions is a fairly recent development.[26] They have a particular concern for the preservation and application of knowledge, and thus with the control and direction of resources, and are therefore, as social institutions inherently conservative and deferential to the status quo.[27] They are thus apt to be tardily responsive to social change, reflecting the vested interest of senior members in protecting tradition rather than encouraging innovation. Furthermore, increasing specialisation conflicts with the need to tackle problems on an inter-disciplinary basis.

Established professions have certain general characteristics and powers: the provision of a competent service to individual clients and the community, and to ensure this competence by the control of professional education and training and of admissions to the profession by appropriate tests of knowledge, skill and experience. Professional bodies determine standards of conduct usually through a code of ethics embodying ideals and a code of practice which sets the standards, and defines the nature of unprofessional conduct. Under the impact of social change, their public responsibilities have been clarified and regulated, and because of the explosion of knowledge, education has become increasingly generalised and transferred to institutions of higher education. One major example of change is the engineering profession, which until recently was fragmented into fourteen different professional institutions. They combined in 1965 to form the Council of Engineering Institutions,* but its functions and relationships remain subject to debate (Chapter 12, reference 17).

General or liberal studies

Concern about the nature and provision of a *liberal* higher education has a long history.[28] The term 'general' has replaced 'liberal' because of the 'illiberal' implications about the rest of the curriculum, which technological and scientific staff resented. *'If we didn't have it, why should they need it?'* Conversely, *'It should apply not only to science and technology students but to the social sciences as well'* – a view expressed many times in discussion. The term 'complementary studies' has increasingly found favour as expressing the general intent while leaving options wide open.

The bias towards safer, more utilitarian studies was reinforced by increasing pressure on the timetable, and because the directness of their appeal gained the support of those teaching science and technology. *'There came the choice between time for management studies and general studies, and of course it was the first that the staff made compulsory.'* The subordinate service status of general studies and of the staff involved was a subliminal but tense issue. It surfaced intermittently, sometimes in direct controversy over status, but most frequently in struggles for resources, for proper teaching conditions and fair timetabling.

General studies – on the Dip.Tech. pattern – were not seen as a University concept by most members of Academic Advisory Committees, and were often deliberately played down or opposed. More-

* The Council of Engineering Institutions (CEI), 2 Little Smith Street, London SW1P 3DL.

over, from recorded evidence, it appeared that general studies were politely but very firmly played out of court by the UGC on their visitations; the U-non-U basis of rejection was quietly assumed for reasons which could not but be of the best! General studies could not be seen as a discipline and a professorship in general, liberal or complementary studies was an evident nonsense. This ensured much greater difficulty in recruiting staff of ability and experience comparable to University staff generally: *'We are not going to get first-rate people if all they can do is service-teaching at a modest level'* ... and conversely ... *'For young staff, with their way still to make, going for interviews at Civic Universities, to mention they teach general studies puts them at a positive disadvantage.'*

In all this, issues of academic autonomy, integrity and status were inextricably involved.[29]* Academic autonomy meant the power to control one's own subject and teaching, academic integrity, the ability to maintain standards in one's own discipline against free and rational criticism; and together, these entailed intense specialisation to satisfy the criteria and desiderata for academic advancement. Research and study in depth for the enlightenment and appraisal of fellow specialists was required rather than the enlightenment, however scholarly, of those in other academic fields: *'I don't think we can live by service-teaching alone'* ... *'Just being part-time purveyors of culture really isn't good enough'* ... *'General studies was interpretive but lacked the edge of disciplinary awareness – it lacked the challenge of a discipline.'*

General studies also incurred charges of superficiality: even at best the scholarly overview of a wide terrain is assumed to be inferior to digging deep with specialist or scholarly thoroughness in a very small part of it. In any case there is apt to be the academic assumption that no course of presentation could possibly be of any significance unless it were of honours degree standard, and that general studies was merely an attempt to apply a cultural veneer to an otherwise illiberal course. With this often went the assumption that all honours degree courses (single discipline best of all) being intellectually demanding, were self-evidently self-sufficient for all needs.

One awkward practicality was that of the assessment of general studies. Cumulative assessment was widely employed, but there was

---

* Staff relationships and academic issues were akin to those experienced initially in the operation of *'course teams'* established to prepare curricula and methods for foundation courses in the Open University.

prolonged controversy as to whether students should be examined, and whether a pass should be required in the final examination. No examination would inevitably lead to no interest on the part of the overworked student, and general studies would simply be crowded out: if there were an examination, it would have to be on the same basis as other final examinations, but professional attitudes were completely against results in general studies examinations adversely affecting a student's final result. *'Why make a peripheral subject a pass/fail factor? . . . Why set it up on a pedestal?'* This confrontation has generally been avoided by counting the general studies marks as part of the final total where they improve the overall average, but otherwise ignoring them. Thus lack of success does no harm, but good attainment is rewarded . . . *'Not all take it but formerly the non-takers were the have-nots, the disadvantaged – now the difference is between the unintelligent and the intelligent, because anyone who does his sums can see he can get benefit as well as find something of interest.'*

Another awkward reality was the lack of support among senior staff, varying from total indifference to outright opposition: *'I hardly know what complementary studies are: I have been in the University three years,'* said one professor, *'and I don't know how they operate and I get no feedback from the students'* . . . *'Liberal studies was a low-status activity, in which students had very little interest, and the departments which sent them had little intention of doing more than pay lip-service to the importance of these studies . . .'* A member of staff responsible for general studies was concerned to claim *'Some of my strongest supporters are engineering professors'* (but they were a small proportion of the total establishment).

Even granted a sufficient commitment among science and technology staff, there was the awkward lack of acceptance of general studies by staff in the social sciences for *their* students. This was on the assumption of superfluity or superiority – on the grounds that their courses already dealt with all essential issues, as distinct from the inherent narrowness of scientific and technical studies. These attitudes are quickly caught by the students concerned, who also are not slow to relate the superior grades of A-level required by social science students for admission to University as compared with those in science and technology. Such attitudes and tensions are minor but not insignificant parts of the polarisation between these disciplines, inherent in the emergence of social sciences as competitors for resources within institutions hitherto almost entirely scientific and technological in character.

Staff resistance may be rationalised in a variety of ways – thus *'general studies will prove to be a transient phenomenon when the sixth forms have been liberalised'* (pass the buck there), which entirely overlooks the growing maturity and understanding of the student in relation to adult affairs. Not everything is timely at the sixth-form stage. Or another reaction – *'If a student comes to University and is not interested in anything outside his engineering or maths or physics, you could make out a case that he ought not to be here anyway'* (pass the buck again!). This ignores the view that being at University should be a challenging, stimulating experience not only in the particular academic studies pursued, but in other aspects as well. Obviously a sense of proportion is needed as indicated by one member of staff . . . *'it would be a pity if it is abandoned, but as a Head of Department, I am worried that it is becoming almost a degree in general studies.'*

The attitudes of science and technology students appeared to vary from enthusiasm (especially for project work) to complete indifference. The staff concerned had formidable obstacles to overcome, in the attitudes of some of their students, of which perhaps the classic expression of resistance was: *'I didn't come here to be bloody educated, I came here to study my subject.'* But the attitude of students as recorded in discussion with student officers and members of committees was a genuine concern for a wider education rather than training, of exposure to general ideas and to the demands for social responsibility: *'The bulk of students are in favour so long as it doesn't become another discipline. It can be a relaxation; it could be an added stimulation.'* These students tended to be the more active socially and more articulate, but a more general reaction could perhaps be expressed as one of moderate involvement through a tolerant acceptance of an official requirement.

However, despite all the efforts made – which were substantial – the position of general studies was further eroded as provision for a broader education became possible in ways more compatible with University traditions. There were two mutually reinforcing trends. First, broadening was sought through establishing combined honours degree courses, by devising fertile hybrids, and by introducing interdisciplinary courses. Secondly, there was a proliferation of disciplines and courses to first degree level which satisfied the academic ambitions of the general studies staff and made them feel academically respectable at last: *'Over the long period there was constantly a tension between the responsibilities that existed* (for general studies) *and had to be discharged by somebody, and the ambitions of members of staff to teach their own disciplines. This tension is only now resolved, and with the setting-up of Departments, the end of the liberal studies concept is in sight.'*

The establishment of new Departments (modern languages, linguistics, history, European studies, economics, psychology, sociology and other social sciences) was irresistible, and inescapably entailed the establishment of postgraduate courses and the development of research. This general development has been heavily criticised as a prime example of passive acquiescence with conforming influences on joining 'the University club'. This view, however, wholly ignores the upward pressures for maintaining and raising standards in scholarly original work of whatever discipline. Institutions of *higher* education are inherently upwardly mobile, and for their academic well-being and effectiveness must secure adequate opportunities for development and progress at postgraduate level.*

The effect on staff attitudes towards general studies of the setting-up of the new Departments was most marked: *'General studies staff were absorbed into the social sciences, and quite honestly the attitude they then displayed towards service-teaching was pretty irresponsible . . . they said, "we cannot teach a subject unless it is done in depth academically".'* Exceptional instances of non-co-operation served to gather support for what proved to be major changes. In one case part of the responsibility was returned to the Departments, and the other part allocated to a small administrative unit under a Director of Complementary Studies. The unit organises a series of general lectures, seminars and conferences, involving either staff from other departments, or external specialists. These are generally on contemporary issues, and in addition a varied list of optional courses – some twenty or so in number in each of two or three successive years – are an integral part. The gathering of support from Departments calls for great determination wrapped in all the skills of delicate diplomacy . . . *'The Director plays a diplomatic game of chess with*

---

* The question naturally arises as to whether the provision of postgraduate studies and research will be conceded by government to be an inherent and significant aspect of the work of Polytechnics. This has been a central issue in the current controversy about the uncertain role of the Polytechnic. But see recent S R C Report, Chapter 12, reference 9A.

Departments: it is very complex as Departments play it differently, with extraordinary variations . . .'

The dispersal of responsibility to Departments is wise, as this is where the main effort should lie. The first objective should be the broadening of their own courses, so that students are helped to gain an historical perspective and an awareness of social relevance in their main subjects. The demands on the staff are inevitably exacting, in the joint planning of courses with their immediate colleagues, but the added intellectual stimulation in company with their students is a sufficient reward: *'We cannot have so much of the cultural side of our students' education left to a laissez-faire method.'* If all works well within the Departments, then the atmosphere engendered and the self-evident support of the staff will the more readily encourage the response of students to complementary studies. Curriculum reform in the physical sciences is beginning to affect the teaching of the basic sciences in technological courses, leading towards common first-year courses and course credits. Similar changes have affected introductory professional subjects, but these are not necessarily specific as in the case of the technological subjects, since they involve economic, humanistic and sociological studies. Ideological and cultural time-lag affects all education and training and there is now a special need not only to keep abreast of the American scene but with the European dimension as well.[30]

Despite their chequered history, there are many signs that concern for general and social education within the Universities is still a live issue. Sir Derman Christopherson[31] maintained that the sponsoring of these studies in Dip.Tech. courses contributed to 'the minor revolution in University thinking and practice about liberalising the overcrowded curricula of engineering courses'. In March 1973 Dr David Brancher at Aston was awarded a Nuffield Foundation grant for a 'General Education in Engineering' (GEE) project. It involved teachers in nine Universities (two of them technological) and two Polytechnics,* and aims to make engineering education more responsive to the needs of society.

* Universities of Oxford, Newcastle upon Tyne, Warwick, Liverpool, Birmingham, Aston, Exeter, Bath and Nottingham, and the Portsmouth and Oxford Polytechnics. The total Nuffield Foundation grant for the project was £57,950, and the co-ordinator was Dr David Brancher at Aston. For a comparison of the SISCON and GEE projects see Clive Cookson: *Two Science sisters take very different paths, THES,* 18th February 1977.

A series of articles in the Journal of the American Society for Engineering Education (ASEE)[32] noted that an increasing number of engineering graduates are successfully undertaking careers in other fields, including law, medicine, business, government, bio-engineering and educational technology. The papers seek answers to the consequential questions – 'are there intrinsic qualities in engineering education that prepare for careers in other fields? ... Can an engineering curriculum be viewed as a new kind of liberal education? ... Can modifications of the present engineering curricula be designed to better serve as preparations for other traditional careers?' Answers to these questions are of importance to the future of the technological Universities, particularly in relation to the recruitment of students.

Whatever the student's subject or discipline, it is but part of a vast ever-changing domain, in which perspectives need frequent readjustment and values need to be clarified and reasserted at various times throughout life. For this uncertain journey, 'the proper study of mankind is Man'[33] – man in society, man in his profession, in his leisure and work and institutions, man in himself, with his motives, duties and obligations, his fears and aspirations. Any topic thus relevant to mankind, examined with intellectual rigour and warmly perceived with imaginative insight and social responsibility, is pertinent to a University education.

However good the provision, a general education clearly cannot be acquired simply by what is 'taught'. It is fostered and might be 'caught' in less formal situations: in relationships with staff and fellow students and by means of the various extra-curricular activities associated with students' unions, residences and sporting and social events on the campus.

We stand on the threshold of a commitment to lifelong or continuing education,[34] and we must provide an appropriate basis for it in the undergraduate years. We cannot anticipate the future but we can prepare for it to the best of our ability, not only in respect of the professional or vocational side but in relation to human, social and political problems as well.

Chapter 4: Sources

---

1. Peter Venables, 'The Technological Universities: education for the professions', *Universities Quarterly*, Winter 1967.

2. Compare Asa Briggs (now Lord Briggs) 'Drawing a New Map of Learning', Chapter 4 in David Daiches (ed.), *The Idea of a New University*, (André Deutsch, London 1964).

3. See Lord Robbins' address as Chancellor of Stirling University, reported in *THES*, 30th June 1972.

4. See F. M. Willis, 'Linguists for a united Europe', *THES*, 5th May, 1972.

5. F. M. Willis, 'Sending languages students abroad: is it efficient?', *THES*, 26th January 1973. Compare also Chapter 9.

6. For an account of the language courses at Bradford University, see M. Binyon, *THES*, 11th August 1972.

7. See Michael Gibbons, 'Liberal Studies in Science', Chapter 10 in J. Knapp, M. Swanton, F. R. Jevons (eds), *University Perspectives*, (Manchester University Press, 1970).

8. Press release, Leeds University, 14th March 1973.

9. Professor E. Braun, Aston University.

10. See W. H. Dowdeswell, University of Bath (Co-ordinator of the project), 'Inter-University Biology Teaching Project', *J. Biol. Educ.*, Vol. 4, 1970, pp. 197–203. See also *Nature*, 11th August 1972, pp. 313–15.

    Roger E. Levien *et al.*, *The Emerging Technology – instructional uses of the computer in higher education*, Carnegie Commission Report (McGraw Hill, New York 1973).

    Anne Howe and A. J. Romiszowsky (eds): *International Yearbook of Educational and Instructional Technology* (APLET, 1976).

11. UGC provisional figures as at 31st December 1975.

12. Sir Brian Flowers, 'Engineering in the Universities', Maitland Lecture, Institution of Structural Engineers, *The Structural Engineer*, January 1973.

13. F. M. Powicke and A. B. Emden (eds), *Rashdalls' Mediaeval Universities* (Clarendon Press, Oxford 1936).

    A. M. Carr-Saunders and P. A. Wilson, *The Professions* (Oxford University Press, 1933, 2nd impression 1964).

    See also *Year Book of Higher Education*, 1959.

14. Hugh Kearney, *Scholars and Gentlemen: Universities and Society in Pre-Industrial Britain* (Faber & Faber, 1970), p. 33.

    A. M. Carr-Saunders and P. A. Wilson, *as 13*, pp. 314–18.

15. Report of the Cambridge University Commission, 1852.

16. W. H. G. Armytage, *Civic Universities* (Ernest Benn, London 1955).

17. David Daiches (ed.), *The Idea of a New University* (*as 2*).

18. Peter Venables, 'The Technological Universities and the Professions', *Universities Quarterly*, Winter 1967.

19. Eric Ashby, *Technology and the Academics* (Macmillan, London 1958), p. 66.

20. D. G. (Sir Derman) Christopherson, *The Engineer in the University* (English Universities Press, 1967).

21. But note an exception: J. A. Jackson (ed.), *Professions and Professionalisation* (Cambridge University Press, 1970).

22. See Lord Butler, *The Responsibilities of Education: The Professions, Industry, the Universities and Government* (Longmans, London 1968).

23. J. P. Powell, 'Vocational training and the Universities', *Universities Quarterly*, Spring 1973, pp. 223–34.

24. R. H. Tawney, *The Acquisitive Society* (G. Bell & Sons, London 1921), Chapter VII: The Liberation of Industry, p. 106.

25. UGC *Annual Survey* 1975–76 (HMSO), paras. 71 and 72, and Appendix IV pp. 36–52.

26. As 21. In the present context, see especially the first three chapters: J. A. Jackson, Editorial Introduction: 'Professions and Professionalisation'; C. Turner and M. N. Hodge, 'Occupations and Professions'; G. Harries-Jenkins, 'Professionals in Organisations'.

The first major study was by A. M. Carr-Saunders and P. A. Wilson: *The Professions* (Oxford University Press, 1933, 2nd impression Frank Cass & Co., 1964).

A. H. Halsey and Martin Trow, *The British Academics* (Faber & Faber, London 1971), Chapter 2, pp. 47–52.

27. See Frank Musgrove, *Patterns of Power and Authority in English Education* (Methuen, 1971) in relation to the general background.

28. J. H. Newman: *The Scope and Nature of University Education* (9th edition Longmans, London 1889).

The Idea of a University defined and illustrated (9th edition Longmans, London 1889).

Sir Walter Moberly, *The Crisis in the University* (Macmillan, London 1949).

Liberal Education in a technical age: A Committee Report (Chairman, Sir Robert Wood, Vice-Chairman, Peter Venables) National Institute of Adult Education (Max Parrish, London 1955).

29. See Sir Walter Perry, *Open University – a personal account by the first Vice-Chancellor* (Open University Press 1976), pp. 83–95.

Jeremy Tunstall (ed.), *The Open University Opens* (Routledge 1974).

John Ferguson, *The Open University from Within* (University of London Press 1975), p. 36.

30. Sir Frederick Warner, 'Education and the professions in the European Economic Community', Mond Memorial Lecture, *Chemistry and Industry*, 7th May 1973. Debate, *EEC Regulations and the Professions*, Lord Bowden *et al.*, *Hansard* (House of Lords), cols 524–615, 10th April 1973. Paul Moorman, 'EEC Ministers find way out of degree deadlock', *THES*, 14th June 1974.

Carnegie Commission Reports (McGraw Hill, New York):
Lewis B. Mayhew, *Graduate and Professional Education 1980*, 1970.
Edgar H. Schein, *Professional Education: some new directions*, 1972.
College Graduates and Jobs, April 1973.

31. *As 20*, Chapter 8, 'Liberal Studies – Colonialisation or Expansion'.

32. February 1973, pp. 331–68. The first article is 'The New Phase in Engineering Education: Engineering and the New Liberal Education', by George Burgliarello, the Editorial Co-ordinator of the papers. Compare Duncan Davies, Tom Banfield, Ray Sheahan: *The Humane Technologist* (Oxford University Press, 1976).

33. Alexander Pope, *Essay on Man*, Epis. ii, 1744.

34. Open University Report *On Continuing Education* (1976).

5

Sandwich Courses

'SANDWICH courses' are so called because substantial 'layers' of full-time study and of organised industrial experience alternate over a period of years, as for example for first-degree courses, six months in industry succeeding six months in college and so on turnabout for four years.* This type of course was supposed to have originated in 1906 at the University of Cincinnati, but some form of sandwich course was in fact started at the Royal Technical College, Glasgow, about 1880, and in 1902–3 at Sunderland Technical College and at Northampton Polytechnic.[1] However, the early schemes lacked some of the significant features which were introduced from 1950 onwards, especially the efforts to integrate study and training, the visits of teaching staff to students in training, and the introduction of project work.[2]

Many causes contributed to fifty years' delay in development, of which the chief were insufficient support from industry and a lack of co-operation between firms and colleges.[3]† There was also a persistent unawareness of the defects of part-time education, first of evening classes and later of the shortcomings of part-time day release courses. The insoluble problem was the lack of time to provide a basic grounding in science and general education on which more advanced studies could be built.

The first real impetus from industry came at the Royal Technical College, Salford, in 1950–51, strengthened in 1953 through the appointment of Dr Willis Jackson FRS (later Lord Jackson of Burnley) as Director of Research and Education at Metropolitan Vickers Ltd. This development had the active approval and support of the Ministry of Education through C. R. English

* Though separately listed in DES official returns, sandwich courses are regarded as full-time courses (and not part-time or block release courses) provided that the minimum period of full-time study is 19 weeks per annum.
† Not for nothing were the American ones called 'co-operative courses'.

HMI.* Similar developments were planned in 1953 at the Birmingham College of Technology between Dr J. J. Gracie CBE, a director of the General Electric Company (GEC) and chairman of the governing body, and Dr J. Wilson, principal of the College. The resulting course for the College Associateship was designed to gain full recognition by the Institution of Electrical Engineers. It subsequently received retrospective recognition for the Diploma in Technology awarded by the National Council for Technological Awards (NCTA), so that the first 34 Diploma students – all GEC employees – graduated in September 1958.

Following these and other developments, the National Advisory Council on Education for Industry and Commerce (NACEIC) saw in sandwich courses an important means of producing the required number of technologists and technicians of the right quality. This was adopted as Government policy in the White Paper in February 1956 and the Council's Report was included as an Appendix. Shortly before this the same policy led to the establishment of the National Council for Technological Awards (NCTA) in July 1955 for the award of the Diploma in Technology (Dip.Tech.). In May 1956 the NCTA published its first 'Memorandum on the recognition of courses in Technical Colleges for the Diploma in Technology, the courses for which will be equivalent in standard to honours degree courses of a British University'. By 31st March 1959 there were 2,518 enrolments in 66 courses, mainly in engineering, but some in various sciences. The expansion to 8,718 enrolments in 118 courses, with 1,073 awards made, is shown in Table 5.1.[4]

In view of the figures in Table 5.1, and the fact that developments of sandwich courses in the CATs did not fall off when they became Universities, it is remarkable how over the last few years, propagandists for the Polytechnics have rarely mentioned the existence of this substantial system of sandwich courses in the Technological Universities. By 1973–74 there were 12,696 sandwich course students enrolled in nine former CATs, compared with 20,647 enrolled in CNAA degree courses in 28 Polytechnics and in eight other Technical Colleges.

General principles and objectives

Sandwich courses provide a mode of professional education in which

* Later Sir Cyril English, and Director-General of the City and Guilds of London Institute.

Table 5.1 Expansion in Diploma in Technology sandwich courses under the National Council for Technological Awards

Position at 31st March each year	10 CATs			Other colleges			TOTAL		
	No. of courses	Student enrolments*	Dip.Techs. awarded	No. of courses	Student enrolments*	Dip.Techs. awarded	No. of courses	Student enrolments	Dip.Techs. awarded
1958	28	1,038	—	13	325	—	41	1,363	—
1959	44	1,899	34	22	619	—	66	2,518	34
1960	61	2,876	106	28	938	23	89	3,814	129
1961	65	3,641	268	35	1,328	41	100	4,969	309
1962	72	:	526	34	:	94	106	6,201	620
1963	73	:	776	35	:	151	108	7,310	927
1964†	73	:	899	45	:	174	118	8,718	1,073
TOTAL Dip.Techs.‡			2,609			483			3,092

Notes: * Figures for CATs and other Colleges not shown separately after 1961.
† Robbins Report 1963. No new Dip.Tech. courses started thereafter.
‡ By 31st March 1967, total Dip.Techs. awarded 4,328: 3,585 (83%) in CATs, 743 in other Colleges.

off-campus training is an integral part of the overall period of study. They are not a panacea for all the ills and defects of traditional forms of professional education and training, but have their own particular merits and advantages. These appeal particularly to students who are concerned to relate theory to practice as soon as possible.

The requisite full-time study must be soundly based scientifically, concerned with theoretical concepts and with the principles underlying practical applications, and not with the details of endless practical processes and manufacture. Sandwich courses, otherwise called integrated courses, do not imply a direct one-to-one correspondence or relatedness of theory to every practical instance (a sheer impossibility), but study which is illustrated by applications of fundamental principles, whenever possible within the students' practical training in industry.*

Experience in the workaday world through simply taking a job is one thing, but training is quite another as it involves *organised experience* with certain declared objectives in mind. These include acquiring specific skills and knowledge, insights and values, and relating to colleagues and co-workers of a particular firm under the inherent constraints of the working conditions and economics. This off-campus activity in the everyday working conditions of factory or business must be an integral part of the whole. Simulation of these conditions and constraints may be attempted intramurally, but inherently cannot succeed. On this practical criterion the training at the workshops provided at Loughborough College from Dr Schofield's day onwards does not suffice to qualify them as sandwich courses.†

From the career standpoint, the firm has a first-hand opportunity during the in-works periods of observing the student's abilities and capacity for development, a form of selection through training which

* Unless the context indicates otherwise, the word 'industry' is used to cover all the extramural works-based periods of a sandwich course, e.g. in industry, commerce, hospitals, government establishments, etc. There is in fact a substantial case for a revision of the nomenclature of sandwich courses – see *Recommendations on Nomenclature* by J. A. R. George, submitted to the Universities' Committee on Integrated Sandwich courses, January 1976.

† L. F. Cantor and G. F. Matthews (*Loughborough: from College to University*, Loughborough University of Technology, 1977, p. 124) have recorded that Dr H. L. Haslegrave (Principal and subsequently Vice-Chancellor) agreed with the Ministry that the training of an engineer must include periods of training with outside firms, 'for only in this way could students become accustomed to the real economic conditions of modern industry. This represented a significant break with Schofield's "Training on production" . . .' (see Brief History).

is more effective than an interview. At the same time, the student has a good opportunity to look at the firm, its efficiency, its management and personal relationships.

Patterns of provision

Assuming that both parts of the sandwich course – study and training* – are well-organised and stimulating, bringing them into

Diagram 5.1 Sandwich courses: patterns of study and training

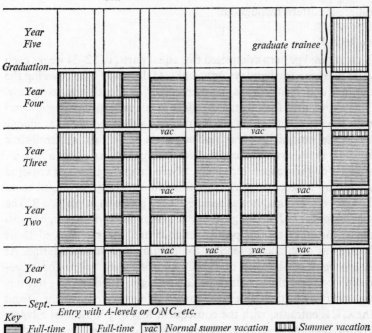

Pattern A 6 months/ 6 months	Pattern B End-on 2 groups Box and Cox	Pattern C.1	Pattern C.2	Pattern C.3	Pattern D 2.1.1	Pattern E 1.3.1
		Variants of general pattern 1.2 mixed.1				

Key *Entry with A-levels or ONC, etc.*

Full-time study | Full-time training | [vac] Normal summer vacation / Reduced vacation period | Summer vacation experience

* As the sandwich course principle has been applied to non-industrial occupations in which the economic/production factor is not paramount, there is a problem of description. For our purposes it is convenient to identify the period in University, Polytechnic or College as '*study*', and the period 'off-campus' in works, offices, on sites, in laboratories or wherever, as '*training*'.

relationship raises important educational issues and poses definite practical problems. The various patterns of study and training are therefore considered in turn, in relation to the operational, teaching and industrial aspects, including points made in the recorded discussions. The main patterns are set out in Diagram 5.1.

In the 1950s sandwich courses developed most quickly in engineering, and were almost entirely of pattern A (see below). Science courses – especially chemistry, physics and mathematics – were originally of this pattern also, but over the period moved fairly quickly to other patterns, especially C.3 and D. Biological sciences most readily adopted patterns C.1 to D, especially the latter. At a later stage sandwich courses were established in the social sciences and very largely adopted pattern D. These general observations do not apply at Brunel and Surrey, each of which has a single but different pattern throughout.

Pattern A

This original pattern comprised two equal parts, of 22–24 weeks each after allowing for holidays or vacations; the study part covering the autumn and spring terms, i.e. September to March approximately. This allows time for substantial effort to be made in each section and with the periods of study closely related to the traditional academic terms the sandwich course students are able to mix with full-time students in social and other activities during their periods of academic study. For this reason especially, where increasing intakes required setting up a second course this was almost always arranged from January to July, and not as an alternating group as in pattern B. The second intake in January gave a peak load in the spring term, but also an opportunity to run post-experience and other advanced short courses as a balancing load in the autumn and summer terms. At Aston separate intakes of ONC students were taken for three-month periods, thus balancing the loading in another way, but this was properly criticised because these students were segregated from the GCE entrants, with the consequent loss of educational advantage to both groups. In recorded discussions, those committed to pattern A held strongly that it fosters competence, maturity and motivation through the sequence of training periods in a cumulative way not possible in a single period of training as in pattern D, i.e. the 2.1.1 arrangement.

The main criticism of pattern A from the industrial point of view was the uneven loading between College and industry, and the consequent difficulty of finding the large number of training places (as distinct from jobs) needed, especially in the summer months when students from other Universities were seeking vacation experience. This led to experiments to establish pattern B. One criticism from students applied to pattern A, in regard to the first and final years, was that two terms in College or University was too short a period for a student *'to find his place'*, *'to settle in before being dragged off/plunged into industry'*. Such emotive phrases seemed to be preferred to a calmer description, e.g. 'being placed in a firm'.

This was undoubtedly the feeling of some students, but it was countered by a staff view that the sandwich course put a premium on adaptability and flexibility and the best students throve on these recurrent challenges. Social science students tended to feel that the six-month pattern did not allow time for sustained reading and an adequate use of libraries. As for taking part in student union activities, attendance for two terms virtually prevented election for office, especially for the senior positions, unless special arrangements were made. In any case, because no special arrangements could be made in respect of sports, some were excluded altogether, such as cricket and tennis for the September intake and football for the January groups. The January intake join the student community when the societies and clubs are already well set in their ways, and thus feel that their opportunities are much more limited than for other groups. The total effect of all the foregoing was a strong move for a full-time first year, and some courses have persisted with this single change.

As for the final year, it is a period of maximum stress, making severe demands on students through the final examination *and* the completion of the special project: the first could be reduced by cumulative assessment but not the second, which has its own inherent stresses. In addition, the students see themselves as graduating in March after the examinations, and although this is not the official view and graduation ceremonies are deferred till after completion of the final training period, its value is undoubtedly affected. There can be no feedback from the final training period to the studies, and the students are concerned to be done at last with training and also to be paid wages at the rate for graduates. All these considerations add up to an argument – with special appeal to academics – for making the final year one of full-time study only, resulting in some variation of pattern C, i.e. the 1.2 mixed. 1 pattern. The single pattern throughout at Brunel goes part-way to C, being pattern A with the final year (only) taken full-time.

Pattern B

This arrangement of two end-on groups, alternating Box and Cox fashion, is meant to ensure full use of capacity in University, Polytechnic or College and of each training place in industry throughout the year. The practical gains to industry are important and self-evident: other effects are less apparent but nevertheless far-reaching for the teaching institution concerned. Since they operate in sequence timewise, the two groups are totally unrelated and never meet. Their lack of alignment to the normal academic terms sharpens the criticisms of pattern A in respect of student involvement and activities, especially for the group which starts the course with a period in industry. This group, however, has the advantage of finishing with full-time study for examinations and completion of the project.

While maximum use of capacity is a prime factor in favour, the supply and utilisation of staff may be a source of serious difficulty. It may be impossible to attract or retain able academic staff unless all Universities are committed to a four-term year (which the end-on arrangement is, in effect), or to two semesters plus summer schools or sessions (with extra income for staff) on the American pattern; it is scarcely possible for those concerned with sandwich courses to go it alone. Moreover, there is the question of the continuing cost of additional staff to be set against the non-recurrent cost of buildings and equipment. One important aspect is the impact on research conducted by or under the supervision of academic staff: in the event of staff absences or shortages, this would be the first casualty as the teaching of the students would have to be regarded as top priority. If academic staff serve for three terms out of four, there is the particular problem of the use of comparatively rare specialists throughout four terms. The assumption may be made that economies of scale apply to the end-on arrangements in that there is a twofold use of the same buildings and equipment by twice the number of students for the cost of the requisite extra staff. However, if normal staff conditions of service and staffing ratios are maintained for end-on courses, the over-staffing which results from falling enrolments is more serious. This has already happened with engineering and science as students have switched to arts and social science courses.

One point, which might have been made in respect of pattern A, is that the students go into training for the same period of the year throughout four years, and never experience training under working conditions in the other half of the year. For example this particularly affects training periods in industries dependent on climate, such as building, civil engineering, agriculture, horticulture and fisheries. Such considerations apply to both groups under pattern B, as each repeats its original first-year arrangement throughout the course. In sum, while the advantages of pattern B are manifest for industry, the consequences for the University and its students are likely to be disadvantageous. This may explain the very limited development of the end-on pattern which has been tried at City University (two courses remaining), Salford (two courses remaining) and at Bradford (three or four courses) with an enrolment of 1,554, being 12·2 per cent of all sandwich first degree course enrolments in 1973–74.

Before cost-benefit considerations are pressed very strongly in favour of pattern B, there should certainly be the most careful appraisal of the effects on the work and life of the Universities concerned. As Polytechnics are, by Government policy, to be primarily and largely teaching institutions closely linked with the needs of industry and commerce, it will be of great interest to see whether they will accordingly establish sandwich courses on pattern B.

Pattern C

Three variants of this pattern which have been tried are shown as C.1, C.2 and C.3 Diagram 5.1. They all have a first year of study, but relate differently to the normal University vacations. With these coming next to periods of study it is possible for students to enjoy them in the traditional ways, including travel abroad, a matter of importance in relation to being in Europe. Patterns C.1 and C.2 have the longest initial period of study, and this is advantageous to acquiring competence in a language prior to training in Europe or vacation travel, and especially desirable for certain inter-disciplinary courses. It is also argued that C.1 and C.3 give adequate time to attain the necessary minimum level in scientific subjects, especially mathematics, physics and chemistry, for profitable training in science-based industries. Patterns C.1 and C.3 have ample periods for examinations and the final project work, more indeed than any other patterns.

The total time for training is halved in pattern C, as compared with patterns A and B, which those who prefer A and B find quite inadequate. Pattern C.3 is criticised on the grounds that a continuous twelve months away from disciplined study creates a serious backlog of difficulty for the student for the next session. As the study periods follow the traditional terms, there is very much greater involvement of students in societies and other activities, but the holding of representative office is still difficult to achieve. Placement with different firms follows the practice under patterns A and B, but the continuous period in C.3 was stated in discussion to be favoured by the large firms. Mistakes in placement cannot always be remedied, and adverse effects are disproportionately greater in comparison with the four shorter periods of A and B. Moreover in C.3 the cumulative maturing effect of several training periods over two to four years can hardly occur in a single period of one year, an adverse judgement which applies still more strongly to pattern D.

Pattern D

This is the logical sequel to the changes indicated by the patterns C.1, C.2 and C.3, and it evokes strong loyalties and equally strong antipathies. The pattern fits most neatly into the traditional University setting, being strictly based on the normal academic year. It maximises the use of capacity, and makes no unusual demands on staff apart from visits to students in their third year. The opportunities for student involvement and the sense of belonging are comparable with those of students in normal full-time courses for the first two years, but in the final year the students return to a community in which they are relative strangers.* It is argued that the year's training and experience 'outside' is sufficient compensation, and in any case there is usually a marked withdrawal from student activities in the final year owing to preoccupation with a project and the final examinations.

A major consideration is whether a whole year away from disciplined study makes settling back in the final year too difficult. At Surrey, where pattern D prevails throughout, opinion in recorded discussions was firmly against this view, or at the very least that there were no undue difficulties to offset against the advantages. At Brunel and elsewhere, opinion of those committed to pattern A is

* One critic asserted that '*the 2.1.1 pattern is merely an interruption in a full-time course.*'

that six months is the maximum period a student should be away, as this causes difficulty enough. In each and every case, once the choice has been determined, rationalisation prevails and the arguments are marshalled to demonstrate its inherent rightness, while difficulties are minimised.

Another advantage claimed for pattern D is that the full range of staff is available and there are no undue demands on them, so opportunities for research are not seriously affected as they are by other patterns.

In determining staffing ratios and equivalent full-time students, the UGC gave notice in 1970[5] of a ratio of 0·85 for staffing for a sandwich course as compared with a full-time one, i.e. 3·4 staff would be a reasonable allocation for a basic unit of a four-year sandwich course as compared with 3·0 for a three-year full-time course. In effect, 0·4 staff was to be allowed for arranging places in industry and visiting the students, whatever the pattern of the courses. This total staffing allowance would favour pattern C.3, and especially pattern D; for them the allowance would be optimised; for A and B it is a liability, and if maintained the direction of change would not be hard to predict. However, in response to representations from the Technological Universities, the UGC advice was modified[6] and apprehensions greatly reduced. However, as with other cost-benefit implications already discussed, there is still need for a critical watchfulness to maintain the best educational conditions for the operation of sandwich courses.

Pattern E

This was a pattern of training favoured by some traditional University Engineering Departments in the post-war period, and when sandwich courses (as described here) were successfully established in the 1950–60s, this pattern was claimed to be a sandwich course. Generally speaking, however, under the 1.3.1 scheme the University was not ultimately responsible for placement in the firms: if none was arranged the student simply took the full-time course with short periods of industrial experience in the vacations.[7]* Furthermore, visits by University staff to students in training were not a regular commitment, nor did the University accept any responsibility for the sequence and quality of the training received. For Dip.Tech. sand-

* As regards the first year in industry, UCCA defines the period in effect as 'pre-entry'.

wich courses, this responsibility for placement and training was recognised by recording the name of the firm(s) on the Diploma and this practice has been continued for succeeding degree courses, or a separate certificate has been issued.

So far as relationship to study is concerned, the value of pattern E, in comparison with all the other patterns, turns on the significance of the one year of prior industrial experience plus two possible vacation periods in industry (one of which may be a summer practice school, arranged specially for a group of students in a large firm). Much is currently being made of the educative value of a substantial break from school before taking up full-time study at University or College, but on that basis any kind of employment will presumably suffice. However, scepticism is justified about the adventitious educational gains of the unplanned experience of being thrown into the industrial deep end.[8] Even at best, success despite an unorganised experience is not a sound basis for a professional education, or indeed for education generally. That 'it sorts out the men from the boys' used to be a favourite argument for the first year of the 1.3.1 arrangement, as it was of the part-time route by those 'who came up the hard way', in both cases seemingly oblivious of the disadvantages of the process.[9]

If the experience is organised and not merely adventitious, it is best taken *within* the overall period of study to which it is related. This fosters the student's motivation and both study and training are more effective. Over the years the major innovations introduced with the Dip.Tech. sandwich courses have affected some of the practices on the 1.3.1 arrangements just as the study content of sandwich courses was affected by University standards and practices.

There was a considerable interchange of ideas and experience, in which external examiners, initially mostly University staff, were particularly influential. Nevertheless when all is allowed for, and while there are no absolute distinctions between all the various patterns indicated in Diagram 5.1, arrangements under pattern E lack the characteristics, general practices and responsibilities which obtain with sandwich courses in the Technological Universities.

Industrial training

The *organised* experience which constitutes training should be based on a scheme agreed by the firm and the University, Polytechnic or

College in advance of the placement of the student in the firm. This does not mean that every detail needs to be finalised in advance, or that beneficial modifications are ruled out. In such a complex relationship perfection is improbable and defects, mentioned in evidence, include the following: insufficient sustained interest on anyone's part in the firm in the 'student-employee', or in the scheme as a whole; insufficient and inadequate visits from University or college staff; sudden and inconsequential changes without explanation or notification; repetitive work unduly prolonged, which happens especially when the student has proved valuable to a particular department or section, to the detriment of his progress through the agreed scheme.

On the other hand there are students who do not co-operate, or expect far too much to be done for them as privileged trainees (as they tend to see themselves); non-co-operative foremen or other staff, who resent the additional time-consuming responsibility, for which they may not have been prepared or consulted; inadequate preparation of the student by academic staff for his period in industry, and little interest thereafter in what he has gained from it; students sacked from firms as a result of mergers, with other places then to be found for them at very short notice (in a general industrial recession); academic staff recruited from traditional Universities with research as their highest priority are reluctant visitors to firms and give a very poor impression of University or College commitment: *'Academics are not always welcome in industry and you have to tread very carefully.'*

For appraising this catalogue of errors of omission and commission a sense of proportion and perspective is essential. Some of the defects mentioned[10] belong to the early stages of schemes and have tended to disappear with growing experience, goodwill and co-operation. Some derive simply from the fact that human nature is widely distributed, indicating that the human and administrative aspects need at least as much care and preparation as the technical aspects. However, the volume of criticism in recorded evidence was small, and there was general acceptance that the industrial training provided was on the whole satisfactory, some of it excellent. The main concern was properly about improvement and, to secure this, some Universities and Departments decided it was not profitable to go it alone, but to establish small discussion groups composed of representatives from the firms and the University staff. These training committees or panels broadly approve schemes of training and related practical matters, and are available to offer advice and support when difficulties arise. The experience proved encouraging and gave rise to another and still somewhat contentious development, that of certification.

Certification of industrial training

A separate award is unacceptable to those who argue for the indissoluble unity of the sandwich course principle, involving as it does the integration of study and training: and that to give two awards for *one* course is both misleading and damaging. Several contrary arguments are urged in favour of a separate certificate of industrial training: the two aspects can never be directly and wholly integrated; training within a firm cannot and should not be part of an academic certification, as the criteria and procedures are so very different;* the greatly varying circumstances of industrial work make it impossible to arrive at assessment of capacity and performance in any way commensurate in rigour and accuracy with that on the academic side; and a separate certificate from a joint body – such as an Industrial Training Institute of the University – could be a valid and valuable statement in its own terms. One further practical point is likely to appeal to students – by the end of four years a full-time student could gain an honours first degree and then an M Sc., but a sandwich course student will have only a first degree: he should therefore have a second award, i.e. for industrial training. This has been pressed as important in attracting students to sandwich courses, but the contrary argument is that different first degree awards should be made for the respective courses, e.g. B Sc. for three-year full-time, and B Tech. or B Sc. (Tech.) for the four-year sandwich.

Unfortunately that differentiation was not established by the Technological Universities altogether at the outset, and regaining that opportunity by collective consultation and action on the part of the eight Universities (of similar origins) seems quite improbable. As things are (1976) a B Tech. is awarded at Brunel for all first degree (sandwich) courses, and at Bradford for sandwich courses as distinct from full-time ones, and at Loughborough a B Tech. plus a Diploma in Industrial Studies.

* This relates to schemes for the recognition of work experience in other countries as credits towards degree requirements.

Assessment of training has a number of important benefits, apart from underlining the importance of the industrial training; its regular appraisal by staff visits and by the periodic completion of specially designed reports; facilitating reasonable changes where necessary in the training programme or in the student's welfare, and in increasing his motivation. Reports by the firm, academic staff, and by the student himself are usually integral parts of the total assessment, but students' reports may be contentious in scope and treatment, especially if of a critical nature or dealing with confidential matters.[11] Cumulatively, however, it is likely to result in a firm and accurate body of knowledge upon which more realistic policies of industrial training could be developed.[12] In 1972 a Committee on Integrated Sandwich Courses was set up composed of representatives from the Technological Universities.[13]

Forms in use set out questions to be answered by the visiting tutor and employer respectively, together with the basis of assessment and allocation of marks: to give one example – extramural course work, 10 per cent; written report 30 per cent; oral report 10 per cent; employer's report and rating 30 per cent; visiting tutor's report 20 per cent.

Sandwich courses provide an established route to professional status, with recognition of the training by professional bodies. Thus the statement No. 6 of the Council of Engineering Institutions (CEI November 1969) outlined general principles for the training of professional engineers. Each of its member Institutions has reviewed the effect of these principles upon the professional training and experience they require for election to their own corporate membership. As sandwich courses were progressively established for a widening range of disciplines and occupations, beyond science and technology to the social sciences, commerce, banking, public services, welfare and social services generally, similar practical questions of assessment and recognition of training had to be settled.[14] It is imperative that joint action should not be delayed as hitherto but established as soon as possible. It is nonsense to suppose that such participation would be an invasion of academic or institutional autonomy, and the Universities concerned should take a clear lead as each new related group of courses and occupations becomes involved. Ten years after the transfer of the Colleges to University status the Vice-Chancellors' Committee established a special committee to consider the problems of sandwich courses, stimulated by the increasing difficulty of finding industrial training places. The Joint Working Party Report deals briefly with some important aspects of sandwich courses, including assessment of training, rate of expansion of courses, administration and finance. However, it fails to deal with the changing pattern of courses, and with the nomenclature of degrees awarded.

The courses can only succeed with well-motivated students, but their motivation is very susceptible to factors outside their control. These include the following: the particular pattern of study and training periods; the attitudes of teaching staff; the design and balance of courses, and the relevance and effectiveness of industrial training and the attitude of management at all levels; the degree of interrelatedness established between academic studies and the knowledge and experience gained in training. If these are openly, and if need be critically, discussed with students by the staff, and their own very firm commitment to sandwich courses is clearly evident, then the motivation of students can be well sustained. Again, at the risk of underlining what should be very evident, a similar commitment on the part of firms is no less essential to the success of the joint enterprise.

The future of first degree sandwich courses

Ordinary three-term, three-year, full-time courses are much easier to initiate and maintain than four-year sandwich courses which involve significant off-campus training. The factors affecting the success of sandwich courses are complex, and genuine sustained co-operation and good relationships with very many firms must be ensured for them. In times of economic stress industry's commitment may be severely tested, and this and other factors may be cumulative in the institutions concerned. The net effect may be a reduced expansion of sandwich courses leading to a net decline in enrolments, taking place simultaneously with an increase in enrolments to full-time courses. Diagram 5.2 exemplifies such trends.

Diagram 5.2 shows that recruitment to ordinary/other full-time courses remains buoyant, not so that for sandwich courses, but the decline is not necessarily caused by the rise in the number of full-time courses and enrolments in them. The factors are compounded of a varying mixture of attitudes in schools and in industry, practical difficulties, and with communications and publicity quite inadequate

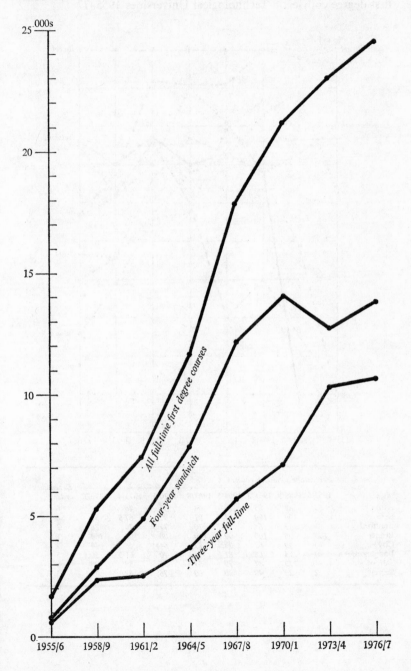

Diagram 5.2 Enrolments in sandwich and all other full-time first degree courses: 8 institutions now Technological Universities 1955–76

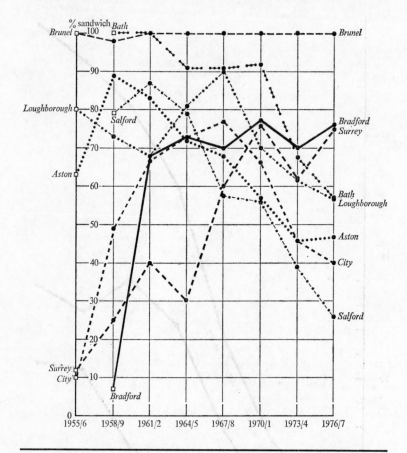

Diagram 5.3 Sandwich courses as percentages of all full-time first degree courses: 8 Technological Universities 1955–77

	Percentage sandwich courses								Descending order
	1955/6	1958/9	1961/2	1964/5	1967/8	1970/1	1973/4	1976/7	
Aston	63	89	83	72	68	57	46	47	6
Bath	—	100	100	91	91	92	67·5	57	4
Bradford	—	7	68	73	70	77·5	70	76	2
Brunel	100	98	100	00	100	100	100	100	1
City	10	49	67	73	77	64	46	40	7
Loughborough	80	73	68	81	90	70	61·5	56·5	5
Salford	—	79	87	79	57·5	56	39	26	8
Surrey	12	25	40	30	60	76	62	75	3

to surmount the problems involved. It might be surmised that staff recruited from traditional Universities may be showing a preferential passive resistance to sandwich courses: but this is hardly likely to be so, with the sustained policy of recruiting staff with industrial experience as shown in Table 8.9. However that may be, the essential point is, that the problems are urgent and require national action, as discussed in Chapter 12.

The changes in the former CATs over the years 1954–1974 are shown in Diagram 5.3. The two extremes are Brunel, with 100 per cent sandwich courses, and Salford, recently declined to 26 per cent. Chelsea College never achieved more than 10 per cent of sandwich courses, and these terminated in 1970–71. UWIST had 31 per cent of sandwich courses in 1975–76. The majority of the Technological Universities have a substantially mixed economy, though showing varying trends finishing within wide limits of about 45–80 per cent. The questions remain of what is a reasonable, viable admixture of sandwich and other full-time courses; and below what lower limits sandwich courses are likely to be in jeopardy because the critical mass of commitment no longer exists among the staff.

Postgraduate sandwich courses

The customary ways forward from first degree courses to full-time graduate studies and research, outlined in Chapter 4, do not readily obtain for students from sandwich courses.* With the professional orientation of sandwich courses, often accompanied by a strong occupational link for particular students, a sequence of postgraduate work has taken much longer to establish. Professionally trained graduates could be expected to want to practise their profession forthwith, and this is borne out by the facts shown in Table 6.1. For those who show promise and inclination for taking a research degree, some consultation with the sponsoring firm is obviously essential. Other graduates may return in small numbers after some years in industry to do research for a higher degree either full-time or, if the nature of the research requires it, by continuing on a sandwich course basis. The latter is valuable for graduates from full-time courses, as their contact with industrial conditions is no longer delayed. This is especially important if such graduates are to make

* This is a persistent residual cause of disapproval of sandwich courses among some academics, albeit rationalised in other ways.

successful careers in for example, production and management. The research projects should be chosen accordingly, preferably be sponsored by a firm, and be studied and tackled on an inter-disciplinary basis.

The Inter-disciplinary Higher Degree (IHD) Scheme, pioneered at Aston from 1968, is one of the largest schemes supported by the SRC/SSRC Joint Committee.[15]* The Scheme provides the student with the opportunity to learn one or more new disciplines to complement his first degree and to provide the theoretical bases for the research work. Supervision is by a team drawn from relevant Departments of the University and one member of the collaborating firm or organisation, co-ordinated by an IHD tutor. In this way the student analyses the problem in its practical context and has the opportunity to develop proposals which, it is hoped, will be implemented and evaluated in the period of the research project. By exposing him to the hazards and tribulations of 'action research', the student is enabled to gain experience of practical problem-solving that will equip him for a career in the central areas of industry, commerce and public bodies.

In 1973 the SRC published a report on 'Total Technology',[16] prepared by a special panel, the main recommendation of which was in effect an extension of the Aston IHD Scheme leading to Ph.Ds in so-called Total Technology. The term itself was introduced by the panel's chairman, Professor H. Ford FRS, to cover all the stages of the technological process in industry, their inter-relationships and the management skills for welding them all together. The aim is to rectify the imbalance of Ph.Ds in engineering which are almost entirely oriented towards careers in research and development, and in teaching in higher education, with very few in production, manufacture and management. The basic principle – following the Aston IHD Scheme – is to combine relevant inter-disciplinary study with practical experience on a project of direct interest and concern to a particular firm, which is prepared to co-operate in all aspects of the work. The report saw 'a need for both Master's and Doctor's degrees which must of course be developed in close col-

* By 1971–72, 83 studentships had been awarded on 18 different schemes, 25 awards being held at Aston. The SRC policy of diversifying awards in such ways at MSc and Ph.D levels has been a very welcome development of recent years: see statement: *SRC's support of postgraduate training:* SRC Bulletin, February 1977.

laboration with industry, *perhaps even* on a sandwich basis: there is no place in such a scheme for exercises in the abstract.'[17] Nevertheless, despite the last assertion, it may not be too fanciful to sense in the two words here italicised an unfortunate residual reluctance to embrace a full partnership with industry: how much better to have suggested *'preferably on a sandwich basis'*. The Total Technology Scheme began in 1974.

Chapter 5: Sources

---

1. Peter Venables, *Technical Education* (G. Bell & Sons, 1956), p. 86.

2. Peter Venables, *Sandwich Courses for Training Technologists and Technicians* (Max Parrish, London 1959).

3. For the history of US developments see 'The Cooperative Division of ASEE – a brief history', *Engineering Education*, April 1971, pp. 785–826, F. O. and Asa S. Knowles and Associates, *Handbook of Cooperative Education* (Jossey-Bass Inc., San Francisco 1971).

4. Source: NCTA *Annual Reports*. For details see Table A III b.

5. Letter to Vice-Chancellors, 8th October 1970. Note 14. (2) of *Notes for Completion of Quinquennial Estimates – 1972–77.*

6. *Letter to Vice-Chancellors,* 9th June 1971.

7. UCCA leaflet: *Industrial Awards and the Universities Central Admissions Scheme.*

8. Peter Venables, letter to *The Times*, 28th December 1974.

9. *15 to 18. Report of The Central Advisory Council for Education – England* (Chairman, Sir Geoffrey (later Lord) Crowther) (Ministry of Education, HMSO, 1959), paras. 513–517: 'Success and Failure in Technical Courses'.

Ethel Venables, 'Placement problems among engineering apprentices in part-time Technical College courses' Parts I and II, *B. J. Educ. Psychol.*, Vol. xxx No. 3, 1960 and Vol. xxx No. 1, 1961.

10. F. Musgrove and A. G. Smithers, 'Attitudes to Industrial Training of Engineering Students on Sandwich Courses', *Educational Sciences*, Vol. 3, 1969.

F. Musgrove (ed.), *Sandwich Course Studies* (University of Bradford 1970 (duplicated)).

F. Musgrove, 'Industry's Doubts About the Sandwich Course', *Durham Research Review*, Vol. vi No. 28, Spring 1972.

11. See publications/papers of Brunel University Institute of Industrial Training, e.g. S. A. Urry and B. Morgan, *Current methods of assessing industrial training in sandwich degree courses.*

12. Compare American experience; see Asa Knowles (*as 3*).
13. Chairman, V. C. Marshall, University of Bradford Schools of Chemical Engineering. *Draft report on assessment of training* published November 1973.

    See also R. A. M. Thomson, 'Assessment of Industrial Training', *Education in Chemistry*, July 1973.
14. W. W. Daniel & Harriet Pugh, *Sandwich Courses in Higher Education* (P. E. P. Broadsheet, No. 557, 1975).

    Joint Working Party Report of CVCP, CDP, ACFHE, & CBI: *The Future Development of Sandwich Courses* (April 1975). See also the related report of the *National Conference on Sandwich Courses* published by the University of Bath, April 1976.

    C. Hanson, 'European Methods of Training Technologists for Chemistry and Industry' (*Chemistry & Industry* (1965) 838).
15. See the Joint Committee Report: *Broader Education for Graduates*, September 1972.
16. Note also UGC *Annual Survey* 1972–73, para. 37.
17. *Ibid.*, para. 3.8. Note that the term 'sandwich' used in the Appendix, para. 15, of the Report, includes the 1.3.1. pattern.

6

Relationships with Industry and Commerce

SINCE 1900, and particularly since the Second World War, it has been increasingly recognised that Universities and industry must work closely together,[1] and complaints about the inadequacies of the Universities have recurred from time to time right up to the 1970s. For example, in evidence to the Education and Arts Sub-Committee of the Parliamentary Expenditure Committee, Session 1972–73, University curricula for engineers were stated by representatives of industry 'to encourage narrow specialisation too frequently and to fail to develop the more generally needed skills . . . and that the importance of the profit motive as the heartbeat and the generation of cash as the lifeblood of private-enterprise industry is insufficiently understood . . . The encouragement of specialisation – which seems to attract esteem in the academic world – may be an inhibiting factor in the development of the personal attributes and breadth of outlook, two contributory elements to the quality of man management and administration which is so essential in the industrial environment.'[2]

Many further examples could be quoted from the press and professional journals, but the wide-ranging nature of the following contribution will serve for an analysis of the reasons why the disagreements between the 'practical men' and the 'academics' still persist so strongly. As so often happens when an argument is pressed unduly, wellnigh perfect attributes in one respect are opposed to carefully selected defects in the other as in the following speech:

'British Universities are not meeting industry's recruitment needs, and a radical change is needed to provide graduates who will make British industrial management the best and British industry the most competitive in the world. Industry needs men educated in sciences, mathematics, economics, foreign languages, the humanities, company law and modern business methods; men of good character and

115

with energy, initiative, dedication and loyalty. This should be coupled to a humane outlook, a knowledge of trade union attitudes and organisation, and a willingness by students to recognise the need to continue learning about their particular industry.

'The Universities seem, probably for political reasons, to have based selection on equality of opportunity before all other considerations and on an examination system . . . that fails to meet the desired goal of selecting the best individuals. What is required is a small number of honours graduates of exceptional brilliance, coupled with a larger number of men who have been required to achieve a lower standard of academic achievement over a broader field . . . Too many University places are given to those taking courses in sociology and kindred subjects, which are ill-defined and are matters of dogma or opinion rather than of fact and where degrees seem to be acquired as a matter of course. In consequence those requiring places for courses designed to supply industry's needs are excluded.'[3]

A variety of considerations intermingle here. First, a time-lag is inevitable in making good the defects in complex relationships, even when the parties concerned are both aware of the need for action and have the will and common understanding to take it. Even if we assume agreement on objectives, and that action will be sustained and effective, the time-scale required to achieve a successful outcome of educational change has to be reckoned in terms of years, not months. An awareness of the need for educational change can be reinforced by changes – actual or impending – in industry, which in turn produce further demands on Universities and Colleges. Thus the gap between the hopes of mutual understanding and achievement widens, and where there could be a proper sense of achievement, there is instead a disabling sense of dissatisfaction expressed in the kind of criticisms quoted. Annoyance energises criticisms of selection on egalitarian grounds, of the fallibility of an examination system which is implicitly felt to bear no comparison with the efficiency of a mechanical 'go-no-go' gauge system, and of the integrity and significance of new academic disciplines. The sociological scapegoat is no surprise, indeed almost a natural from the engineering standpoint, as was repeatedly made clear in the recorded evidence from academic staff.

Such industrial criticisms can be matched by corresponding ones from University administrators and academics, for example in relation to post-experience courses: 'Industry has not accepted the responsibility of ensuring the continuation of employment of its middle-grade staff in an industrial society based on a rapidly changing technology ... unless the situation is changed, middle management and middle grade technologists would be thrown on the scrap heap of redundancy at post-middle age.'[4] Complaints are made also about the lack of support for sandwich courses, and all too often about complacency – about the way in which students and graduates are received on entering industry for the first time. Cotgrove and Box write: 'If we found less evidence of strain among industrial scientists than we had expected, we *did* find considerable evidence to suggest that industry is failing to use the skills and capacities of many of its scientists to the full – a major factor in the failure of industry to attract the best graduates.'[5] A contrary view is that in future 'increasing numbers of graduates are going to have to adjust their sights and be content with jobs as foremen, for example, and section leaders in offices'.[6]

Modern science-based industries, which tend to take the lead in representative bodies, as in management and production, are still exceptional in many respects. They are not typical of industry as a whole, a fact which affects relationships with Universities and Polytechnics, and the other side of the picture was put sharply in 1972 as follows: 'A more rapid response is needed from industry in recognising social change, in which higher education tends to be a generation ahead ... There are still whole sections of commercial enterprise in this country who look with deep-rooted suspicion at those who have been tainted with higher education. There are still too many companies in this country who regard the employment of a graduate other than the boss's son as a certain step to bankruptcy. Too many companies are looking for the promising school-leaver of 15 or 16, whom they can bring up on the shop floor, send to night school, and at some time in the distant future have him take over as works manager.'[7]

Defensively the reaction from industry can instantly be: 'Isn't this another stereotype which is outdated?' – for the proportion of industry affected is very small but gets disproportionate publicity. Within higher education, academics often retreat to the traditional view of the nature of their institutions, and their separation from practical ends.[8] Some in the Universities go so far as to reject any orientation towards industry at all, whether in classifying degrees for the convenience of employers, or in accepting industrially-sponsored research projects. Such heavily defensive reactions rarely lead to constructive outcomes, any more than do recurrent blasts of criticism from leading employers. The relationships are complex, and continuously need a more involved but cooler concern.*

Interactions between industry and Universities respond not only to changes within each group but also to changes within society at large. The early consequences of the scientific and technological revolution were seen as a liberation from toil and squalor, but nowadays the social and political consequences come under close scrutiny. Earlier élitist systems are being challenged and educational opportunity is being extended in a move towards mass higher education. Visions of universal higher education and permanent or recurrent education are on the horizon.[9] Education, including vocational education at all levels – operative, craft, technician, professional, managerial and executive – is also increasingly seen and felt to have wide social and political effects beyond the narrow and particular aims of individuals and their employers.

Growth of itself poses severe problems. The impact of science and technology on industry and the consequent need to extend educational facilities has meant that the Technological Universities and the Polytechnics are attempting to cater for a larger number of firms spread over wider catchment areas, which in turn involves the shedding of lower-level courses. More important from the point of view of industry is the problem of overlap in the provision of courses, and competition for industrial support, particularly in relation to sandwich and post-experience courses. Some representatives of the CBI have defended the calibre of graduates entering industry, and have also expressed satisfaction with the output from the higher and further education systems, especially where vocational-type courses are concerned. Reservations and criticisms were made in evidence to the Committee on Postgraduate Education,[10] arising particularly

* The Vice-Chancellors' Committee (CVCP) in December 1976 established a special group to consider the report of the Select Committee on Science and Technology 'to advise on ways of reacting to those of the Select Committee recommendations on which the Universities might take the initiative' (DES Expenditure Committee: Government observations on Third Report 1973–74, *Postgraduate Education*, Cmnd. 6611 (HMSO)). Even so it has already been stated that there is 'a danger of higher education over-reacting to the problems of industry, to the point where short-term needs may dictate long-term policies'. See Henry Chilver: 'Relevance must be seen in a long-term perspective', *THES*, 18th February 1977. (But see Chapter 12, reference 17.)

from the experience of science-based industries. A memorandum by ICI[11] exhibits very clearly the changing demands of modern scientific industry far beyond those of traditional industries.

The enormous range of British industries and their greatly differing degree of scientific sophistication makes generalisation difficult, and sound practical relationships with higher education institutions can only be established over a substantial period of time. With the Technological Universities there have been decades of effort and change, accelerating since the early 1960s. Vocational classes began in response to the demands of employees, and encouragement from their employers came later with their reimbursement of fees to successful students. Part-time day release courses began to be strongly supported during the First World War, and the second significant advance came with the development of sandwich and block release courses after World War II.

Collaboration developed through the setting up of college advisory committees with members nominated from employers' federations, from the trades unions, and from relevant professional institutions. They discussed curricula, practical training, the provision of workshops and equipment, and encouraged interest and support from their fellow industrialists. Similar representatives served on college governing bodies with some overlap to provide a link with the college advisory committee. The chairman of a governing body was often a leading industrialist, and a great majority of the staff had had previous industrial experience. Representatives served on the Regional Advisory Councils which influenced, even if they could not determine, the distribution of vocational courses in the colleges.

On becoming Colleges of Advanced Technology, representation of industry on governing bodies tended to increase. On the University councils the proportion was in general less. The risk of undue industrial influence on the autonomy of the University could be a matter of concern,[12] but there was no evidence in recorded discussions that this was a serious issue in any of the Technological Universities. In such discussions, however, students expressed concern on a broader basis, that of the undue influence of *any* external group or sector of society through having a disproportionate representation on Council.

A marked change in the CATs was the termination of the advisory committee system, and this mainly because the rising standard of work and increasing specialisation in the institutions, especially at postgraduate level, made all-inclusive College-based advisory committees ineffective and time-consuming for gathering advice and support. They were replaced, as needed, by specialised panels at departmental level, recruited *ad hoc* for the period of each particular project. With the rapid development of sandwich courses, the degree of direct involvement with industry increased very substantially.[13] This was inherent in the recruitment and placement of students, in the schemes and arrangements for training, and in the supervision of students' projects in the final year. Contacts with industry were also maintained through part-time courses at postgraduate level in post-experience courses, and more recently by courses for postgraduate diplomas and MSc. degrees, and in IHD schemes for MSc. and Ph.D degrees on the sandwich course principle. Modern science-based industry has a particular interest in such collaboration.

Most of the Technological Universities are committed by their Charters, and all by their history, to close association with industry, and in extending their research interests the large number of staff with previous industrial experience made a significant contribution. With the attainment of autonomy and consequent changes in conditions of service, the institutions were enabled to fulfil objectives which had hitherto eluded them. After 1956 the post of Reader was established in the Colleges of Advanced Technology, and some visiting Readers were appointed. However, the rank of Professor was not available. After 1963 most of these institutions proceeded fairly quickly to establish posts for visiting Professors in order to involve distinguished practitioners in industry, commerce and the professions in the work of the University. They are variously concerned, as befits their own interests and background, in the design of courses, in research projects and in teaching. They may attend faculty boards but attitudes are strongly against using their limited time in administration. The conditions of appointment vary, but they are usually part-time posts, of three to five years' duration. By 1972–73, there were 78 Visiting Professors in the eight Technological Universities.*

* There is some variation in nomenclature, and some Universities reserve 'Visiting Professor' to denote an established Professor from another institution seconded or on sabbatical leave for a substantial period of full-time service. Alternative titles for the part-time posts discussed above include Associate Professor and Professorial Associate.

The reverse involvement of academic staff in industry has long been advocated, but apart from visits to sandwich course students in the firms, and the selection and supervision of their final year projects, the results have been very small and uneven. Sandwich course arrangements lead to other contacts and activities, such as special investigations and research projects, or to postgraduate courses which, it is hoped, will lead to more substantial and permanent involvement. Very early in their history as Colleges, the secondment of staff to industry for periods of six months or more was strongly recommended,[14] but the results were not encouraging. There was little incentive for industry to receive the weaker members, and the best who could hardly be spared were easily persuaded not to return, in view of salary differentials.

Another arrangement which is theoretically desirable, but apt to be very difficult in practice, is the interchange of a teacher with some equivalently qualified and experienced person in industry.[15] Quite apart from the capacity of each in the other's job, all sorts of practical problems arise to frustrate proposals: the problem of matching differing career expectations and prospects; the safeguarding of pension rights; travel and accommodation problems – not to mention inherent personal difficulties, the impossibility of moving house, and the unlikelihood of exchanging use of homes for the period. Thus local interchanges are the only ones likely to be feasible. So the pressures are very strong to settle for less, e.g. would it not be more feasible and at least adequate to arrange ample visitation and consultation both ways on a part-time basis?

No real system of interchange was established during College days, and no significant progress has been made since becoming Universities. Sabbatical leave, which is one possible solution, does not appear to have been used for the purpose of gaining or regaining direct experience in industry. Conversely the move from industry to a University post has its problems. It can be seen as a soft option, but quite a proportion of those who choose to take it find the responsibilities involved, including the need for sustained disciplined study in the preparation of lectures and seminars, much more arduous than they expected.

For small institutions and departments, liaison with industry is simply a matter of direct contact by the staff concerned, mostly within the locality. With large ones having a wide range of interests and expertise, special appointments to facilitate work with industry became desirable and presently essential. By May 1973, 65 posts of Industrial Liaison Officer had been established in 58 institutions with a view to establishing liaison centres – four Universities (Aston, City, Strathclyde and UMIST), 22 Polytechnics, two Scottish Central Institutions and 30 Technical Colleges. However, the results were uneven: some liaison centres were successfully established, but by July 1973 some 25 centres were due to close and others were at serious risk.[16]

Establishing working relationships is apt to be difficult anyway, but disproportionately so with the far greater number of small firms than with the small number of large firms. The latter are generally very well established and equipped, have highly specialised manpower, and have their own training staff and facilities. Small firms are very widely dispersed and have little or no resources for training staff, and yet their specialised needs and particular problems have received little response from Colleges or Universities until recently.

The first specific pilot development was the establishment in Birmingham (the home of small businesses) of the Small Business Centre at Aston University as from 1st January 1967,* with a grant of £45,000 from the Department of Economic Affairs. Progress was made, but in July 1973 the whole effort was reorganised† and staff were transferred to form the nucleus of Aston Technical, Management and Planning Services Ltd. (briefly Aston Services) a subsidiary company owned by the University which started operations on 1st August 1973. The services cover management consultancy, technical facilities, prototype facilities and links with specialist centres within the University. Altogether some 28 UK Universities have now established special links with industry, as Liaison Office, Industrial Unit or University Company,[17] yet another marked change from the 'ivory tower' stereotype.

Generally speaking the foregoing companies provide a bridge between the particular University and a wide variety of organisations, public and private, for the purpose of attracting research and/or development contracts, and of gainfully marketing appropriate consultancy expertise and facilities. At the same time greater opportunity

* The grant was obtained on the initiative of Sir Joseph Hunt, Chairman of Council at Aston University.

† Following the recommendations of the Committee of Inquiry on Small Firms (Chairman, J. E. Bolton) (Cmnd. 4811, HMSO, November 1971). The CBI has in recent years given increasing attention to the problems of small firms.

is provided for academic staff to gain valuable and relevant consultancy experience, with beneficial effects on the teaching of students. Such companies are an expression of the practical commitment of the University to the application of knowledge, but each one must remain firmly under the control of the University. As indicated, definite advantages can accrue to the individual teacher and researcher, but no academic should be *required* to undertake work for the company, and contracts must be freely negotiated.

University Appointments Boards and employment of graduates

Universities generally found it necessary some decades ago to establish Appointments or Careers Advisory Boards to deal with the placement of students in employment.[18] In its 1972 quinquennial *Notes for Guidance*, the UGC recommended an increase in expenditure on careers advice of 5 per cent per student. An important step was that taken in 1971–72 by the Committee of Vice-Chancellors and Principals in setting up a Central Services Unit (CSU) for Appointments Services. As a result any employer can notify immediate vacancies to the CSU which then circulates details to all Universities.

At first, with a large proportion of works-based or works-sponsored students in sandwich courses, and a small proportion in most cases in full-time courses, there did not seem the same necessity for establishing Appointments Boards in the Colleges of Advanced Technology. However, the worsening of national economic conditions sharply reduced the number of works-based/sponsored students and there was a consequent rise in College/University-based students. In addition more full-time courses were started, and increasingly students were pressing to enter arts and social science courses, and interdisciplinary courses. For all these groups career prospects were very different from those sponsored students in the original sandwich courses, and as already indicated establishing Appointments and Careers Advisory Boards became as necessary in the Technological as in other Universities, and were set up by 1973.

In 1972 a Parliamentary question as to the percentage of those graduates who were still unemployed at the end of the year in which they graduated elicited the facts given in Table 6.1.[19]

The percentages generally were very small and the differences between the means for Technological and traditional Universities negligible. However, the range was wider in the traditional sector,

Table 6.1 Unemployment of graduates 1970–71 and 1975–76

| | Believed to be unemployed | | | | In temporary employment | | | |
| | 1970–71 | | 1975–76 | | 1970–71 | | 1975–76 | |
Institution	N	Percentage of total first degree graduates	N	Percentage of total first degree graduates	N	Percentage of total first degree graduates	N	Percentage of total first degree graduates
Aston	18	2·6	28	3·4	6	0·9	14	1·7
Bath	15	3·7	21	3·3	9	2·2	11	1·7
Bradford	46	6·4	28	3·8	18	2·5	24	3·2
Brunel	16	5·4	16	4·5	8	2·7	18	5·1
City	10	1·9	19	4·2	19	3·5	13	2·9
Loughborough	30	6·1	38	5·5	13	2·6	24	3·5
Salford	35	4·9	37	4·9	8	1·1	17	2·2
Surrey	26	5·6	25	5·0	28	6·0	20	4·0
TOTALS								
Technical Universities	196	4·6	212	5·3	109	2·7	141	2·2
All UK Universities	2,331	4·7	2,944	5·3	1,499	3·0	2,461	4·4

six of them having values ranging from 8·0 to 13·8. The range for all eight Technological Universities was 1·9 to 6·4. The low values gave no support for the alarmist views of the preceding years, that the market for graduates was exhausted. What appeared to be happening, and it was certainly desirable, was that graduates were moving into new types and levels of occupations. Too much can be made of short-term market fluctuations, and in any case there is no question of trying to find *the* one job which will fit the particular graduate. Such occupational determinism is an absurdity, and a much more resilient vigorous attitude has been recommended by Duncan S. Davies:[20] 'Don't let us waste time in worrying about "a surplus of graduates". Let us get on with the business of helping them to batter their way into society; they alone can decide where to batter and what sort of things it is best to do when they are in. But let us avoid perpetuating the idea that a degree confers a right to be a centurion, with appropriate status and badges of rank. Have graduated, will travel hopefully.'

Chapter 6: Sources

1. See *Industry and the Universities—Aspects of Interdependence*: Report of a conference convened by CVCP and CBI (published by ACU, March 1966).

   Committee on Manpower Resources for Science and Technology, *The flow into employment of scientists, engineers and technologists*. Report of Working Group (Chairman, Professor (now Sir) Michael Swann FRS, FRSE) Cmnd. 3760 (HMSO, September 1968).

   The Relationship between University Courses in Chemistry and the Needs of Industry Report of Committee (Chairman, Professor Colin Eaborn), sponsored by a joint committee of The Royal Society and Royal Institute of Chemistry, (published RIC, London December 1970).

   Industry, science and Universities: Report of a working party on Universities and industrial research to the Universities and Industry Joint Committee (London July 1970: Appendix No 1, June, 1971; No. 2, February 1972).

2. Report from the Expenditure Committee (Education and Arts Sub-Committee) Session 1971–72, *Further and Higher Education*, Volume I, Report (HMSO), Minutes of evidence, GKN submission 28.2.73, p. 278.

3. Sir John Hunter, Chairman of Swan Hunter Group Ltd. Address to the Association of University Teachers, University of Newcastle, reported in *The Times*, 26th January 1972. Original copy supplied by courtesy of the author.

4. Dr J. A. Pope, Vice-Chancellor, University of Aston in Birmingham, reported *THES*, 16th June 1972.

5. S. Cotgrove and S. Box, *Science, Industry and Society* (Allen & Unwin, London 1970), Chapter 5.

6. GKN Evidence, Education and Arts Sub-Committee (*as 2*), 6th March 1972.

7. Revd. Dr George Tolley, Principal, Sheffield Polytechnic, reported *THES*, 10th March 1972.

8. K. R. Minogue, *The Concept of a University* (Weidenfeld & Nicolson, London 1973).

   J. MacCallum Scott, *Dons and Students: British Universities Today* (Ward Lock, London 1973).

   Compare Evidence to the Expenditure Committee (Education and Arts Sub-Committee) (*as 2*), 12th February 1973, p. 72, Question 234.

9. Martin Trow: *Reflections on the transition from mass to universal higher education, ibid.*

   T. R. McConnell, R. O. Berdahl, Margaret A. Fay, *From Elite to Mass to Universal Higher Education* (University of California, Berkeley 1973).

   Logan Wilson and Olive Mills (eds.), *Universal Higher Education* (American Council on Education, 1972).

10. Expenditure Committee (Education and Arts Sub-Committee) Session 1972–73, *Postgraduate Education*: Minutes of Evidence, 2nd April 1973: Memorandum submitted by Confederation of British Industry, pp. 236–247 (HMSO).

11. See ICI Memorandum to the Parliamentary Committee, 12th February discussing its experience with 2,243 employees with postgraduate qualifications of which 1,586 had Ph.D, and 558 MSc., and 6,707 at level of first degree or equivalent professional qualification (i.e. 8,950 out of 37,500 monthly-paid staff).

12. See E. P. Thompson, *Warwick University Ltd.* (Penguin, Harmondsworth 1970).

13. Despite the contrary views expressed by Tyrrell Burgess and John Pratt, *Policy and Practice* (Allen Lane Penguin Press 1970), Chapter 5, p. 40.

14. *The Supply and Training of Teachers for Technical Colleges* (Chairman, Sir Willis Jackson) (Ministry of Education, HMSO London, 1957).

15. Compare the CBI Evidence to the Expenditure Committee (Education

and Arts Sub-Committee) on Postgraduate Education (*as 10*), 2nd April 1973, p. 246.

16. *Hansard* (House of Commons), Written Answer, 8th May 1973, Cols. 76–79. Government support grants to industrial centres were withdrawn as from 31st July 1973: see Pamphlet 5, *Assistance of Small Firms*, Industrial Liaison Service, October 1972.

17. See *Directory of University Industry Liaison Services* (Brunel University, 1976). See also UGC, Annual Survey 1975–76 (Cmnd. 6750, HMSO): para. 19 refers to the 'development of industrial liaison units which now exist in some two-thirds of the universities'. Paras. 56–59 detail progress made as a result of pump-priming schemes over eight years of industry/university collaboration, e.g. in industry-oriented courses and in research and consulting activities. Of 58 collaborative projects supported from the reserve (fund), 46 were judged to have been wholly or partially successful.

18. See the following: 63rd *Annual Report*, May 1973, Careers Advisory Board, University of London. The Board has 'the task of providing careers guidance and appointments services for the benefit of students and graduates of the University, and of publishing periodic reports on progress'.

    UGC Reports, *First Employment of University Graduates*, annually from 1963–64, but see criticisms by Gareth Williams (reference below).

    Ernest Rudd and Stephen Hatch, *Graduate Study and after* (Weidenfeld and Nicolson, London 1968).

    A. G. Watts, 'HE Careers Services rethink their role', *TES*, 16th March 1973.

    Ernest Rudd, *The Highest Education:* a study of graduate education in Britain (Routledge and Kegan Paul, London 1975).

    R. Keith Kelsall, Anne Poole, Annette Kubin: *Six Years after – a first report on a national follow-up survey of ten thousand graduates of British Universities in 1960* (University of Sheffield, 1971).

    Harriet Greenaway and Gareth Williams (eds.): *Patterns of Change in Graduate Employment* (SRHE Monograph, London 1973).

19. UGC: *First Destination of University Graduates* (HMSO, 1971 and 1975).

20. Dr Duncan S. Davies, General Manager for Research and Development, ICI, in his chapter in *What kinds of graduates do we need?* ed. R. F. Jevons and H. B. Turner (Oxford University Press, 1972).

7

Teaching and Research

THE Technological Universities, like the Polytechnics, began as Technical Colleges which have always been strongly orientated towards the vocational needs of their students, whether already in employment or in preparation for it. Teaching staff had in many cases 'come up the hard way' and could empathise with their students who were continuing the struggle.[1] Their teaching methods reflected those they had themselves experienced: strict adherence to the prescribed syllabus, and endless note-taking as a safeguard against the difficulties of part-time study. The attitude was usually paternalistic and their unsophisticated students were generally grateful. Change came about gradually in response to internal needs and external pressures. For example the extension of the range of studies within the Colleges lowered the proportion of staff with an exclusively industrial background and the manifest need for technical teachers to be trained led first to part-time and short courses run by the Regional Advisory Councils or the Ministry of Education. In 1946–47 three Technical Teachers' Training Colleges were set up,[2] a fourth was added in 1961 and the Further Education Staff College at Coombe Lodge was established in 1963.[3] The challenge of the McNair Report – 'The good technical teacher is no mere technician: he is an interpreter of the modern world'[4] – remained the ideal, but the hazards of the examination system, the lack of continuity and the overcrowding of syllabuses and timetables made it virtually impossible to achieve.[5]

Perhaps one of the most potent forces for change has been the emergence of the non-assenting student, which has affected all teaching institutions including the technical ones, even though their alumni are among the more conforming members of the student body. Concomitant with this has been the change in emphasis in Colleges of Education from the teaching teacher to the learning student.[6]

128

Educational technology

The application of systems analysis and the devising of special technological equipment and other resources have been a progressive feature of the last decade, with a consequential voluminous literature on educational technology,[7] and new national bodies to promote the desirable changes have been established.[8] The computer has of course had very important effects in the last decade, for example on the storage of information and promoting, to quote but one example, the more effective use of libraries. Computer-Marked Assignments – CMAs – are an integral part of the assessment of course work in the Open University, and indeed working at a distance with about 50,000 students would be impossible without the aid of the computer in dealing with the despatch, return and assessment of scripts, the recording and analysing of examination results and the general monitoring of all the University's operations. Its use is likely to spread to other Universities.[9] 'While many people fear the impersonality of technology, others welcome it at least for certain tasks and situations. As David Riesman points out, computers and other teaching devices are not susceptible to threatening prejudices or attitudes that students – often minority students – sense in their human teachers and which can become blocks to effective learning'.[10]

Programmed instruction based on the work of Skinner[11] was much in the news in the 1960s, giving rise to somewhat premature obituaries of 'The Teacher'.[12] While clearly such techniques cannot provide the whole answer to teaching problems, their emergence has stimulated a close re-examination of traditional teaching methods. Lecturing, for example, has been subject to critical assessment and its efficiency as a method of imparting information severely challenged.[13] Again, because of a preoccupation with teaching rather than learning aspects, note-taking by students has not been seriously investigated.[14] The tendency has been to provide them with more and more facts and assume that they will be able to process them. Experimental psychologists[15] have been investigating the problems of learning and instruction for at least two decades, and the assimilation and application of their findings has been a slow process. Thanks to the learning theorists we now recognise that the educational problem is not *if* a pupil can learn but rather *how* he is to learn. There has been a profound reorientation of thinking on the problems of learning and

E

instructing, as is manifest in the publications of the course teams in the Open University.

Professor Alec Mace was a pioneer in teaching students how to learn, arising from his experience of teaching mature students attending Birkbeck College part-time, and produced his book in 1929.[16] The Open University produces a Study Guide in three sections: *Studying in the Open University, Some techniques of study,* and *Studying your course*; clearly a guide of this kind should be available for all students. Some instruction in the use of the library is also advisable. A report published by the National Book League of a survey of Sheffield University students showed that one out of four never used the University library, and nearly half said that guidance from lecturers was only fair or poor.[17]

Adolescence is a time for learning about ourselves and our attitudes as well as about our favourite subjects. This is best promoted within the safety of a small group, but requires staff knowledgeable about group dynamics and syndicate methods developed in training courses for management.[18]

The project method, as a means of testing a student's capacity to apply his knowledge to the solution of a specific problem, was introduced in the Dip.Tech. courses and has continued in the succeeding University courses. Generally the project is of interest to the firm in which the student is doing his training, and the ever-present question is how to avoid the Scylla of a narrow exercise devoid of intellectual demand and the Charybdis of a demanding research programme beyond the student's resources and the time available. In view of the wide use of projects in sandwich courses there has been insufficient critical appraisal of their value as a method of learning.[19] They appear to be very highly regarded by students, staff and external examiners alike and the best ones are quite frequently published in the appropriate journals. This is clearly an advantage to a student at the outset of his career; the hazard is that he may be tempted to spend an undue proportion of his time on something of such intrinsic interest to the neglect of the rest of his studies.

Standards, examinations and assessments

From the outset, the standard of the Dip.Tech. was to be that of a British first- or second-class honours degree, and awards at pass level were to be exceptional. Establishing and maintaining standards allegedly equivalent to those in other institutions of differing histories is self-evidently a difficult operation. In the Universities as a whole, the award of a degree is a pragmatic exercise in interdependence based on shared experiences and judgements. This derives partly from the movement of staff between institutions, but also from the system of external examiners. These are usually chosen from another University doing similar work, and may be involved in the design of sessional examinations and of cumulative assessments throughout the course, but their crucial role is the assessment of the final examination.

This traditional system was taken over by the CATs so that the Diploma in Technology was accepted as equivalent to a British University degree for entry to postgraduate study at master's or doctorate level. Thus on transfer to University status, no major change in examination procedures was needed. The same system, including classified degrees, was continued by the CNAA for degree courses in Polytechnics and Colleges. No single institution or even a group of them could hope – even if they wished – to change such an inbuilt custom, which ensured its comparability with British Universities generally.

Concern has frequently been expressed about the possible decline in the standard of British degrees. One fear is that by increasing opportunities for higher education more is likely to mean worse; another, that the vast increase of knowledge has led to cram courses and rote learning at school and also grossly overloaded curricula at undergraduate level, with consequent ill-preparedness for postgraduate work.

The question about declining academic standards is non-specific and capable of very ambiguous treatment – is it that the standard of first-class honours has declined over the years? – or of all degrees? – or that the *relative* level of attainment decreases with expansion of opportunities in higher education? The *standard* of first and upper seconds is not necessarily reduced by larger *numbers* of less able candidates, and there is no significant evidence that this is so despite all the wishful thinking of those intent on halting expansion.

In recent years, examinations have come increasingly under critical attack on grounds of unreliability, irrelevance, or unsuitability in that they defeat the academic purposes of the courses and above all impair the relationships between staff and students as senior and junior members of an academic community. The necessity of

131

examinations and of grading results – 'students marked for life' – is vehemently denied by critics on humanistic, social and academic grounds and on experimental evidence, but is as vigorously defended on the grounds of integrity, academic excellence and social responsibility. We cannot deal here with the growing literature on examinations,[20] but a number of trends are discernible. For example, it is likely that final examinations will diminish in importance and will be modified in character with the use of objective testing and self-pacing methods, as well as being replaced in part by cumulative assessment throughout the course as a whole. However, these in turn have their own defects.

'The sole duty of a University towards its students is to educate them. Certification of students in professional subjects is a duty toward the public, which Universities have undertaken since the Middle Ages . . . Grading of students is a function which Universities have undertaken only recently in their long history, as a convenience to employers, including themselves.'[21] The debate about grading will doubtless continue, but present practices and structures will probably persist for a long time because of the immense practical difficulties of changing them,[22] including the task of devising more reliable alternatives.

Until recently in British higher education, assessment of the effectiveness of the teaching-learning process has been in terms of content, methodology and the assessment of students' attainments.[23] Despite experience in the USA and elsewhere, the assessment by students of the effectiveness of the teaching is a highly contentious issue in Britain.[24]* It is likely to become more acceptable as the training of University teachers becomes established and with the greater involvement of students on University bodies. That changes are taking place is evident enough, if present practices are compared with the recommendations of the UGC Report of 1964,[25] that is before the widespread student unrest.

Inter-relationship of teaching and research

The conventional wisdom about the inherently close relationship

* As witness the disproportionate uproar which followed the suggestion by the Government Prices and Incomes Board in 1968 that part of the evidence to be taken into account in assessing teaching ability, as affecting University staff salaries, should be the views of students.

between teaching and research in Universities can be briefly summarised. Teaching is a prime commitment of all educational institutions. If a University were to abandon its teaching entirely in favour of research, it could become a research institute, but without the commitment to research, most University staff would feel that as teachers they had lost an essential source of inspiration and drive.[26]

Table 7.1   Use of staff working time in the Technological Universities

University	Proportions of total working time (percentages)					
	Under-graduate time	Graduate course – work time	Graduate research time	Personal research time	Un-allocatable internal time	External profes-sional time
Aston	35	9	6	17	20	12
Bath	44	7	4	16	17	11
Bradford	38	5	8	21	19	8
Brunel	45	9	6	14	15	11
City	43	5	5	19	19	8
Loughborough	36	8	7	19	18	12
Salford	40	4	6	26	15	8
Surrey	37	5	7	18	20	13
Heriot-Watt	49	4	4	18	16	9
Chelsea College	35	7	8	22	16	11
UWIST	45	4	4	18	18	12
Range within the Technological Universities	35–49	4–9	4–8	14–26	15–20	8–13
Range within all other Universities and University Colleges	21–51	1–8	2–14	17–39	15–23	5–14

Any challenge to this basic tenet provokes a vigorous defence from representatives of the Universities, whether it arises from worsening economic conditions, or through inadequacies of Government policy, or serious lack of public understanding.[27] With the likely increase in numbers of students and the decrease in resources, the Universities will have acute problems in determining the balance between teaching and research. Major Universities may experience a conflict of interest between the needs of individual scholarship and large-scale research, which is writ large nationally and internationally in the competitive claims between Big Science and Little Science.[28]

Given the dual nature of their role, University staff are faced with

133

priority problems: between undergraduate and postgraduate course teaching, the supervision of research students, and the conduct of their own research. Replies to a questionnaire on this subject initiated by the Committee of Vice-Chancellors and Principals are shown in Table 7.1.[29]

The pattern of commitment of working time within the Technological Universities is very similar to that of the Universities generally, suggesting that by the early 1970s they had substantially increased their involvement in research. On the assumption that the Universities had reached the 'right balance' between these two activities any doubling of their size would inevitably have required a similar increase in research time and resources. This would pose severe, if not impossible, problems in the expansion of higher education.[30] The question then arises as to *how much* research is necessary to achieve the best teaching? The economics of higher education make it imperative to find an answer – and one which will not render it more difficult to answer the questions of what kind of research, and where. These considerations were a sensitive issue in the transition of the Colleges to University status, and as recorded in Chapter 3 the opinions of members of Academic Advisory Committees (AACM), University Council members engaged in industry and commerce (CMI) (as well as academic staff) have been monitored and individual comments recorded.

The reactions of the first two groups to various aspects of the changes, including the increased emphasis on research, are recorded in Tables 3.3 and 3.4. Of the 43 AAC and 54 CMI members who responded* to their questionnaires, 77 per cent and 76 per cent respectively approved the change in favour of more research and only four altogether disapproved. A few individual comments follow:

'The ideal proportion cannot be specified. Staff research must be an aid to teaching and not an interest that subordinates the interests of students' (AAC).

'It is essential to prevent the image of "Research" from causing disparagement of teaching. Promotion Committees should make sure that the claims of excellent teachers with little research are not overlooked' (AAC).

'Present proportions and trends are about right, and will continue to

* Percentages recorded in Tables 3.3 and 3.4 are based on the sample at risk: here non-respondents have been excluded.

be all right so long as good solid teaching, the tradition of the past, retains its premier role. The danger lies with the young academics, brought up to assess achievement solely in quantity of published work' (AAC).

'Research is valuable in giving life to a department, but should not be carried so far as to devalue the primary function of a teaching department' (CMI).

'Research is necessary to attract the right calibre of staff, but should have a practical bias, and should not be undertaken at the expense of undergraduate teaching' (CMI). This view of one member expressed the views of several of those who rated themselves 'uncertain'.

Tables 3.3 and 3.4 deal with the question in two parts, the second one being whether the institution had changed in the traditional direction, and comments from the two groups of respondents strongly favoured applied research.

'The considerable change in a traditional direction refers mainly to the volume of the activity made possible by University status, new staff, etc., but if one were to think mainly of the type of research and the emphasis on applied problems, one would have to record that the University had changed hardly at all' (AAC).

Approval: *'Provided the research is industrially oriented, it is desirable'* (CMI).

'Distilling experience and developing new knowledge is essential to any University – but especially to any higher education unit which is linked to external, recognised professional-type occupations. This point is incompletely accepted. Far too much research is simply graduate education and with effects totally absorbed in a minor thesis or publication' (CMI).

'As always it is important to select potentially useful subjects for research' (CMI).

'The direction of research is what matters. I'd hope to see more liaison with the industrial research associations, sharing practical and academic projects, instead of the negative competition which often seems to exist' (CMI).

Results obtained from the staff enquiry are recorded in Tables 7.2–7.12 below: they include comparative figures from Halsey and Trow's study where available. The tables are followed by individual comments made either on the questionnaire or during discussion sessions.

Table 7.2 records the replies to question 13 (of the questionnaire) analysed by rank, and the differences are in the expected direction.

135

Table 7.2 Q.13; Do your own interests lie primarily in teaching or in research? Differences by rank: 10 institutions

Rank*	N	Balance of interests (percentages)			
		Very heavily in research	In both, but with a leaning towards		Very heavily in teaching
			research	teaching	
Professors	93	7	60	32	1
Readers	16	25	62·5	12·5	nil
Senior lecturers	69	6	22	55	17
Lecturers	176	3+	40+	43−	14−
Research staff	15	60	20	20	nil
TOTAL	369	8	42	40	10
Research orientation			50		
Teaching orientation				50	
Research and teaching				82	

Note: * Halsey and Trow do not report analysis by rank.

Table 7.3 Q.13; Do your own interests lie primarily in teaching or in research? Differences by period of appointment: 10 institutions

Period of appointment	N	%	Balance of interests (percentages)			
			Very heavily in research	In both, but with a leaning towards		Very heavily in teaching
				research	teaching	
O Before August 1956	40	11	2·5	12·5	50	35
I August 1956–July 1962	92	25	7·5	32·5	51	9
II August 1962–July 1966	83	22	4	47	41	8
III August 1966 onwards	154	42	12	52	31	5
TOTAL	369		8	42	40	10
Halsey and Trow Table 12.1, p. 278	1,368		10	54	36	*

Note: * Column 4 was omitted from the Halsey and Trow study.

62 of the 93 Professors (67 per cent) and 14 out of 16 Readers (87·5 per cent) endorsed a primary interest in research compared with only 19 of the 69 senior lecturers (28 per cent) and 77 out of 176 lecturers (44 per cent). The comparison between Readers and senior lecturers is of interest since it illustrates the generally accepted view that the difference between these ranks lies in the balance of interest between research and teaching respectively. The difference is unrelated to period of appointment: 9 of the 16 Readers (56 per cent) were originally appointed during periods O and I and only 46 per cent of the senior lecturers (32/69). The designation of the CATs in 1956 made it possible to appoint Readers, which enhanced the development of research. The appointments of 27 of the 93 Professors (29 per cent) date from periods O and I also. There was wide variation depending, as research output always does, on individual appointments to particular institutions, but inevitably in view of the heavy weighting of science and technology before 1962 most of the research was in these subjects, often done in conjunction with industry.

Table 7.3 shows that the interaction between period of appointment and commitment to research is in the expected direction. The percentages shown for respondents recruited in the final period when the institutions were established as Universities are very close to those given by Halsey and Trow's sample. It must be remembered however that the present sample – to whom the questionnaire was sent – though random within each rank, was weighted to increase the contribution of the senior staff. The ratios were 1 in 2 for Professors, 1 in 4 for Readers, senior lecturers and research staff and 1 in 7 for lecturers to give an overall 20 per cent sample of the 3,000-plus staff at risk.* Response rates decreased with rank and the sample of respondents consisted of 8 per cent of lecturers, 14 per cent of Readers and senior lecturers and 37 per cent of the Professors. If valid comparisons are to be made with the Halsey and Trow figures, the research/teaching orientation by rank must be examined. This is done in Table 7.4 in a simplified form, since the numbers in each cell are too small for a more detailed analysis. The increase in research orientation with recency of appointment is shown to be true for lecturers as well as Professors and Readers, but not for senior lecturers where the proportion among later appointees is actually less. This means that broad comparisons with the Halsey and Trow figures for research/teaching orientations are acceptable.

* See Appendix, Table AIVI.

Table 7.4 Research/teaching orientation by period of appointment and rank: percentages

	O		I		II		III		TOTALS	
Rank	N	Research/teaching	N	Research/teaching	N	Research/teaching	N	Research/teaching	N	Research/teaching
Professors	8	25/75	19	63/37	25	68/32	41	76/24	93	67/33
Readers	5	80/20	4	75/25	3	100/0	4	100/0	16	87·5/12·5
Senior lecturers	9	0/100	23	35/65	13	38/62	24	25/75	69	28/72
Lecturers	18	0/100	46	30/70	41	39/61	71	66/34	176	44/56
Research staff	—	—	—	—	1	0/100	14	79/21	15	80/20
TOTALS	40	15/85	92	40/60	83	51/49	154	64/36	369	50/50

Table 7.5 Teaching orientation by University group: Halsey and Trow 1964 survey

	Oxford and Cambridge		Sussex		London and major Redbrick		Wales		Scotland		Minor Redbrick		CATs	
	N	%	N	%	N	%	N	%	N	%	N	%	N	%
Percentage of respondents orientated towards teaching rather than research	148	31	119	35	228 + 451	38	114	40	236	44	451	52	373	58

For their 1964 enquiry, Halsey and Trow developed a research/ teaching orientation scale and the results are presented for various types of institutions, including a small sample from three CATs. The percentages of respondents oriented towards *teaching* are shown in Table 7.5.[31]

The figure of 58 per cent for this 1964 sample is comparable with the figure of 60 (51 + 9) per cent for the second group in Table 7.3, i.e. those recruited between 1956 and 1962. Thereafter orientation

Table 7.6 Staff interests in research and teaching by institution (all groups)

		Balance of interests (percentages)			
		Very heavily in	In both, but with a leaning towards		Very heavily in
Institution	N	research	research	teaching	teaching
Aston	60	8	39	43	10
Bath	30	—	57	30	13
Bradford	44	7	27	57	9
Brunel	31	10	29	42	19
City	34	9	47	32	12
Loughborough	31	10	38·5	38·5	13
Salford	45	11	42	40	7
Surrey	38	11	47	37	5
Chelsea	22	—	50	36	14
UWIST	34	6	38	47	9
TOTAL	369	8	42	40	10

primarily towards teaching within the ex-CATs decreased markedly and the overall 36 per cent for the most recently appointed group (III, Table 7.4) is comparable with the figures for Sussex, London and Major Redbrick in Table 7.5.

When analysed according to institutions, the two Technological Universities with a long association with the University of London (City and Surrey) showed a balance in favour of research of 56/44 and 58/42 respectively. Bradford and Brunel had the lowest research ratios – 34/66 and 39/61. The Bradford figure could be related to the low response rate among its Professors* but Brunel had the highest

* See Appendix, Table AIVI.

Table 7.7 Opinions on research and teaching:
percentages agreeing with each statement, by period of appointment: 10 institutions

Statement	Period of appointment								All respondents		Halsey & Trow results	
	O		I		II		III					
	%	N	%	N	%	N	%	N	%	N	%	N
9. Promotion in academic life is too dependent on published work	87	39	79	89	64	79	67	149	71	356	76	1,228[32]
31. The distinguishing feature of the University don is his ability as a research worker	49	39	41	88	46	79	57	149	51	355		
14. An academic man's first loyalty should be to research in his discipline	28	39	19	89	28	79	32	149	27	356	35	1,372[33]
33. There should be more academics in Universities whose main commitment is to teaching	79	39	76	89	60	78	57	150	65	356		
15. Successful research in my subject requires teams of full-time research workers	51	39	51	88	39	80	53	149	49	356		
24. In my subject I have no problem in combining good teaching with effective research	55	38	62	86	63	80	60	146	61	350		

total response rate of all the institutions. It is of course a special case, with its total commitment to sandwich courses which may attract more staff whose interest lies mainly in teaching. The figures simply relate to staff attitudes and reveal nothing about the amount of research actually being done.

The next Table deals with six statements (three pairs) relating to teaching and research which were included in Part II of the questionnaire. Comparable data is available on two of the three pairs. The overall impression, which is not contradicted by any of Halsey and Trow's data, is that the dual function is endorsed, and that any undervaluing of the teaching function is deplored.

The increasing orientation towards research, in contrast to the inherently strong predisposition to teaching in former times, could be

Table 7.8 Q.15; Do you feel under pressure to do more research than you would actually like to do? By period of appointment and rank: percentages

		Professors		Senior Lecturers		Lecturers*	
Period of appointment		Yes, a lot	Yes, a little	Yes, a lot	Yes, a little	Yes, a lot	Yes, a little
O	Before August 1956	*12·5*	—	*9·0*	*36·0*	*6·0*	*31·0*
I	August 1956 – July 1962	*10·5*	*10·5*	*9·0*	*24·0*	*17·5*	*33·0*
II	August 1962 – July 1966	*8·0*	*8·0*	—	*8·0*	*10·0*	*39·0*
III	August 1966 onwards	*5·0*	*7·0*	*4·0*	*25·0*	*7·0*	*18·0*
	TOTAL	*7·5*	*7·5*	*6·0*	*23·0*	*9·0*	*28·0*
	N	93		69		176	

			Yes, a lot	Yes, a little	None
All staff	N	367	27	77	263
	%	*100*	*7*	*21*	*72*
Halsey and Trow	N	1,231	49	172	1,010
Table 13.23, p. 348	%	*100*	*4*	*14*	*82*
Range according to subject and research orientation			*0–9*	*2–29*	*61–98*

Note: * Readers and research staff who are, by definition, committed to do research have been excluded.

felt by some staff to be an unwanted pressure to do research. Table 7.8 shows the response to this question according to period of appointment and rank.

Some pressure to do research is felt by some staff in all Universities, as shown by the Halsey and Trow figures. Additional pressure within a developing institution is to be expected. Professors felt the need to justify their appointments and increase the status of their Departments, and this exerted pressure on their staff to do likewise. Most staff accepted the need and welcomed the increased opportunities: they felt no unwanted pressure. Even among the lecturers, who recorded the greatest unwanted pressures, 63 per cent endorsed the option 'None'. When analysed according to institution, the 'None' column varied between 87/86 per cent at Brunel and Surrey down to 62 per cent at Salford and 56/59 per cent at UWIST and Chelsea, leaving those in between similar to Halsey and Trow's totals. Their figures are analysed into fifteen groups according to research/teaching orientation within five subject areas, with the 'None' column varying between 61 per cent and 98.

Most respondents to the questionnaire added some additional comments following the structured responses and nearly 300 staff took part, mostly in small groups, in the recorded discussion sessions. Main topics, broadly related to the headings of chapters in this book were abstracted from these records of all the discussions and then combined to see if any consensus obtained, e.g. on sandwich courses, staff-student relationships, teaching and research, etc.

Most of the quotations which follow are examples of opinions expressed in various ways by many contributors. In every case an attempt has been made to maintain a balance between opposing views, as a necessary background to making judgements on the changes taking place in the institutions.

'It seems literally tragic that the CATs have not recognised and firmly established "the teaching Professor" ... Although my own position is secure, I regret the continual necessity to advise junior academics to concentrate on research. In so many cases their inclination is towards their teaching role – but one must point out to them that this gives their career a ceiling as senior lecturer: obviously they must research but not, one would hope, as the sole criterion of professional worth ... Senior lecturers as well as readers should be "cadet Professors".'

'Too much emphasis on research, which determines promotion prospects. Poor researchers dabble in research and teaching suffers in

consequence. Sympathetic teachers become overloaded by students who genuinely need help and advice about many "professional problems".'

'It is now quite clear that the efficiency bar is in fact a research bar – lip-service is paid to teaching but is ignored when considering efficiency bar transfers. This was certainly not the spirit of the old CAT ... teaching ability and teaching techniques are deteriorating as a result of over-emphasis on research publications. I do not object to research but I do object to my ability being measured by the number of published papers produced by me.'

'It is unfortunate that research has become almost the only criterion for major promotion. This is undoubtedly the case. It is not only in teaching but also in the organisation and administration of teaching that there really is no incentive to improve their methods. People are thinking about new ways of teaching, new ways of doing things, new ways of selling courses ... and there's an enormous amount of work to be done, but very little incentive to get on with it. Formerly there was too little research, now there's enough, but it is unfortunate that all senior personnel will get there by the research route, and that will influence the Department all the way down.'

'Promotion has come to a colleague and myself for our teaching and general administration and other contributions, and we have not been discriminated against on research grounds. As far as younger lecturers are concerned it is probably important for them to turn out as much research work and publish as much as possible if they look forward to promotion to Readership level and beyond.'

'If the Universities as a whole throughout the country had attached importance to teaching, they would by now have found a way of measuring it. The real truth is that research was the thing that really mattered. It was almost the sole criterion in promotion, but that is beginning to pass now.'

'In the two Departments I know well research is highly regarded, but in practice it is teaching and administration work which occupy people, and research does tend to be pushed out. There is an expressed desire to take up research but it doesn't come into practice. There is more tension than there used to be, and a defensive feeling that teaching ought to be more valued'.

'Essentially the challenge for me (as a new Professorial Head) was to try to induce a new balance between teaching and research which I consider to be absolutely fundamental to any University institution worthy of the name ... There is the old familiar problem of having to

143

take staff with one in this exercise. This can't be done brutally. It has to be done gently and by persuasion . . . I don't want to over-emphasise this difficulty but it is a difficulty nevertheless, but I certainly can't complain about not having had the whole-hearted co-operation of my colleagues concerned.'

'The arrival of people from other University contexts with other expectations and patterns of activity changed the balance between teaching and research: this acted as a stimulus to research and publication, but also the experience was threatening to those who had different expectations of advancement under the former regime. It is not easy for people to accept this.'

'One mustn't assume that because he is research-minded he is going to be a good teacher.'

'If the student has been properly taught at undergraduate level, he will be self-sufficient, self-searching and self-critical, and if he cannot find information from elsewhere, then God help him. If we always have to feed him with a silver spoon full of treacle he hasn't much hope of standing in a competitive world.'

'It is often difficult to conduct research unless a reasonable time period, say six hours, is available: two periods of three hours is never as helpful.'

'The academic world's almost total neglect of teaching is very dis-heartening.'

'I'm too committed to teaching undergraduates and postgraduates to want to return to industry.'

'Am nearly drowned in a sea of admin. paperwork (including questionnaires).'

Research and postgraduate study

Research and postgraduate studies are integrally related in the indispensable flow of new knowledge from one to the other – the point has been picturesquely put by Ernest Rudd[34] 'that learning from someone who is extending the boundaries of knowledge is like drinking from a running stream, whereas learning from someone who has himself ceased to learn is like drinking from a stagnant pool'.[35]*

* Rudd used this interrelatedness as the basis of classifying Universities in respect of their most advanced work, i.e. in terms of the research grants received by the University as a proportion of its total income, and the number of full-time postgraduate students.

Table 7.9 Q.14: What are the major handicaps that you experience in carrying on research?
By period of appointment: percentages

Item No.	Item [*Note*: respondents could endorse more than one item.]	Period of appointment to staff			Halsey and Trow sample (all institutions)	
		Up to July 1962	Aug. 1962 and after	TOTAL	All Subjects	Science, social science, technology
2	Insufficient time because of teaching commitments	*46*	*38*	*41*	*52*	*52*
3	Insufficient time because of other than teaching commitments	*58*	*51*	*53*	*54*	*51*
4	Insufficient financial resources	*16*	*36*	*29*	*39*	*41*
5	Slowness of machinery for obtaining equipment and/or books etc.	*5*	*8*	*7*	*21*	*23*
6	Insufficient contact with other workers in your field	*10*	*15*	*13*	*24*	*26*
7	Insufficiencies in your library	*5*	*13*	*10*	*25*	*23*
8	Unresponsiveness of your Departmental or College administration to your needs	*11*	*19*	*16*	*28*	*27*
	Number of respondents experiencing handicaps	100	196	296	1,153	713
	Number responding to Item 1: 'I experience no major handicaps'	26	39	65		
	TOTAL responding to the question	126	235	361		

Table 7.10 Q.14; What are the major handicaps that you experience in carrying on research?
By rank: percentages

Rank	Col. 1 Total at risk	Col. 2* Number answering 'None'	Col. 3 $\frac{\text{Col. 2}}{\text{Col. 1}} \times 100$	Col. 4† N	Handicaps % 2	3	4	5	6	7	8	Col. 5‡ T = Total number of choices	Col. 6§ Ratio T/N
Professors	93	15	16	78	14	81	27	3	4	12	13	128	1·6
Readers	16	4	25	12	17	50	58	—	—	—	33	20	1·7
Senior lecturers	69	10	15	54	43	52	22	6	4	7	6	83	1·5
Lecturers	176	32	18	141	59	41	31	9	21	11	17	283	2·0
Research staff	15	4	27	11	9	27	36	27	36	27	27	24	2·2
TOTAL	369	65	18	296	41	53	29	7	13	10	15	538	1·8

Notes: * Item 1 on the list of possible responses was 'I experience no major handicaps'.
† N in Col. 4 is the number of respondents who experienced some handicap(s). Percentages add up to more than 100 since multiple choices were allowed.
‡ T = Total number of responses made by N respondents.
§ Average number of handicaps scored by rank.

The problem of resources for research and the conditions necessary for its effective pursuit were explored in the academic staff enquiry, and the results are presented in Tables 7.9[36] and 7.10. The major handicap was time: as it was for the Halsey and Trow sample. The latter registered considerably more complaints on the other items (4 to 8) than the technological sample. Certainly all governing members of the ex-CATs, which had established themselves as good teaching institutions, were aware of the need to expand their research activities. However, the academic staff appointed after 1962 made more complaints than those already in post at that time, probably because their expectations about research facilities were greater.

The spectrum of academic studies may affect comparisons between the two samples. The Halsey and Trow figures were therefore abstracted for science, social science and technology, which together comprise the greater part of the work of the Technological Universities. Surprisingly the deletion of arts, medicine and other subjects, which reduces N from 1,153 to 713 in the Halsey and Trow sample, makes little difference to the percentages, as the two right-hand columns of Table 7.9 show.* Similarly, the same group of subjects (science, social science, technology) when abstracted from the present sample show no significant difference from the figures in the 'Total %' column of the table. The persistently low responses for item 5, both in themselves and in comparison with the Halsey and Trow sample, are surprising and at variance with criticisms made in recorded discussions.

In their chapter on teaching and research orientations, Halsey and Trow describe as their 'most striking finding . . . that the teachers of technology . . . are so little inclined towards research'. They go on to discuss the fact that many University technologists do in fact engage in research and speculate that 'It may be that there is in technology, to a higher degree than in other University subjects, a marked division of labour between the men who carry the research work of the subject and those who only teach it.' They also suggest that future changes in the size and shape of British higher education (i.e. post-Robbins) will inevitably change the distribution of research activities within the University system. 'One outcome may be to strengthen the research functions of technology in the Universities

* The difference is greatest for item 3, but the probability that it is due to chance is not low enough to make it statistically significant, i.e. $p > 0.05$.

and former CATs.'[37] As this study makes clear, this has certainly happened in the case of the former CATs.

When we turn to a more specific question on the adequacy of resources, the difference between the two samples is reversed, with the 1964 Halsey and Trow University sample showing greater levels of satisfaction. The Halsey and Trow CAT sample investigated by Oliver Fulton was drawn from staff at the three Colleges, Birmingham, Salford and Brunel, in 1964 'when these Colleges were in the position of "Universities designate" ',[38] and comparison of the results with those of the present study indicates a recognition of some improvements since then. Among the small sample (36) of 'old stagers' no fewer than 29 (81 per cent) found their research facilities adequate and even excellent, and among more recent recruits this rating fell to a low of 53 per cent and then up slightly to 56 per cent. Since in objective terms facilities undoubtedly improved during that period, the figures convey something about the increase in levels of expectation during the transition.

Table 7.11 Q.16; Apart from time, are the resources available to you (library space, technical assistance, etc.) adequate for the kind of scholarly or scientific research you are doing? By period of appointment: percentages

			Respondents: percentages			
Period of appointment		Excellent	Adequate	Somewhat inadequate	Highly inadequate	N
	N	32	188	110	30	360
O	Before August 1956	11	70	19	nil	36
I	August 1956–July 1962	7	61	28	4	90
II	August 1962–July 1966	6	47	32	15	82
III	August 1966 onwards	11	45+	34+	9	152
	TOTALS	9	52	31	8	100
Halsey and Trow samples 1964[39]						
	CATs	7	42	37	13	366
	Universities[40]	17	44	31	7	1,384
	Technology only[40]	19	52	26	3	176

The findings in Table 7.11 tally with impressions from recorded discussions: no complacency but considerable numbers expressing satisfaction with the resources available. Many of the newer recruits emphasised that they had chosen the University *because* it was technological and because of the developing opportunities and resources offered.

Finally there remains the last question on this topic: is research possible during term-time? Table 7.12 gives the results. The pattern of response from the two samples is very similar to the Halsey and Trow sample (Professors in particular) finding it rather less easy to do their research in term-time. When the present sample is analysed according to period of appointment, the figures for the three options change progressively over time from 24/33/43 per cent in the first period to 27/53/20 in the fourth, indicating considerable improvements in conditions for research during the transition.

Table 7.12 Q.17; Are you able to carry on research during term? By rank: percentages

Research in term time	Professors		Readers		Senior lecturers		Lecturers		TOTALS	
	(a)	(b)*	(a)	(b)	(a)	(b)	(a)	(b)	(a)	(b)†
N	92	192	16	127	62	210	170	727	340	1,256
A substantial part	25	21	56	41	29	23	22	21	26	24
Only a little	53	44	31	46	39	44	52	49	49	47
Almost none	22	34	13	13	32	32	26	30	25	29

Notes: * (a) Column records results for the present study.
　　(b) Column calculated from Halsey and Trow Table 12.16, p. 293.
　　† Excludes research staff under (a) and 'others' from Halsey and Trow under (b).

The different types of arrangements for postgraduate and post-experience courses have been discussed in Chapter 4,[41] and the application of the sandwich course principle at graduate level in Chapter 5, the latter including innovations such as IHD and CASE schemes, Total Technology and, most recently, 'Teaching Companies'.* Here we have been concerned with the significance of these

* Altogether the SRC's newer schemes to encourage broader training and academic/employer collaboration have helped to increase the variety in the forms of postgraduate education. These include Total Technology, Cooperative Awards in Science and Engineering (CASE), and the joint SRC/SSRC Scheme for Multidisciplinary Training. It is very encouraging that the Council has declared its policy of supporting these schemes with an increased proportion of studentships, to support other closely related developments. See *SRC Annual*

developments for the traditional relationship between teaching and research among academic staff. Table 8.8 shows that 30 per cent of staff were appointed direct from industry, and Table 8.9 that 54 per cent of all staff and 63 per cent of Professors had been employed in industry. From this firm basis stems their support for collaborative ventures with industrial firms and other extra-mural enterprises. This is true of undergraduate courses, but at the postgraduate level there must also be a firm commitment to and experience of applied research.

The progress made in research facilities and appointments since 1966 indicates that at least an adequate basis has been developed to sustain these innovations. The benefit for staff in these co-operative schemes and courses, in sustaining close contacts with industry and commerce, are as important as the benefits derived from them by their students. Recent developments are thus encouraging in kind and diversity, but are not yet on a scale commensurate with the need to update British industry.

Chapter 7: Sources

1. Ethel Venables, *The Young Worker at College*: A Study of a Local Tech. (Faber and Faber, London 1967), Chapter 6.
Beryl F. Tipton, *Conflict and Change in a Technical College*, Brunel Further Education Monograph No. 6 (Hutchinson, London 1973), Chapter 4.

2. Peter Venables, *Technical Education* (G. Bell & Sons, London 1955), p. 535.

3. Leonard M. Cantor and I. F. Roberts, *Further Education in England and Wales* (Routledge and Kegan Paul, London 1972), pp. 195–211.

4. Report of Board of Education Committee (Chairman, Sir Arnold McNair), *Teachers and Youth Leaders* (HMSO, 1944), para. 383.

5. Crowther Report, *15 to 18* (HMSO, 1959), Chapter 31. *As 1*, pp. 138–9.

6. See Torsten Husén, *The Learning Society* (Methuen, London 1974), 'We have grossly over-emphasised the didactic aspects of education', p. xvii.

7. *British Journal of Educational Technology* (Since 1970; the journal of the Council for Educational Technology).

Report, 1976–77, pp. 11–12, and pp. 44–45 (HMSO, 1977). These developments are most pertinent to the future of the technological universities, and a challenge to them.

Programmed Learning and Educational Technology (Since 1963; the journal of the Association for Programmed Learning and Educational Technology, APLET).

Visual Education (The magazine of the National Committee for Audio-Visual Aids in Education).

Educational Media International (The journal of the International Council for Educational Media).

T. Cantrell, 'A cybernetic approach to University teaching', *Brit. J. Medical Education*, Vol 7, 1973, p. 211.

International Yearbook of Educational and Instructional Technology 1976–77, APLET (Kegan Paul / IPS, New York).

8. *Audio-Visual Aids in Higher Scientific Education*, Report of the Committee (Chairman, Dr (now Sir) Brymnor Jones) appointed by the UGC, DES and SED (HMSO, 1965).

Central arrangements for promoting educational technology in the United Kingdom, Report of a DES Working Party (Chairman, J. A. Hudson) (HMSO, 1972).

See *THES*, 4th February 1972, 1st December 1972 and H. D. Perraton, 'Non-plan for technology', *TES*, 25th February 1972.

9. See the Carnegie Commission Reports:

Roger E. Levien *et al.*, *The Emerging Technology – instructional uses of the computer in higher education* (McGraw Hill, New York 1973), and

J. F. Rockart and M. S. Scott Morton, *Computers and the Learning Process in Higher Education* (McGraw Hill, New York 1975).

10. Clark Kerr, Chairman of the Carnegie Commission, in his Preface to the 1973 Report.

11. B. F. Skinner, *The Technology of Teaching* (Appleton-Century-Crofts, New York, 1968).

12. Fred Keller, 'Goodbye Teacher . . .', *Journal of Applied Behaviour Analysis*, Vol. 1, 1968, pp. 79–89.

Compare Martin Sherwood, 'Educational Innovators', *New Scientist*, 7th June 1973.

L. R. B. Elton, 'Teach yourself paradigm – the Keller Plan', *Chemistry in Britain*, April 1973.

13. Donald A. Bligh, *What's the Use of Lectures?* (University Teaching Methods Unit, 55 Gordon Square, London WC1H 0NT, 1971).

D. G. Christopherson, *The Engineer in the University* (English University Press 1967), Chapter 4, 'A Defence of Lectures'. J. Fletcher and T. Knott, 'Abolishing the lecture', *Universities Quarterly*, Winter 1971.

John P. Powell, 'University Teaching Methods', in *Educational Research in Britain*, Vol. 2, H. J. Butcher and H. B. Pont (eds) (University of London Press, 1970).

Colin Flood-Page, 'Students' reactions to teaching methods', *Universities Quarterly*, Autumn 1971.

Norman Mackenzie, Michael Eraut, Hywel C. Jones, *Teaching and Learning – an introduction to new methods and resources in Higher Education* (UNESCO Press, 1971).

Norman Mackenzie, Richmond Postgate, John Scupham, *Open Learning – systems and problems in post-secondary education* (UNESCO Press, 1975).

Ruth M. Beard, *Research into Teaching Methods in Higher Education* (SRHE monograph, London 1969).

14. Michael Howe, 'Note-taking students remember more', paper to the British Advancement of Science, September 1973, edited version, *THES*, 31st August 1973.

15. For example: B. F. Skinner, 'The Science of Learning and the Art of Teaching', *Harvard Educational Review*, Vol. 24, 1954, pp. 86–97.

B. S. Bloom *et al.*, *Taxonomy of Educational Objectives* (Longmans, London 1956).

J. S. Bruner *et al.*, *A Study of Thinking* (Wiley, New York 1956).

J. S. Bruner, *Toward a Theory of Instruction* (Harvard University Press, Cambridge, Mass., 1966).

See also: Edgar Stones, *Learning and Teaching* (Wiley, Chichester 1968).

Readings in Educational Psychology (Methuen, London 1970).

Torsten Husén, *as 6.*

16. *The Psychology of Study* (Methuen, London 1929; re-issued Penguin, 1962).

See also Harry Maddox, *How to Study* (Pan Books, London 1963).

17. *Books and Students*, reported *THES*, 25th May 1963; booklet available from 7 Albemarle Street, London W1X 4BB.

B. V. Loen, 'Why don't engineers read books?', *Engineering Education*, November 1973, pp. 116–18.

18. See *Newsletter* of the Nuffield Foundation Group for Research and Innovation in Higher Education, and particularly No. 3, October 1973.

Margaret MacNamara, 'Group Dynamics in University Tutorials', *Universities Quarterly*, Spring 1972.

M. L. J. Abercrombie, 'Teaching in Small Groups', Chapter 9 in *Contemporary Problems in Higher Education*. (eds) H. J. Butcher and Ernest Rudd (McGraw Hill, Maidenhead 1972).

Maurice Broady, 'The conduct of seminars', *Universities Quarterly* Summer 1970.

19. But see A. G. Harding, Sheffield Polytechnic, 'The Objectives and Structure of Undergraduate Projects', *Brit. J. Educ. Technology*,

Vol. 4, No. 2, May 1973, and 'The Project: its Place as a Learning Situation', *Brit. J. Educ. Technology*, Vol. 4, No. 3, October 1973.

20. Symposium on Examining in Universities, *Universities Quarterly*, June 1967. *Assessment of undergraduate performance*, Background paper, Universities UK Conference, Spring 1969, CVCP and AUT.

 D. A. Allen, 'The anxious examiner', *Universities Quarterly*, Spring 1970.

 W. Isbister, 'The University Assessor', *Universities Quarterly*, December 1968.

 R. S. Scorer, 'Examinations Examined and Found Wanting', *Bull. Inst. Mathematics*, February 1971.

 See also *THES*, 19th January 1973.

 H. V. Wyatt, 'Examining Examined', *J. Biol. Sci.*, Vol. 7, No. 4, 1973, pp. 11–17.

 B. Butterworth and A. Powell, 'Examining the Examiners', *THES*, 7th September 1973.

 D. Greenslade, 'A degree of change', *Further Education*, Summer 1972.

 SSRC study: 'How sex affects examination performance', *THES*, 11th February 1972.

 R. L. Holder, 'Sex, social class and student performance', *Universities Quarterly*, Spring 1970.

 Roy Cox, 'Value of objective examinations', *Nature*, 30th June 1972.

 'Traditional examinations in a changing society', *Universities Quarterly*, Spring 1973.

 D. L. Nuttall and A. Wilmott, *British Examinations: Techniques of Analysis*, (NFER, Slough 1972).

 A. James, 'What does course work predict?' *Universities Quarterly*, Spring 1973.

 Ian Inkster, 'Some criticisms of a course mark system', *Higher Education Review*, Summer 1971.

 B. A. Driver and B. W. Pashley, 'Patterns and Trends in Degree Performance', *Universities Quarterly*, Summer 1971.

 Edward Nevin, 'How not to get a Degree', *Economic Journal*, Vol. 82, 1972, p. 658.

 See editorial comment, *Nature*, June 1973, p. 419.

21. Eric Ashby, *Any Person, Any Study* (McGraw Hill, New York 1971), p. 51: 'Tests, Certification and Grading'.

22. See S. J. Eggleston, 'Exams – integral part of the social system', *TES*, 25th September 1970.

 Anton Powell, 'Marked for life', *THES*, 11th February 1972.

 Tom Fawthrop, *Education or Examination* (Radical Students' Alliance, 1968).

Lawrence Lerner, 'Assessment and examinations: who wants a degree?', *THES*, 27th October 1972.

Antony Flew, 'Not so much a difference of degree', *THES*, 23rd February 1973.

Replies to Flew: L. Lerner and H. Robinson, *THES*, 9th March 1973, and P. B. Taylor, *THES*, 16th March 1973.

23. See Society for Research into Higher Education (SRHE) Abstracts, 1966 to date. Also:

W. J. McKeachie, 'Research on teaching at College and University level', Chapter in *Handbook of Research on Teaching*, (ed. N. L. Gage) (Rand McNally, Chicago 1963).

J. P. Powell, 'Experimentation and teaching in Higher Education'. *J. Educ. Research*, Vol. 6, 1964, pp. 179–191, and *Universities and University Education: a select bibliography* (NFER, Slough 1966).

24. See Sir Sydney Caine, *British Universities* (Bodley Head, London 1969). Colin Flood-Page, 'Teaching and Research – happy symbiosis or hidden warfare?', *Universities Quarterly*, Winter 1972, p. 103.

Alan Smithers, 'What do students expect of lectures?', *Universities Quarterly*, Summer 1970.

25. *University Teaching Methods*, Report of the UGC Committee (Chairman, Sir Edward Hale) (HMSO, 1964).

See also:

R. C. Wilson, 'Teaching effectiveness – its measurement', *Engineering Education*, March 1972.

Barbara Falk and Kwong Lee Dow, *The Assessment of University Teaching* (SRHE monograph, London 1972), particularly Chapter 4, 'The use of student evaluation'.

J. M. Foy, 'A note on lecturer evaluation by students', *Universities Quarterly*, Summer 1969.

M. Parlett, 'Evaluating Innovations in Teaching', Chapter 11 in *Contemporary Problems in Higher Education* (*as 18*).

L. A. MacManaway, 'Teaching methods in higher education: innovation and research', *Universities Quarterly*, Summer 1970.

H. Maddox, 'University teaching methods – a review', *Universities Quarterly*, Spring 1970.

Otis E. Lancaster, 'Measuring Teaching Effectiveness', *IEEE Trans. on Education*, E.16, No. 3, August 1973.

A. Smithers and F. Musgrove, 'Students' reactions to their teaching', *Durham Research Review*, Vol. 6, No. 29, 1972, p. 211.

D. Magin, 'Evaluating the role performance of university lecturers', *Universities Quarterly*, Winter 1973.

26. See the following:

Sir Sydney Caine, *British Universities* (Bodley Head, London 1969), Chapter 4.

Sir Derman Christopherson, *The University at Work*, (SCM Press 1974), particularly Part I.

Higher Education and Scientific Research, Report of British Association Study Group (Chairman, Lord Ashby), December 1973.

27. See for example, Sir Alan/Lord Bullock, Oration by the Vice-Chancellor, University of Oxford *Gazette*, Supplement No. 2 to No. 3842, 13th October 1971.

28. James A. Perkins, 'Missions and organisation – a redefinition', Chapter 14, p. 246 in *The University as an Organisation* (McGraw Hill, New York, 1973).

29. *Report of an Enquiry into the Use of Academic Staff Time*, The Committee of Vice-Chancellors and Principals of Universities of the United Kingdom, 1972 (bottom line of Table 1 *ibid.*, pp. 16–18).

30. See C. F. Carter, 'Can we get British higher education cheaper?', paper read to Manchester Statistical Society, 15th December 1965, reprinted in *Economics of Education 2*, (ed. M. Blaug) (Penguin Readings, 1970), p. 334.

31. Extracted from Halsey and Trow, *The British Academics* (Faber & Faber, London 1971), Table 12.11, p. 288, Items 4 and 8 combined.

32. *Ibid.*, Table 13.24, p. 350.

33. *Ibid.*, Table 12.4, p. 280.

34. Ernest Rudd, 'The Research Orientation of British Universities', *Higher Education*, Vol. 2, 1973. The operative phrase is 'ceased to learn', not 'ceased to do research'.

35. As 34, pp. 301–24.

36. As 31, Table 13.36, p. 359.

37. *Ibid.*, pp. 321–322.

38. *Ibid.*, Appendix A, p. 469.

39. *Ibid.*, Table A.11, p. 479.

40. *Ibid.*, Table 13.37, *ibid.*, p. 361.

41. For some criticisms, see *Postgraduate Education*, Third Report (Vol. 1) from the Expenditure Committee (Education and Arts Sub-Committee) paras. 83–88, 94, (HMSO, 20th December, 1973) see also Vol. 2., and Government Observations on the Third Report 1973–74, Cmnd. 6611 (HMSO, August 1976).

8

Academic Staff

THE role, function and objects of Universities have been widely discussed over the last two decades and the debate continues. Whatever the aspect under consideration the academic staff are of central importance – be it egalitarian demands or élitist assumptions; the pursuit of truth and the need for academic autonomy and freedom or the social obligations of discovery and of the application of knowledge; whether 'publish or perish' for the academic must give way to teach or perish for the institution; or the extent to which loyalty to a discipline as a professional, or loyalty to a union as a worker, conflicts with loyalty to the institution as an academic community. No wonder then that in the last twenty years, academic staff also have been subject to increasing criticism and their roles and responsibilities to searching analysis.[1]

In 1961, T. H. Matthews remarked, 'University teaching might be called the hidden profession. It is practised as a secret rite behind closed doors and is not mentioned in polite academic society'.[2] Just over a decade ago, and what worlds away! And there is no going back, especially with the positive catalytic influence of the Open University virtually teaching in public. Moreover, as the Universities became so largely dependent on public money the principle of accountability for its effective use was quite inescapable. Expenditure on teaching no less than on research must be broadly accountable, and academics who rigorously apply analysis and criticism in their own disciplines can hardly expect to escape similar treatment of their own work in Universities.

Thus a strong interest has arisen in the role and work of academics, of which the major study by A. H. Halsey and Martin Trow, *The British Academics*, is the most recent and authoritative. Certain aspects of the present study were strongly influenced by it, and comparisons with it have been valuable. A prime concern in this present study has been to see whether the changing nature of the institutions

156

is reflected in the changing characteristics and views of the academic staff, and the ways in which the evolution of these institutions has been affected by staff changes over the major periods of transition to date.

The increases in staff in the eight Technological Universities between 1967 and 1974 are shown in Table 8.1.[3]

Table 8.1 Increase in full-time academic staff wholly financed from University income: 8 Technological Universities 1967–75

	Number of staff		
Institution	Dec. 1967	Dec. 1975	Percentage increase 1967–75
Aston	348	452	*30*
Bath	244	331	*36*
Bradford	370	493	*33*
Brunel	189	268	*42*
City	278	302	*9*
Loughborough	227	380	*67*
Salford	396	476	*20*
Surrey	262	311	*19*
TOTALS	2,314	3,013	*30*

Taken together the increase was 30 per cent. City, which has had the greatest difficulty in expanding because of its Central London site, shows the least increase and Loughborough, which started from a low figure, and had the greatest space available, shows the greatest gain.

The appointment of Readers, and Professors (posts not available to the CATs) increased the proportions of senior posts as shown in Table 8.2.[3] At a time when the Universities as a whole were expanding considerably the Technological Universities were allowed to expand at a faster rate and by 1974 were approaching equality in the proportions of senior staff.

The Robbins Committee (para. 469) envisaged that the Technological Universities should each expand to a total of 4,000–5,000 enrolments. This could of course result from increasing the size of the subject groups without altering their relative proportions in the total enrolment; or by altering those proportions to give a revised 'mix';

157

Table 8.2 Establishment of senior academic posts (wholly financed by University funds) in 8 Technological Universities and in all UK Universities in 1967/8 and 1975/6 respectively

| Posts | 8 Technological Universities | | | | Other UK Universities | | | | Percentage increase 1967 – Dec. 1975 | |
| | Dec. 1967 | | Dec. 1975 | | Dec. 1967 | | Dec. 1975 | | Technological Universities | Other UK Universities |
	N	% of all staff	N	% of all staff	N	% of all staff	N	% of all staff		
Professors	158	6·8	284	9·4	2,924	11·3	3,989	12·4	79·7	36·4
Readers and senior lecturers	378	16·3	706	23·4	4,830	18·7	7,617	23·6	86·8	57·7
TOTALS	536	23·2	990	32·8	7,754	30·0	11,606	36·0	84·7	49·7

or, yet again, by diversifying the academic spectrum of work by the addition of new subject groups during the expansion. In their evidence to the Robbins Committee the Principals' Committee favoured some diversification of the academic spectrum by the development of social sciences and other studies in addition to the existing engineering, applied and pure sciences. This development began with independent status and has continued over the years as Universities, but has not proceeded as far in the direction of the traditional Universities as the Robbins Committee appeared to envisage (paras. 505–508).

Staff structure, and social and professional background

In order to monitor such changes, a staff questionnaire including an attitude survey was developed. The details of the rationale and planning are set out in Appendix IVc, which includes a discussion of

Table 8.3   Q.1; Staff numbers by institution in 1971 in relation to response

Institution	Total sample		Respondent sample	
	N	%	N	%
Aston	434	*13·9*	60	*16·3*
Bath	257	*8·3*	30	*8·1*
Bradford	411	*13·2*	44	*11·9*
Brunel	205	*6·6*	31	*8·4*
City	309	*9·9*	34	*9·2*
Loughborough	292	*9·4*	31	*8·4*
Salford	451	*14·5*	45	*12·2*
Surrey	293	*9·4*	38	*10·3*
Chelsea	210	*6·8*	22	*6·0*
UWIST	249	*8·0*	34	*9·2*
TOTALS	3,111	*100·0*	369	*100·0*

response rates and some results, but the main results are presented here.* Changes are most marked among the eight institutions which became Universities in their own right. Chelsea and UWIST, which

* Q numbers at the head of a table refer to the number on the questionnaire. In a few cases responses are not tabulated but simply narrated.

Table 8.4 Q.2: Academic staff in post at 31st March 1972 analysed by date of first appointment: row percentages

Institution	Period O Appointed before 1st Aug. 1956	Period I Appointed Aug. 1956–July 1962	Period II Appointed Aug. 1962–July 1966	Period III Appointed since 1st Aug. 1966	TOTALS	N i.e., Number of staff in post 31.3.72	Col. %
Aston	17	23	24	36	100	443	14·3
Bath	7	24	28	41	100	250	8·1
Bradford	8	25	27	40	100	410	13·2
Brunel	11+	24	26	38+	100	215	7·0
City	14	27	22	37	100	313	10·1
Loughborough	10	22	25	43	100	266	8·6
Salford	6	27	26	41	100	453	14·6
Surrey	15	28	23	34	100	287	9·3
SUB-TOTAL	12	25	25	38	100	2,637	85·2
Chelsea	16	28+	13+	42	100	207	6·7
UWIST	12	25	23	40	100	252	8·1
GRAND TOTAL N	370	773	740	1,167		3,096	100·0
Row %	12	26	24	38	100		
Respondent sample N	40	92	83	154		369	
Row %	11	25	22	42	100		

were each affiliated to an existing University, are special cases and are discussed separately. Respondents to the questionnaire were divided into the four groups according to the dates of the periods* in which they joined the staff of a technological institution.

Table 8.3 gives numbers in post in 1971 and the numbers of respondents from each institution.

To have asked for the breakdown of the 1971 figures by date of appointment would have threatened the anonymity assured to respondents,† but the figures for 1972 were obtained by direct enquiry and are shown in Table 8.4 together with a comparable analysis of the respondent sample.

The proportions of the respondents in each of the four periods are satisfactorily close to the proportions at risk in 1972. Over-representation in period III is due to two factors: the higher proportion of Professors in that category and the higher response rates of high-ranking staff. The final column percentages by institution in Table 8.4 (for 1972 staff) are very close to the proportions given in Table 8.3 for 1971. The sample in this study can thus be assumed to be adequately representative of the four periods of recruitment.

The dynamic interaction between 'the old stagers' and incoming staff was an important influence determining the nature of the institution at the time this study was undertaken. By 31st March 1972 only 12 per cent (ranging from 6 to 17 per cent within institutions) of those in post had been appointed in the Technical College days. They had had a major say in development (including staff appointments in the early days after designation as CATs) but as the College expanded, so their numerical proportion declined and their influence diminished. This still continues and, for example, the proportion of 17 per cent at Aston had declined to 10 per cent by 31st July 1976.

One point, repeatedly confirmed in recorded discussions, was that if institutions are to be upgraded it had better be done in a period of rapid expansion, as the normal flux of appointments could not possibly provide the staff changes required. Expansion needs to continue beyond the first few years, and the curtailment of development in the current quinquennium could have marked effects on the functioning of the Technological Universities. A marked renewal of

* Four periods, i.e. O, before August 1956; I, August 1956–July 1962; II, August 1962–July 1966; and III, after July 1966.
† This applies also to the analysis by subject. See Table 8.5.

expansion in the 1977–82 quinquennium is essential if they are to reach their full potential, but the omens are unfavourable and the severe stresses and strains of the 'steady state' will be pressing.

The numbers of respondents in the four main subject groups are analysed according to the four periods of appointment in Table 8.5.

Table 8.5 Q.5; Academic staff in subject groups by period of appointment: 8 Technological Universities*

Subject Group	Period O Appointed before 1st Aug. 1956		Period I Appointed Aug. 1956– July 1962		Period II Appointed Aug. 1962– July 1966		Period III Appointed since 1st Aug. 1966		TOTALS	
	N	%	N	%	N	%	N	%	N	%
Technology	13	38	32	45	23	35	42	34	110	37
Natural sciences	17	50	33	45	25	38·5	25	28	110	37
Social sciences	2	6	5	7	16	25	33	26	56	19
Others	2	6	2	3	1	1·5	15	12	20	7
TOTALS	34	100	72	100	65	100	125	100	296	100
Row percentages	11·5		24·3		22·0		42·2		100·0	

Note: * Chelsea and UWIST (N = 73) not included.

The increased recruitment of social scientists after 1962 is very clear and the consequent reduction in the *percentages* (not necessarily in actual numbers) teaching technology and science. Official statistics do not provide a breakdown of staff by subject but in 1971 the percentages of *students* in the four subject areas were 49:27:12:12 (see Table 8.11).

The distribution of appointments across the four periods, O–III, affects the staff age-profile, which is likely to have important consequences for the future. The age of respondents by rank is shown in Table 8.6.[4]

The variation in average ages in the senior posts is small, and movement to posts elsewhere is unlikely, especially among Professors. Thus many holders of senior posts can be expected to serve for a substantial number of years, 15 to 20 or more, with two important consequences. First, that the direction and quality of development is already largely determined for years to come; and

Table 8.6 Q.4 & 6; Ages of respondents by present rank

Rank	Under 30 N	Under 30 %	30–34 N	30–34 %	35–39 N	35–39 %	40–44 N	40–44 %	45–49 N	45–49 %	50–54 N	50–54 %	55 & over N	55 & over %	TOTALS N	TOTALS %	Average age in years
Professors	—		—		7		18		26		22		15		93		47·0
Readers	—		—		2		5		5		4		—		16		45·5
Senior lecturers	—		3		10		19		18		10		9		69		45·5
Lecturers	26		37		44		36		18		6		9		176		38·0
Research staff	12		2		1		—		—		—		—		15		30·5
TOTALS	38	10·3	47	12·7	64	17·3	78	21·1	67	18·2	42	11·4	33	8·9	369	100·0	41·5
H & T TOTALS	220	16·4	255	19·0	283	21·1	194	14·5	387 (Age 45 and over)	29·0					1,339	100·0	
UGC 1968 TOTALS		20·3		21·0		16·4		14·7		11·2		6·7		9·7	29,179	100·0	

second that the promotion of able young staff is likely to be seriously reduced. Halsey and Trow[5] showed that an increased rate of expansion is reflected in a greater proportion of younger staff at a later date, and the converse is implied. Financial stringency will reduce mobility within and between Universities and have adverse effects on staff morale.

These are the facts of life within any organisation, but for emergent institutions a slowing-down of expansion could be particularly disadvantageous. For example, there is one aspect of particular importance to the Technological Universities, with their high proportion of staff with experience in industry and commerce. Such staff will

Table 8.7 Q.2 & 4; Senior ranking respondents by period of appointment

| | Period O | | Period I | | Period II | | Period III | | | |
| | Appointed before 1st Aug. 1956 | | Appointed Aug. 1956– July 1962 | | Appointed Aug.1962– July 1966 | | Appointed since 1st Aug. 1966 | | TOTAL | |
Rank	N	Row %	N	Row %	N	Row %	N	Row %	N	Row %
Professors*	8	9	19	20	25	27	41	44	93	100
Readers and senior lecturers	16	19	25	29	16	19	28	33	85	100
Total senior staff	24	13	44	25	41	23	71	40	178	100
Total respondents	40	11	92	25	83	22	154	42	369	100

Note: * Visiting, Consultant and Associate Professors were not included in this study.

tend to be older, even much older, on recruitment than University staff on average, and thus relatively expensive. Insofar as financial stringency permits any staff replacements, only much younger persons could be appointed in order to save salary payments but at the cost of experience indispensable, for example, to the conduct of sandwich courses, management studies and applied sciences generally.

The senior appointments were spread through the four phases of development as shown in Table 8.7.

Of the Professors 71 per cent had been appointed after July 1962, but nearly half the other senior staff were appointed before that date, suggesting that few Professorial posts were filled from within. There was a higher proportion of promotion below Professorial level, mainly as a result of regarding senior lectureships as the internal career grade (as in British Universities generally).

A number of factors determine academic appointments, and the type of post held at the time of the application is self-evidently important. Table 8.8 presents the range of such appointments held by respondents.

Table 8.8 Q.9; Type of appointment held by respondents at time of application for present post

Type of previous appointment	N	%
Universities	110	30
Colleges*	64	17
Schools	10	3
Industry†	109	30
Public service‡	24	6
Other§	26	7
None§§	26	7
TOTAL	369	100

Notes: * includes Technical Colleges, Colleges of Further
　　　　　Education, Colleges of Education
　　　　† includes commerce
　　　　‡ mainly comprises Civil Service and Local
　　　　　Authorities
　　　　§ includes professional institutions
　　　§§ University graduates taking up their first lectureship
　　　　　or research post

Nearly a third of the academic staff were appointed direct from Universities, a marked change from the former phases as Colleges of Technology or CATs under Local Authorities. Another third came direct from industry, presumably as the result of a positive recruitment policy. If the commitment of the Technological Universities to the application of knowledge is to be maintained, a continuing substantial recruitment of staff with experience of industry at some time in their careers is very important. Table 8.9[6] shows that over half the respondents had had industrial experience at some time during their employment.

In his comments on Table A.10,[7] Oliver Fulton contrasts the 1 per cent of University natural science and technology staff with 41 per cent for CAT teachers 'ever employed in industry: research and development', and attributes this higher figure to the fact that 'the history of development of the CATs was very different from that of the Universities', especially in their contacts with *local* (my italics)

165

industry, which thus affected the careers of their staffs. This is to oversimplify the picture by too great an emphasis on the local situation for the connection of the CATs with industry. Their enrolment of students had become largely regional before they became independent, and became increasingly national thereafter, but the

Table 8.9 Q.9; Respondents ever employed in industry by rank

	TOTAL	Ever in industry	
Respondents	N	N	%
Professors	93	59	*63*
Readers	16	10	*62·5*
Senior lecturers	69	37	*54*
Lecturers	176	88	*50*
Research staff	15	6	*40*
TOTAL	369	200	*54*

Halsey, Trow and Fulton samples		
All staff		
Universities	1,408	*1*
CATs	383	*41*
Natural science only		
Universities	410	*2*
CATs	153	*34*
Technology only		
Universities	179	*4*
CATs	175	*53*

figures in Table 8·9 suggest that the proportion of staff 'ever employed in industry' had not declined at all. Moreover, about two-thirds of the Professors had had such past employment. In short, Table 8.9 shows a persistent recruitment policy at work for all levels of staff up to 1971, through seven years of expansion in which appointments were being made also in the social sciences and humanities.

'One-third of all the CAT natural scientists had worked in industrial research and development, and over half their technologists', remarked Fulton, and concluded, 'In this respect at least, the CAT teachers were much less solidly connected to the academic world than their University colleagues, very few of whom had ever held a non-academic job.' The implication might be that this is a sign of weakness, whereas the significance and strength of such previous employment for the Technological Universities goes unremarked.

It is somewhat surprising that nowhere else in Halsey and Trow's comprehensive book is the employment of existing academic staff in industry and commerce discussed, nor the particular significance of previous industrial employment of technologists and natural scientists. A small percentage may indeed have seemed a proper sense of involvement at the time and if so, the strictures of representatives of industry about the attitudes of Universities and their graduates might stem from this basic cause. For the same reason, it is not surprising that other Universities did not establish sandwich courses, since the necessary degree of industrial involvement of the academic staff was not there. (Medical students would not be expected to undertake medical studies and walk the wards of hospital under non-medical supervision.)

At various times there were discussions, in the period prior to designation as CATs, suggesting that certain Colleges of Technology should be incorporated within the local University, for example at Manchester and Birmingham respectively. Had that happened the outlook for sandwich courses would have been very bleak in view of the strength of the internal conforming influences with Senates so largely lacking in prior experience of industry. Sandwich courses have not been part of the traditional University pattern, as for example Imperial College and UMIST demonstrate, despite the industrial aspects of their particular histories. Moreover, sandwich courses were allowed to lapse at the Royal College of Science and Technology, Glasgow, with the imminence of University status as the University of Strathclyde, and they have not developed significantly at Chelsea, which has always had a strong university orientation. (See Appendix II, Sources, No. 8, p. 79.)

The evidence in Table 8.9 of a sustained policy of appointing staff with prior industrial employment is analysed further into the four phases of appointment in Table 8.10. The more detailed picture shows an overall decline across the four periods from 60 to 44 per cent, which is most marked among lecturers and senior lecturers. This is due in part to the recruitment of staff for the social sciences and humanities, but may result from other factors affecting recruiting to science and technology.

167

Table 8.10 Q.2, 3 & 9; Respondents 'ever in industry' by rank and period of appointment: percentages

| | *Period of appointment* | | | | | |
Rank	O	I	II	III	N/Total N	% overall
Professors	60	53	68	61	59/93	63·0
Readers	60	50	100	50	10/16	62·5
Senior lecturers	55	76	38	42	37/69	53·6
Lecturers	50	60	63	35	88/176	50·0
Research staff	—	—	100	36	6/15	40·0
TOTAL	60	62	63	44	200/369	54·0

Table 8.11 Q.5; Student enrolments 1971 and 1974 by subject group: percentages

| | 8 Technological Universities: Student enrolments | | Halsey, Trow and Fulton samples of teachers 1964 | |
Subject group*	1971	1974	CATs	UK Universities
Engineering and other applied sciences Technology [3 & 4]*	49·3	43·0	46	13
Science [5]	26·2	24·6	40	29
Social, administration and business studies + other vocational subjects [6 & 7]	14·5	19·6	10	16
Others [1, 2, 8 & 9]	10·0	12·8	4	42
TOTAL N	22,261	25,078†	383	1,404

Notes: * See Table 10.3, where subject groups are numbered 1 to 9. Here integers indicate which of these groups have been combined to give the four-point-scale.
† An increase over 1971 of 11 per cent.

In recorded interviews many Professors were concerned to emphasise that they had sought their appointments because of the increased opportunities of working closely with industry in the discovery and application of knowledge, and in teaching those already set on industrial careers through sandwich courses.

The academic programme of the Technological Universities has widened over the years, and Table 8.11[8] gives the classification of students by subject groups in 1971 and 1974 respectively.

Judging from recorded discussions, the evident increase in the social sciences had been felt by other staff in particular Universities to be larger than in fact it was, provoking and sustaining the debate about the spectrum of studies appropriate to a Technological University, and as to whether they should have arts faculties. At present, however, there appears no likelihood of conformity with the traditional University in this respect.

The main change was the substantial increase in social sciences, and the proportionate decline in natural sciences and technology. This change of policy coincided with the markedly changed pattern of student applications throughout the University world – a sharp increase in the ratio of applications to places in the social sciences, and a decline for natural sciences and technology.

Table 8.12[9] exemplifies the social basis of educational opportunity, and the very great importance numerically of the grammar schools to the staffing of higher education.

Table 8.12   Q.10; Type of secondary education of respondents: percentages

Type of school	Technological Universities 1971	Halsey and Trow sample 1964	
		CATs	Universities
Grammar	69	68	55
Direct grant	11	8	10
Public	10	10	21
Other*	10	13	13
Total N	368	372	1,387

Note: * For the Technological Universities this includes secondary technical (4%), modern (1%) and the remainder (5%) includes overseas.

Halsey, Trow and Fulton's figures showed how closely the figures for the CATs approximated to those for the Universities, and the 1971 figures show no significant change in this period of expansion. The age of leaving school is another indicator of varying social opportunity, and Table 8.13 gives the analysis for the respondents.

Table 8.13   Q.11; Age of leaving school by rank: percentages

	Age of leaving									
	18 and over		17		16		15 and below		TOTALS	
Rank	N	%	N	%	N	%	N	%	N	%
Professors	49	53	21	23	17	18	6	6	93	100
Readers	7	44	6	37·5	2	12·5	1	6	16	100
Senior lecturers	30	45	16	24	15	22	6	9	67	100
Lecturers	103	58	37	21	26	15	10	6	176	100
Research staff	13	86+	—	—	1	6+	1	6+	15	100
TOTALS	202	55	80	22	61	16·5	24	6·5	367	100 (2NA)

Table 8.14   Q.2 & 12; First and higher degrees by period of appointment: percentages

	Technological Universities 1971			Halsey, Trow and Fulton sample 1964	
Degree Qualification	Periods O + I	Periods II + III	TOTAL	CATs	Universities
First degree	35	27	30	41	35
Master's degree	25	27	26	17	13
Doctorate	37	45	42	33	46
No degree	3	1	2	9*	6
Total N	132	237	369	383	1,402

Note: * Two-thirds of these had professional qualifications.

Of the 367 respondents 23 per cent had left school before the age of 17, and since only 2 per cent had no degree (Table 8.14), it can be assumed that at least 21 per cent had graduated 'the hard way' by part-time study at 'the Tech'.

The Technological Universities, from their origins, have placed a high value on professional training and qualifications, and those of their staff are set out in their prospectuses or calendars. When the CATs gained University status and were thus to be detailed in the Yearbook of the Association of Commonwealth Universities, representations had to be made for the inclusion of professional qualifications of academic staff in addition to the customary list of University degrees. A small point, but not insignificant in relation to the different traditions. Table 8.14[10] compares the first and higher degrees of respondents in three samples, and Table 8.15 gives other types of postgraduate qualifications including professional qualifications; significantly no data are available for the Universities.

The comparison between phase (O + I) and (II + III), i.e. before and after August 1962 when independent status had been attained and the prospect of University status became more likely, shows a definite trend towards close comparability with the Universities as of 1964. Alongside the marked increase in doctorates, there was a decline over the two main phases in the proportion of Fellowships and Memberships respectively, as shown in Table 8.15.

The decline in professional qualifications may be more apparent than real, being simply a numerical consequence of the growth of the social sciences and humanities in the Technological Universities, which also contributes to the increased proportion of staff appointed direct from other Universities. While recruitment of staff from industry and commerce is maintained, and sandwich courses are fostered, professional qualifications are likely to command a high regard in the Technological Universities.

In the debates of recent years on equality *v.* quality, on educational routes, and on lifelong learning, the need for diversity and flexibility has been an insistent concern. A detailed analysis of the varied patterns of study followed by respondents is summarised in Table 8.16.

Only 6 per cent of staff over-all had studied part-time only, decreasing from 12 per cent in the earlier years to 3 per cent in the most recent periods. The increase in recruitment of social scientists prob-

Table 8.15 Q.2 & 12; Types of postgraduate/professional qualifications by period of appointment in Technological Universities 1971: percentages

Period of appointment		Fellow-ship*	Membership and Associateship†	Diplomas and Certificates	None	TOTALS
O+I Up to and including July 1962		30	20	19	31	100
II+III From August 1962 onwards		24	16+	19+	40+	100
TOTALS	%	26	18	19	37	100
	N	96	66	71	136	369

Notes: * i.e. the senior grade of professional membership. There has been some confusion as professional institutions have been changing their nomenclature in recent years, e.g. the former first and higher grades became MICE and FICE for civil engineers from the former AMICE and MICE respectively; for mechanical engineering the change was from AMIMech.E and MIMechE to MIMech.E and FIMech.E.; for electrical engineering from AMIEE and MIEE to MIEE and FIEE respectively. In the Royal Institute of Chemistry, ARIC has become MRIC, with FRIC as the senior grade.

† i.e. the first grade of professional membership following graduation plus approved professional training and experience, one which for professional engineers is equivalent to CEng., indicating the status of chartered engineer: likewise C Chem. for chartered chemists.

Table 8.16 Q.2 & 12; Patterns of study by period of appointment: percentages

		Patterns of study				TOTALS	
Period of appointment		All full-time	All part-time	Full-time undergraduate and part-time post-graduate	Mixed	%	N
O+I Up to and including July 1962		51	12	22	15	100	131
II+III From August 1962 onwards		65	3	19	13	100	236
TOTALS	%	60	6	20	14	100	
	N	220	22	75	50		367

ably accounts for most of this difference, and among the technologists increased opportunities to attend full-time courses would account for the rest.

About one-fifth undertook part-time postgraduate study, and this proportion may be expected to increase if the recent strictures on full-time study for Ph.D take effect, and the Technological Universities continue to afford opportunities to take higher degrees by part-time study. The mixed patterns of study – about one-seventh of the whole – indicate flexibility and diversity in the system,[11] and these are likely to increase in the future because of the effects of occupational mobility, the changing nature of industry which demands recurrent retraining and, perhaps most of all, by the economic situation with consequent lack of grants.

Turning to personal and social characteristics, 95·6 per cent of the sample were men, of whom 89 per cent were married. The small proportion of women staff is not surprising in view of the restricted opportunities which have prevailed for women. Awareness of discrimination against women has grown in recent years, and there has been increasing activity to rectify the situation, in pressure for equal pay and for equal opportunity in employment for example, leading to legislation.[12]

The discrimination against women in higher education is complex and cumulative both in this country and abroad.[13] Women as a proportion of all full-time students at UK Universities increased from 24·0 per cent in 1959–60 to 32·0 per cent in 1973–74. In 1973–74 they were 33·7 per cent of women in undergraduate courses, but only 24·8 per cent among the postgraduates. 50·8 per cent of the men as against only 31·6 per cent of the women postgraduate students were doing research for a higher degree.

In 1973 the proportion of women staff in Technological Universities was about 1 in 15 (6·6 per cent) compared with about 1 in 9 (11 per cent) in all UK Universities; and this lower ratio is largely due to the preponderance of science and technology, since for these two subjects jointly the ratio was only about 1 in 19 (5·3 per cent). When the percentages are calculated in descending order of rank the nature of the differentiation is more marked. Among professors in all UK Universities the proportion of women was 1·7 per cent, and for science and technology alone it was 0·4 per cent. For Readers and senior lecturers the two figures were 6·3 and 2·7 per cent; for lecturers and assistant lecturers 12·1 and

173

Table 8.17 Q.27: Social origins (father's occupation), Technological Universities (1971), CATs and Universities (both 1964), by age: percentages

Father's occupation	Age −30			30–34			35–39			40–44			45 +			All		
	Tech. Univs	CATs	Univs	Tech. Univs	CATs	Univs	Tech. Univs	CATs	Univs	Tech. Univs	CATs	Univs	Tech. Univs	CATs	Univs	Tech. Univs	CATs	Univs
Professional	16	14	19	14	13	21	9·5	9	15	16	12	18	17	9	25	15	11	20
Intermediate	30	34	35	38	30	33	41	35	43	34	39	45	41	42	43	38	35	41
Skilled	51 (54)	43 (52)	38 (46)	45 (48)	45 (57)	38 (46)	40 (49·5)	49 (57)	37 (42)	43 (50)	39 (48)	30 (37)	40 (42)	46 (50)	25 (32)	42 (47)	44 (53)	33 (39)
Semi-/unskilled	3	9	8	3	12	8	9·5	8	5	7	9	7	2	4	7	5	9	6
Total N	37	65	227	42	95	259	63	78	287	76	56	198	130	57	397	348*	373	1,368

(In the Skilled row the figure in brackets gives the combined Skilled + Semi-/unskilled percentage.)

Note: * 21 of the Sample of 369 did not respond to this question.

5·6 per cent; and for the 'others' 26 per cent and 16·3 per cent.[14]*

An enquiry of the eight Technological Universities produced figures for the same period which were similar to those for science and technology in all UK Universities viz: 1·6 (range 0–4·8), 2·9 (1·2–5·4), 7·9 (5·1–14·7) and 31·4 (0–100) (0·7 updated). These proportions are neither fortuitous nor genetically determined but originate in deep-seated economic factors, and in personal, family and social attitudes generally which together largely determine unequal access to higher education for women, and still affect progress in it once an appointment has been gained. Despite recent changes, still more effort and resources are required to rectify the situation, including positive official recognition of the necessity of change – as in the belated official stand by the Vice-Chancellors' Committee against the quotas of places for women students in medical schools.[15]

Opportunity for higher education has been shown to be linked with father's occupation,[16] and among the respondents to the questionnaire (Q.27) academic rank was again found to be so related, in line with the findings of Halsey, Trow and Fulton. The proportion from the professional class was highest for Professors and lowest for lecturers, and the converse was roughly true for the working class.

Halsey, Trow and Fulton went on to show that the analysis of staff by age revealed a trend towards an 'increasing democratisation' within the Universities, while the position in the CATs was 'more complex', though it showed signs of 'convergence' towards the University pattern.[17] Table 8.17[18] shows the social origins of the three samples. 20 per cent of all University staff came from social class 1, and by 1971 the Technological Universities were not very far behind. Conversely it is important to note that 75 to 80 per cent did *not* come from a professional background. Moreover the younger the member of staff the more likely is he/she to have been born into the working class.

Items 28 and 29 on the questionnaire asked for the school-leaving age of both parents, and whether either parent had had any further or higher education after leaving school.

Almost a fifth of the respondents did not know the age of leaving

* One 'subject group of all full-time teaching and research staff' of the seven groups listed is entitled 'Engineering, technology, architecture and other professional and vocational subjects'. This group is referred to above as 'Technology' and the figures combined with those in the group labelled 'Science'.

school of their parents, but most of them gave a categorical answer about post-school education. The results are compared with Halsey and Trow's figures in Table 8.18.[19] Their response was also, apparently, 20 per cent short on this variable. The discrepancies between the patterns of school-leaving among the two samples of fathers are not large and are readily accounted for by the higher proportions of respondents in the 1964 Halsey and Trow sample who attended public and direct grant schools and graduated at Oxford and Cambridge. The pattern for the mothers in the present sample, compared with the fathers shows, as may be expected, much less post-school education and a greater proportion leaving before eighteen. In only twelve instances (3 per cent) had both parents had a University education.

Table 8.18   Q.28 & 29; Parents' education

Age of leaving school		No further education		Some further education		University		TOTALS		H&T Totals	
		N	Col. %	N	Col. %	N	Col. %	N	Col. %	N	Col. %
15 or	F	193	85·6	16	50·0	4	10·3	213	72·0	657	58·7
earlier	M	208	80·9	7	28·0	0	nil	215	72·1	—	
16	F	17	7·5	5	15·6	3	7·7	25	8·4	115	10·3
	M	31	12·1	3	12·0	1	6·2	35	11·8	—	
17	F	9	4·0	1	3·1	7	17·9	17	5·7	106	9·5
	M	15	5·8	4	16·0	3	18·8	22	7·4	—	
18 and	F	6	2·7	10	30·3	25	64·1	41	13·9	240	21·5
over	M	3	1·2	11	44·0	12	75·0	26	8·7	—	
TOTAL reporting age of	F	225	100·0	32	100·0	39	100·0	296	100·0	1,118	100·0
leaving	M	257	100·0	25	100·0	16	100·0	298	100·0	—	
Age of leaving	F	55		11		5		71		290	
not known	M	67		3		0		70			
TOTAL responding	F	280		43		44		367		1,408	
Row %			76·3		11·7		12·0		100·0		
	M	324		28		16		368			
Row %			88·0		7·6		4·4		100·0		

Key: F = Father, M = Mother.

Of the male staff themselves, 98 per cent were graduates, 67 per cent had higher degrees and 25 per cent of the married men had wives who were graduates (Q.30). These figures represent a very great change in educational opportunity in a single generation, and show a sharp contrast in parental background and educational influence within the family life of two generations of children.

An age analysis shows that the intermarriage of graduates has increased with increasing democratisation of higher education. Fulton in his 1964 study found that one-fifth of the staff in his three CATs were married to graduates, as compared with two-fifths of the University staff. The total of 25 per cent in this 1971 study showed a range from 39 per cent to 16 per cent, roughly in descending order of age. He remarks that the differences between CAT and University teachers probably derived in part from the lower social origins of the CAT teachers, but more substantially from the fact that so many of them had held industrial or non-University jobs, 'which would provide them with greater chances of exogamy than University lecturers a large part of whose feminine company is provided by their students'.[20]

Academic and other activities

The extent to which teaching staff are able to engage in advanced study and to travel on leave of absence is related closely to their conditions of service, and these were an important aspect of the changing status of the CATs, first to independence in 1962, and then in becoming Universities in 1966. Some improvements were gained at the first stage, but they were not commensurate with expectations. These included an improved balance between teaching and research, more study leave and foreign visits for professional purposes. Substantial leave of absence was infrequent and was only a potential rather than an actual condition of service in the Technical College days, and this remained true for the CATs. Fulton noted in the 1964 survey that they 'were considerably worse off than their University counterparts'.[21] The position did not alter immediately upon achievment of University conditions of service, if only because of the greater demands on staff time in a period of reorganisation and growth. Table 8.19[22] sets out the picture presented by responses to items 18 and 19 on the questionnaire.

The Professors were clearly the first to benefit from the changing

177

conditions and the figures for the rest of the staff suggest that they have had to await their turn. The next three tables, 8.20,[23] 8.21[24] and 8.22,[25] relate to Q.21, 22, 23 and 24, which deal with publication of articles and books and to national and international connections.

Table 8.19 Q.18 & 19; Leave of absence by rank: percentages

Rank	N	While on the staff of a CAT	Ten Technological Universities & Colleges after 1966
Professors	93	9	25
Readers	16	19	6
Senior lecturers	69	9	4
Lecturers	176	7	7
Research staff	15	0	7
All ranks	369	8	11
Halsey, Trow and Fulton 1964:			Universities 1964
CATs	383	6	—
Universities	1,361	—	26

Table 8.20 Q.22; Number of articles published, by rank: percentages

Rank		N	*Number of articles*			
			None	1–4	5–10	11–20 +
Professors		91	2	3	12	83
	H & T	190	1	1	8	90
Readers		15	0	7	13	80
	H & T	125	0	2	13	85
Senior lecturers		69	14	28	25	33
	H & T	216	1	14	25	60
Others		15	40	40	7	13
	H & T	114	20	40	22	18
TOTALS		365	18	24	19	39
	H & T	1,375	7	22	23	47

Table 8.21   Q.23 & 24; Books published or in
preparation, by rank: percentages

Rank	Book published	Book in preparation
Professors	60	55
Readers	44	56
Senior lecturers	30	48
Lecturers	18	27
Research staff	7	20
TOTALS (N = 369)	32	39
Halsey and Trow 1964 (N = 1,405)	35	50

Table 8.22   Q.21; Proportion of staff who have held office in a national or
international academic, learned or professional society

Rank	N	%	Subject	N	Range according to age %
			Halsey and Trow		
Professors	93	60	Natural sciences	403	4–62
Readers	16	44	Technology	177	8–36
Senior lecturers	69	30			
Lecturers	175	13			
Research staff	15	7			
TOTALS	368	29			

Note: Ages ranged from −30 to 45+.

Fulton in his 1964 study of the three CATs found that 22 per cent
of staff teaching natural sciences and 43 per cent of those in technology departments (N = 151 and 195 respectively) had published
no articles. 17 per cent and 9 per cent respectively had published ten
or more.[26] Table 8.20 shows the overall figures for the ten institutions by 1971 to be 18 per cent publishing none and 39 per cent in the
11 to 20 category. In relation to books published or in preparation,
Table 8.21 again shows a narrowing of the gap between the Tech-

nological Universities and the rest. Halsey and Trow comment that publication is the most visible evidence of research activity, and holding office in a scholarly or scientific society is a rough though useful indication of academic distinction. Detailed comparison between their figures and ours is not possible, since on this item they do not provide data on subject groups.

As would be expected, the holding of such offices is closely linked with age. The older staff in fact have more publications to their credit than the younger members in absolute terms, but the big spurt comes in the early years,[27] especially in the natural sciences. Recognition in academic and learned societies by election to office tends to

Table 8.23 Q.26; Public activities outside the University that take up an appreciable amount of time, by rank

Rank	N	%
Professors	93	*47*
Readers	16	*31*
Senior lecturers	69	*30*
Lecturers	175	*21*
Research staff	15	*13*
TOTAL	368	*29*

come in the later years of a professional career, and Halsey and Trow wryly remark, 'Perhaps that is just as well for the research productivity of young scientists.'

Table 8.23 sets out the proportions of respondents by rank who claimed to spend an appreciable amount of time on public activities outside the University and, again, the higher the rank (and the older the respondent) the greater the proportion committed in this way. The extent of such activities is of some interest in view of the current debate about the social responsibilities of the Universities. Some of the activities are undertaken with the encouragement, indeed nomination, of the University, e.g. representation on Local Authority committee or governing body, but most are entirely on the person's own initiative as in the case of religious, political, social or welfare activities.

The Vice-Chancellors' Committee Report defined and separated External Professional Time (EPT) from other self-imposed social activities, which amounted to 11 per cent of the working year and about 5·5 mean hours per week over the working year for staff as a whole. For Professors the proportion of EPT was 18 per cent (10 hours), readers and senior lecturers 13 per cent (7 hours), lecturers 9 per cent (4·5 hours) and others 4 per cent (1·5 hours).[28] EPT covers a range of commitments such as external examinerships, service on CNAA Boards, Open University tutorships, and service as governors of schools and colleges, as well as work for professional, governmental and other national bodies already mentioned.

Respondents listed a wide variety of other activities, not included in the definition of EPT, including involvement in local party politics, membership of Local Authority councils and committees, and service as a magistrate. A wide range of voluntary work included social welfare, community relations, youth work, scouting, careers guidance and various kinds of counselling. Work in support of charities included particularly those for the physically and mentally handicapped. Concern with the environment was evident, with repeated mention of work for housing trusts and co-partnership societies, area development associations; and likewise for conservation societies, the restoration of canals for leisure purposes, the preservation of buildings and civic amenities, and membership of archivist and archaeological societies. Church activities were quite frequently listed, and to a lesser extent, drama and the arts, and also learned societies, including recent ones such as the European Society. All in all, a not insignificant involvement in the life of the community.

Attitude change and status

The Attitude Inventory of the staff questionnaire consists of six pairs of statements built around a concept plan explained in detail in Appendix IV. The six concepts relate to ideas and attitudes associated with the Colleges of Advanced Technology, i.e. the value of sandwich courses; the need for practical training at undergraduate level; the advantages for staff of continuing contact with industry; the importance of maintaining close relationships between industry and these institutions; the desirability of some degree of special emphasis within individual Universities; and finally, in this same context, the inadvisability of following other Universities by the addition of Arts Faculties.

Table 8.24 Attitude Inventory: percentages of high scorers by period of appointment

		Period of appointment				
		O	I	II	III	TOTALS
	N	34	72	65	125	296
Sandwich courses						
1. The advantages of sandwich courses do not justify the extra difficulties involved in arranging them.	D	94	90	74	70	79
35. The Technological Universities would be losing their greatest asset if they abandoned sandwich courses.	A	79	81	55	50	62
Real-life experiences						
38. There is no overriding argument for the provision of supervised practical training during the period of a degree course.	D	76	72	52	55	61
18. The argument that professional training should be provided within the overall period of undergraduate study is a sound one.	A	71	78	63	72	71
Value for staff						
34. The supervision of industrial periods on sandwich courses is a waste of academic staff time and needs a special establishment of non-academics.	D	88	97	78	83	86
21. Supervisory visits to sandwich course students in training are advantageous to staff in their academic work.	A	85	92	65	83	81
Relationships with industry and commerce						
2. After a year in a job the three-year trained engineering graduate is indistinguishable from a four-year sandwich course graduate.	D	85	81	62	55	66
32. Industry and commerce have a great need for graduates who have had a sandwich course type of training.	A	85	81	72	66	73
Special identity						
13. The ex-CATs should not aim to preserve a distinctive role for themselves in the University world.	D	62	75	62	44	58
6. It would be bad for technological education in this country if the ex-CATs lost their special identity.	A	82	83	51	42	58

Key: D=Disagreement scores high; A=Agreement scores high.

Scoring was on a 4-point scale (Agree strongly – Disagree strongly) orientated so that endorsement of these concepts scored high. By this device scores on the statements could be added together to give a total score. Responses on ten of the twelve statements were internally consistent, but those dealing with the inadvisability or otherwise of adding Arts Faculties were not.* There was little support for rejecting Arts Faculties out of hand, and in fact most institutions were already running some courses in the Arts and Humanities, but without full faculty organisation. As a result scores on the attitude inventory have been based on the five concepts only (ten statements) and the Arts Faculty responses are reported separately in Appendix IV. The maximum possible score was thus 40, indicating total agreement with each concept, and the minimum 10, indicating total disagreement.

Respondents placed themselves on a continuum between a stereotypical 'CAT-man' scoring high on all statements and an equally notional stereotype of the traditional University man who rejected all that the Colleges of Advanced Technology had endorsed. By grouping respondents according to period of appointment, institution, rank and subject group, mean scores on these vectors were calculated. These are shown in Tables AIV Nos. 4 to 7, since they are mainly of technical interest. The use of mean scores masks the differences in response to individual statements, and these differences are best shown by calculating the percentage of respondents scoring high† (i.e. 3 or 4) on each statement, and these results are shown here in four Tables from 8.24 to 8.27 inclusive.

As shown by Table 8.24, the greatest support was for the concepts underlying statements 1, 21 and 34. Sandwich courses were not rejected as being too difficult to organise, and there was very little support for using non-academic staff to supervise them. However,

* The plan of the pilot run was inadequate to detect this inconsistency – each institution should have been represented. To avoid two postal enquiries, Aston staff, who could be approached in person, were used, but they, along with Brunel staff, proved to be less in favour of Arts Faculties than any other group. The most important point in relation to the preliminary survey was to try out the wording of the statements, to ensure that each respondent dealt consistently with each pair, and for this purpose it was perfectly satisfactory (see Appendix IV).

† *Disagreement* with the first statement in each pair scored high, and *agreement* with the second thus the two sets of figures for each pair should be reasonably congruent.

Table 8.25 Attitude Inventory: percentages of high scorers by institution

				Institutions						TOTAL	Range
	N	Aston	Bath	Bradford	Brunel	City	L'boro	Salford	Surrey	296	
		60	30	40	27	33	29	41	36		
Sandwich courses											
1. The advantages of sandwich courses do not justify the extra difficulties involved in arranging them.	D	83	87	73	93	67	79	76	75	79	67–93
35. The Technological Universities would be losing their greatest asset if they abandoned sandwich courses.	A	63	63	53	82	58	48	73	56	62	48–82
Real-life experiences											
38. There is no overriding argument for the provision of supervised practical training during the period of a degree course.	D	60	63	53	78	61	62	59	50	61	50–78
18. The argument that professional training should be provided within the overall period of undergraduate study is a sound one.	A	68	80	80	74	70	83	63	50	71	50–83
Value for staff											
34. The supervision of industrial periods on sandwich courses is a waste of academic staff time and needs a special establishment of non-academics.	D	82	83	85	96	76	90	88	86	86	76–96
21. Supervisory visits to sandwich course students in training are advantageous to staff in their academic work.	A	85	73	78	85	67	86	83	92	81	67–92

Relationships with industry and commerce

2. After a year in a job the three-year
   trained engineering graduate is
   indistinguishable from a four-year
   sandwich course graduate.

   D 77 63 71 62 61 78 55 71 58 66   55–78
   A 72 87 71 83 70 93 73 71 64 73   64–93

32. Industry and commerce have a great need
    for graduates who have had a sandwich
    course type of training.

Special identity

13. The ex-CATs should not aim to preserve
    a distinctive role for themselves in the
    University world.

    D 60 53 89 45 39 58   39–89
    A 57 63 82 42 50 58   42–82

2. It would be bad for technological
   education in this country if the ex-
   CATs lost their special identity.

Key: D = Disagreement scores high; A = Agreement scores high.

the recent worsening financial circumstances may induce a different attitude towards supervision, especially with the need to conserve staffing resources, and this may gain support from the addition of certification of industrial training to that of academic studies. An Institute established primarily to deal with such certification, as at Brunel, could conceivably become a powerful lever for the transfer of staff supervision; and thus to move strongly towards American practice with their 'Co-ordination Staff' appointed specifically for the training programs in their 'Co-operative Courses'.[29]

Statements 1 and 35 relate to the value of sandwich courses, and on each there is a steady falling-off with recency of appointment. If we turn to Table 8.25 it is clear that this is partly due to differences between institutions. Thus percentages scoring high on statement 35 range from 48 per cent at Loughborough to 82 per cent at Brunel. The latter had the highest percentage of high scorers on eight of the ten statements, which is not surprising since the entire programme at Brunel was based on the sandwich course and, moreover, essentially the original 'thin' (6 month: 6 month) pattern.

As shown in Table 8.26, differences of response according to rank are negligible, but analysis by subject group shows important differences.

Recency of appointment is related to the increased number of social scientists on the staff, and as a group they show a relative lack of enthusiasm for sandwich courses (Table 8.27). Less than half of them regard such courses as the 'greatest asset' of the Technological Universities. Indeed in every case the social science group are less in favour of the CAT-man ethos than the technology and natural science groups. In some cases the differences are very marked indeed, e.g. statements 38, 2, 13 and 6.

Two-thirds of the technology and natural science respondents scored in favour of the ex-CATs aiming to retain a distinctive role (statement 13), and in agreeing that it would be bad for technological education if they lost their special identity (statement 6), but only one-third of the social science group did so. Since the staff enquiry which yielded these results was made, the problems of obtaining training places for sandwich course students have markedly increased, owing mainly to economic recession, with such consequences as mergers and reorganisation which have reduced the number of placements still further. The reduction in places available plus a reduced staff commitment may together engender a cumulative loss of confidence in sandwich courses. This may explain the undue caution, even timidity, of the most recent report on sandwich courses.[30]

However, we may note here that in Table 8.27 nearly 80 per cent felt that the advantages of sandwich courses did justify the extra difficulties involved in arranging them, and 62 per cent overall believed that the Technological Universities would be losing their greatest asset if they abandoned sandwich courses.

The respondents in periods O and I scored higher than those in periods II and III in every case, and this is of special interest in relation to statement 35. Staff in the earlier periods were closely identified with re-establishing sandwich courses, while those in the later groups, who had to sustain them, were increasingly committed to establishing research. While the staff in Technical College days felt sandwich courses to be their prime asset, because educationally they were a very great improvement on part-time courses, those appointed in the later periods would naturally compare this asset with others integral to all Universities, namely postgraduate courses and research. The somewhat lower figure does not necessarily imply a substantially reduced commitment (especially in view of the responses to statement 1), but may indicate a discerning revaluation in a different context.

In Table 8.24, statement 18 shows less falling-off among the later recruits to the staff, although there is diminishing disagreement with 38, which is a more extreme statement. 45 per cent of the most recent staff thought that students of engineering trained by the two different methods were indistinguishable after a year on the job (i.e. agreed with statement 2) but rather more of them (66 per cent) thought that employers had a great need of graduates with a sandwich course training. This was the view of nearly three-quarters of the staff as a whole, but the greatest support of over 80 per cent came predictably from staff in periods O and I. The same two groups were equally strongly of the opinion that students from four-year sandwich courses were distinguishable from those from three-year full-time courses after one year on the job (statement 2), and presumably by implication, advantageously so.

As would be expected, there is much variation between the responses by institution to the statements as shown in Table 8.25. Statements 1, 18, 34, 21 and 32 show over 70 per cent of high scorers, but the range of responses to each statement indicates that

Table 8.26 Attitude inventory: percentages of high scorers by rank

		Rank			
	Professors	Readers & senior lecturers	Lecturers	Research staff	TOTAL
N	76	71	135	14	296
Sandwich courses					
1. The advantages of sandwich courses do not justify the extra difficulties involved in arranging them. — D	80	79	76	85	79
35. The Technological Universities would be losing their greatest asset if they abandoned sandwich courses. — A	62	62	63	60	62
Real-life experiences					
38. There is no overriding argument for the provision of supervised practical training during the period of a degree course. — D	62	58	61	60	61
18. The argument that professional training should be provided within the overall period of undergraduate study is a sound one. — A	67	76	67	80	71

Value for staff

34. The supervision of industrial periods on sandwich courses is a waste of academic staff time and needs a special establishment of non-academics.	D	84	87	87	95	86
21. Supervisory visits to sandwich course students in training are advantageous to staff in their academic work.	A	83	87	74	95	81

Relationships with industry and commerce

2. After a year in a job the three-year trained engineering graduate is indistinguishable from a four-year sandwich course graduate.	D	62	72	67	65	66
32. Industry and commerce have a great need for graduates who have had a sandwich course type of training.	A	72	80	76	85	73

Special identity

13. The ex-CATs should not aim to preserve a distinctive role for themselves in the University world.	D	61	63	53	55	58
6. It would be bad for technological education in this country if the ex-CATs lost their special identity.	A	62	66	56	75	58

Key: D = Disagreement scores high; A = Agreement scores high.

Table 8.27 Attitude inventory: percentages of high scorers by subject group

			Subject group			
		Technology	Natural sciences	Social sciences	Others	TOTAL
	N	110	110	56	20	296
Sandwich courses						
1. The advantages of sandwich courses do not justify the extra difficulties involved in arranging them.	D	81	81	67	85	79
35. The Technological Universities would be losing their greatest asset if they abandoned sandwich courses.	A	72	61	41	60	62
Real-life experiences						
38. There is no overriding argument for the provision of supervised practical training during the period of a degree course.	D	71	62	43	60	61
18. The argument that professional training should be provided within the overall period of undergraduate study is a sound one.	A	79	66	59	80	71

34. The supervision of industrial periods on sandwich courses is a waste of academic staff time and needs a special establishment of non-academics.	D	88	87	75	95	86
21. Supervisory visits to sandwich course students in training are advantageous to staff in their academic work.	A	84	78	77	95	81

Relationships with industry and commerce

2. After a year in a job the three-year trained engineering graduate is indistinguishable from a four-year sandwich course graduate.	D	75	66	48	65	66
32. Industry and commerce have a great need for graduates who have had a sandwich course type of training.	A	85	72	57	85	73

Special identity

13. The ex-CATs should not aim to preserve a distinctive role for themselves in the University world.	D	61	64	32	55	58
6. It would be bad for technological education in this country if the ex-CATs lost their special identity.	A	65	62	37·5	75	58

Key: D = Disagreement scores high; A = Agreement scores high.

193

there is no close uniformity or identification of view between the eight Technological Universities. It would indeed be surprising were this the case, since little has been done severally or collectively to arrive at a consensus of views on these matters.

Using Table 8.25, it is possible to rank each of the eight Technological Universities on each statement. For example, as already indicated, Brunel has the highest score on eight out of the ten statements, whereas City and Surrey each have four statements on which their scores are the lowest. By scaling their positions on each of the ten statements, a ranking order was devised as shown in Table 8.28.

Table 8.28 Technological Universities: continuing identification with characteristics of CATS

Close identification					Less close identification		
1	2=		4=		6	7	8
Brunel	Loughborough	Bath	Aston	Salford	Bradford	Surrey	City
		2=					

The use of such an approximate scale, based on the responses to the statements, is but one attempt to try to evaluate the transitional changes undergone by these institutions. Table 8.28 may be read from right to left as a scale of increasing identification with the ethos of the CATs, headed by Brunel for reasons already discussed; or from left to right as a 'flexibility scale' of response to changing conditions; or even as a traditionalist-conformist scale, having at the furthermost right-hand side two Universities formerly closely linked with London University. Either way the gradient of differentiation is not substantial, and four of them could reasonably be included in position 2. The question remains as to how far these differences will grow in the future – will they have ceased to be an identifiable group of institutions by – say – the late 1980s?

Attitudes towards expansion

Quite apart from the exigencies of the 'steady state', discussed in Chapter 11, changes in the identity of the Technological Universities will be influenced by the attitudes of staff. This chapter concludes with recording and discussing the responses of academic staff to the

192

three pairs of statements dealing with expansion in the Universities; the possible transfer of numbers to other forms of higher education; and the Polytechnics.*

61 per cent of respondents agreed that there are plenty of able young people available to justify the expansion of the Universities, and interestingly enough, agreement was somewhat greater (65 per cent) among recently appointed staff (period III) than for the 'old stagers' (51 per cent). Responses to statement 39 'more means worse' were not completely consistent, for only 52 per cent rejected this. Opinion was in fact fairly evenly divided on the pros and cons of expansion. One implication seems to be: the Universities are not

Table 8.29 Size of Universities; élitist/expansionist: percentages agreeing with each statement, by period of appointment

	Period of appointment								All respondents	
	O		I		II		III			
	%	N	%	N	%	N	%	N	%	N
10. We have by no means reached the limit of able young people who could benefit by a University education.	51	39	62	87	55	78	65	149	61	353
39. In relation to University expansion 'more' *does* mean 'worse'.	53	38	40	88	52	79	49	145	48	350

catering for all young people who could benefit from higher education, but – let them go elsewhere. This result is broadly similar to that obtained by Oliver Fulton,[31] in which he found the attitudes of the then CAT teachers to be 'astonishingly like those in the Universities'. He speculates whether further expansion (beyond the upgrading of the CATs) 'might be seen as a dilution' of their 'newly acquired status'. He also makes the point that they are on average more conservative than University teachers, a fact which is in turn related to the predominance of scientists and technologists.

There are various ways in which higher education might be expanded, and attitudes will vary with the method which is favoured. Some have argued for major increases in the older foundations in order to retain 'centres of excellence'; others with a different axe to grind argue for the expansion of smaller institutions. Arguments

* See Concept Plan B.3 and 4, Appendix IV.

have been made for granting new charters to a few Polytechnics recognisable already as 'crypto-Universities', and meanwhile opportunities to graduate are increasing in the Colleges of Technology, Art and Education through the agency of the CNAA. Some indication of the attitudes to these questions is to be found in the responses to statements 12 and 28 in Table 8.30.

Statement 12 of Table 8.30 is essentially similar to statement 49 in the Halsey and Trow questionnaire. In their survey (1964), 37 per cent of the small sample of CATs (3 colleges) agreed that the Universities should be left alone, as did 49 per cent of the University

Table 8.30 Preserve quality / expand other forms of higher education: percentages agreeing with each statement, by period of appointment

	Period of appointment								All respondents	
	O		I		II		III			
	%	N	%	N	%	N	%	N	%	N
12. Non-University forms of higher education should be expanded, leaving the Universities as they are.	64	39	49	88	45	80	59	149	54	356
28. Local or regional mergers between all forms of higher education would be advantageous.	36	39	47	88	37	80	48	149	44	356

sample. Oliver Fulton commented that this was 'a very large proportion of the CAT faculty' to fall into what they called 'the élitist teacher category': this they regarded as the most unsuitable one 'for what are intended to be flourishing Technological Universities which might become the spearhead of the once-promised technological revolution'.[32] The most élitist group in the 1971 survey is period O, with the two middle periods I and II falling below 50 per cent. The rise to 59 per cent in period III is not encouraging to those like Fulton who hoped to see the Technological Universities expressing a strong commitment to mass higher education.

The third set of statements poses the question of whether the staff of the Technological Universities thought the creation of the Polytechnics was a mistake or a good answer to the problems of expansion in higher education. As Table 8.31 records, only a quarter of the respondents thought it was a mistake, with only period O being less sure; and altogether nearly two-thirds (64 per cent), with 67 per cent in periods I and III, thought they did provide a good answer.

The very substantial balance in favour of Polytechnics probably depended on certain assumptions obtaining in 1971–72, especially that Government policy would inhibit any attempt by Polytechnics to compete seriously with the Technological Universities. The staff appointed in the Technical College days of period O possibly felt less

Table 8.31 Polytechnics welcome/unwelcome: percentages agreeing with each statement, by period of appointment

	Period of appointment								All respondents	
	O		I		II		III			
	%	N	%	N	%	N	%	N	%	N
30. The establishment of the Polytechnics is a great mistake.	40	38	22	89	23	78	23	148	24	353
36. The creation of the Polytechnics is a good answer to the problems of expansion in higher education.	50	38	67	87	63	78	67	148	64	351

secure and might well have been more concerned about them as a potential threat. However, the difference may have been due to a residual feeling of regret over the change of status of the CATs. Certainly some of the staff of that time would have preferred to remain at the apex of the further education system: they would have retained their status (and would not have had to undergo apparent demotion from being a senior lecturer in a CAT to a lecturer in a University), and would have avoided the stresses and strains indicated in Chapter 3, not least the stress of holding their own among the incoming staff recruited from established Universities.

Chapter 8: Sources

Note: throughout this list, references to A. H. Halsey and Martin Trow, *The British Academics* (Faber & Faber, London 1971), to the figures quoted from their statistics in the Tables, and to the figures in the Appendix to this work by Oliver Fulton, are so numerous that they have simply been distinguished by an asterisk * to avoid repetition.

1.

(A) For the British scene, the statistical works are:

* *The British Academics* (see Note above).

Tessa Blackstone and Gareth Williams, 'Structural Aspects of the Academic Profession in a Period of Expansion', Chapter 22 in *Contemporary Problems in Higher Education* (eds H. J. Butcher and E. Rudd) (McGraw Hill, Maidenhead 1972).

Gareth Williams, Tessa Blackstone, David Metcalf, *The Academic Labour Market: Essays on economic and social aspects of the University Teaching Profession* (Elsevier, The Hague 1974).

(B) The following are discursive appraisals:

Sir Derman Christopherson, *The University at Work* (SCM Press, 1973).

Ibid., Chapter 4, 'The Academic Profession'.

J. MacCallum Scott, *Dons and Students, British Universities Today* (The Plume Press – Ward Lock, London 1973).

Ibid., Chapter 6, 'The Academic Profession'.

Kenneth R. Minogue, *The Concept of a University* (Weidenfeld & Nicolson, London 1973).

Eric Ashby, *Adapting Universities to a Technological Society* (Jossey-Bass, London 1974).

W. Roy Niblett, *Universities Between Two Worlds*, (University of London Press, 1974).

Alan Montefiore (ed.), *Neutrality and Impartiality: The University and Political Commitment* (Cambridge University Press 1975).

(C) For the American scene:

Clark Kerr, *The Uses of the University*, Godwin Lectures (Harvard University Press, Cambridge, Mass. 1963), pp. 42–44.

Christopher Jencks and David Riesman, *The Academic Revolution* (Doubleday, New York 1968).

Jacques Barzun, *The American University* (Oxford University Press, 1969), Chapter 2, 'Scholars in Orbit'.

Th. M. Hesburgh, Paul A. Miller, C. R. Wharton, *Patterns for Lifelong Learning* (Jossey-Bass, San Francisco 1973).

Martin Trow, 'Reflections on the transition from mass to universal higher education', *Daedalus*, winter 1970, 99, 1–42.

T. R. McConnell, Robert O. Berdahl, Margaret A. Fay, *From Elite to Mass to Universal Higher Education* (University of California, Berkeley 1973).

Talcott Parsons and G. M. Platt, *The American University* (Harvard University Press, Cambridge, Mass. 1973).

'American Higher Education: Towards an Uncertain Future', *Daedalus*, Vol. I, Fall 1974, Vol. II, Winter 1975.

Philip Rieff, *Fellow Teachers* (Faber & Faber, London 1975).

Martin Trow (ed.) *Teachers and Students* (McGraw Hill, New York 1975).

Other Carnegie Commission publications (McGraw Hill, New York)

Seymour E. Harris, *A Statistical Portrait*, 1972, pp. 453–539.

Report: *Governance of Higher Education*, April 1973, Chapters 4, 6, 7.

E. C. Ladd and Seymour M. Lipset, *Professors, Unions and American Higher Education*, 1973.

David Riesman, V. A. Stadtman *et al.*, *Academic Transformation*, 1973, Chapter 19, David Riesman, 'Commentary and Epilogue'.

Irwin T. Sanders, 'The University as a Community', Chapter 4 in James A. Perkins (ed.), *The University as an Organisation*, 1973.

Edward Gross and Paul W. Gramboch, *Changes in University Organisation 1964–71*, 1974.

2. Quoted by Sir Douglas Logan, *Universities: The Years of Challenge*, The Rede Lecture, 1963, p. 28, from Dr. T. H. Matthews, *Improving College and University Teaching*, Vol. IX, No. 1 (Oregon State College, 1961). Logan remarks that 'I think it must be conceded that the undue importance attached to research has produced an imbalance in higher education'.

3. From *Statistics of Education*, Vol. 6 (UGC), HMSO, 1967: Table 57, p. 103; 1975, UGC Communication, April 1977.

4. * p. 158.

5. * Table 12.7, p. 282; UGC 1968 figures quoted in Table 7.6, p. 158.

6. * pp. 478–480.

7. * Table A.10, p. 478; 1962 sample for Universities 'ever employed in industry: research and development'. CATs, Appendix A, 1964 sample by Oliver Fulton.

8. Student enrolment calculated from *Statistics of Education*, Vol. 6 (UGC), HMSO, 1971: Tables 8 and 12 combined, pp. 18 and 28; and Vol. 6, 1974: Tables 7 and 10 combined, pp. 16 and 24. Samples of teachers * Appendix A, Table A.2, p. 471.

9. * Appendix A, p. 475.

10. * Appendix A, Tables A.7 and A.9, pp. 475 and 477.

11. Compare A. G. Watts, *Diversity and choice in higher education* (Routledge & Kegan Paul, London 1972).

12. Sex Discrimination Act, January 1976 (HMSO).

13. Gareth Williams *et al.*, *The Academic Labour Market (as 1)*, Chapter 19. Tessa Blackstone and Oliver Fulton, 'Sex discrimination among University teachers: a British comparison', *B. J. Sociology*, Vol. XXVI, No. 3, September 1975, pp. 261–275.

Margherita Rendel: 'Men and Women in Higher Education', *Educational Review*, June 1975.

For the USA, see Carnegie Commission Studies (McGraw Hill, New York): Report and recommendations: *Opportunities for Women in Higher Education*, 1973.

Saul D. Feldman: *Escape from the Doll's House – Women in Graduate and Professional School Education*, 1974.

Florence Howe (ed.) *Women and the Power to Change*, 1975.

For Europe, see UNESCO and OECD Reports.

14. All figures in the two paras. calculated from Statistics of Education 1973, Vol. 6 (UGC), HMSO, Tables 7, 10 and 30. In the comparable tables for 1975 the proportion of women students, undergrad and postgrad, are about 1·6 per cent higher, and among the staff the proportions of women in the different grades show no substantial changes.

15. A memorandum submitted by the Committee of Vice-Chancellors and Principals at the invitation of the DES in relation to the Government's consultative document *Equal Opportunities for Men and Women:* the memo reprinted in *THES*, 1st March 1974, under the heading 'No discrimination in admissions'.

16. Robbins Committee Report, Chapter VI, and Appendix One, Part II. * Table A.5, p. 473.

17. * pp. 472–474.

18. Figures for CATs and Universities: * Table A.5, p. 473.

19. Numbers extracted from: * Table 15.16, p. 411 and percentages added. Mother's education not recorded. Bottom right-hand figures from 'Achieved' sample,* p. 509.

20. * p. 490.

21. * pp. 490–491. Fulton goes on to point out that the technologists in the University sector were the least privileged in this regard and that the CAT technologists were relatively well treated.

22. * Table A.28, p. 491.

23. Figures for Professors from: * Table 12.15, p. 291. Totals taken from: * Table 12.2, p. 278. The totals figures in the two tables do not tally. It has been assumed that the total of 1,404 quoted in Table 12.2 includes 29 non-respondents to this item.

24. * Table 12.3, p. 279.

25. * Table 12.33, p. 318.

26. * Table 12.22, p. 304.

27. * p. 317.

28. *Report of an Enquiry into the Use of Academic Staff Time*; the Committee of Vice-Chancellors and Principals of the UK, 1972.

29. Asa S. Knowles and Associates, *Handbook of Co-operative Education* (Jossey-Bass Inc., San Francisco 1971), Part 3.

30. *The future development of sandwich courses*, Report of a Joint Working

Party (UPIC) or representatives of CVCP, CDP, ACFHE, CBI,
April 1975.

31. * p. 481.
32. * p. 495.

9

Students and their Concerns

WITHIN the CATs the transition to University status covered two quite different periods as far as students were concerned. The period of independence of the CATs from 1962 to 1966 was un- affected by the ominous signs of student unrest gathering momen- tum abroad, and the impact was felt only after 1966 when nearly all the charters had been granted without serious representations being made, for example, on student membership of Council and Senate.

In the earlier days of the Technical Colleges life was in some ways simpler for both students and staff. Admission to a College was relatively easy, and if a student was not equipped to take a particular course he (infrequently she) could take the course preparatory to it. However, over the years, the requirements of external bodies – such as London University, professional bodies and NCTA – imposed an increasingly rigorous control of entry standards.

Surveys conducted by the Robbins Committee showed that differ- ences in family background between full-time students in Uni- versities and further education (FE) were not large, and that even among part-time FE students the children of manual workers were grossly under represented. The FE figures are given in Table 9.1,[1] which also shows the differences in parental education.

Not only were the FE students excluded from more advantageous forms of study, but generally their opportunities for extra-curricular activities – social events, music, drama, games and athletics – were severely limited as compared with those of University full-time students. For part-time students in employment leisure time is clearly more restricted, and the facilities available to them were meagre and often quite unsuitable.

To achieve full professional status by part-time study for the Higher National Certificate followed by graduateship of a pro- fessional institution was a gruelling test of dedication for any man,

200

Table 9.1 Parental occupation and education of students by method of study, 1961–62: percentages

Student groups by method of study	Father's occupation					Percentage of parents either graduates or Certificated Teachers	N
	Professional & managerial	Clerical	Skilled manual	Other manual	NK		
Further Education, full-time[2]	44	14	28	10	4	13[4]	2,178
Further Education, part-time day[2]	26	16	39	16	3	4[4]	837
Further Education, part-time evening[2]	27	14	39	15	4	6[4]	921
University[3]	59	12	18	7	4	29[5]	3,725

and entailed a severe restriction of his extra-curricular activities and social life generally. He tended then to be seen as a narrow technical man with inadequate social skills (a stereo-typical view much favoured in modern science-based industry preponderantly staffed by graduates from full-time University courses and research). This in turn prejudiced his advancement to managerial responsibility. As things were, the system could hardly have been better designed to produce this result, but it must not be forgotten that there were many success stories despite the system.

Many factors are involved in the progress of students in higher education: conditions of entry and admission, and of selection for courses; the choice of courses; the extra-curricular activities and facilities, and types of residence available; student health as a factor affecting ability to concentrate on study; graduation and prospects of employment, research or further study. The impact of these has changed substantially in the period of transition to University status, and they have demanded very close consideration within the Technological Universities.

Recruitment, admissions, and selection

Ensuring an adequate supply of able students is a matter of first importance to institutions of higher education, and Universities live in a highly competitive world in this regard.[6] It is a problem of special significance to emergent institutions, as the Polytechnics have also discovered. For Universities the ability needed is primarily intellectual: the capacity and power to use and generate concepts in whatever field of study is chosen: without the selection and fostering of intellectual ability, a University would be quite unable to maintain its integrity and standards. In that parlous condition it would fail inevitably in the long term to sustain a concern with vital objectives in the life and work of the community. If, for example, the flow of intellectual ability into sciences, engineering and technology declines as compared with other disciplines, severe – even disastrous – consequences for the future economic and social life of the nation will inevitably follow.[7]

The immediate practicalities of recruitment were particularly urgent for the emerging Technological Universities. Their potential catchment had widened from the city and locality to the region, and was becoming nationwide. Though we are but a short way along the progression from 'élite' to 'mass education', and still less in sight of 'universal higher education', there has been some widening of recruitment towards a more even representation of the social classes in higher education, to which the Technological Universities have made a contribution.

The acute problem of communicating with thousands of secondary schools was significantly reduced, first, when the CATs became members of the Universities Central Council on Admissions (UCCA), following the Robbins Committee Report, and secondly, on their transference to the UGC list from 1st April 1965.[8] They were able then to appoint sufficient staff to deal with recruitment, and in due course to establish a University registry broadly on traditional lines.

For good or ill, Universities have become 'publicity-minded' and use the mass media to ensure that their major academic developments and discoveries, new buildings and facilities receive adequate coverage. The design of calendars and other publications has been greatly improved, stimulated by justifiable criticisms from the schools, but 'trendy' publications, the 'hard sell' and 'the holiday brochure treatment' have been criticised as inappropriate and misleading.[9]

Sixth-formers may be quite unable to choose between particular Universities because their information is insufficient and mostly second-hand.[10] They have no face-to-face contact with any University until they are called for an interview, by which time their UCCA forms have long been completed and the choice made. Universities should take the initiative for more direct contact with potential students, but of course many pupils will be beyond daily travelling distance of a University, with consequent substantial expense involved. Quite a number of Universities hold well-organised Open Days and vacation conferences for fifth- and sixth-formers, which are generally appreciated.

In the early days of the CATs, all applicants were interviewed, but this has become impossible with the increasing number of applicants since joining UCCA. It becomes a very time-consuming burden for the staff, one liable to generate stress, especially with realisation that interviewing can add to the errors of the whole selection process. On the other hand interviews do not lack defenders,[11] even if only as public relations exercises. Personal experience of a cordial reception and well-conducted visits and interviews can be valuable – in the words of one student, *'It was the first place where I felt I really mattered to somebody.'*

Undoubtedly schools have a very difficult task. Quite apart from the problem of maintaining accurate, up-to-date information on all the competing institutions, it is difficult to resist the temptation to play safe, stick to the known contacts and established routines, rather than recommend a course which is new and unproven (especially to able students): but how does an institution – or a course – make an impact without a reasonable proportion of students of good or superior ability? Such resistances were very evident in the early days of the CATs, and of Dip.Tech. sandwich courses.[12]

Though we have become used to the system, the selection and placement of some 73,932 students a year in Universities out of 142,307 applicants of all grades in a very wide variety of subjects in 82 institutions is nevertheless a very remarkable achievement.[13] The UCCA scheme has made an invaluable contribution to the smooth expansion of higher education.

The problems of admission and selection are of general concern to all Universities, and differing aspects receive periodic bursts of attention. These include, for example, the predictive value of A-levels for academic success,[14] confusion about entry standards,[15] the untoward effects of differential standards,[16] the acceptability of new certificates that may be devised for sixth-form leavers,[17] and the criteria for the admission of 'mature students'. Social discrimination in selection must be of concern to all Universities, but recruitment is still very small from the lower social groups, and of women students as compared with men in all social groups.

Students' grants are another factor affecting educational opportunity and response: if they are inadequate they can seriously affect the students' academic progress, not least as regards the use of vacation time for study. We create the headache and reserve the right to complain about the effect. Inadequate grants deter students from applying to enter a University, especially those from the lower income groups. The long-term effects are damaging to society as well as to the individual, and the husband's income test-limit on grants for married women was a particularly glaring example. It provided a strong financial incentive for students to 'live in sin' until they graduated. Again very few women have been sponsored by firms for sandwich courses.*

* Some of the instances cited have been overtaken by administrative action

Such evidence as there is suggests that the social catchment of the Technological Universities is not significantly different from that of Universities generally, which is perhaps surprising in view of their origins as Technical Colleges. However, it was mainly the part-time courses, for technicians and craftsmen, which were of direct interest to working-class students, and it was these courses which were shed as standards were raised, and the CATs concentrated on developing full-time and sandwich courses. These courses attracted more A-level than ONC holders, and this meant an increased proportion of students from the professional and other related classes. However, it must be emphasised that these trends were under way *before* designation as Colleges of advanced Technology, as is shown in Table 9.1. They were accelerated by the influence of NCTA in its insistence on a high proportion of advanced courses in Colleges as an important condition of recognition. Its successor, CNAA, has been equally insistent for the Polytechnics. So it is not surprising that the social class of students going to a polytechnic has been found to be not much different from that of University students.[18]

In this country women students are generally not encouraged to take engineering courses and they favour the arts faculties, so inevitably their numbers in the Technological Universities are below the average in the Universities as a whole. Table 9.2[19] gives the figures for 1975–76.

The proportion of women students has increased with the addition of social science faculties and education departments. As regards technological subjects no comparable increase is in sight in Universities as a whole, and consequently the proportion of women staff teaching these subjects is likely to remain very low – an unequal and self-perpetuating situation.*

The minimum standard of entry to a University is two A-levels plus three O-levels, but this constitutes no right of entry, only one of consideration. Faculty or departmental requirements are often well

anticipating legislation, as for example, the revised regulations early in 1975 concerning grants to married women, made in advance of the Sex Discrimination Act, which became effective on 29th December 1975.

* Long-term trends are revealed in UCCA statistics. Among the home – i.e. UK – applicants the percentage of women has increased from 30·0 to 36·2 over the period 1967 to 1976 while among the home admissions the percentage of women increased from 29·7 to 36·4. However, the differential subject recruitment remains – more women than men apply for arts, fewer for science and very few for technology (see UCCA Fourteenth Report 1975–76 p. 3).

Table 9.2 Proportions of women students in Technological and all UK Universities 1975–76

	8 Technological Universities			All UK Universities		
	Undergraduate full-time (including sandwich)	Postgraduate full-time (including sandwich)	Part-time*	Undergraduate full-time	Postgraduate full-time	Part-time*
Total number	22,772	4,282	3,133	218,088	50,626	22,502
Number of women students	5,606	679	485	77,276	13,365	5,188
Women as per cent of total	24·6†	15·9	15·5	35·4	26·4	23·1

Notes: * Part-time undergraduates numbered 133 in the Technological Universities (46 per cent women) and 3,815 in all UK Universities (48 per cent women).
† At December 1976 the proportion of women in sandwich courses was 23 per cent; in full-time undergraduate courses 28 per cent; in all undergraduate courses 25 per cent and among all students including postgraduate 24 per cent. The range for this latter figure was 16 to 34.

beyond this, requiring three A-levels with high grades. While Universities expressly advise students that A-level is only one of several criteria used for admission, and that a high grade does not guarantee admission nor a low one rejection, some have nevertheless published median scores and median grades as a rough guide to applicants.* Ambivalence about this practice is inevitable: but in the long run news of good teaching and care of students (which items are difficult to tabulate), good facilities and congenial living conditions, will circulate on the grapevine through satisfied students and their schools. The experience of Technological Universities has been encouraging in this respect.

Reasons for entering University

Students' motives for entering University are often mixed and, contrary to a superficial moral judgement, this is realistic and healthy, as life and its choices are far from simple. Not all applicants are single-minded dedicated academics – for the rest vocational/professional ambitions, personal and family pride and social expectations are there alongside the intellectual drive. The balance between these varied motives must be of some interest, if not concern, to University staff as teachers.[20] One question (and challenge for staff) is how many of these students acquire strong intellectual interests by the time they graduate – to what stimulating intellectual challenges have they been exposed? It would be unwise to regard reasons for entry (however accurately evaluated in retrospect after one year's experience at University) as permanent determinants of progress.

In a survey 90 per cent of students indicated strong occupational considerations for seeking entry to University;[21]† about half felt that the University would lead to better paid occupations, and to a wider choice of occupations. The possibility of working with more interesting colleagues was another significant consideration. Contrary to accepted wisdom in some traditional quarters, a strong occupational motivation is not mutually exclusive of intellectual commitment, not even in technology. Moreover, J. A. Wankowski

* Grade A = 5, B = 4, C = 3, D = 2, E = 1; thus three grades can range in total from 15 down to 3.

† A survey of the views of 500 sixth-formers in Yorkshire schools showed strong expectations that learning at University or College would be a preparation for a definite vocation or profession.

found that those who were vocationally motivated on entry did better than others in their courses.[22]

Students entering the Technological Universities generally have strong vocational/professional predilections, and especially those entering sandwich courses. However, discussion with students showed that some enter Technological Universities because they are Universities, rather than not enter a University at all. Not surprisingly, such students were apt to be 'agin the government' within the University, arguing vehemently in favour of generalising the University. In one instance they earnestly hoped that this change would be symbolised in the removal of 'Technology' from the title of the University. Social science students took the lead in this, but they had allies among the science students. The articulateness and committed critical stance of such students contrasted sharply with the large quiescent majority of conforming students in science and technology. The involvement of this majority in discussing controversial matters was in any case strongly discouraged by their having much heavier class timetables because of practical work required in laboratories and workshops.

Pre-entry experience for students

Students' expectations on entry to a University may soon be jarred by realities, and this unfortunate hiatus may be partly due to the student's immaturity, his lack of knowledge of other possibilities and to the alleged conveyor-belt or escalator effect of being carried forward unwittingly from school to University.*

With the experience in mind of war-service veterans returning to the Universities, and of the quality and commitment of mature students in adult education,[23]† it has been argued increasingly over the last decade that students should have at least a year's gap between school and University in which 'they can sort themselves out'. Optimistically it is hoped that the adventitious benefits of a year's experience of work and/or travel will be more positive than a year

* Sustained, it is said, only by the projected ambitions of parents and school-teachers. However, rigorous comparative studies are lacking and much is made of such evident cases as there are, especially if they can supposedly be linked to the small minority of dissidents.

† And most recently because of the graduation results gained by Open University students.

spent at University – with – some may hope – fewer arriving back at the doors in consequence.[24]

More generous in spirit is the view urged that 'channelling the creative urges, and the desire to help young people into service to the community either here or overseas, on a wider scale than is possible at present, must be of immense service to the community and also to the individuals involved'.[25] Anyone with close knowledge of the difficulties of the work of placement in Voluntary Service Overseas, or of the practical difficulties on a far bigger scale of arranging industrial periods for sandwich course students, will appreciate how substantial will be the problems of establishing a widespread effective provision of social service and 'real life' experiences. It is quite unrealistic to suppose that 'it just needs a little practical encouragement'.[26] Indeed, substantial institutional changes at the interface between secondary and higher education would appear essential if the arrangements are to be commensurate with the need.[27] However, it is at least encouraging that a survey of some 15,000 sixth-form leavers, not previously traced to a University or college immediately after taking A-levels, were heavily in favour of the year's gap.[28]* A survey by second-year sociology students at Reading University reported feeling that they had gained by the experience of a year's interval.[29]

If adequate, flexible means were established for a valuable and effective year's experience this could become the norm – i.e., in effect a required voluntary activity. Those without it would then somehow be supposed to lack some essential qualities; orthodoxies grow by subtle accretion on practices and it would be foolish to impose this view on those students who are dedicated academics and who cannot get to University fast enough to pursue their studies. So far as the Technological Universities are concerned, the industrial periods of sandwich courses provide a significant and varied social experience with growing responsibility. It must not be implied that this is really less meaningful than the year off, as it would be regrettable and untrue to assume that preparation for a profession is less significant in social terms, or that working for the community through industry necessarily has less social meaning or value.

However, the numbers of students taking full-time courses in the Technological Universities are continuing to rise, and the one-year gap considerations apply to them. In addition, arguments are being

* Note that the UCCA facilitates applications in relation to a year off.

presented that all full-time courses should have planned periods of social experience or community work.[30] If the Technological Universities give serious consideration to these two aspects for their full-time students, their experience with sandwich courses could be a useful guide. This would also render the walls between University, work and the community more permeable, with exchange of help and experience for the general good.[31]

Student health

Most students of Technical Colleges live at home. If need be they consult the family doctor or, as the case may be, the works doctor. With students increasingly recruited more widely, nationally and internationally, there was an increasing need in each of the CATs for a student health service on lines established in the Universities. With the exception of Loughborough, with its early, relatively large, residential basis, full development did not take place until after University status was gained. Even then progress for some years was generally not equal to the needs because resources were not granted in competition with demands made for other developments. Naturally the students had a strong interest, were properly articulate about it, and the provision is now comparable with that of other Universities.

The absence of the family doctor is not alone a sufficient reason for a student health service, for students in lodgings or flats can register in term-time with a local doctor. What more do they need – and the carping comment has been frequently made that just at the time when students become legally recognised as adult citizens at eighteen, at the outset of their University careers, they were demanding more and better student health services, including psychiatric treatments when necessary. This is but another sign of a tense public ambivalence about students, for no one appears to make similar criticisms of medical services for workers and occupational groups with particular hazards. Being a student is a stimulating experience but it is a peculiarly stressful demanding one, sustained over a long period. Coming towards the end of the uncertainties and changes of adolescence, these particular stresses and strains are apt to induce problems, which can adversely affect the student's well-being and academic progress.

Confidentiality is an indispensable condition for a student health service to be acceptable to students. The range of problems is very wide – emotional disorders, physical illnesses, anxiety and depression, examination stress, sexual relations, pregnancy, drugs, drop-outs, self-injury and potential suicide. Fortunately the incidence is not large.[32]

Extra-curricular activities

Opportunity for students to choose freely from a wide range of activities – social, sporting, dramatic, musical, literary, political and religious – is an integral part of University life. As important educationally as the freedom of choice is the opportunity to mix with students of other Departments. The third important aspect is that in British Universities nearly all the activities are organised by the students themselves, mainly through their own largely autonomous student union. Advice and support may be sought from academic staff, but this is decided by the students themselves.

Much of the foregoing is in marked contrast as regards scale of provision with the earlier Technical College days – when perhaps an intermittent academic paternalism encouraged students despite the prevailing lack of appropriate facilities. The pace of remedying this during the decade 1956–66 was nowhere adequate: teaching facilities (other than libraries) were added first and facilities for extra-curricular activities were a long way behind. The diversity of student societies despite the conditions was commendable, but especially for city-based institutions providing really adequate facilities was a depressingly long-drawn-out task; for example, to obtain playing-fields for Aston students took eight years, once a decision to start had been made. As a student president in the early years remarked, *'It's pie in the sky for us, and for many more to come'* – and that was for suitable use of land in a Green Belt. Hazards on the way included two public enquiries, refusal by two Local Authorities to act on behalf of the College, and this led to reference of the case to the Lands Commission, which was almost immediately disbanded by the next Government. Thanks to the vision of Dr Herbert Schofield, Loughborough University had been exceptionally well placed as regards residence and grounds since its early days, and most of the Technological Universities are now provided for reasonably well.

Student unions

The existence of a students' union, well provided with amenities and a wide range of facilities, is understandably a factor in the recruitment of students, as between Universities and other institutions of higher education. Former deficiencies were not only in buildings and facilities, but in support services. The inherently intermittent nature of student activities throughout the session, and especially from one academic year to another, puts a premium on having adequate administrative, secretarial and maintenance staff to secure continuity and to maximise the students' efforts. In earlier years it was relatively easy to justify with governing bodies, Local Authorities and the Ministry of Education/DES the addition of new laboratories and services, but far more difficult to secure grants for buildings and services necessary for the wider education of students – owing to an underlying puritanical utilitarianism which still dies hard.

The transformation of roles and relationships over the last decade has been stressful at times. Democratically speaking, definitive gains have been made, despite the understandable shock felt by many traditional academics at these major changes, and quite apart from the deplorable incidents which took place. However, it remains true that the opportunity to organise in furtherance of individual and group interests is a basic right of a democratic citizen. Students in higher education are now adult citizens and they have many important interests and concerns which can be protected and furthered by well-organised joint action. The exercise of individual judgement and responsibility in making decisions after adequate and fair discussion and debate are matters of the greatest moment to the self-education of students.

The students' right to organise is generally recognised in individual British Universities through the existence of the students' union, or a guild of students, a students' representative council, or other such body;[33]* and nationally through the National Union of Students, founded in 1922. In the past the benefit of NUS cheap travel facilities was an outstanding example, but recently these schemes have been in severe financial straits. Other valuable schemes, e.g. for ex-

* Oxford University approved the institution of a Central Student Union as late as January 1974.

change visits abroad, should not be overlooked.[34]* The NUS contributed to a smoother transition than happened abroad,† but subsequent changes and the continuing relevance of the NUS have been called in question.[35]

Student–staff relationships have changed markedly in the last decade or so, but 'student–institution' relationships even more. This became evident when student unions – especially when dominated by rather left-wing minorities – promised or actually provided grants from union funds for external purposes which were not in any way directly part of the purposes of students or University. These student union monies were derived from grants made to individual students by Local Education Authorities for their wider education. This raised acute controversy about the misuse of public funds, the limited degree of autonomy which should be accorded to student unions, and the ultimate responsibility of each University for such misuse. The highly political debate raged over many months,‡ especially concerning proposals in Parliament to establish a Registrar of Student Unions as an official appointment external to the Universities and the UGC. Wisely, Government action was shelved in January 1972 for legal and administrative reasons, but also, we may hope, because this would have been yet another step in reducing the autonomy of the Universities and the UGC: there were no irregularities sufficient to justify so serious an action and none since then.

However, the issue of the *degree* of autonomy to be enjoyed by student unions remains unresolved as far as (militant) students[36] themselves are concerned; but in relation to University Charters as at present devised, and as far as the views of University Councils and Senates can be discerned, complete autonomy is out of the question.[37]

Student grants

The principle laid down in the Anderson Committee Report,[38] that no able student should be debarred from a University for financial reasons, was widely accepted, but inflation supervened. By 1972 the

---

* Central Bureau for Educational Visits and Exchanges, 43/45 Dorset Street, London W1.

† e.g. the concordat with CVCP and Local Authorities respectively in 1968.

‡ As an abundance of varied and vigorous Parliamentary speeches, the promotion of a Parliamentary Bill, press editorials and letters too numerous to record here, showed over the period December 1971 to July 1972.

principle no longer applied because in real value maintenance grants were significantly below the minimum needed. Inflation worsened and the Vice-Chancellors' Committee protested strongly to the Government,[39] as did the NUS, and grants were much improved[40] (though still with a residual discrimination against married women students).[41] Non-payment of assessed parental contributions entailed serious hardship for many.[42] The whole period was one of serious disquiet concerning grants, and University residences were not excluded from contention, as under UGC rules they had to be self-financing (apart from capital costs) and could not be subsidised from University funds. The consequent unavoidable increase in charges eroded the value of grants, and led to student rent strikes, a great embarrassment to University authorities who strongly favoured an increase in grants.

The contrast of full-time students on grants with sandwich course students on adequate wages during their industrial periods may have strengthened a proposal that students be paid wages rather than grants.[43] There was also a strong revival of proposals for loans to students, in addition to or in place of grants,[44] and evidence from other countries was an integral part of the debate.[45] The arguments in favour of loans are allegedly not merely financial, but social and egalitarian in that they aim to ensure that the student repays (over a period of years) a large proportion of the cost of his education, from the benefits of which he will derive an income disproportionately higher than that of the majority of the population throughout his working life. The most serious criticism of loans is that they will inhibit still further the enrolment of students, generally from the lower income groups. Prior to 1976, this deterrent effect would have been even greater for women students. Late in 1976 it appeared that the Government did not propose to institute a system of loans because of administrative difficulties.

Student residence

Some advocates present residence as an indispensable quintessential experience. However, on that view, considering the small proportion of students, minute among the population generally, who have been full-time in residence between 18 and 22 years, the outlook for the human race must be parlous indeed. The truth is that residence does have educational and other advantages, but it need not be on the

214

same pattern or at the same age for everyone, still less administered on the same traditional paternalistic basis.[46]

Inescapably with the rapid growth of higher education, residence in traditional terms has raised acute problems of resources. These have beset development in all new Universities, including the technological ones. In recent years the trend has been towards a more varied provision, a diversity of environments for ever-changing groups of students, whose needs and attitudes change through the years of study. The range includes the following: traditional halls of residence, flat units,[47] bed-sits and communal feeding, self-help flats provided by the University or sponsored by student organisations, and 'digs' provided by landladies. Digs, however, have become much more difficult to find, for the increasing number of students, in the changed circumstances of the Welfare State and with an increasing proportion of two-income homes.

The Colleges of Advanced Technology moved as soon as they could to provide halls of residence on traditional lines because they were recruiting students increasingly from the whole country and accommodation had to be found. For example at Aston, the proportion living at home was already down to 43·4 per cent in 1965–66, but fell to 29·1 per cent by 1969–70. For lodgings the figures were 42·8 per cent and 50·4 per cent respectively, and for University accommodation 8·2 per cent and 15·6 per cent. By December 1974 the home-based proportion was down to 21·5 per cent, in lodgings and flats was at 39·0 per cent, and University accommodation stood at 37·2 per cent, out of a total full-time enrolment of 4,137 as compared with 2,038 in 1965–66.[48]* Overall in the Technological Universities in 1975–76 the proportions were as follows: 47·3 per cent in University residences; 20·2 per cent in lodgings (with meals); 15·2 per cent at home (parental or own home) and 17·3 per cent other accommodation (flats, self-catering).†

Many students who live in lodgings or at home (chores are inescapably involved for women students) would ideally prefer not to do so. This is a finding persistently overlooked by the advocates for regional recruitment of students and a consequent increased propor-

* The proportions for all Universities in December 1974 were: colleges or halls of residence 43·7 per cent; lodgings or flats 36·6 per cent; at home 16·3 per cent, others 3·4 per cent. Reference *48*, Table 5, p. 14.

† The figures are approximate, as replies from the eight Universities covered only 27,747 students out of the 29,064 enrolled in full-time courses.

tion of students living at home, which has been strongly urged on grounds of financial stringency.[49] The students' wishes stem not merely from the avoidance of chores but primarily from psychological need[50] (recognised by the Government in granting adult citizenship): in noting this psychological fact, no disparagement is implied of the value of the family as a social unit.

The assessment of academic progress

In more authoritarian times students accepted the dual role of academic staff as both teachers and examiners, but over the last decade assessors and their methods, with the resulting failure and wastage, have come under fire from student activists and – let it not be overlooked – increasingly from academic staff also.[51]

Within the Technological Universities, certainly, students entering courses leading towards their chosen professions generally accepted the traditional methods, but in recent years project work, assessed essays, dissertations, and cumulative assessment of course work during the year have been added to the customary three-hour examinations. While the debate about the accuracy and subjectivity of examinations has continued, closed examinations are still staunchly defended, and the effort to do away with all assessment has made no headway against determined resistance.

We must not fall into the error of supposing that those who wish to change the content and orientation of existing courses have no concern for standards. The two issues of content and assessment must be kept separate, but the question remains as to how those standards should be tested and secured. The proper recognition of excellence involves judgements and this fact of academic and professional life cannot be set aside simply by the pseudo-egalitarian sentiment that student achievement should not be graded. Nevertheless, students' future careers and lives may be profoundly affected by damaging assessments, and constant vigilance over the fairness and accuracy of the methods used is essential. Part of the students' concern about the effects of examinations and assessments is due to lack of understanding of what is involved. Academic staff should, with each new set of entrants, make an early opportunity to explain and discuss the currently established procedures, and invite comment and criticism on possible changes when they are being considered. Such discussions do not constitute an abdication of academic responsibility, but an intelligent, sympathetic fulfilment of it in co-operation with the students concerned – a pertinent instance of the change from *assent perforce* to *consent perhaps*. In this context it is desirable that the important role of the external examiner, and the protection which this affords the students, should be emphasised.

That academic decisions concerning students' progress are made with great care and sense of responsibility should be manifest to the student, particularly if failure appears likely to entail his exclusion from the University of which he is a member. Considerations of natural justice require that the student be properly informed of the decision, and that he has the right of appeal to an appropriately constituted body in the University. No matter how carefully and sympathetically the case may be considered by any other University body, however prestigious (e.g. Senate or Council), the right to appeal to the board of examiners concerned with the course against expulsion on academic grounds must be upheld. This was the upshot of the Aston case, where students appealed to the High Court against adverse academic decisions on grounds of natural justice. Despite the Lord Chief Justice's judgement that the conclusion that there had been a breach of the rules of natural justice was justified only on the particular facts of the case, the case led to a re-examination of procedures in most British Universities.[52] The recognition of considerations of natural justice applying to students as individual citizens and as members of the academic community was but one aspect of the changing relationship between the University and the student body, and was related to the general context of student unrest in Great Britain in the 1960s, itself part of a worldwide phenomenon.

Student unrest

Though the Technological Universities have not been seriously disrupted (so far) by student protests – demonstrations, sit-ins and the like – this chapter must take note, albeit very briefly, of the relevant matters of student concern. The urgent phenomena of student unrest have been recorded in a very wide range of publications, from colourful polemic to intellectually disciplined attempts to disentangle the complex problems involved. The context of particular incidents and campaigns, in higher education institutions the world over, is enormously diverse, and space permits only a brief summary of the main underlying causes in the British scene. These may be set

217

broadly in four main groups, though the interplay between them is complex and often highly specific:

Personal: home circumstances; financial worries; difficulties in personal relationships; and health problems.

Academic: inadequate schooling; unsuitable choice of course; inadequate options in courses; poor teaching and indifferent relationships with teaching staff; lack of advice on, and facilities for, study.

Administrative: unsuitable lodgings; poor communications and lack of clearly established procedures; lack of clear structure and relationships in the institution; outmoded regulations, and apparently arbitrary decisions; lack of consultation.

External context and contrasts: socio-political inequalities and injustices in contrast/conflict with the idealism of youth; students increasingly better informed of standards and practices elsewhere, e.g. in differences of University governance and representation; in range and quality of facilities provided; in the standards of attainment required; as to the range and suitability of methods of teaching and assessment used elsewhere; and as to the consideration given to 'drop-outs' from courses. Latterly in some at least of these respects there has been comparison with the methods and published material of the Open University.

There are several possible reasons why the Technological Universities have been relatively free from such troubles. Most of their courses have a firm vocational orientation, and generally the students are strongly motivated towards the profession of their choice.[53] These Universities are closely linked with industry and commerce, and a high proportion of their graduates do in fact take up jobs in industry and commerce. The courses generally are well structured and, while broadly based, are progressively designed towards clear objectives, which is in strong contrast with the uncertainties of inter-disciplinary courses and other educational experiments.[54]

The effects of isolation were the subject of comment on the structure of Essex University in relation to its persistent and severe disturbances. They derive, according to Professor Mary Douglas,[55] from a mistaken social theory which '. . . supposes that people can best work together when hampered by the minimum of institutional rules, separated by no formal distinctions, but only inspired by their commitment to a common aim.

'Such a theory might do well for disembodied spirits. But humans need their identity made visible and their responsibilities defined. The Annan Report[56] is the case-history of the failure of a social theory. It records the new students' sense of loneliness in the broad-based first-year course common to them all: it notes the deliberately weak spatial symbolism (no junior common room, no senior common room, no territorial identity for the teaching departments) and it notes the ambiguous allocation of responsibility . . . the institution's lack of structure is to blame for the place deserted at weekends, the lack of student societies, the difficulty of making friends except at student demos. . . .'

It would be as easy to overemphasise the importance of structure as it is to underestimate it – one student's structured course may be another's strait-jacket. However, the value of such structures greatly depends on the 'degrees of freedom' associated with them, of options available, of variations in methods and pace. Fruitful study and creative work can and do arise within the freedom of structured conditions, and it is usually against the rigidities of a structure that students protest, rather than the existence of a structure as such.

A perennial cause of unrest is the frustration of youthful idealism by the elderly remaining unduly long in power. They are a markedly growing proportion of the population in western countries, and their retarding influence is reinforced generally through society's obsolescent institutions. Idealism is renewed in each generation (else it were a tragic day for human progress) and it is unwise to add unnecessarily to the tensions involved.[57] Students in recent years have confronted the established adult world with their idealist campaigns for charities (e.g. Oxfam, Shelter), and against injustices and abuses. The latter have included issues very contentious in the University world, such as dependence on investments held in racialist countries, the acceptance of classified and other research sponsored by armed forces and related Government departments,[58] and the undue intrusion of external influences within the University (e.g. by big business,[59] but no criticism was made on this score in the course of this study).

A report published in 1974[60] showed that although 80 per cent of the University teachers sample had experienced student unrest at their Universities, nearly 94 per cent of them (75 per cent of all teachers) thought it had been beneficial. It had given the system a jolt and made Universities take more notice of the needs of their students. Moreover, the teachers were largely opposed to harsher disciplinary proceedings against student protesters, and almost entirely against any admissions policy designed to exclude potential protesters. However, student demonstrations have without doubt sharply affected public opinion and generated opposition to paying grants to students, increasing the pressure to introduce loans instead. Such consequential 'student-bashing' has become a preoccupation likely to have unfortunate effects in the public mind for the Universities, the more so because the role of the Universities is not very widely understood, particularly as regards the vital importance of intellectual enquiry.

Freedom of intellectual enquiry in a University must embrace the whole of human knowledge, thought and experience, including speculation about society and its institutions: such freedom of its very nature is disputatious, and challenging to accepted values and traditions. The crucial practical distinction to be made is in the choice of means which are to be used in the pursuit of such ends: this is the fundamental question which lies at the centre of arguments about discipline, and about what should constitute sufficient grounds and procedures for exclusion from the University. No blueprint for action, no panacea, can be devised to solve or remove continuing problems of this sort, changing in context and impact as they will from generation to generation. The burden of responsibility for wise decisions and action will continue to lie inescapably with the University Council and Senate. Much progress has been made in recent years in removing or mitigating the causes of unrest discussed above, by bringing the concept of natural justice to bear wherever it is applicable, by involving students more actively in decisions over academic work and by their increased participation in University governance.[61] The awareness of the need to create and foster a sense of community in large institutions has grown over the last decade, and with it a greater responsible involvement of students: but much still remains to be done.

Chapter 9: Sources

---

1. Based on Surveys conducted by the Robbins Committee and taken from the report *Higher Education* (HMSO, 1963), Appendix Two (B), as detailed on the tables (*2–5*, top of facing page).

2. Table 135, p. 128.
3. Table 5, p. 4.
4. Table 134, p. 128.
5. Table 2, p. 2.
6. Guides across the binary system are essential. See for example: Brian W. Heap: *Degree course offers: your place at University and Polytechnics* (Career Consultants Ltd.) 1975.

   Higher Education in the United Kingdom (British Council and Associations of Commonwealth Universities – Longman 1976–78 and biennially).

   Handbook of Polytechnic courses (Committee of Directors of Polytechnics, 1976–77 and annually).
7. Lord Bowden, *Annual Report*, 1974–75, as Principal of UMIST, reported *THES*, 2nd January 1976.
8. UGC *Annual Survey* 1963–64 (HMSO), paras. 33–36.
9. *THES*, 26th July 1974, 2nd August 1974.
10. J. Lines and A. Novak, *The Market for University Places: a Pilot Study* (University of Bradford Management Centre, June 1973), and *THES*, 16th November 1973.
11. David A. Reibel, 'University admissions: a defence of the interview', *THES*, 14th April 1972.
12. Some resistances are deeply embedded in educational and social history. See exposition by John Dancy: 'Academic idealism and the challenge of technology', *THES*, 4th March 1977.
13. UCCA *Fourteenth Report*, 1975–76 (published February 1977).
14. *The Prediction of Academic Success*, Report by the University Research Unit of the National Foundation for Educational Research (NFER), June 1973; for comment see *TES*, 6th July 1973.

    John L. Powell, *Selection for University in Scotland* (University of London Press, 1975).
15. Brian MacArthur, 'Schools confused over admission policies'. *THES*, 31st March 1972.
16. Edwin Cox, 'Arts-science disparity a source of "gross injustice" to students', *THES*, 24th November 1972.

    And note: L. A. Moritz, 'Value of A grades', *THES*, 8th December 1972.

    See also: Edwin Cox, 'Opinion' article, *THES*, 7th April 1972, and note correspondence, *THES*, 21st April 1972 and 5th May 1972.

    Also, 'Turned away at the gates', *THES*, 16th November 1973.
17. *THES*, 25th August 1972.

    TES, 25th August 1972, 21st July 1974, 28th July 1974, 5th August 1974.
18. 'Social class of Polytechnics students same as University', report of an

221

investigation at Kingston Polytechnic by Peter Marris, *THES*, 27th July 1973.

R. A. Draffon, 'Working-class students still too rare', *THES*, 23rd February 1973.

Note the recent setting up of the National Institute for Careers Education and Counselling (NICEC) at the Hatfield Polytechnic, sponsored also by CRAC, the Careers Research and Advisory Centre, Cambridge.

19. UGC Communication April 1977 and Communications from each of the eight Technological Universities.

20. R. Startup, 'Why go to University?', *Universities Quarterly*, Summer 1972.

21. L. Cohen, *Journal Curriculum Studies*, 1970.

22. J. A. Wankowski, *Random sample analysis: Motives and goals in University studies* (University of Birmingham, 1969), Author's abstract, SRHE Abstracts, 1975, Vol. 9, No. 2.

23. See Norman Mackenzie, Richmond Postgate, John Scupham, *Open Learning: systems and problems in post-secondary education* (UNESCO Press, 1975), pp. 344–48.

24. Sir John Masterman, letter 'Break before University', *The Times*, 5th December 1974; see other correspondence on this topic, following statement by Sir Keith Joseph, *THES*, 15th November 1974; in *The Times*, 23rd November 1974, 29th November 1974, 2nd December 1974 (S. L. Bragg, Vice-Chancellor, Brunel University), 4th December 1974, 10th December 1974, 16th December 1974, 27th December 1974 and 28th December 1974 (Peter Venables).

25. D. G. H. Sylvester, Medical Officer in Charge, Bristol University Students' Health Service, letter, *The Times*, 15th February 1972.

26. Another letter to *The Times*, 15th February 1972.

27. Edmund King, 'Between school and University', *THES*, 30th June 1972.

28. Ken Fogelman, *Leaving the Sixth Form*, NFER Report, 1972.

29. Reported *THES*, 30th June 1972, 'Student attitudes to delayed entry'. Also *Education Notebook*, Stephen Jessel, *The Times*, 12th June 1973.

30. S. Thomas and S. Murgatroyd, *Education beyond School* (Fabian pamphlet, 1974).

31. Peter Venables, 'Dissolving the Walls', *Universities Quarterly*, Summer 1974.

32. Dr Nicholas Malleson, *A Handbook on British Student Health Services* (Pitman, London 1965).

Dr Anthony Ryle, *Student Casualties* (Allen Lane The Penguin Press, 1969).

Dr Philip Cauthery, *Student Health* (Priory Press, London 1973).

33. *THES*, 25th January 1974.

    See Digby Jacks, *Student Politics and Higher Education* (Lawrence and Wishart, London 1975), Chapter 3, 'The development of students' unions and the NUS'.

34. See report of Conference, Keele University, *THES*, 27th April 1973.

35. e.g. editorial, 'Why the NUS is losing its relevance', *The Times*, 14th April 1975.

36. Up to 1975 see Jacks (*as 33*) pp. 155–158.

37. Graeme C. Moodie and Rowland, Eustace: 'Power and Authority in British Universities', *The Student Challenge* (Unwin, 1974), pp. 196–207.

38. Anderson Committee: *Grants to Students* (HMSO, 1960).

39. Vice-Chancellors' Committee statement published December 1973 (*TES*, 14th December 1973), following earlier warnings (*THES*, 19th October 1973 and 13th October 1972).

40. Secretary of State for Education and Science, *Hansard* (House of Commons), 14th May 1974, reported *THES*, 17th May 1974.

41. See *THES*, 17th May 1974 and 5th July 1974.

42. Ernest Rudd, 'Parents should not be forced to pay', *THES*, 24th October 1975.

    Colin Cross, 'Students want end to the means test', *The Observer*, 9th November 1975.

43. But see Sir William (now Lord) Alexander, 'The student wage proposal', *Education*, 27th November 1970.

44. Ernest Rudd, 'Who pays for undergraduate study?', *Universities Quarterly*, Winter 1970.

    Ernest and Fiona Rudd, 'Parental wealth and student poverty', *THES*, 13th April 1973.

    Lord Robbins, interviewed by Peter Hennessy, 'Strong arguments in favour of repayable student grants', *THES*, 12th January 1973.

45. Maureen Woodhall, *Student Loans: a Review of Experience in Scandinavia and elsewhere* (Harrap, London, for the University of London Institute of Education, 1970).

46. See Report of the UGC Committee (Chairman W. R. Niblett), *Halls of Residence* (HMSO, 1957).

    Also Joan Brothers and Stephen Hatch, *Residence and Student Life* (Tavistock, 1971).

47. Alan Doig, 'Flat Units', *THES*, 1st November 1974.

48. UGC *Statistics of Education* 1974 (HMSO), Vol. 6.

49. Noel Annan, 'The Accommodation Crisis: should more students live at home?', *THES*, 22nd October 1971 – a summary of a report of a Working Party (Chairman, Lord Annan) set up by the Vice-Chancellors' Committee.

See also: NUS Report: *Regionalisation of Intake*, April 1973, *THES*, 6th April 1973, and 'How to dragoon students back to their homes?', *THES*, 29th December 1972; and AUT criticisms, reported *THES*, 23rd June 1972.

The DES sponsored a three-year study at the University of Kent on Student Housing, reported *THES*, 7th September 1973.

50. Derek Pike and Jill Gardener, *Neighbourhood Universities* (Reading University, 1975).

51. Gordon W. Miller, *Success, Failure and Wastage in Higher Education* (University of London Press, 1970).

52. Copy of Judgement: High Court of Justice, Queen's Bench Division, No. 218/68: before the Lord Chief Justice of England (Lord Parker), Mr Justice Blain, Mr Justice Donaldson: the Queen *v.* Senate of The University of Aston, *ex parte* Roffey and Another: 27th March 1968.

53. cf. Wankowski (*as 20*).

54. Clive Church, 'Modular Courses in British Higher Education: a critical assessment', *Higher Education Bulletin* (University of Lancaster), Vol. 3, No. 3, Summer 1975.

55. Letter to *The Times*, 3rd August 1974.

56. *The Report of the Annan Inquiry*, published by the University of Essex, but largely reported *THES*, 2nd August 1974, under the heading 'What went wrong at Essex'. See editorial of that issue, and much ensuing correspondence, and articles by Jo Grimond MP, and Colin Beardon, *THES*, 9th August 1974, and by Michael Mann, *THES*, 16th August 1974.

57. Sir Frederick Dainton, 'Failing to match the dreams of the angry young', reported *THES*, 9th August 1974.

58. Zoë Fairbairns, 'War research at British Universities', *New Scientist*, 8th August 1974.

59. E. P. Thompson (ed.) *Warwick University Ltd* (Penguin Education Special, 1970).

60. Gareth Williams, Tessa Blackstone and D. Metcalfe, *The Academic Labour Market: Economic and social aspects of a profession* (Elsevier, The Hague 1974).

61. The authors and works listed below are recommended from a voluminous literature on student unrest. Reference has already been made to the following writers whose works are relevant: Eric Ashby, Sir Sydney Caine, Sir Derman Christopherson, David Martin, Graeme Moodie, W. R. Niblett and E. P. Thompson. Further works:

Margaret S. Archer, *Students, University and Society* (Heinemann, 1972).

Bernard Crick and W. A. Robson (eds), *Protest and Discontent* (Penguin, 1970).

Colin Crouch, *The Student Revolt* (Bodley Head, 1970).

A. Cockburn and R. Blackburn, *Student Power* (Penguin, 1969).

Paul Jacob and Saul Landau, *The New Radicals* (Penguin, 1967).

Harry Kidd, *The Trouble at LSE* (Oxford University Press, 1967).

Roger Poole, *Towards Deep Subjectivity*: Chapter 2 (Allen Lane The Penguin Press, 1972).

B. G. Salter, 'Student Militants and counter-culture', *Universities Quarterly*, Autumn 1974.

Select Committee on Education and Science, 1968–69: *Student Relations: Report and Evidence* (HMSO, 1969).

B. R. Williams: chapter 13, 'Student Problems', *Year Book of Education 1971–72* (Evans Bros).

Also mainly for the scene in the USA:

Daedalus: following special issues: Fall 1964, Winter 1968, Summer 1970, Winter 1970.

H. L. Hodgkinson and L. R. Meeth (eds), *Power and Authority – Transformation of Campus Governance* (Jossey-Bass, San Francisco 1971).

Dissent and Disruption, a Report and Recommendations by the Carnegie Commission on Higher Education (McGraw Hill, New York 1971).

Academic Transformation: seventeen institutions under pressure, David Riesman and Verne A. Stadman (eds), a volume of essays sponsored by the Carnegie Commission (McGraw Hill, New York 1973).

H

10

The Polytechnics

THE structure of further education in 1956 was substantially as shown in Diagram 1.1, with four levels of institutions and the Colleges of Advanced Technology at the apex. After they were designated as Universities in 1963, the truncated triangular diagram showed 25 regional colleges at the apex. These then became by Government policy[1] the main body of the Polytechnics, and some combined with other institutions, such as Colleges of Art and of Commerce, before being designated as Polytechnics.

Their origination from the *second* tier of the structure coloured the feelings about the Polytechnics, generating at first a mixture of uncertainty, defensiveness and aggression concerning their work. However, many thought that the Robbins Committee had under-estimated the Further Education Colleges: 'Certain it is that within weeks of the issue of the (Robbins) Report, leading Technical Colleges that could be counted in tens rather than units were urging their claims to be promoted to University status ... the general anxiety and sense of uncertainty in the FE world of which the race for promotion was a symptom must be included in any statement of the general problems presented.'[2]

An aggressive tone was unfortunately set by the vigorous speech of the Secretary of State for Education and Science on the occasion of the seventy-fifth anniversary of the Woolwich Polytechnic on 27 April 1965.[3] Such occasions are apt to be euphoric, so perhaps such an appeal as: 'Let us now move away from our snobbish caste-ridden hierarchical obsession with Universities' might seem excusable in the circumstances. Be that as it may, the speech was later issued, in a reduced form and with a cover note, as an Admin. Memo.[4] Subsequently the Minister candidly described the timing and presentation of his speech as 'an appalling blunder',[5] and he followed it with a mollifying clarifying speech at Lancaster University in 1967.[6] However, Mr Crosland held firmly to his thesis of a binary system,

226

and Polytechnic advocates have unfortunately often maintained the tone of his original speech about the two sectors of higher education. Consequently the detailed criticisms of the time cannot be completely forgotten.[7]

The Woolwich speech characterised the system of higher education as comprising *'the autonomous sector'* of the Universities and *'the public sector'* represented by the leading Technical Colleges and the Colleges of Education. 'The public sector' was identified as being 'under social control, directly responsive to social needs', with the implication that Universities were less – or even not at all – responsive to such needs.* These were not identified as to whether they were short-term and concerned with more immediate needs (as could be argued for the public sector) or with the less direct and longer-term needs which are nevertheless indispensable to society (as for example, fundamental research in the Universities). Again, the close identification of the public sector with vocational and certain kinds of professional education carried the implication that such education was of little or no interest to the Universities, and that they were unconcerned with professional and technological expertise, as for example in medicine and engineering.

Furthermore, while the importance of sandwich courses was rightly stressed for the public sector, no comparable statement was made about the professional sandwich courses in engineering and other technologies in the new Technological Universities. In fact as CATs they had played the leading part in establishing these courses, and were undoubtedly continuing them as a prime commitment for the future, and in a wider range of subjects. Above all, the significant fusing together of the main characteristics of the two sectors in the development of the Technological Universities was tacitly ignored, as if to recognise this would somehow weaken the case for the public sector and for the Polytechnics in particular. Pre-emptive claims have been made about the Polytechnics' contribution to, and close co-operation with, industry, again seemingly regardless of the work of the Technological Universities, and of the Technological and Science Departments in other Universities.

Against this initially confused and contentious situation we turn to appraise the latest available facts about the growth and work of

* In his Lancaster speech Mr Crosland denied that he intended this implication, but in the 1970s it proved a handy assumption in public discussion and criticism of the Universities, especially with politicians and industrialists.

227

the Polytechnics, bearing one very important aspect in mind – that the first of the Polytechnics was designated in January 1969 and the last in September 1973. The latest available list* shows that thirty Polytechnics have been formed from some ninety separate institutions, many of which had already developed considerably in size and range of work. None of them has had adequate time to establish the *combined potential* of all its constituent institutions. With reorganisation hardly completed, with plans made for expansion (but under serious threat of financial curtailment), it is too early to make firm judgements about their future, and one must remain sceptical about any claim to a unique role.[8]

Volume and range of work

The enrolments at November 1975 in six different modes of attendance are shown in Table 10.1.[9] The total number of enrolments is substantial, and 54 per cent are in full-time and sandwich courses,

Table 10.1 Enrolments in Polytechnics, November 1975

	Men	Women		Totals	
Courses (N = 30)	N	N	Row %	N	Column %
Full-time	38,726	27,190	*41·3*	65,916	*37·1*
Sandwich	25,746	4,368	*14·5*	30,114	*16·9*
Release (day and block)	35,762	6,160	*14·7*	41,922	*23·6*
Other part-time day	4,526	2,796	*38·2*	7,322	*4·1*
Evening only	23,054	7,603	*24·8*	30,657	*17·2*
Short full-time	1,482	388	*20·8*	1,870	*1·1*
TOTAL	129,296	48,505	*27·3*	177,801	*100·0*

Source: DES. Provisional figures.

which represents a very much higher proportion of the volume of work done than the 46 per cent enrolments in part-time courses. In contrast to their earlier years as Technical Colleges, the Polytechnics are becoming full-time institutions, particularly in relation to degree work.

* See Appendix Table AIIIf.

Table 10.2 Advanced course enrolments in Polytechnics, November 1975

Courses	Full-time	Sandwich	Part-time day	Evenings only	TOTALS	Column %
University first degree	1,068	123	51	813	2,055‡	1·4
CNAA first degree*	31,237	20,932	2,903	739	55,811	38·3
	(5,453)	(371)	(—)	(—)	(5,824)‡	
Higher degrees	552	63	933	422	1,970	1·4
Research for higher degrees	2,116	18	3,085	1,264	6,483	4·4
TOTAL degree enrolments†	34,973	21,136	6,972	3,238	66,319	45·5
Row %	52·7	31·9	10·5	4·9	100·0	
Professional courses	8,507	949	14,626	10,179	34,261	23·5
Other advanced courses	18,801	7,731	15,684	2,895	45,111	31·0
GRAND TOTALS	62,281	29,816	37,282	16,312	145,691§	100·0
Row %	42·7	20·5	25·6	11·2	100·0	

Notes: * Students on the former Dip.AD course shown in brackets.
† Full-time and sandwich courses only = 48,623, of whom 1,776 (under 4 per cent) were registered for higher degrees and just under 40 per cent were on sandwich courses. 2,869 (6 per cent) were taking University degrees.
‡ First degree courses: 50,792 enrolments 1974. Figure for 1975 was 59,801: increase 18 per cent (CDP figures).
§ Approximately 82 per cent of all enrolments shown in Table 10.1.

Table 10.2 sets out the enrolments in advanced courses, which numbered 126,106, i.e. 79 per cent of the total enrolments of 159,190 shown in Table 10.1. Higher degrees (including course and research) were 5·5 per cent of all advanced course enrolments.

If we consider total degree enrolments only (which comprise about half of all advanced enrolments) 4 per cent of full-time and sandwich course students were registered for higher degrees and among part-time students there were 3,511 out of 5,170, i.e. 68 per cent. Just under 16 per cent of degree enrolments were part-time but for all advanced work the proportion was just over 39 per cent. Within the Universities for the period 1974/75, 19 per cent of all full-time students registered for degrees, diplomas and other courses, were postgraduates[10] and among the part-timers the figures are 21,968 out of 25,373, i.e. 85 per cent.[11] Combining all courses – full (including sandwich) and part-time – the postgraduate population was 25 per cent of the total of 283,057, compared with 5·5 per cent for the Polytechnics (Table 10.2, final column). The Polytechnics are of course concentrating much of their effort on essential professional and other non-degree advanced courses. In a press release dated November 1976 a further 11 per cent increase of students on full-time and sandwich courses was recorded. A similar growth in enrolments in science, mathematics and technology courses is reported in addition to the growth of teacher training resulting from the mergers with Colleges of Education. The statement reiterates their major commitment to advanced education by means of part-time and short courses, which were expected to reach 80,000 and 40,000 respectively in 1976 to give a total population of 230,000 students for the academic year 1976–77. The figures conform to the Government view that the Polytechnics should be substantially orientated towards teaching rather than research and should cater for part-time students.[12] Whether the balance will change is a question for the future.*

In Table 10.3[13] the range of degree courses is analysed by subject groups.

Within the Polytechnics the largest group is social, administrative and business studies (37 per cent) and for the Technological Universities, engineering and technology still top the list with 43 per cent; more than double the proportion in the Polytechnics. The profile of

* In 1977 the Polytechnics were criticised by the Secretary of State, Mrs Shirley Williams, for their low rate of part-time expansion in a report of a Conference *THES* 4th January 1977. See also editorial: *Ten Years on for Polytechnics.*

the latter looks rather more 'poly' than 'technic'. Within the Universities as a whole the spread is much more even since they are responsible for all of the provision in medicine and for most of the arts. When the total enrolments are divided by the number of institutions in each of the three groups the average numbers per institution are 1,925, 2,953 and 5,709* respectively, i.e. a ratio of 1:1·5:3·0.

Table 10.3 Degree course enrolments in Polytechnics, Technological Universities and all UK Universities, by subject groups

Subject group	Polytechnics (N = 30)		Technological Universities (N = 8)		All UK Universities (N = 44)	
	N	Col. %	N	Col. %	N	%
1. Education	734	*1·3*	317	*1·3+*	10,571	*4·1*
2. Medicine, dentistry and health	1,247	*2·2*	1,674	*6·7*	28,092	*10·9*
3. Engineering and technology	11,790	*20·4*	10,717	*42·7*	35,907	*13·9*
4. Agriculture, forestry and veterinary science	—	—	75	*0·3*	4,840	*1·9*
5. Science	10,069	*17·4*	6,177	*24·6*	61,228	*23·8*
6. Social, administrative and business studies	21,327	*36·9*	4,234	*16·9*	57,423	*22·3*
7. Architecture and other	3,918	*6·8*	688	*2·7*	5,307	*2·1*
8. Language, literature and area studies	2,069	*3·6*	1,103	*4·4*	29,990	*11·6*
9. Arts other than languages	6,584	*11·4*	93	*0·4*	24,323	*9·4*
TOTALS	57,738	*100·0*	25,078	*100·0*	257,684	*100·0*

In 1969 Martin Trow[14] raised questions about the kind of education the Polytechnics would provide in relation to industry, and particularly as to whether the training of engineers and technicians was feasible within the same institution. 'Engineers who enter the

* The inclusion of part-time figures in the University totals increases the average numbers per institution by over 500 and the ratios become 1:1·8:3·2. The average for all UK Universities is unduly high because the Universities of London and Wales each count as one institution.

economy ought not to be trained to accept the going conceptions of how to make things and service people, but rather should acquire the lively scepticism regarding the efficiency and economy of current practice that in most cases it deserves. This critical attitude towards current practice is the essential difference between the engineer and the technician, and it, rather than the less important differences in their skills and knowledge, is why they should be educated differently and separately. For the tone and climate of institutions which aim to produce technicians, of whatever degree of skill, is basically different from that which produces men who are to reform or modify current practice.'

That is a special problem for the Polytechnics, but we should not readily accept a contrast between the best kind of training for professional engineers and an inadequate form of training and education for technicians, nor overlook the advantages of educating within the same institution those who subsequently in employment have to work together if industry is to be productive. In a footnote Martin Trow draws attention to the human and social consequences of technological change visible in the urban environment as in the factory, and raises questions as to how consideration of these is to be brought within the education of engineers; he adds 'The growth of the social sciences within the Colleges of Technology in Britain may make this task easier than it has been in all but a few American institutions.'[15]

However, technicians will be concerned with the same problems whether as workers or as citizens, and should not be denied a similar education in this respect. The volume of social, administrative and business studies in 1974, shown in Table 10.3, is encouraging, provided three things obtain: first, that Polytechnics do not discourage or shed advanced technician education, such as HND courses; second, that this group of associated social science and other studies are not simply technical: and third, that the staff of other disciplines – science, engineering and technology – co-operate from the outset in solving the difficult educational problems involved.[16]

In accordance with the policy of the 1966 White Paper, the Polytechnics have concentrated increasingly on 'advanced work', and have transferred a considerable volume of other work to Further Education Colleges. In this they closely followed the example of the Colleges of Advanced Technology in their first few years. Similar considerations obtained, and the major influences were those of the

NCTA and the CNAA respectively, in their insistence that the particular institution must have (or expect reasonably early to have) a high proportion of advanced work before courses could be recognised for a Dip.Tech. or a CNAA degree.

The minimum entry standard to degree courses in Polytechnics is comparable with that of such courses in Universities, but the proportion of students with more than the minimum standard (in number of subjects and grades attained) is markedly higher in the Universities, though there is significant variation between institutions and disciplines. Both the Polytechnics and the Technological Universities accept ONC/OND of appropriate standard for entry to degree courses in relevant disciplines. A variety of GCE A-level, ONC/OND and other qualifications gives entry to A.2 courses in Polytechnics.

For school-leavers seeking a full-time or sandwich course, the thirty Polytechnics by September 1976 offered a very wide choice of courses leading to CNAA first degrees, Higher National Diploma and other advanced courses such as Polytechnic diplomas or to qualifying examinations of professional bodies.[17]

For graduate and other mature students there is a small range of full-time and sandwich courses leading to CNAA higher degrees, of other advanced non-degree courses leading to postgraduate diplomas, and yet others mainly geared to professional qualifications. Many if not most of the first group are similar to Master's degree courses in the Universities, but there is more variety in the other two groups. Part-time courses for students in employment include those for Higher National Certificates and for meeting the various requirements of professional bodies, as well as some part-time degree courses. In addition there are many short courses of a few days' or weeks' duration, designed mainly to meet specific needs of individuals or, more frequently, of occupational groups.

Initially it was feared by many critics that the former CATs and then the Polytechnics would, under status-seeking pressures, conform to the traditional patterns of University courses[18] (generally assumed scarcely to have changed at all). Some conformity is inescapable in view of the facts of academic life: that in every discipline there is a core of knowledge which every serious student must master whatever institution he joins, and furthermore there is in all cases an obligation regularly to review the content and methodology of a course in order to update it. Nevertheless there can never be uniformity: courses of the same or similar titles in different institutions vary substantially with the interests, ideas, and present motivation of the staff concerned: as determined, for example, by their past experience, industrial or academic. The geographic, economic and social contexts of the institution are also powerful factors in the recruitment of staff.

Whatever its administrative importance, the binary system presents no impermeable academic barrier to the flow of ideas, nor is there a totally one-sided distribution of good practice, modes of operation, standards and design of courses – nor of the seemingly inescapable jargon and fashions. In the Polytechnics, at the apex of the 'alternative University system'[19] (i.e. the Further Education sector) similar discussions and controversies recur as in the traditional University sector – though pressed in rather different directions – about studies and disciplines which are pure, not so pure, applied and even technological; about professional and vocational education, and the seemliness of certain subjects for inclusion; the degree of relevance which is advantageous, indispensable or meretricious.

With a burgeoning educational press in a publicity-dominated period, claims for uniqueness and 'first-evers' are apt to abound, especially from emergent institutions. However, the froth is not the substance of the matter, as their handbooks and directories demonstrate. Despite a strong approximation to University degree courses,[20] there has been some progress in the imaginative design of new courses in recent years, more perhaps at degree level than otherwise, but there are signs that increasing attention is being paid to the needs of emerging professions as, for example, in the paramedical sphere and the social services. The publications make evident the wide diversity of subjects and course arrangements,[21] but some important areas have been subject to acute uncertainty and even bitter controversy.

The Diploma of Higher Education (Dip.HE) for a two-year course was recommended by the James Committee[22] as an innovation designed to afford greater flexibility and choice at entry into higher education. The Dip.HE was recommended as the first of three cycles of teacher education, but its potential is much greater than that.[23] It did not have a ready acceptance, but the first two courses were started in September 1974.* Few Universities have shown any inclination even to consider establishing courses for Dip.HE. The Committee thought the courses would have a terminal

* With about 100 students, about 75 of them at North-East London Polytechnic.

234

value for those students who wish to enter employment rather than undertake further study,[24] but it is hoped that a significant proportion will make enough progress to justify proceeding to a degree course.

Diplomas of Higher Education stand in the same relation to CNAA degree courses as does the Dip.AD for art students. The James Committee recommended that 'while possession of two A-levels should be the normal requirements for entry to a diploma course, exemptions should be generously given *at any rate for several years*' (italics mine). A rigorous academic orthodoxy of two A-level entry* will inevitably frustrate the potentially much larger numbers who might value the Diploma as a terminal qualification. However, lack of entry qualifications would affect the curriculum design, but the Open University exemplifies what can be done.

The possibilities of Diploma students transferring to degree courses or returning to full-time study from employment will be largely determined by the grants available to students; if awards for the final years are few in number, the Dip.HE by setting the standards unduly high could become in effect a resuscitated scholarship system; secondly, after some years in employment, the student (by then probably married) could not be expected to return at the same rate of grant as he would have had initially. In 1976 the DES clarified this issue and confirmed that, provided he had qualified to proceed to a degree course he would be entitled to a new award for the third and subsequent years of the course and that the award would be calculated according to his circumstances at the time.

The spectrum of courses in some Polytechnics has been widened in important respects by the inclusion of neighbouring Colleges of Education and Schools (or Colleges) of art. In other instances Polytechnics have established their own Education Departments. In both art and education courses Government policy has been highly controversial, generating bitter opposition from the respective Colleges.[25] In the case of education, the policy has almost entirely disrupted the long-standing links between the Colleges and the Universities which arose from the policy recommended by the McNair Report of 1944.[26] In May 1976 there were 130 Colleges of

* In May 1976, CNAA issued a circular to institutions concerned with CNAA awards, stating it had been 'rigorous in its validation of Dip.HE courses – whether linked to degree programmes or otherwise – to ensure that the courses are of a standard equivalent to the first two years of a degree programme', and discusses matters of transfers to degree courses accordingly.

Education, 4 Colleges of Education (Technical) and 16 Polytechnic Education Departments. No Colleges had amalgamated with Universities, but negotiations were in progress for 5 Colleges so to do. It was anticipated that 37 free-standing institutions would continue to provide teacher training either as monotechnics or as diversified Colleges. 94 Colleges would become constituent parts of Polytechnics or merge with other Colleges of Education or Colleges of Further Education. The future of 33 Colleges still had to be settled.[27]*
Among the factors which led to this profound reorientation were unsatisfactory relationships with Universities in some cases, and the strong desire of Local Authorities to retain – or where necessary to regain – control over the Colleges which produced most of the teachers for their schools. The Polytechnics were favoured because they also are Local Authority institutions. There was also a growing feeling that future teachers should be educated and trained alongside students entering other professions and occupations and, on the whole, this had not happened when the Colleges were linked with the Universities.[28] The amalgamations present a special challenge to the Polytechnics to establish mutually beneficial relationships for the staff concerned.

For many decades there have been Departments and Schools of Art in Technical Colleges, but there was generally a quite marked sense of difference or separateness, typified by a separate institutional number in Board of Education and Ministry of Education records. Examinations were conducted under different regulations, and courses and teaching methods reflected different values and an ethos which was sustained in the main despite the 'unaesthetic insensitive Technical College influence': in sum, they were in the Tech, but not of it. Over the years shining examples of fruitful co-operation have emerged, but the bitter and prolonged controversy indicated a deep-seated fear of being dominated by technologists, with the loss of their long-standing academic autonomy. By the same token the transfer of the awarding of qualifications in art, the Dip.AD and the NDD, to the CNAA were likewise resisted. Unless the defensive attitudes are resolved the educational and economic future of design in this country will be at stake.

* The stresses in the system continued throughout 1976, owing to the predictions of a sharply declining birthrate. This afforded the DES an unprecedented opportunity to reduce the supply of teachers and reorganise the Colleges of Education.

Courses in the arts, including modern languages (which could involve experience in Europe), have long been taught in Technical Colleges and Colleges of Commerce, but the scale and scope have increased in recent years. These courses tend to emphasise modern as distinct from ancient literature, and are usually combined with studies of the social institutions of the related country. Social science courses have also increased greatly in number and scope in response to student demand. We may wonder what will be the fate of general studies for scientists and technologists with the increasing provision of fully-fledged professional courses in arts and the social sciences. It is at least probable that the decline and reorientation of general studies which took place in the CATs will be repeated in Polytechnics.

Some Polytechnics offer English literature as a single-subject degree course, as compared with the many combined honours degree courses with English either as a main or an optional subject. However, the criticism has been made that arts courses in Polytechnics have followed traditional lines far too closely and are consequently 'boring, academically antediluvian and make little or no contact with other subject areas'.[29] However, there has in fact been quite a strong trend towards developing inter-disciplinary courses, composed of elements of science, social science, technology and arts variously chosen and related. With this there usually goes a degree of relevance to contemporary professional, vocational and social needs, backed up with practical experience and training in this country and abroad.

Fashions prevail, even in matters academic – from the single to the combined honours course, to multi-disciplinary (parallel lines which may never meet?) to inter-disciplinary (and creative inter-relationships?), to modular courses and timetable slots (the ultimate in student choice: highest bid to December 1975 – 300 options). As a result of validation of such courses the CNAA reviewed the problems and opportunities involved, and in September 1974 circulated a paper, *Reflections on the Design of Modular Courses,* to Colleges for discussion. A modular course is mainly composed of integral units which are assessed on the credit system. The units are chosen initially by the student, but subsequent choices can be varied in the light of performance. Motivation, so the argument goes, is likely to be increased as compared with the passive acceptance of studies wholly laid down by the academic staff. While the modular course

237

thus gains mainly in terms of flexibility and increased motivation, another advantage is the avoidance of duplication and overlapping of courses in different Departments so that scarce resources are conserved.

However, there are inherent disadvantages which are not negligible.[30] Certainly the degrees of freedom available to staff and students are not as great as might appear when a modular course is said to offer 20, or 60, or 120 modules, still less with 300 units.[31] A completely open choice cannot be offered to all the students all of the time. With so many options available in the week, some must be held simultaneously, though the proportion will be less if self-instruction systems are used. Moreover, constraints of timetabling become cumulatively more severe as the course advances, and these problems must be foreseen from the outset of planning. Satisfactory performance of some subjects – indeed any performance at all – requires prior knowledge, and these academic pre-requisites have to be clearly specified and choices determined accordingly. In the choice made, and even in the design of a course as a whole, the distinction between modular and the traditional courses is not always necessarily substantial or clear-cut.

Courses in business studies, and later in management studies, have been established in major Technical Colleges in the last two decades, but their development was hampered by uncertainty over objectives and consequent changes of policy. A definitive stage seemed to have been reached with Government recognition of certain Colleges as Regional Management Centres, and some twelve of the Polytechnics were so involved or recognised in 1975. There remains anxiety about the duplication of management studies in the two sectors of the binary system, and the view that the Polytechnics should not provide postgraduate management courses was emphatically expressed to a Select Committee.[32]

Advocates of the Polytechnic philosophy properly stress the relevance of their courses to the needs of industry, commerce and a wide variety of occupations.

If this trend should continue, then the factors which are likely to accelerate the process will be much the same as those for the Technological Universities. In sum, the factors are trans-binary, and joint action by the Technological Universities and the Polytechnics to deal with urgent common problems was regrettably very belated.[33] They have followed the lead of the former CATs in establishing

238

sandwich courses, and have also positively orientated the content of many full-time courses in practical directions. For the Polytechnics as for the Technological Universities, a lasting commitment to sandwich courses is a touchstone of their development. As a result of the development of arts and social science courses, however, the proportion of sandwich courses out of the whole volume of work has declined.

Validation of courses

The establishment of the CNAA proved a powerful preamble to the designation and development of the Polytechnics: having regard to the inherent complexity of its operations concerning the consideration, visitation and recognition/rejection of so many subjects in so many widely dispersed institutions, its achievements are remarkable.[34]

1975 marked the end of its first ten years of operation and enrolments in approved full-time first degree courses had grown to a total of 72,627 of which about 54,000 were studying in Polytechnics (see Table 10.2). There were 853 courses in operation of which 49 per cent were in science and technology (including paramedical), 28 per cent in arts and social studies (including administration and business studies) and 19 per cent in art and design. The remaining 4 per cent were in education, apart from 0·4 (3 groups) in modular courses. Proportions of students registered were 42 per cent in science and technology (40); 35 per cent in arts and social studies (52), 15 per cent in art and design (6·8) and 7 per cent in education. (1·3).[35] The figures in brackets are taken from Table 10.3 and illustrate the very large congruence between students registered for CNAA degrees and those attending Polytechnics. Art Schools, Colleges of Education and Advanced Technical Colleges in Scotland and Northern Ireland account for most of the other institutional customers.

Detailed consideration of courses submitted for recognition is carried out by over forty Subject Boards composed of experts from Universities, Polytechnics, industry, commerce, the professions and the Civil Service, supplemented as required by specialist Subject Panels.

To cope with the rapid and substantial growth of work the Council's structure of Committees, Boards and Panels was reconstituted in 1971. The changes reflected the widening spectrum of

Table 10.4 The polytechnics: distribution and qualifications of the academic staff (May 1974)

Post	Highest level of qualifications held					TOTAL	% of all academic staff
	Doctorate	Master's degree	Good hons. degree or recognised equivalent	Other first degree or recognised equivalent	Other quals.		
Above Head of Department	50	24	25	12	—	111	*1*
Head of Department	145	129	128	120	17	539	*4*
Reader	28	1	4	2	—	35	*—*
Principal Lecturer	388	519	533	392	65	1,897	*13*
Senior Lecturer	670	1,149	1,268	1,290	321	4,698	*33*
Lecturer LII	695	1,180	1,655	1,456	621	5,607	*40*
Lecturer LI	19	53	138	102	116	428	*3*
TOTAL established staff N	1,995	3,055	3,751	3,374	1,140	13,315	94
%	*15*	*23*	*28*	*25*	*9*	*100*	
Research fellow	40	8	18	6	3	75	*1*
Research associate/assistant	19	94	482	131	31	757	*5*
GRAND TOTAL	2,054	3,157	4,251	3,511	1,174	14,147	*100*
% of grand total	*15*	*22*	*30*	*25*	*8*	*100*	
Technological Universities 1971*	*42*	*26*	*30*		*2*	*369*	*100*
Halsey & Trow sample 1964*	*46*	*13*	*35*		*6*	*1,402*	*100*

Note: * See Table 8.14.

work and increased confidence in the ability of Polytechnic staff. Their proportionate membership of Committees and Boards has increased, which has of course meant a relative decline in University membership.

Three major developments within the CNAA have been the addition of the approval of Dip.HE courses in 1973–74, of BEd. degree courses, and as from 1st September 1974 amalgamation of the work of the National Council for Diplomas in Art and Design. To these the Diploma in Management Studies was added in September 1976.* These major changes, together with the increasing volume of postgraduate courses and research, have encouraged, if not compelled, a reappraisal of the relationships between CNAA and the institutions concerned. The growth of mutual respect between the Polytechnics and the CNAA is reminiscent of the supportive role played by NCTA in the emergence of the CATs to independent status. The signs are that the CNAA is ready to move fairly quickly towards greater academic independence for the Polytechnics in the design of their degree courses.[36]†

However well the CNAA and its constituent bodies carry out their work, the centre of gravity of the system is in the Polytechnics, and the success of the work educationally is determined primarily by the quality of the staff and students.

The results of a survey in May 1974 by the Committee of Directors of Polytechnics are shown in Table 10.4,[37] together with some comparative figures from the Universities. Of the Polytechnic staff, 67 per cent had at least the equivalent of a good honours degree, of whom just over half (37 per cent) had higher degrees. 15 per cent of the total in Polytechnics in 1974 had doctorates, as compared with 42 per cent of the staff of the Technological Universities in 1971, and 46 per cent in the Universities in 1964. Without doubt the Houghton Report[38] was regarded by many as justifiably closing the gap between the salaries of teachers doing degree (and equivalent) work in the Polytechnics and the Universities, and the change is not without implications for the binary system.

* The CNAA Annual Report for 1976 shows continuing growth. The total enrolments of 77,548 in 1975–76 rose by 22 per cent to 94,523 in 1976–77. With the addition of the Diploma in Management Studies to the awards offered by the Council, there was a further 9 per cent increase reaching the impressive grand total of 101,502.

† For further discussion on this issue see Chapter 12.

The emergence of institutions is a stressful period for staff concerned, and salary negotiations are apt to reveal hidden as well as open resentments. Most of the staff of the CATs were members of ATTI, but University Charters transferred them to the other side of the binary line where ran the writ of the AUT, and so transfers were generally made without serious difficulty.[39] Designation of the Polytechnics had no such effect, and their staff remained within ATTI, the body officially recognised by the DES and TUC. Many felt that the interests of these thirty institutions would not be adequately or specifically represented by the ATTI, concerned as it was with the interests of full-time and part-time staff in more than 500 institutions. A separate body was formed,[40]* and increasingly acrimonious correspondence filled the columns of the *THES* prior to the Houghton Report, but the DES and the TUC have not officially recognised the APT as a negotiating body.

Rises in salary carry with them recognition of increased status and both aspects influence staff recruitment. In 1971 the Polytechnic of Central London announced their intention to confer the title of Professor 'on the basis of personal merit, not automatically or necessarily on Heads of Departments'. The move was seen as one of expressing confidence in the future of the Polytechnics and their senior staff, appointed as they would be after rigorous examination of each case, as with University Professorships.[41] The move was criticised,[42] not least because of the serious differences in salary which would unavoidably obtain, and only a few appointments have been made in a small number of institutions. The Houghton Report could accelerate this change considerably† and could also affect staff mobility, though staff trends are conflicting.[43] However, if a 'steady state' replaces continuous expansion 'bunching' or distortion of the age-structure of the staff will become an acute problem. One regrettable aspect of staff recruitment, shared with the Universities, is the low proportion of women appointed to the Polytechnics,[44] and the related uncertainty of their future prospects.[45]

The need to train staff has long been recognised in the Further Education sector – as distinct from the Universities, and there are four Technical Teacher Training Colleges involved as well as the

* Association of Polytechnic Teachers, APT.

† After the Houghton Report, the title in reference 41, 'Professors in the Polys will establish parity', might well become 'Parity in the Polys will establish Professors'.

Further Education Staff College.* The users of these five institutions are mainly from the staff of technical and Further Education generally, and the signs are that the Polytechnics may wish to make separate arrangements,[46]† perhaps on a regional basis and possibly with Universities. Student assessment of the quality of staff teaching is still in a preliminary and contentious phase, and is itself being assessed.[47] Nevertheless, in an age of consumer demand for satisfaction, the art and practice of teaching will hardly be exempt from critical assessment by its consumers.

Research and other postgraduate work

There is considerable variation in the proportion of research and postgraduate work within the Polytechnics, and the extent and nature of their provision compared with the Universities has been a problem since their designation. Not long thereafter the question was raised whether the committees of the Science Research Council (SRC) were properly constituted or their terms of reference appropriate to the consideration of research and courses in institutions other than Universities – with the implication that the Polytechnics' needs were special and different. In their day the Committee of Principals of the CATs considered these selfsame questions and decided that there were no grounds for special treatment. Their critics would no doubt feel that this was because they were merely aiming to be traditional Universities and not basically different institutions: they themselves felt that there was no fundamental divide in research and postgraduate courses, and that their proposals would have to be judged by the same criteria of quality and of special timeliness and promise as applied elsewhere. The results in terms of the nature and range of work supported by the SRC have generally justified this view, and research in the CATs and subsequently in the Technological Universities has continued to be mainly directed towards application and the needs of industry.

In March 1972 the SRC set up a Polytechnics Working Group, with the result that a new SRC Committee on Postgraduate Training in the Polytechnics was set up for three years until 31st August 1976 with appropriate terms of reference.[48] The Report stated that 'pro-

* Coombe Lodge, Blagdon, Bristol, B18 6R.

† e.g. A staff Development and Educational Research Unit, Manchester Polytechnic.

243

posals received from Polytechnics are accorded the same treatment and are judged by subject committees on the same criteria as those received from Universities'.[49] At March 1976 figures for grants from the Science Research Council were £61,031,000 for the 68 Universities (including £3,934,000 for the 10 former CATs) and £1,337,000 for 28 listed Polytechnics.[50] These figures take no account of other research monies and in 1972 the DES estimated that the total amount spent by the Polytechnics on research and development was £4·3m: £1·24m on basic research, £2·4m on applied research and £0·7m on development. Specific grants from Government and other sources were estimated at £0·6m.[51]

Students

From their designation at the outset, there has been a widespread assumption – especially in the Polytechnics themselves – that the social background of their students was much wider, and much less middle-class, than that of University students. In a paper published in 1971, Lex Donaldson concluded that 'the current evidence suggests that they are assimilating to the University pattern of social class composition'.[52] This relates closely not only to what should be the philosophy and function of the Polytechnics, but more widely to the growing questioning of the social responsibilities of all institutions of higher education. Increasing egalitarian concern has led to various experiments such as specially favoured entry conditions for particular groups – e.g. the handicapped – and in setting aside normal A-level requirements for those socially disadvantaged who are 'likely to succeed in the course' or 'likely to benefit from the course'.[53] However, these raise problems which cannot be solved unaided by the institutions themselves: there are very difficult practical problems to be resolved as to the means – political, economic, social and institutional – to ensure that such social responsibilities are undertaken. It is one thing to analyse the social catchment of students, quite another to widen it by making procedures more effective and opportunities better known.[54] A new enterprise needs time to establish itself and to overcome the inertia and natural resistances of, for example, schools and parents.[55]*

As with the Technological Universities, and Universities generally, the Polytechnics are finding it essential to establish counselling and

* See Table 9.2.

careers advisory services for their students.[56] 'The ways in which students differ in their educational and vocational objectives seem to depend to a large extent on their subjects of study, and it is mainly in this respect that Polytechnic students might be expected to differ from students at a University.'[57]

Discussions have been held to try to bring Polytechnic recruitment within UCCA,[58] which would ensure for them the same access to sixth-formers as is enjoyed by the Universities, but it would be very complex and costly.[59]*

In respect of CNAA degree courses, grants for full-time and sandwich course students are on the same basis as for similar students at Universities. However, students attending other advanced courses have not been so fortunate, as grants from the Local authorities have been discretionary, i.e. constituting a long-standing discrimination, which is particularly unwise in view of the economic importance of the occupations to which these advanced courses lead. At last a start has been made with mandatory grants for Higher National Diploma.[60]

Governance and administration

The Secretary of State announced the list of thirty proposed Polytechnics on 5th April 1967,[61] and issued *Notes for Guidance* (DES Admin. Memo. 8/67) to the Local Authorities concerned. These were applied with the liberally intentioned Weaver Report[62] very much in mind. This led to the passing of the Education (No. 2) Act 1968, which required both FE Colleges and Colleges of Education to have autonomous governing bodies with articles of government approved by the Secretary of State.[63]

Throughout this period the Local Authorities showed considerable resistance to such delegation,[64] as is apparent in their continuing reluctance to implement the approved schemes in full.[65] These difficulties, and other factors such as the widening catchment of students, and the pooling of expenditure, repeat the experience of some of the CATs from their designation in 1956 to gaining independence in 1962. The Committee of Directors of Polytechnics (CDP) in September 1973 reaffirmed 'its commitment to the development of Polytechnics within the public sector of higher education, but is firmly of the view that the important national objectives

* DES estimate of cost about £700,000.

245

set for the Polytechnics can be attained only if their distinctive function and purpose are appropriately recognised by elected members
and administrators', and stressed 'the urgent need to review the
nature of the controls under which the Polytechnics currently
operate, in order to establish a more appropriate structure for
their government, financing, development and effective management'.[66]

Increased Local Authority resistance was not surprising,[67] not
least because such a review could lead to separation and a repetition
of the painful loss of the CATs. Closely linked with this question of
governance by the Local Authorities is that of approval of courses
through the Regional Advisory Councils (RACs), on which they
are strongly represented. Generally speaking, institutions have found
these Councils irksome, as the Councils have become increasingly
outmoded by events, and critics press for substantial reform, or even
discontinuance in their present form.[68] One strong indication of their
inadequacy in respect of higher education was the move by Local
Authorities to establish the Local Authorities Higher Education
Committee,[69] but this was overtaken by the reorganisation of Local
Authorities in 1974.

The changes in the structure and administration of Polytechnics
will accelerate as they increase the proportion of degree and higher
degree work and widen the catchment of their students. The rigid
departmentalism of the past has been modified and in some instances
is giving way to schools of study[70]* in which the role of a Head of
Department tends to be less authoritarian. How significant will be
the change of role from a Principal of a College to that of a Director
of a Polytechnic? It will be of interest to observe whether the
Director's role begins to resemble that of a Vice-Chancellor[71] – a
change from the exercise of power to that of influence. Such changes
are unlikely to be adventitious, but will arise as inherent characteristics of upwardly mobile institutions, as most of the Polytechnics
manifestly intend to be.

Again like the CATs before them, most of the Polytechnics are
having to recruit and train their own administrative staff, and again
the academics are ambivalent about efficient administration.[72]

* Note also, for example, a structure of Boards of Study and Resource Centres at
  Middlesex Polytechnic.

Philosophy and function

The 1966 White Paper identified some characteristics considered desirable for Polytechnics: developing degree courses without prejudicing opportunities for less advanced students who wish to take courses at intermediate and lower levels; providing part-time day and evening courses for those in employment; and in sum, to be 'comprehensive' in the sense of providing for all levels of work for students in full-time and sandwich, part-time day and evening courses. Such a comprehensive range of work, it was argued, would broadly distinguish them from other higher education institutions, and they would have closer and more direct links with industry, business and the professions.[73] These proposals did not prove completely satisfying to the Polytechnics, and the debate about their function has continued for years, including complaints about aping the Universities[74] and about the lack of a common philosophy.[75] In June 1974 Sir Norman Lindop, in justification of the continuance of the binary system, wrote: 'It will be some years before the non-University sector, with its identifiably different philosophy and criteria, will be strong enough to face the merging of the two streams without loss of identity.'[76]

A review by Joanna Mack of the progress of the Polytechnics ten years since designation concludes that their role is still uncertain and muddled further 'by the newborn Institutions of Higher Education'.[77] However, the fact remains that the thirty Polytechnics were very diverse institutions at their designation – in the range and standards of their work – and could hardly be expected to become very similar in a decade. In defining the role of the Polytechnics, a strict uniformity would be most undesirable. A broad characterisation is all that is required, and the end of the first decade has brought encouraging reaffirmations along these lines. Most positive among them is the address by Sir Alex Smith to the Standing Conference of Regional Advisory Councils (SCRAC) Annual Meeting.[78] Sir Alex contended that the 1966 White Paper initiated the development of the Polytechnics as 'a group of institutions which were no longer aspirant Universities but institutions on a par with them, and it gave the local authorities the responsibility for accomplishing that splendid purpose'.

Two characteristics of Polytechnic education were stressed by Sir Alex: first, that three groups of students are welcomed – those taking degree courses, those taking other qualifications and those who study on a part-time basis; and secondly, the aim is to achieve an excellence complementary to scholarship, for which there is no simple word. 'It is design, it is action, it is synthesis, it is professionalism, it is the application of knowledge.' Beyond this, Polytechnic education would be characterised by awareness of other human qualities and virtues, including, it is hoped, a re-emphasis on the work ethic. The role of the staff is seen as that of a new strain of educators, 'polytechnicians' for the modern world. Whereas staff development in Universities is through research and publishing papers, that in Polytechnics is seen positively by Sir Alex 'as encouragement to go out and work for a period in industry or the professions (a kind of sandwich course) – an approach much more satisfactory and positive than the negative one that Polytechnics should not do research but should be teaching institutions'.[79]

However, Sir Alex goes on to insist on a rigid separation of characteristics between Universities and Polytechnics across the binary line: the Universities' *sole* function (italics mine) being that of scholarship, and he links this with the quite unproven assertion that the University 'is weakened and distorted when it is diluted and when it tries to do something for which it is unsuited, by background, experience and ethos'.[80]

So simplified a view is not in accord with the complexity of the facts, as this study shows, for example, in the overlapping functions of institutions of higher education; the long-standing commitment of Universities to professional education, their adaptability in meeting the changing demands of society and the economy, exemplified in the history of Civic Universities; the viability of the former CATs as Technological Universities and their continuing commitment to objectives which, apparently, Polytechnic advocates would like to regard as uniquely their own. Instead of a misleading uniqueness, we should be looking for a characteristic but not exclusive orientation of functions,[81] and this we do in Chapter 12.

Chapter 10: Sources

1. White Paper, *A Plan for Polytechnics and other Colleges* (HMSO, May 1966).

2. View expressed by Mr T. R. (later Sir Toby) Weaver, then Deputy

Secretary, DES; Address to a joint meeting of the Association of Chief Education Officers and Association of Education Officers, *Education*, 20th August 1965.

3. Rt. Hon. Anthony Crosland MP, Woolwich speech, 27th April 1965, reported *Education*, 30th April 1965. (See John Pratt and Tyrrell Burgess, *Polytechnics: A Report* (Pitman, 1974). Relevant parts of the speech are reproduced pp. 203–207.)

4. Administrative Memorandum No. 7/65 (6th May 1965), *The Role in Higher Education of Regional and other Technical Colleges engaged in advanced work*.

5. The Politics of Education, Edward Boyle and Anthony Crosland in conversation with Maurice Kogan (Penguin Education Special, 1971) p. 193.

6. 20th January 1967, reported *TES*, 27th January 1967 (reproduced in *Polytechnics: A Report* (*as 3*), pp. 208–213).

7. For example, Peter Venables, 'Dualism in Higher Education', *Universities Quarterly*, Winter 1965.

8. *Polytechnics: A Report* (*as 3*), was criticised on these grounds – e.g. Sir Norman Lindop, Director, Hatfield Polytechnic, *THES*, 15th March 1974.

   Dr George Tolley, Principal, Sheffield Polytechnic, *Universities Quarterly*, Summer 1974.

   Sir Alex Smith, Director, Manchester Polytechnic, *THES*, 2nd January 1976.

9. Figures from Committee of Directors of Polytechnics (CDP).

10. UGC *Statistics of Education* (HMSO, 1974), Vol. 6, Table 2, p. 9: 1.7 per cent (N = 3,587) were classified as 'diploma and other courses'.

11. *Ibid.*, Table 12, p. 31.

12. Notes for Guidance for Polytechnics: Parliamentary statement by Secretary of State for Education and Science, 5th April 1967; later circulated as Admin. Memo 8/67, Appendix B, Research in Polytechnics, para. 2.

13. Figures for Polytechnics from CDP, November 1974; includes part-time enrolments, which were about 16 per cent of the total.

    Figures for Technological Universities and all UK Universities from *Statistics of Education* 1973, Vol. 6: Universities (UGC), Tables 7 & 10, pp. 16 & 24; includes full-time and sandwich but not part-time.

    1974 figures (*ibid.*, 1974, pp. 17 and 25) show an increase of 2·6 per for all UK Universities and 6 per cent for the Technological Universities. In 1974, part-time students numbered over 25,000 in UK Universities (*ibid.*, Table 13, p. 31).

14. Martin Trow, 'Problems for Polytechnics', *Universities Quarterly*, Autumn 1969.

15. *Ibid.*, p. 396, footnote 19.

16. See *General Studies*, Chapter 4.

17. See *Handbook of Polytechnic Courses in England and Wales* (full-time and sandwich courses) (published annually for the CDP, since its formal establishment in April 1970, by Lund Humphries, 12 Bedford Square, London WC1).

18. R. Oxtoby, 'Polytechnics and the sanctity of the honours degree', *Universities Quarterly*, Winter 1969.

D. W. Jary, 'General and vocational courses in Polytechnics', *Universities Quarterly*, Winter 1969.

Julia Whitburn, Maurice Mealing, Caroline Cox, 'The Blackbrick Universities', *THES*, 5th November 1971.

19. *Alternative University Structures*, UNESCO international project, UK Report by Dr Colin Adamson, Director, Polytechnic of Central London, August 1972.

20. Joanna Mack, 'The Polytechnics' unhappy birthday', *New Society*, 22nd January 1976. A senior CNAA official is quoted as saying, 'When it comes down to looking at courses in Polytechnics and University, you often cannot tell the difference.'

D. Astle, 'What CNAA Boards need', *THES*, 5th April 1974.

Valerie Pitt, *THES*, 19th April 1974; D. Robbins and D. Astle, *THES*, 19th May 1974.

21. The span of educational provision is emphasised in a Statement by the Committee of Directors of Polytechnics, *Many Arts, Many Skills – The Polytechnic Policy, and requirements for its fulfilment*, November 1974.

22. *Teacher Education and Training*, Report of a Committee of Enquiry (Chairman, Lord James of Rusholme) (HMSO, 1972).

23. Lesley Bleakley, 'What students want a two-year diploma?' *THES*, 27th December 1974.

Alan Jones, 'Dip.HE's begin to take shape and substance', *THES*, 27th December 1974.

T. R. McConnell, 'The Diploma of Higher Education: some dilemmas and opportunities', *Higher Education Review*, Spring 1974.

24. 'Report on James' of conference discussion group – Lord Boyle, Lionel Elvin, Alan Evans, Boris Ford, Joyce Skinner, George Tolley, Martin Trow, *Universities Quarterly*, Spring 1972.

Gerald A. Cortin, 'The James Report: attitudes of senior staff in the Colleges' (of Education), *Higher Education Review*, Summer 1972.

T. R. McConnell and Margaret A. Fay, 'Flexibility or rigidity:

University attitudes to the James Report', *Higher Education Review,* Summer 1972.

DES Circular 6/74: approval of advanced courses, *TES,* 21st June 1974.

25. e.g. Patrick Heron, 'Murder of the Art Schools', *The Guardian,* 12th October 1971.

Patrick Nuttgens, 'No murder of the Art Schools', *The Guardian,* 2nd November 1971.

A. M. Smith 'No evidence of Art School murder', *THES,* 26th November 1971.

The concern remains active, e.g.

Ken Rowat, 'The threat of respectability hanging over the new degree courses in art', *Education Guardian,* 10th February 1976.

26. *Teachers and Youth Leaders,* Board of Education Report, (McNair Committee) (HMSO, 1944).

27. Provisional figures from UGC, May 1976.

28. But see an account of the relationships from McNair to the 1970s: W. Roy Niblett, Darlow W. Humphreys and John R. Fairhurst, *The University Connection* (NFER, Slough 1975).

29. Bill Scott and Jeremy Hawthorn, 'Arts courses in Polytechnics: case for change', *THES,* 5th January 1973.

30. D. F. Billing, 'The pros and cons of modular courses', *THES,* 8th November 1974.

'Modular courses: students need much more guidance than in conventional courses: extracts from CNAA report on design', *THES,* 27th September 1974.

Clive Church, 'Modular Courses in British Higher Education: a Critical Assessment', *Higher Education Bulletin,* Vol. 3, No. 3, Summer 1975.

31. *THES,* 9th August 1974, 1st September 1972, 14th June 1974, 9th April 1973.

32. R. J. Ball, Principal, London Business School, reported *THES,* 6th July 1973. Expenditure Committee (Education and Arts Sub-Committee) on Postgraduate Education. Witness examined 2nd July 1973.

Note also Joanna Holland, 'Further Education's answer to the business schools', *THES,* 24th November 1972.

33. See the CBI-CVCP-CDP *Joint Report on Sandwich Courses.*

34. Few details can be given here; see the informative *Annual Reports* and the *Directory of First Degree Courses,* obtainable from CNAA, 344–354 Gray's Inn Road, London WC1X 8BP.

See also a history of its first ten years: Michael Lane, *Design for Degrees* (Macmillan, London 1975).

But note review 'CNAA's untold success story', Bill Gutteridge, *THES*, 15th August 1975.

35. Figures from CNAA Annual Report 1974-75, which records enrolments up to the end of 1975 and the beginning of 1976: Tables B & D, pp. 17 and 19.

36. CNAA Discussion Paper, *Partnership in Validation*, July 1975.

37. From evidence submitted by CDP to Houghton Committee on pay of non-University teachers (see next note).

38. *Report of the Committee of Inquiry into the pay of Non-University Teachers* (Chairman, Lord Houghton), Cmnd. 5843 (HMSO, 1975).

    Fully reported *THES*, 27th December 1974 and editorial, 'Justice from an historical document'; see also *THES*, 17th January 1975.

39. In addition University salaries were considered by the National Incomes Commission (Report No. 3, *Remuneration of Academic Staff in Universities and Colleges of Advanced Technology*, Cmnd. 2317 (HMSO, March 1964) to which the Committee of Chairmen of Governing Bodies and Principals of CATs gave evidence, and the revised salary scales applied to the staff as from 1st April 1964, i.e. before Charters were granted.

40. Reported in *THES*, 11th May 1973. See also:
    D. Farnham, 'Collective bargaining and the Poly teachers', *THES*, 20th July 1973.

41. T. E. Burlin, 'Professors in the Polys will establish parity', *THES*, 19th November 1971.

42. Eric Robinson, 'Polytechnics do not need conventional Professors', *THES* 17th April 1972. See also Colin Adamson, T. Burlin, *THES*, 31st March 1972; also *THES*, 16th June 1972, 5th November 1972, 10th November 1972, 26th October 1973.

43. Julia Whitburn, Caroline Cox, Maurice Mealing, *THES*, 14th January 1972.

    Julia Whitburn, *Career Patterns of Polytechnic Teachers*, paper to SRHE, 14th May 1974; reported THES, 24th May 1974, 'One in five Poly teachers expects to move' (see corrected tables, *THES*, 14th June 1974) and 'Newer Poly teachers more academic', *THES*, 31st May 1974.

44. M. Richards and Alexandra Withall, 'Unsure about job prospects', *THES*, 2nd February 1973.

45. For general background see J. S. King, *Women and Work: Sex Differences and Society* (HMSO, 1974), and *Women and Work: a statistical Survey* (HMSO, 1974).

46. Reported in *THES*, 26th July 1972, See also:
    'More Polys training their staff', *THES*, 26th July 1974.

Staff Development in Further Education, Report of a Joint ACFHE/ APTI Working Party, 1973.

A standing Conference on educational development services in Polytechnics, *THES*, 26th April 1974.

47. Paul Ramsden, 'Polytechnic Students' Expectations of their Teachers ... A Preliminary Report', *Higher Education Bulletin*, Vol. 3, No. 2, Spring 1975.

    R. Rumery, D. Rhodes, H. Johnson Jr, 'The Role of Student Reports in the Evaluation of Teaching in Higher Education', *Higher Education Bulletin*, Vol. 3, No. 2, Spring 1975.

48. Stated in the Preface to the *Report of the Polytechnics Working Group* (SRC, London, December 1973). But see subsequent SRC Report, *Research and Postgraduate Training in the Polytechnics* (HMSO, 1977).

49. *Ibid.*, pp. 7, 8, 12 and 13.

50. SRC Report 1975–76 (HMSO, October 1977). The comparable awards from the 1976–77 SRC Report are respectively: £64,650,000/ £4,535,000/£1,569,000.

51. Evidence to Select Committee on Science and Technology (Science sub-committee). Minutes of Evidence 1972, p. 183, Annex A. (HMSO).

52. Lex Donaldson, 'Social class and the Polytechnics', *Higher Education Review*, Autumn 1971, and *Policy and the Polytechnics* (Saxon House, D. C. Heath Ltd, Farnborough 1975), Chapter 3.

    See also:

    Sarah Bills, Maurice Mealing, Caroline Cox, Julia Whitburn, 'Safety net for the middle classes', *THES*, 1st September 1972.

    Robert A. Draffan, 'Working-class students are still too rare', *THES*, 23rd February 1973.

    Annabel Ferriman, 'Social class of Polytechnic students same as University', *THES*, 27th August 1973.

53. 'Likely to benefit – new test of student entry/admission', *The Times*, 13th January 1972; *The Guardian*, 15th January 1972, *THES*, 21st January 1972.

    John Pratt and Tyrrell Burgess, *THES*, 16th June 1972.

    Jane Howells, 'Self-selected students', *THES*, 24th May 1974.

54. David Moore, 'Why teenagers do A-levels at the Tech', *THES*, 21st April 1972.

    See: K. Farnell, L. P. S. Piper, *THES*, 12th May 1972; also: 'More and more students choosing FE courses and freedom,' *THES*, 16th June 1972.

55. Laura Kaufman, 'Polys "need to attract more women" ', report of a speech by E. Simpson, Deputy Secretary, DES, *THES*, 5th April 1974.

'Information on Polytechnics sparse in schools', *THES*, 28th September 1973.

Anne Riggs and Sarah Robinson, 'How you know depends largely on who you know', *THES*, 6th September 1974.

56. S. Stander, 'Student counselling and the new Polytechnics', *Universities Quarterly*, Spring 1974.

Robert Oxtoby, 'Role conceptions and perceived expectations of students entering a Polytechnic', *Durham Research Review*, Vol. 6, No. 29, 1972.

George Tolley, 'Career development in Polytechnics', *TES*, 17th April 1972.

See also: Alan Corbett, *TES*, 30th April 1971; Keith Hammond, *TES*, 14th July 1972.

57. Robert Oxtoby, 'Objectives of Polytechnic students', *Universities Quarterly*, Winter 1971.

58. 'No clearing-house for Polys', *THES*, 27th November 1970.

'50 per cent of Poly students prefer University', *THES*, 15th September 1972.

Philip Venning, 'Time for a re-think', *THES*, 25th May 1973.

Annabel Ferriman, 'Two Polytechnics to boycott standard application form' (i.e. pending entrance to UCCA), *THES*, 18th May 1973.

59. Reported *TES*, 26th July 1974.

John Gibbins, 'How to supply the demand', *THES*, 15th February 1974.

A. N. Black, 'The problems of estimating Poly student numbers', *THES*, 5th April 1974.

Frances Gibb, 'Great selectivity in Poly applications, survey shows', *THES*, 3rd January 1975.

60. *Education Act 1975*, with effect from 1st September 1975.

61. Hansard (House of Commons), Vol. 744, cols. 151–55: 28 on provisional list, one invited from Staffordshire and Stoke-on-Trent LEAs, and one other to be in Northern Lancashire.

62. DES *Report of the Study Group on the Government of Colleges of Education* (Chairman, Mr T. R. (later Sir Toby) Weaver) HMSO, 1966.

63. DES Circular 7/70: *Government and conduct of establishments of Further Education*.

64. Michael Locke, 'Government', Chapter 4 in *Polytechnics: A Report* (*as 3*).

D. A. Fiske, *Some thoughts on the Government of Colleges*, paper to AGM, 1973, The Association of Colleges for Further and Higher Education, reported *THES*, 16th February 1973.

65. e.g. reported cases include: Trent Polytechnic, *THES*, 5th July 1974

(editorial), 12th July 1974, 19th July 1974, 29th November 1974, 24th January 1975.

Sheffield Polytechnic, *THES*, 9th February 1973, 25th March 1973.

John Fairhall, 'Ties that bind', *The Guardian*, 3rd April 1973.

North East London Polytechnic, *THES*, 10th August 1973.

Bristol Polytechnic, *THES*, 15th November 1974, 29th November 1974.

'What Poly directors want on controls, pay and validation', *THES*, 12th October 1973 – being edited extracts of Statement issued by the Committee of Directors of Polytechnics.

Philip Venning, 'Polytechnic expansion depends on independence', *THES*, 5th October 1973.

'Polys air their grievances', *THES*, 19th October 1973.

'Poly directors attack London HE policy', *THES*, 16th February 1973.

66. CDP Statement *On Polytechnics and the expansion of Higher Education*, 3rd October 1973. Compare CDP Statement – *Many Arts, Many Skills*, November 1974, paras. 63–67.

67. Annabel Ferriman, 'Polytechnics must stay under Local Authority control' and also editorial, *THES*, 19th October 1973.

George Brosan, 'Where the Polytechnics stand in the debate with LEAs', *Education*, 5th April 1974.

'LEAs should keep Polys' – Sir Toby Weaver, reported *THES*, 25th October 1974.

Eric Briault, 'Why the Polytechnics should not go independent', *THES*, 29th November 1974.

68. Eric Robinson, 'RACs and the economics of the madhouse', *THES*, 3rd January 1975.

69. Roger Grinyer, 'Polytechnic Committee will be stopgap until 1974', *THES*, 18th August 1972.

Report of Standing Conference of RACs: *Co-operation in the Planning and Development of Higher Education*, 1972.

70. 'Polytechnic (Central London) deserts tradition in favour of schools system', *THES*, 11th October 1964.

71. Graeme C. Moodie and Rowland Eustace: *The Student Challenge* (Unwin, 1974), Chapter IX, 'The Vice-Chancellor'.

John Griffith, 'Growth of the polycrats', *THES*, 21st September 1973.

72. Keigh Houghton, 'Poly planning needs new approach', *THES*, 24th March 1972.

'First step towards training the admin. men', *THES*, 9th June 1972.

'Are the town halls inhibiting the Polytechnics?', *THES*, 15th October 1971.

'Administration in the Polytechnics', *THES*, 15th December 1972.

73. W. A. C. Stewart, 'Rediscovering identity in higher education',

chapter in *Higher Education: Patterns of Change in the 1970s* (ed. John Lawlor) (Routledge & Kegan Paul, London 1972).

74. Rt. Hon. Anthony Crosland, 'Polytechnics are abandoning their original role by aping Universities', reported Stephen Jessel, *The Times*, 10th June 1972 but see editorial, 'Polytechnics need time', *TES*, 16th June 1972.

   Rt. Hon. Reg Prentice, then Secretary of State, DES, praised Polys but warned against dropping part-time and sandwich courses, reported *THES*, 21st June 1974.

   Peter Scott, 'The Bowdlerised Universities', *THES*, 8th March 1974, being a review of *Polytechnics; A Report (as 3.)*; see also Sir Norman Lindop, *THES*, 15th March 1974.

   Tyrrell Burgess, 'Applying scientific methods to public policy', *THES*, 26th April 1974; and correspondence, *THES*, 10th May 1974.

75. 'Lack of common philosophy in Polys attacked by NELP head (Dr Brosan)', reported *THES*, 19th April 1974.

76. Sir Norman Lindop (Director of the Hatfield Polytechnic), 'Polys: spearhead for the public sector', *THES*, 21st June 1974.

77. *As 20.*

78. Annual Residential Conference Proceedings pp. 6–15 (published by SCRAC, Tavistock House South, Tavistock Square, London WC1H 9LR, 11th-13th September 1975).

   See also *A Philosophy for Polytechnics*, address by Sir Alex Smith to the Conference of Principals of Colleges of Advanced Education in Canberra. Reported *THES*, 5th September 1975.

79. Sir Alex Smith, Proceedings SCRAC. *Ibid.*, pp. 8–9.

80. *Ibid.*, p. 7.

81. cf. H. J. Habakkuk (Vice-Chancellor Oxford University), *The University at the approach of the 21st Century*: Address to the International Conference in Moscow. Reported *THES*, 5th September 1975.

11

Aspects of Expansion
and the Steady State

THE national planning of institutions of higher education – their distribution, scope and size – is a very recent development in Britain. The UGC was founded in 1919 and there ensued a twenty-five-year transition towards an overall State policy for Universities.[1] The gradual rate of involvement and change was quickened by a growing concern about increasing the supply of scientific manpower. The Percy Committee had reported that 'the greatest deficiency in British industry . . . shown by the war [was] the shortage of scientists and technologists who can administer and organise, and can apply the results of research to development.'[2] The Report emphasised the contribution of the Technical Colleges, which was not surprising as their output in 1943 of civil, electrical and mechanical engineers was somewhat greater than that of the Universities. This Report was quickly followed by that of the Barlow Committee on *Scientific Manpower*,[3] the chief recommendation of which was that the Universities should double their output of scientists within the next ten years, but it also asserted that 'Even if the total student population in British Universities were doubled, this country would still fall far short of a number of European countries and the United States of America in the relative provision which it made for higher education.' Another important expression of this concern was the establishment of the Advisory Council on Scientific Policy in 1947, which continued until 1964, when it was replaced by the Committee on Manpower Resources for Science and Technology: this in turn was absorbed into other more widely based Governmental means for considering national manpower problems generally.[4] As for the expansion in higher education, narrowly based predictions such as that of the Barlow Committee for the Universities only, also gave way to more widely based indications. Of particular interest, in view of the later emergence of the Polytechnics, is the comment in the UGC's *A Note on Technology in the Universities* that 'developments in the Universities, on the lines discussed here, would leave for the 'Technical Colleges a large and expanding field of work of great importance.'[5] There was then no unified planning of technological education, let alone of higher education as a whole, a problem which remains to this day.

The 1956 White Paper on *Technical Education,* in which the creation of the Colleges of Advanced Technology was announced, devoted a chapter to 'The Role of the Universities' and their expansion as determined by the UGC since the war. It suggested expansion in the Technical Colleges also to increase the annual output of advanced courses from 9,500 to about 15,000. Not to act can be a very positive decision of policy, and such was the failure to ensure that the whole of this increase was concentrated in the designated Colleges of Advanced Technology. Applications for establishing advanced courses, especially four-year sandwich courses, in other colleges were encouraged. With concentration the impetus to expand the CATs would have been much more powerful and rapid in effect, allowing them to draw level with the 'new Universities'. As it was, the Committee of Principals of the CATs had considerable difficulty in obtaining Ministry approval for adequate targets to ensure effective expansion, despite the lessons of the long drawn-out development of Keele and other University Colleges, in contrast with the rapid establishment of Sussex. Speculation on the possible rapid emergence of ten and perhaps ultimately twenty CATs, each with about 8,000 full-time and sandwich students, and the consequences for the balance of the system of higher education, including the non-emergence of Polytechnics and institutes of higher education is interesting, but unprofitable.

The definitive stage in the expansion of higher education was the publication of the Robbins Committee Report (1963), and its immediate acceptance by the Government. In the years preceding the Report the proportion of the increasing number of school-leavers with two or more A-level subjects, *who actually entered Universities,* fell from nearly 80 per cent in 1956 to 65 per cent in 1961, and to 59 per cent in 1962. The Committee recommended a crash programme of expansion and the first part of Appendix Table AIIId shows that by 1967–68 the Robbins numbers for the Universities were well maintained, but the Colleges of Education and Further Education

Colleges were overshooting their Robbins targets substantially. However, the number of qualified A-level candidates from the schools continued to rise over the period and the percentage of these actually entering the Universities declined further from 59 to 53 per cent, thus eroding one of the major principles of the Robbins Report.

Against this general background we may recall that when the CATs became Universities it was frequently predicted that they would do worse at the tail end of the long queue of suppliants for resources from the UGC than by staying with the DES at the head of the other queue as direct grant institutions. What in fact happened is shown in Appendix Table AIIIa, which gives the comparative figures for the quinquennium 1967–72 between the ex-CATs and the other Universities. Taking all Universities other than the ex-CATs the increase in student numbers was 17 per cent and in the Technological Universities it was 26 per cent. In terms of cost per student place, Universities other than the ex-CATs increased on average from £733 to £1,056 (44 per cent): the technological ones from £969 to £1,114 (13 per cent). In other words the ratio of costs between the two groups was 1·0:1·3 at the beginning of the quinquennium and 1·0:1·05 at the end; i.e. the UGC virtually equalised the rate of recurrent grants during the five-year period.

The loss of grant suffered by the Technological Universities in the first year of the quinquennium is evident enough from Table AIIIa, and at the time seemed to justify the forebodings. Relatively, the CATs had been well treated by the Ministry in their initial stages as direct grant institutions, but there were other inherent reasons for their high costs. First was the high proportion of relatively expensive subjects – science, technology and management studies. Secondly, satisfactory recruitment of able staff after responsible experience in industry and commerce cannot be made at the lower salary levels – appointing 'refugees from industry' to train students for successful careers in industry would be an absurd and extravagant economy. Both these factors remain and should be reflected in higher relative grants. It is not clear how far this is taken into account in fixing recurrent grants. The converging costs per place imply that grants relate simply to student numbers. Another factor is the uncertain supply of students for science and technology, and as long as this persists, grants for expansion of these subjects will hardly be forthcoming. However, judgements made over a short period of years, lacking active official moves and publicity to reverse the trend, can be misleading as well as self-perpetuating. There has been an upward move recently,[6]* though it will need to be maintained to meet national needs.

Allocations of capital grants for buildings and equipment depend on a complexity of factors – such as sites actual and potential, the stage of development of the institution, its previous history and particular specialities, 'the timeliness and promise' of its proposals in relation to national policy and the general balance of University development. The eleven brief histories[7] show the very varied situations of the technological institutions.

The White Paper, 1972

The publication of the Government White Paper *Education: A Framework for Expansion*[8] was a major step in its overall review of five main areas: nursery education, school-building, staffing standards in schools, teacher training and higher education, in order to determine

Table 11.1 Grants to Universities 1972–77

Academic year	Recurrent grant £	Equipment grant £
1972–73	252·0	23·5
1973–74	263·0	24·5
1974–75	276·0	25·5
1975–76	292·0	27·0
1976–77	309·0	29·0
TOTALS	1,392·0	129·5

the distribution of available national resources between them. Attention was therefore focused mainly on matters of scale, organisation and cost, rather than on educational content. For present purposes, we note that it dealt particularly with the organisation of higher education, the number of students and staff involved and the implication for public expenditure. Its proposals on grants to Universities are shown in Table 11.1.[9]

The UGC[10] stated that grants for years later than 1972–73 would be

* Admissions to engineering courses at Universities and Polytechnics were up 8 per cent in October 1976, and applications by 17 per cent (Rt. Hon. Mrs Shirley Williams MP, Secretary of State DES).

supplemented to take account of any further increase in salaries and costs in accordance with new arrangements, but inflation proved severe, and the subsequent withdrawal of this assurance caused very serious concern in the Universities about their future.

The grants provided by the Government were for a total of just over 320,000 students by 1976–77, made up as shown in Table 11.2.[11]

Table 11.2 Projected full-time enrolments in British Universities 1976–77

Full-time students on campus	303,000
Full-time students off campus (e.g. sandwich course students)	3,000
TOTAL full-time	306,000
Part-time students = full-time equivalent	15,500
GRAND TOTAL	321,500

Table 11.3 Full-time enrolments, projected and actual, in British Universities 1972–77

	1972–73	1973–74	1974–75	1975–76	1976–77
Projected numbers of full-time students	243,000	251,000	264,500	283,000	306,000
Projected per cent increase over previous year		3·0	5·0	7·0	8·1
Actual numbers achieved	246,813	251,226	257,684	261,258	272,487
Actual per cent increase		1·8	2·6	1·4	4·3
Excess/shortfall in relation to projected figures	+3,813	+226	—6,816	—21,742	—33,513

Note: Increase in numbers on 243,000 over 5 years only 12 per cent.

The growth of full-time enrolments over the quinquennium was expected to take place as in Table 11.3.[12]

As was remarked in the UGC Survey 1972–73,[13] these figures were based on pay and prices at the time of submission of the Universities' quinquennial estimates, i.e. July 1971, and had to be adjusted for subsequent price and salary movements up to January 1973, and various other administrative changes. The resulting revised figures were set out by the UGC[14] as in the upper part of Table 11.4.

The lower part of Table 11.4 takes account of a new procedure for revaluing grants for current prices introduced in the spring of 1973, when the Government announced supplementary grants which had the effect of giving 100 per cent compensation for the expected increase in prices from January 1973 to January 1974, so that in July 1973 the UGC were able to allocate the lower part of Table 11.4. In retrospect the progression of grants made to the eight Technological

Table 11.4   Revised allocation of recurrent grants to Universities 1972–77, as at January and July 1973

	£m				
	1972–73	1973–74	1974–75	1975–76	1976–77
Quinquennial settlement	252·000	263·000	276·000	292·000	309·000
Supplementary grant, price and academic salary increases to January 1973	50·900	48·500	51·750	54·750	58·000
Amounts for minor capital works	—	4·538	4·557	4·557	4·557
Transferred from quinquennial settlement of equipment grant	—	0·675	0·700	0·738	0·800
TOTAL	302·900	316·713	333·007	352·045	372·357
Less transfer from recurrent grant to furniture and equipment grant		1·500	1·570	1·658	1·750
Supplementary grant as at July 1973		16·691	20·704	21·887	23·150
Equipment grant		0·691	0·717	0·755	0·819

Universities in comparison with those to all UK Universities, indexed to 1976–77 values, is set out in Table 11.5.[15]*

In the circumstances the degree of variation in unit costs over the 1972–77 quinquennium, and the preceding one, is remarkably small.

As to the growth of numbers during the 1972–77 quinquennium, the White Paper confirmed the total of 306,000 full-time students in 1976–77, but added 15,500 full-time equivalent for increased part-time student numbers, i.e. a total of 321,500. In addition, the number of postgraduate students was to be increased from 45,000 in 1971–72,

---

* Certain Universities received other supplementary grants because of specific inadequacies in earlier years of the quinquennium,[16] while other, relatively small, once-for-all grants were made for specific purposes to 29 Universities.[17]

to 52,000 out of 306,000 full-time students, but this increased total masked a diminished proportion of postgraduate students out of the whole, i.e. from 19 to 17 per cent.[18] In addition it was assumed that 47 per cent of full-time students in 1976–77 would be arts-based and 53 per cent science-based, which would reduce to a small extent the existing disparity of opportunity between applicants for admission to the arts and the sciences.[19]

The White Paper stated that expansion in the Polytechnics and other non-University Colleges would continue and in fact increase, so that by 1981 there might be a total of 750,000 places in Great

Table 11.5 Total recurrent grants 1972–77: actual payments indexed to 1976/77 value

	£				
	Technological Universities (N = 8)		*All UK Universities*		Unit costs* indexed
	Payment	Indexed	Payment	Indexed	
1972–73	30,156,137	54,944,481	311,195,865	566,998,866	2,475†
1973–74	34,710,800	57,793,482	358,922,565	597,606,071	2,550
1974–75	41,547,687	57,086,522	424,830,116	583,716,579	2,396
1975–76	51,907,672	56,838,900	531,204,674	581,669,118	2,328
1976–77	58,192,898		596,860,330		2,323

Notes: * University recurrent unit costs, representing grant and fee income divided by student numbers at 1976–77 pay and prices.
 † Unit costs for the previous quinquennium were: 1968, £2,362; 1969, £2,262; 1970, £2,251; 1971, £2,225 and 1972, £2,136.

Britain equally divided between the University and non-University sectors.[20] There was, therefore, 'the formidable task' for the non-University sector of providing, on 1972 estimates, for some 335,000 full-time and sandwich places in England and Wales in 1981, the major part to be in the Polytechnics, which had been encouraged to aim for 180,000 places.[21] The other Colleges – of Education and of Further Education – would thus also need to expand to provide a further total of about 155,000 *places* as compared with their 1971–72 total of some 138,000 *students*.[22]*

* It is important to distinguish *places* from *students*: for full-time students they are almost equal, for sandwich course students and part-time students, variously in/out of college, more students can be accommodated in the same number of places.[23]

The Polytechnics are financed annually from two sources: by the Local Authorities out of the rates and by the Government Rate Support Grant from the Advanced Further Education 'Pool'.[24]* The firmest indication therefore of committed growth to come is not the annual estimates, which can only confirm growth retrospectively, but the estimated amount of capital grant for new buildings and equipment for the years ahead. The White Paper stated that £7 million had been allocated for building projects in 1972–73, £19 million earmarked for 1973–74, and £27 million for 1974–75. In addition, £3 million and £5 million respectively had been allocated for residential building in the last two periods.[25] These were the first assurances to the Local Authorities and the Polytechnics of a policy of sustained expansion, and they appeared to justify the assertion that Government support had switched to polytechnics.[26] Subsequent deferments, then cuts, followed by partial restorations of targets, made for a confusing and increasingly dispiriting situation. Representatives of the Polytechnics were concerned to dispel any sense of a 'Poly bonanza' and to claim that the full programme would simply reduce but not remove the disparity in buildings, facilities and amenities between the Polytechnics and the Universities, since the Polytechnics were starting from a much lower base-line.[27] The cumulative disparity was totalled by Pratt and Burgess,[28] namely, £83·4 million for buildings for Polytechnics from 1967–75 inclusive, as compared with £232 million for Universities.

The determination of numbers for the expansion of higher education depends on an assessment of difficult and conflicting factors. For the Universities these include the varying numbers sitting for A-levels, which reflect social and economic changes, and the number of those who qualify but do not in fact wish to enter the Universities.

* The 'Pool' was established in 1959 as a clearing-house for student costs (as mentioned in Chapter 1 in relation to the CATs), thus avoiding claims for reimbursement by many Local Authorities for a large number of widely dispersed students. Authorities claim from the 'Pool' the recurrent cost of all advanced students in their area. One important fact is that capital costs for buildings, etc. are treated as recurrent costs, and consequently a part of these costs is similarly recouped. The 'Pool' was thus proved to be an effective instrument for expanding advanced higher education by enterprising LEAs, with no redress or control by the others, who simply had to contribute in accordance with the formula. Payment without representations proved counterproductive, and generated moves towards control through insisting on standardised costs for courses, staff ratios, etc.; more than that, towards replacing the 'Pool' by a more responsive system.

Others take advantage of the increased opportunities for degree courses in Polytechnics and other colleges; and yet others go direct to a job, since with inflated wages as compared with depressed grants, a job in the hand appears more sure and rewarding than a degree in the bush. In these circumstances 1973 was aptly described as 'a planners' nightmare'.[29]

The White Paper was subjected to prolonged discussion and much criticism in the ensuing two years, but only the major points concerning expansion in the Universities and Polytechnics respectively can be considered here.

An increase of 59 per cent was envisaged from the achieved figure of 236,000 full-time University students in 1971–72 to a projected figure of about 375,000 in 1981.[30] Before the advent of the Polytechnics, the 1970 DES Planning Paper had estimated 460,000 full-time places in Universities out of a total of about 835,000 full-time places in higher education as a whole by 1981.[31] So the 1972 White Paper was predictably described as 'resource-switching – not genuine expansion'.[32] Except for postgraduate studies, the reduction of 85,000 places to be borne by the Universities was not subject to any formal complaint by their representatives, though it was attacked by some outside the Universities who were concerned about the limitation of opportunity in higher education. Within the walls ambivalence could be detected among some staff members between the egalitarian imperative and traditional élitism, the balance of which was altered as the number of students applying to enter began to fall. However, the Robbins Report prediction of 356,000 full-time students in higher education in Britain in 1971–72 was in fact exceeded by 71,000, so if in the event the 750,000 target were to be exceeded by the same proportion, numbers would reach 1,000,000 by 1981.[33]

Gareth Williams examined the various predictions of output of A-level candidates,[34] and he concluded that the curve of increase of eligible A-level candidates would probably be S-shaped, indicating that 'there would be a more or less stable 15 per cent of the population obtaining the minimum qualifications currently necessary to obtain a mandatory student grant', and that 'by 1981 (there would be) about 600,000 full-time students in higher and advanced Further Education'. Factors which in part explain this reduced figure, and which will tend to lower it still further, include the adverse effects of a declining economy, the level of students' grants and their declining power of purchase as compared with the wages of contemporaries in employment, the unemployment rates of fresh graduates wishing to enter occupations, and the decline of salaries of graduates relative to weekly wage rates of manual workers.

Sound predictions should of course be attempted and used with judgement no less sound, but the whole tendency of 'the system' is to play safe, and almost always to take the lower estimate. This could be most unfortunate for the many who are excluded, even if they were able to retrieve their lost opportunities through the Open University in later years. Declining estimates of future need should be examined with great scepticism by egalitarians. However, that is not to say that everyone should go by the same educational routes or at the same age, but that new opportunities should be afforded by modification of the existing system and by innovations – such as extending education intermittently throughout life (lifelong learning), or by 'learning while earning' through part-time, block release and sandwich courses. The egalitarians will have plenty to do to prevent Governments under economic pressure from procrastinating, or from using the Open University on financial grounds only.

By contrast with the planned increase in total numbers, the relative reduction in postgraduate work, combined with silence about research in the White Paper, caused widespread concern, and not only in the Universities.[35] In addition there was fear that the required reduction of as much as 23 per cent in unit costs would mean 1,300 fewer promotions and 3,500 fewer academic posts.[36] Such cuts would mean a worsening of staff-student ratios, with particularly adverse effects at postgraduate level setting limits on flexibility and innovation.[37] In sum the White Paper's intentions were very clear: the acceptance by the Universities of lower standards of accommodation, of teaching and of research for at least ten years following 1972. This unilateral political decision was in sharp contrast with the consultations between the Universities and the Government in 1969 when thirteen possible means of reducing expenditure were suggested by Mrs Shirley Williams, Minister of State for Education: (1) a reduction or removal of student grants aid (first degree level) coupled with a loan system; (2) a similar policy at postgraduate level; (3) a more restrictive policy on admission of overseas students; (4) grant-aided students should enter specified kinds of employment after graduation; (5) the greater use of part-time and correspondence courses; (6) the most able students should have the opportunity to graduate in two years; (7) some students to be able to take two-year courses leading not to a degree but to a diploma; (8) possibly inserting a period or year between school and University; (9) more intensive use of buildings and equipment and the possible reorganisation of the academic year; (10) more sharing of facilities between adjacent institutions; (11) more home-based students; (12) the development of student housing associations and other forms of loan-financed provision of residences; (13) some further increase in student-staff ratio.

The Vice-Chancellors' Committee replied to the thirteen points in April 1970 and opposed nine of them. Mrs Williams became Secretary of State, DES, in 1976 at a time of severe inflation and it is probable that many of her items will appear on educational agenda for the next decade or so.[38]

The economic crisis

The serious deterioration in the national economic situation began in late 1973 and accelerated through 1974 to the menacing levels of 1975 and 1976. In consequence of the Government's decision to rephase the public building programme, the UGC would not approve any tenders (except for student residence) between October and December 1973, later extended to 1st July 1974. In January 1974 the UGC notified Universities of the Government's decision[39] to withhold half the supplementation of recurrent grant,* and not to supplement equipment grant in respect of 1973's increase in prices for the subsequent years of the quinquennium. Because of the energy crisis, supplementation for the remaining part of the 1974–75 year was withheld and the furniture and equipment grants for 1974–75 were reduced by £15 million.[40] The decisions understandably caused grave concern, and in Lord Annan's view, University finance was now in confusion. 'In withholding the whole of the supplementary grant to compensate for inflation in 1974–75 the Government had set the universities on a greasy slide: the worse inflation became the worse their deficit would be.'[41] One immediate effect in the UGC

* The Tress–Brown Index is compiled each year, and measures changes in the costs of all goods and services which the Universities buy and changes in the salary rates of non-academic staff. It is named after its authors, Dr Ronald Tress, Master of Birkbeck College, London, and Professor A. J. Brown of Leeds University.

and the Committee of Vice-Chancellors and Principals was to focus attention again on re-examining the probable numbers of students in the later years of the quinquennium. In the event, the distribution of UGC recurrent grant reserve in February 1974 was insufficient and in some cases the 1974–75 grants were, in real terms, a reduction on the 1973–74 figures. The Government however did award supplementation to cover Value-Added Tax (VAT) of about £75,000–£81,000 per annum.

In May 1974 the UGC notified Universities that the revised building programme for 1974–75 would be £11·5 million at 1973 prices, i.e. only about one-fifth of the value of the work already included in firm building programmes but unstarted at the time of the moratorium in October 1973. To this 80 per cent reduction must be added the postponement of the projects in the 1975–76 'sketch design' list. In allocating the greatly reduced grant, preference was to be given to those requirements for University buildings which were a necessary complement to other forms of public investment, in particular, the DHSS teaching hospital programme, and the Computer Board's investment in computer equipment for Universities. Grants were made preferentially for projects which could be started quickly in areas where there was an identifiable increase in student demand.

In July 1974 the UGC reminded Universities that it had (in the previous February) indicated that supplementary grants for increased costs for 1975–76 and 1976–77 must be related to possible changes in the planned numbers of students. Grants for 1975–76 and 1976–77 had been recalculated accordingly on a realistic assessment of a probable student population in 1976–77. This meant between 8 and 11 per cent below the 1972 White Paper figure of 321,000. The overall reduction was to be reflected in varying ways at individual Universities, and the main criteria in determining particular grants were to be the physical capacity available, including residence, and the University's experience of application and admittance rates in the previous two years. While evidently fair, this basis inevitably reinforced the persistent swing away from science and technology, which was a very disturbing, not to say threatening, factor in the developing programme of the Technological Universities: and this just at a time when national needs required a positive campaign to increase substantially the quantity and quality of students taking up science and technology.

The Vice-Chancellors' Committee made cogent representations to the Secretary of State, DES, that the earlier decision concerning no supplementation was having a disproportionate effect and the government provided a supplementary grant of £4 million in the academic year 1974–75. To this the UGC reluctantly added £1·5 million from the already reduced equipment and furniture grant, and the cost of pension increases and employers' contributions were to rank for automatic supplementation – small amounts by contrast with the total reductions, but very welcome in such straitened circumstances.

Because of the severe financial pressures and the likely shortfall in numbers of students, the UGC in November 1974 asked Universities to consider how to increase their effective capacity in any area of need by the re-allocation of existing accommodation. A further problem was that University submissions for future building programmes were likely to arise from needs not directly related to student numbers, and change in the use of rooms is not a simple matter. The location may be awkward and conversions disproportionately costly, yet the pressures for more effective utilisation were inescapable.

The expected reduction of targets for 1981 was announced by the Secretary of State, DES, on 25 November 1974: from 750,000 down to 640,000,[42] and this was stated to be consistent with the Robbins principle that 'courses of higher education should be available for all those who are qualified by ability and attainment to pursue them *and who wish to do so.'* This author's italics emphasise the crucial condition, for the academic 'wish to do so' may be overborne, as has been noted, by worsening financial circumstances within the family combined with the lessening purchasing power of students' grants as compared with wages. For this reason the Government's action in establishing a special committee to enquire into the falling number of qualified students applying to enter Universities in 1975 was somewhat belated.[43]

On 18th December 1974, following the announcement by the Secretary that there would be a supplement of £15 million to the 1974–75 recurrent grant, the UGC made allocations to individual Universities, and payment began in January 1975. The £15 million plus earlier supplementations approached only about half of the full cost of inflation, assuming this to be about 20 per cent. Welcome though the supplementation was, the impact of inflation remained severe, and there were frequent reports in the press of many academic posts not being filled and other drastic measures unavoidably being taken, in quite the most shaking financial crisis ever before experienced by the Universities in peacetime. The rate of inflation in University expenditure was 28·2 per cent in the calendar year 1974, compared with a rate of 12·8 per cent the year before. This – the 28·2 per cent – was above the national figure. Sir Arthur Armitage* commented that 'this unprecedented increase is causing great anxiety among the Vice-Chancellors and in the Universities, for it shows that the particular costs which fall on Universities are rising at a higher rate than other costs.'[44] He emphasised that 'Universities have instituted and are continuing to apply stringent economy measures. The scale of inflation over the past year makes it vital that the shortly expected Government announcement about resources for Universities in the years 1975–76 and 1976–77 provide for grants based on actual current costs, and which will be fully supplemented to take account of subsequent inflation.'

The continuing inflation led the CVCP to publish in November 1975 *A Statement: Universities in a Period of Economic Crisis,* which presented a thorough appraisal of the adverse effects on the Universities, of their indispensable contributions to the economic life of the nation,† and of the conditions vital to their future well-being. In concluding the Statement, the Committee looked to the Government 'to do three things – none of them unreasonable but together capable of having a decisive impact. The first is to promote a more efficient use of resources by establishing a system of University grants which departs from the *ad hoc* arrangements of the present and immediate past, and which provides a planning perspective and a real terms funding commitment extending beyond a year. The second is to give the firmest possible assurance to the Universities that, at the end of this period, they will be able to resume their programmes of development with financial support at a level in keeping with their national and international standing and commensurate with the burdens they have shouldered. And the third is to give a clear commitment that effective long-term planning and financing ar-

* Chairman of the Committee of Vice-Chancellors and Principals of UK Universities (CVCP).

† This Statement should be required reading for all those who attempt to advance discussions of higher education to meet society's needs on a basis of comparison of supposedly comprehensive, immensely productive Polytechnics, with Universities as ivory towers from whence come only scholars.

rangements will be restored thereafter so that preparations – including consideration of the necessary capital programmes to meet expansion after 1977 – can be made in the intervening period.'

On 28th November 1975 the UGC wrote to Universities about recurrent grant allocations, saying that they would invite from each an appreciation of its needs and problems in relation to a possible medium-term resource distribution. On 27th January 1976, Universities were informed it was probable that only a grant for 1976–77 would be distributed. The UGC, by letter of 16th February 1976, sought from each University an assessment of its position in respect of four specified categories, and a fairly brief review of the University's development over the next five years, assuming very much the same capital stock and including any projects already assured of finance. The White Paper on *Public Expenditure to 1979–80* was published in February 1976[45] and in the following month – at last – the Government announced that Universities were to receive £581 million in recurrent grant for the academic year 1976–77, and that 'the recurrent grant, in common with three-quarters of all central Government-voted expenditure, other than social security benefits, will be treated as a cash limit which will not be subject to supplementation for academic or other salary or price rises.'[46] For the academic year which started in September 1975, the grant was £465 million, followed by a supplementary grant of £58 million, so that the grant for the last year of the current quinquennium represents an increase of about 11 per cent. Though at first this settlement seemed better than had been feared,[47] only time and discussions between the UGC and individual Universities will reveal the realities underlying the White Paper.

Thus ended a quinquennium of financial severity, unprecedented unpredictability, and of planning in disarray. The general reaction would appear to be one of sympathy and respect for the UGC in the performance of an extremely difficult task in straitened circumstances. Nevertheless, with the multiple changes of grant and the fits and starts which perforce served for planning, the future of the quinquennium, and linked with it the future of the UGC itself, have been called in question,[48] which is discussed in Chapter 12. It is interesting that while the CVCP in their Statement urged a return to long-term planning, specific mention of the quinquennial system was avoided. Quite apart from whether crisis conditions do constitute a point of advantage from which to modify the system, there had been very little previous pressure for this particular change: both HM Government and HM Opposition seemed firmly committed to the five-year system for the Universities.

Other possible questions with financial implications await serious discussion:[49] how to enable Universities to build up reserves, placing the system of student fees on a more economic basis, and perhaps even changing the conditions of tenured staff and employing more academic staff – part-time or full-time on short-term engagements (as American practice might suggest).[50]

The proposal of the Secretary of State[51] to raise undergraduate fees for 1977–78 to £500 (home students) and £650 (overseas students) for first degree courses, and to £750 and £850 respectively for postgraduate courses has had a very guarded – in some cases hostile – reception.[52] However, the Robbins Committee (para. 652) thought it 'a source of strength that public finance should come through more than one channel', and recommended 'that the level of fees be revised so that in future they meet at least 20 per cent of current institutional expenditure. Some of us would prefer to see the proportion greater' (para. 654). The increases now proposed would provide 20–30 per cent of University income. The proposals would have little effect on most home students because of correlated changes in the grant regulations and increased funds for Research Councils, but there would be quite disproportionate effects with overseas and postgraduate students. Home students not in receipt of grants will suffer hardship and some could even find it impossible to complete their studies.[53] Increasing the proportion of income derived from student fees could increase the autonomy of Universities but will also affect their relationships with their students. Postgraduate courses are likely to suffer: students will be less able to prolong their studies and Universities will have to choose between expensive postgraduate courses, for example in science and engineering, and less expensive undergraduate provision. Within the Technological Universities in December 1976 there were 956 overseas students in sandwich courses; 1,790 in full-time courses (i.e. 2,746 in first degree courses); and 1,803 in postgraduate courses and research. Thirty-nine per cent of all postgraduate students were from overseas, ranging from 25 per cent at Bath to 45 per cent at Bradford and 53 per cent at Salford.[54]

The annual grants system of the Polytechnics was of course not immune from the economic hazards, and their loss of building programmes was severe in the 1972–74 period. For them there was perhaps a greater sense of disappointment and frustration with such adverse decisions coming so soon after the bright promise of the 1972 White Paper.

Within the Polytechnics the pressure seems to be away from the annual system towards a triennium, even a rolling triennium, though this is unlikely to be implemented while they remain under the Local Authorities with a system of finance based on annual budgets. Were they to become direct grant institutions, a triennial system would be possible, as obtains already for the Open University. Sir Derman Christopherson[55] has suggested a rolling quinquennium for the Universities, so that they could continually plan for five years ahead on the basis of forecasts of future public expenditure on higher education; which is in effect the system used by the research councils. If the financial difficulties continue into the 1980s such a system would be better for the Universities also, rather than an interrupted quinquennium which could become indistinguishable from a system of annual grants.

A changing stereotype

As already indicated, there are those who are concerned to maintain the obsolete stereotype of the Universities as 'ivory towers', unalterable or very slow to alter in their work, structure and external relationships. Arguments are forsworn because they are thus made to appear unresponsive to social needs, in comparison with other institutions of higher education.

The CVCP Statement (November 1975) on *Universities in a Period of Economic Crisis* was properly concerned to dispel this erroneous view, especially within the Government, and cited incontrovertible facts about the Universities which are not widely appreciated. These may be briefly summarised:

1. The Universities are responsible for more than 80 per cent – over 250,000 – of students taking full-time degree courses.
2. Their degree courses range from the least to the most applied, from humanities and prehistory to social work and the latest technology.
3. The Universities have responsibilities in the whole field of vocational training to degree level, and within this field have the sole responsibility for the training of agriculturalists, and of doctors,

273

dentists and veterinary surgeons, the last three to a level leading to a licence to practise.

4. They are responsible for a large part of the nation's research programmes, and a substantial contribution to this, and to other areas of nationally important work, is made by their 25,000 full-time and 13,000 part-time research postgraduates.

5. Also at postgraduate level, the Universities have some 25,000 full-time and 8,000 part-time students following taught courses, mostly of one year's duration, a very substantial proportion of which are concerned with professional education including teachers and social workers. In addition there are the large numbers who take short full-time or part-time vocationally oriented post-experience courses.

6. In sum, the number of University postgraduates studying part-time exceeds the total of all postgraduate degree students, full- and part-time, in all other centres of higher education.

7. University staff are widely used by Government as chairmen and members of a whole range of committees, and their expertise and knowledge are increasingly called upon by the public services, industry, commerce and the professions.

8. Universities have reacted and will continue to react to the challenge of problems which face the nation, as witness the response to the Barlow Committee and Robbins Committee Reports, as well as to a whole series of more recent national reports which called for greater numbers of highly trained men and women in particular fields including science and technology, medicine, law and social work. 135,000 students – well over 50 per cent of the total – are in science and technology courses.

9. Despite the effects of accelerating inflation and consequent reduced resources, the Universities increased their student numbers by 7,000 in 1974, and 10,000 in 1975, and this has entailed a decline of the staff-student ratio to 1:10 (other than for medical subjects).

10. University buildings and facilities have been made available locally, regionally and nationally to a wide range of public, professional, educational and social welfare activities. The work of adult education and extramural departments is important in this context, and the Universities have also rendered valuable public service in accommodating the summer schools of the Open University.

The foregoing summary of the important contributions and services of Universities[56] can be amplified and illustrated in particular from the work of the Technological Universities, including their sandwich courses at first degree and higher levels such as IHD, CASE, Total Technology and Teaching Firms. All in all, it is high time that the 'ivory tower' image, whether leaning or upright, collapsed totally.

Maximising efficiency to offset diminishing resources

Hard times have compelled Universities to give increased attention to their use of resources. No longer is it possible to assume that funds for continuing expansion will be available. There was a remarkable change between 1966 and 1976, not due simply to the changed context wherein the books of the Universities became open to inspection by the Comptroller and Auditor General,[57] nor predominantly to the increasing policy-directing 'influence' of the UGC – as witness the *Notes for Guidance* and various publications. These have been influential of course but there has also been a genuine concern to maximise efficiency and a growing appreciation of the value of the Universities' resources and the need to deploy them wisely, not only for the good of their students but also for the benefit of the surrounding communities.

The analysis of organisations as social systems is by now a well-developed area in the spectrum of sociological studies. National business schools and Departments of Business and Management Studies have been established in Universities and Polytechnics and it was inevitable that, given time, these institutions would themselves be seen as fit subjects for study by the organisational theorists[58] and management experts.[59]

The setting up of a project team at Sussex University in 1971–72, supported by a DES grant, with staff from the University and from Peat, Marwick, Mitchell and Company (Management Consultants), was a significant development. The proposal was 'to examine the existing planning, management and budgeting systems and practices in a sample of British Universities, and, having considered any other management techniques and innovations, to produce recommendations in the form of a handbook of good practice which Universities may find helpful in solving some of their problems'. Five Universities were substantially involved, and twelve others visited, as well as two

275

Polytechnics. There was of course competent University administration before this date, but the report was timely and useful,[60] and the project an example of the growing number of co-operative ventures among Universities.

To optimise the use of existing buildings, equipment and plant is one obvious possible source of increased efficiency, but is by no means simple. There are two main possibilities – first to extend use throughout the year, either by a standard four-term year or by substantial introduction of (and required attendance at?) summer schools. Present indications are strongly against any University being able to go it alone: concerted efforts will be essential.[61] Moreover, the Universities are increasingly being used for other relevant activities in the vacations – short courses, summer schools, conferences – either for their own students or by letting facilities to professional and other bodies. Without all these, the influence of the University would be far less widely felt in the country at large.

The second possibility is to ensure as far as practicable the maximum utilisation of class and lecture rooms, laboratories and other specialised areas throughout the working week.[62] This may be achieved by central planning and control of the utilisation of space, especially in non-specialised teaching rooms. Limits are set by the design, layout, size and contiguity of buildings. Regular surveillance of the use of accommodation is essential – and the same is true of teaching facilities such as visual aids. Central planning is desirable, but academic considerations set definite limits to multiple usage.

The detailed analysis of operational costs occupies an important place in the assessment of efficient performance. Cost-benefit analysis is a device for relating costs, calculated on as full a basis as possible, to a future flow of benefits, discounted to a present value.[63] Against an estimate of all costs, regardless of who bears them, must be set a full estimation of benefits, direct and indirect, over as long a period of time as possible. The problem is to decide what the benefits are – income and other quantifiable effects, yes, but the imponderable effects of intellectual, personal, social and cultural growth are quite a different matter. Eric Ashby rightly emphasises that these imponderables result from personal contact and, for future innovators – master craftsmen, innovators in intellectual life and the pace-setters in cultural and moral standards – 'there is only one recipe: the sustained dialectic with a master whose own intellectual and cultural achievements are distinguished.'[64] True, but not for them only, or else the outlook for humankind would be depressing indeed.

The same applies to a differing degree, but not in a fundamentally different way, to all good teaching – or else why continue to try to improve the education of teachers: or invest in educational technology if it is not to free the teacher for closer relationships with the pupils? Again, Ashby rightly protests that applying cost-benefit analysis to non-vocational education is a nonsense, but notes that it can be applied to vocational education in gauging the rise in earnings on gaining a qualification, or the increased benefit which accrues to the economy. However, even here we should not overlook the importance of the personal and social aspects, which in relation to professional competence cannot be ignored.[65] Cost-benefit analysis, though an important aspect of maximising resources, is a contentious issue in academic circles because of the vulnerability of the qualities and values which cannot be quantified.

The Carnegie Report on *The more effective use of Resources*[66] comments on the process of effecting change in this area: that 'it will cause conflicts – of department *v.* department, of faculty against administration, of administration versus State authorities. Costs will confront quality; the new will challenge the old; the welfare of the total institution will battle against the status quo of its component parts. Unionisation becomes more likely as faculty members face some unpleasant changes, as they seek to defend what they have or what they have come to expect . . . It will cause a greater degree of centralisation of authority on campus – perhaps also in the co-ordinating Council or the State government . . . governance [therefore] becomes more difficult to arrange and to manage. . . .'

These points already echo in the British scene, and some begin to resonate with apprehension, as witness the concern of Alan Bullock about 'the dangerous attraction of cost-benefit analysis'.[67] Nevertheless, studies of costs will continue – as they should – costs of courses, of facilities and administration, of the collection of data, of establishing methods and criteria and determining the limits of application – the long and hard road emphasised by C. F. Carter in 1967.[68] Progress made by 1975 has been analysed by Pickford.[69]

This need to optimise scarce resources has stimulated and reinforced co-operation between Universities. Examples include combined research projects; MSc. courses run jointly to secure the necessary specialist staff and facilities; and access to large-scale and highly specialised equipment particularly if used on short runs for individual projects, as in nuclear physics, electron microscopy and computers. Planned provision of computers in Universities was inescapable, and the Computer Board for Universities and Research Councils was established in 1966.[70] A policy document, published by the Computer Board in January 1977, argues that all Universities and Polytechnics should be linked in a single computer network.[71]

The allocation to institutions of such specialised facilities is influenced by many factors, primarily the high academic standing of the particular department, but also by the needs of other institutions in the region, as well as by national considerations. Initial preeminence is thereby reinforced. Latecomers are likely simply to be participators in such schemes and not leaders: this is true of most of the new Universities including the technological, and particularly true of the Polytechnics, since they are much less committed to research.

The steady state

Clearly no institution can expand indefinitely, and in the case of educational institutions cessation of growth will be determined by student demand and the availability of finance, staff and land within the national plan of educational provision. The recently established Universities, both 'new' and Technological, are perhaps the most threatened by the cuts since they may have to settle for a steady state before they have reached their maximum potential. However, there are difficult and contentious implications in a standstill even for long-established Universities.[72]

In the steady state the number of students remains constant, and as UGC grant allocations relate closely to full-time equivalent (FTE) numbers, so will the main income of the University remain constant (in real terms, assuming full supplementation for inflation). With growth hitherto, money was fed into growing areas, so that senescent studies were not actually cut back but declined relatively. With the steady state, funds for new developments can come only by contracting existing activities. Interference with established practices is bound to create problems: such as, for example, abolishing or modifying life tenure, or by transferring vacancies from a Department to a Faculty or to a central pool for re-allocation in accordance with the changing needs of the University as a whole. Closing down any teaching or research activity is especially difficult but will certainly be unavoidable from time to time if new growth is to be fostered. The central problem, already discussed in relation to cost-benefit analysis, is to establish criteria and procedures for judging the relative importance of the activities at risk and to ensure the growth of important innovations. It is especially difficult to judge multi-disciplinary innovations which span more than one Faculty but are not crucial for any particular one.

The Cambridge General Board regarded an effective cessation of new developments as quite unacceptable and envisaged that 'the University will from time to time have to make decisions to cut out certain fields of study, perhaps even whole Departments. This will mean strengthening and developing the present procedures for reviewing critically the disciplines studied and the resources allocated to these disciplines'. The Board accordingly invited discussion of the criteria for deciding which fields of study should be relinquished, and also of the critically important question of staff redeployment as their subjects and Departments evolve or decline. Assistant lectureships and demonstratorships with limited tenure should be retained, but in most Universities, including the technological, these are rare.

Early retirement with generous redundancy payment offers possible solutions, but this and any of the foregoing changes could be introduced only on a national basis covering all institutions. Moreover, as academic independence is a primary and vital concern, effective safeguards would be needed to ensure that appointments were not renewed for the wrong reasons.

Two difficulties are likely to arise in the support of research. After 'pump-priming' grants made by the Research Councils it was customary, when the grant ran out, for the University to take over responsibility for the project and the staff. To a lesser extent the same procedure tended to apply to projects sponsored by industry, but this cannot continue as the norm in a steady state. Inter-University collaboration in the rationalisation of courses and transfer of staff may help a little, at least if it is transfer to a more prestigious institution . . . but the reverse would hardly be welcomed. Favoured Universities can hardly sustain the traditional arguments about the vital contribution of research to teaching, and simultaneously act in ways which discourage research and postgraduate studies in newly established Universities.

The General Board concluded that 'despite the strong financial pressures for expansion, the unique character of Cambridge would be changed irrevocably by an indefinite expansion, and that steps must be taken now to draw the expansion to a close in an orderly manner whilst developing the necessary procedures for coping with the steady state.'

For most other Universities in very different environments the situation is likely to be viewed differently. Many of them already possess the land required for their planned expansion. The UGC conducts a site capacity exercise every other year for which Universities supply maps showing areas of land available. Their 1971–72 survey showed that land already owned or zoned could accommodate 420,000 students, including residential capacity for 200,000,* and that in addition there was enough land available for purchase to accommodate a further 80,000 with 30,000 in residence. Thus site capacity is not a major problem: the limiting factors are finance and the supply of students. The DES Report 1975[73] indicated lower birth trends for 1980 than previous predictions.

However, Gareth Williams has argued that a gloomy view should not be accepted too readily.[74] From 1930 onwards the figures have shown alternating upswings and downswings, and he suggests that such cyclical behaviour is unlikely to cease. A long run of stability in higher education is improbable in a free society, assuming a dynamic economy: periods of growth which prove too fast to be good for us will alternate with painful periods of stagnation. The same is likely to be true of the demand for graduates in employment, which has its effect on the supply of recruits in the next generation. The mismatch of phases of supply and demand is due in part to the inertial effects of planning in the educational system in relation to economic changes generally, and in part to non-economic considerations such as family background and aspirations. Any cohort of young people refusing to take the chance of higher education will become a generation of parents who, having come up 'the hard way', will, on previous findings,[75] be the more likely to insist that their children commit themselves to full-time study after leaving school. However, in the context of the late seventies the falling birthrate seems likely to have a bigger impact on the demand for higher education than either inflation or unemployment.[76]

---

* See Brief Histories (Appendix II) for the sites available in 1975 for the Technological Universities.

Internationally, the cautious predictions in Britain should be set against the proportionately greater enrolment in the USA and their more optimistic assessments of future developments. Nevertheless, accepting that something like a 'steady state' is likely to last for ten years or so, the Universities and Polytechnics would be wise to prepare themselves for the rigours of limited expansion and lower costs per student place. There are many signs of change which suggest that this is already happening – more part-time degree courses, credit arrangements with the Open University and so on.[77]* Indeed in view of the inherent instability of the present phase, 'the unsteady state' is the better description. Symptoms of this stressful condition are evident, for example, in staff unionisation,[78]† in renewed claims for preferential financial support for some Universities as centres of excellence, and even for the closing down of some others,[79] and in an economic xenophobia inimical to international academic exchange and understanding.[80]

Chapter 11: Sources

1. Robert O. Berdahl, *British Universities and the State* (Cambridge University Press 1959), Chapter IV.

2. *Higher Technological Education*, Report of a Special Committee appointed in April 1944 (Chairman, Lord Eustace Percy), Ministry of Education, (HMSO, 1945).

3. Presented by the Lord President of the Council to Parliament by Command of His Majesty, May 1946, Cmnd. 6824 (HMSO).

4. For the difficulties of manpower prediction and of related educational requirements, see:
Alice Crampin and Peter Armitage, 'The pressure of numbers: speculation for the seventies', *Higher Education Review*, Spring 1970.
K. G. Gannicott and M. Blaug, *Manpower Forecasting since Robbins: A Science Lobby in Action, Higher Education Review*, Vol. 2, No. 1, September 1969.

5. (HMSO, 1950.)

6. Reported *THES*, 3rd December 1976.

7. See Appendix II.

* e.g. with Lancaster in 1975, and with Kent, Salford and Sussex Universities in 1976.

† In March 1976, the AUT voted on affiliation with the TUC. The result was in favour by 13,140 to 7,584, i.e. 20,724 voted out of 31,000 academics in the UK.

8. Presented to Parliament by the Secretary of State for Education and Science, Rt. Hon. Mrs Margaret Thatcher MP, December 1972, Cmnd. 5174 (HMSO).

9. From 1972 White Paper, *Education: a Framework for Expansion* (*as 8*), para. 129.

10. UGC *Memorandum of General Guidance*, pp. 64–71 of report, *University Development* 1967–72, Cmnd. 5728 (HMSO, 1974).

11. *Ibid.*, p. 65.

12. Top two rows *as 11*. Third row: 1972–73, 1973–74 and 1974–75 figures from UGC *Statistics of Education*, Vol. 6, 1972, 1973, 1974 (HMSO). 1975–76, figures from UGC *Annual Survey* 1975–76, Cmnd 6750 (HMSO, 1977). 1976–77 figures (provisional from) *Hansard* (House of Commons) 18th January 1977, col. 84, reported *THES*, 28th January 1977.

13. Cmnd. 5766 (HMSO, 1974) para. 9.

14. *Ibid.*, para. 10.

15. UGC communication, April 1977.

16. *As 13*, para. 13.

17. *Ibid.*, para. 16.

18. 1972 White Paper (*as 9*), paras. 134, 135.

19. *Ibid.*, para. 136.

20. *Ibid.*, para. 120.

21. *Ibid.*, paras, 141, 142.

22. *Ibid.*, para. 144.

23. *As 10*, paras. 148, 151; also paras. 80, 81 re 'full-time equivalent students'.

24. Criticisms are made on these matters in paras. 24–28 of the Report (HMSO, 1976) of the Committee of Inquiry into Local Government Finance set up in 1974 (Chairman, Mr Frank Layfield QC).
    See also Pratt and Burgess, *Polytechnics, a Report* (Pitman, 1974).

25. *As 9*, para. 143.

26. Brian MacArthur, *THES*, 8th December 1972.

27. Sir Norman Lindop, *THES*, 26th January 1973.

28. *Polytechnics, a Report* (*as 24*) p. 113.

29. E. H. Simpson (Deputy Secretary, DES) Council of Europe *Information Bulletin*, 2/1974, p. 7.

30. *As 9*, para. 132.

31. *Student numbers in higher Education in England and Wales*, DES Education Planning Paper No. 2, para. 7.6 (which includes the figures for Scotland) (HMSO, 1970).

32. Vera Morris and Gerry Fowler, *THES*, 12th January 1972.
    See also Symposium, 'Framework for binary consummation', Colin Crouch, Boris Ford, A. H. Halsey, A. W. Merrison, Miss J. E.

Skinner, G. Tolley, *Universities Quarterly*, Spring 1973. But note White Paper (*as 9*), para. 8.

33. Gareth Williams, 'Must we choose between nursery and University?' *THES*, 28th December 1972.

34. Gareth Williams, 'The events of 1973–4 in a long-term planning perspective', Lancaster University *Higher Education Bulletin*, Autumn 1974.

35. *The Times* editorial, 7th December 1972, 'From the Cradle to the Ph.D'.
    Nature editorial, 15th December 1972, 'Squeeze on postgraduates'; also 22nd December 1972.
    THES editorial, 8th December 1972.
    Asa Briggs, Geoffrey Caston, *THES*, 15th December 1972.
    R. C. Griffiths, 'Ominous proposals for University staff-student ratio', *THES*, 29th December 1972.

36. Brian MacArthur, *THES*, 8th December 1972.

37. Alfred Morris, 'Grants squeeze may be more savage than intended', *THES*, 15th December, 1972.

38. See Annabel Ferriman *THES*, 22nd October 1976.
    Sir Alec Merrison, 'The Education of Ministers of State', *New Universities Quarterly*, Winter 1975, and the response from Maurice Peston, 'The Education of Vice-Chancellors', *New Universities Quarterly*, Spring 1976.

39. White Paper on *Public Expenditure to 1977–78* Cmnd. 5519 (HMSO, February 1976).

40. *Hansard* (House of Commons), 21st January 1974, Cols 232–33.

41. Lord Annan, Provost, University College, London, *Annual Report*, 1973–74.

42. Announced by Rt. Hon. Reg Prentice MP, *Hansard* (House of Commons), Written Answer, 25th November 1974, Col. 39.

43. Enquiry initiated by Rt. Hon. Lord Crowther-Hunt, Minister of State DES, early in 1975 – see Report summarising preliminary conclusions: '16 and 19-year olds: attitudes to Education', Gareth Williams and Alan Gordon, Lancaster University, *Higher Education Bulletin*, Winter 1975, Vol. 4, No. 1.

44. Reported *The Times*, 3rd April 1975.

45. Cmnd. 6393 (HMSO, 1976).

46. Rt. Hon. Fred Mulley, Secretary of State DES, *Hansard* (House of Commons), 11th March 1976, Col. 326, reported *The Times*, 12th March 1976.

47. CVCP reaction reported *The Times*, 12th March 1976.

48. Lord Crowther-Hunt, Minister of State, Higher Education, first hinted at change in the quinquennial system (*THES*, 3rd October

1975) and Mr Gerry Fowler MP, his successor, was reported (*THES*, 12th March 1976) as stating that the Government is reviewing priorities in University finance and may well abandon the quinquennial system or modify or replace the dual support of academic research.

49. Tuition Fees: Interim Report of a Joint Working Party, CVCP, November 1975.

Tony Flowerdew and Richard Layard, 'The case for "conditional grants" for home students', *THES*, 26th March 1976.

50. Carnegie Commission Report, *The More Effective Use of Resources; an Imperative for Higher Education* (McGraw Hill, New York 1974).

51. DES Press notice, 25th November 1976.

52. See *THES*, 2nd July 1976, 'Differential is greatest sin', Annabel Ferriman *THES*, 29th October 1976, 'Fee rise may bring first fall in University numbers since 1936'.

John Griffith, 'Taking for granted', *New Statesman*, 4th March 1977.

Ralf Dahrendorf 'Fear is the spur behind this unrest', *THES*, 11th March 1977.

53. Richard Way, Letter to *The Times*, 14th March 1977, 'University Fees'.

54. For general background see *British Universities and Polytechnics and Overseas Development:* report of a working group: Chairman, Sir Michael Swann FRS (published by the Inter University Council in January 1977, copies from 90/91 Tottenham Court Road, London).

55. Report of the Vice-Chancellor 1974–5, University of Durham.

56. For a detailed summary of this stressful quinquennium see the *Report on the Period 1972–76* published by CVCP. Summarised in *THES*, 1st September 1976.

See also Peter Scott, 'Decline and fall of a five-year plan for University financing', *THES* 15th October 1976.

57. See UGC report: *University development 1967–72* (HMSO, September 1974) paras. 183–186, 'Relations with Parliament'.

Also 'Autonomy and Accountability' by Sir Kenneth Berrill, former Chairman UGC, *THES*, 14th June 1964.

58. A. K. Rice, *The Modern University: a model organisation* (Tavistock, London 1970) and *The Enterprise and its Environment* (Tavistock, London 1971).

E. J. Miller and A. K. Rice, *Systems of Organisation* (Tavistock, London 1967).

59. Glenn E. Brooks, 'Administrative modernisation in British Universities', *Universities Quarterly*, Autumn 1973.

Michael Pickford, *University Expansion: Costs, Potential Economies and Finance* (Sussex University Press, 1975), Bibliography, pp. 216–21.

60. J. Fielden and G. Lockwood, *Planning and Management in Universities* (Sussex University Press, 1973).

See Review, *Higher Education*, 4 (1975), pp. 119–20.

61. David S. P. Hopkins, 'An Analysis of University Year-Round Operation', *Socio. Econ. Plan. Sci.*, Vol. 7, 1973, pp. 177–87.

62. K. S. Davies, Report on *The utilisation of non-specialised teaching rooms*, prepared for The Committee of Vice-Chancellors and Principals of Universities of the UK, 1968.

Space utilisation in Universities and Polytechnics, University Building Note 12, UGC and DES Architects, 1974.

63. John Vaizey, *The Economics of Education* (Macmillan, London 1973; also Faber & Faber, London 1962).

See also Michael Pickford, 'Costing University resources', *Universities Quarterly*, Summer 1974.

For the wider context and significance of cost-benefit analysis (CBA, see W. J. M. Mackenzie, *Power, Violence, Decision* (Penguin, 1975), Chapter 17.

64. Lord Ashby, *Adapting Universities to a Technological Society* (Jossey-Bass, London 1974), pp. 142–43.

65. Compare J. A. Bottomley *et al.*, *Studies in institutional management in Higher Education, Costs and Potential Economies* (OECD, Paris 1971).

See also: 'Cost-effectiveness: a study of potential economies per student at the University of Bradford', in *Commonwealth Universities and Society*, the report of the proceedings of the Eleventh Congress of the Universities of the Commonwealth, Edinburgh, August 1973 (Association of Commonwealth Universities, London 1974), pp. 205–20.

John (now Lord) Vaizey, 'The cost of Higher Education', pp. 220–24 of the same proceedings.

Michael Pickford, *Universities Quarterly*, Summer 1974; and 'A Statistical Analysis of University Administrative Expenditure', *J. R. Statist. Soc.*, Vol. 637, part I, 1974; also *University Expansion: Costs, Potential Economies and Finance, ibid.*

G. Wilson and Pamela Lewis, 'Cost Studies in Higher Education', *Higher Education Review*, Spring 1970.

D. W. Verry, 'Rates of return on University education with economies of scale: a comment', *Higher Education*, Vol. 3, 1974, p. 231.

66. *As 50*, para. 16, p. 21.

67. Sir Alan (now Lord) Bullock, 'Why Universities are not a luxury', *THES*, 14th February 1975.

68. C. F. Carter, 'The Structure of University Costs' in *Research into Higher Education 1967*, papers presented at the third annual conference of the SRHE, December 1967, (SRHE, London March 1968), pp. 19–26. The paper discusses an exercise in cost analysis recently conducted by the Committee of Vice-Chancellors.

69. Michael Pickford, *University Expansion: Costs, Potential Economies and Finance* (Sussex University Press, 1975).

70. See Report for 1974–75, Cmnd. 6221 (HMSO).

71. *Computers in Higher Education and Research: The Next Decade* (HMSO, 1977).

72. Report of the General Board on 'The long-term development of the University'. III, Steady-State University (Cambridge University, 17th December 1974).

73. Report No. 82/March 1975, *Teachers for the 1980s: Statistical Projections and Calculations* (DES Information Room).

74. Gareth Williams, Professorial Inaugural Lecture, *Higher Education and the Stable State*, Lancaster University, 27th November 1974.
'Facing up to the problems of steady-state Universities', *THES* editorial, 17th January 1975.

75. Ethel Venables, 'The human costs of part-time day release', *Higher Education*, Vol. 1, No. 3, 1972, p. 283.

76. Pat Healy, *The Times*, 2nd December 1976.
See also Ernest Rudd, 'What a falling birthrate will mean to Universities in 1982', *THES*, 19th November 1976.
John Maddox, 'Facing the facts of Britain's baby slump', *TES*, 9th July 1976.

77. Reported *THES*, 2nd April 1976.

78. *As 50*, pp. 87, 111, 117.
'American Colleges in a Steady State', *The Economist*, 21st September 1974.
Meghnad Desai, 'Industry Bill: is it relevant to University management?', *THES*, 28th March 1975.
Brian MacArthur, 'Unionisation moves as financial squeeze tightens on all sides', *THES*, 28th March 1975.
'Eleven reasons why affiliation should be supported', *THES*, 20th February 1976.
Trevor Marshall, 'Why we should join the TUC . . .'
Graeme Moodie, '. . . and why we should not', *THES*, 27th February 1976.
A. H. Halsey, 'Is a gentlemanly class to be proletarianised?', *THES*, 5th March 1976.
See also *THES*, 26th March 1976 (after the vote).

79. Dr R. B. (now Sir Robert) Hunter, Vice-Chancellor of the University of Birmingham, reported *THES*, 18th July 1975.

80. For a selection from the period of controversy about fees for overseas

students see *THES*, 21st March 1975, 17th October 1975, 31st October 1975, 28th November 1975, 5th December 1975, 19th December 1975; *Guardian*, 4th November 1975; *The Times*, 10th November 1975; *TES*, 30th January 1975, 20th February 1976, and note particularly:

Dr E. G. Edwards, Vice-Chancellor, Bradford University (the only university which still charges the same fees for UK residents and overseas students), letter to *The Times*, 28th November 1975

'Subsidy for overseas students', *The Times* editorial, 23rd January 1976.

Tim Devlin, 'Why overseas students should not be made to pay more', *The Times*, 10th February 1976.

Tony Flowerdew and Richard Layard, 'How much should overseas students pay?', *THES*, 19th March 1976.

'Overseas students and fees', *THES* editorial, 21st March 1975.

12

The Future: Institutional Change and Interdependence

THE two decades 1956–76 span a period of substantial social and educational change against a background of international upheaval, both political and economic, and the final year dawned in an atmosphere of profound uncertainty about the future. In such circumstances it is all too easy to be so oppressed with the problems which have to be faced that the resilience and initiatives needed to cope with them are inhibited. Educators should not add to the gloom by undervaluing the real advances during these years. These are summarised in Table 12.1.[1]

The increase in full-time enrolments is striking, and indicates rising social and educational expectations and a realisation by school-leavers of the importance of further study and training. The increase in numbers was accompanied by an increase in the number and the diversity of institutions and courses. The newly created institutions were not unique in any sense but were set strongly in existing moulds, the 'new' Universities conforming substantially to traditional patterns: the Polytechnics following in the footsteps of the former CATs, using the newly constituted CNAA which was modelled on the NCTA. As with all such emergent institutions they planned to make good former deficiencies and seize new opportunities, but even so marked an innovation as the Open University made no attempt to create a new degree system. As for the Technological Universities, their functions as former CATs have been blended with the new ones made possible by University conditions. Within the range of higher education institutions they can be seen as a bridge between traditional Universities and the Polytechnics.

Sir Alex Smith recognised this in a recent statement:[2]* '. . . one must remember that within the Universities themselves there is a

* Chairman of the Committee of Directors of Polytechnics (CDP).

288

Table 12.1 Growth of higher and Further Education, 1956–57 and 1975–76: enrolments

| | 1956-57 | | | 1975-76 | | | Ratio of increase | | |
| | Full-time | Part-time | | Full-time* | Part-time | | Full-time | Part-time | |
		Day	Evening		Day	Evening		Day	Evening
Universities (UK)	92,100	16,600		268,700†		26,300	1:2·9		1:1·6
Further Education (England and Wales)	66,700	42,000	1,415,800	340,200	729,300	2,628,800	1:5·1	1:17·4	1:1·9

Notes: * Full-time includes sandwich courses. † Includes 7,400 students in Northern Ireland.

very wide spectrum. There are Universities very much on the basic end of science: there are those who concentrate on cultivating relationships with industry just as we do: there are highly technological Universities and you may find it difficult to differentiate between a highly technological University and what is happening in a Polytechnic.' On the other side of the Polytechnics – as it were – are the newly emerging Institutes of Higher Education[3] in which 'advanced work is going on – I suppose that there is much less in the way of research there than there is in the Polytechnics, but it is a spectrum.'*

Range of functions within institutions of higher education

The diversification of institutions and of courses alongside the increases in enrolments has produced the outline of a loosely related system of higher education with a considerable overlap of functions between institutions. For the purposes of this study these have been considered in three separate groups: Polytechnics, Technological Universities and all other Universities. There is no lack of diversity within each of these groups. No single institution can command the whole range of knowledge, if only because of the scarcity of highly specialised staff and of material resources. There are many other factors – historical, geographical and personal – determining the detailed structure and functioning of any one institution but as collectively they attempt to cover the necessarily very wide range of academic objectives, overlapping of functions is inevitable.

'To establish an array of institutions of higher education each uniquely characterised in its functions, and for each of which a uniquely characterised group of students can be selected annually with absolute accuracy, is a task fortunately incapable of achievement; but this appears still to be the unspoken underlying ideal assumption of much discussion about the planning of institutions and

* The Institutes of Higher Education are multifunctional institutions which have been created in line with the policy set out in DES Circular 7/73, though they are not referred to as such. By August 1976 some 24 combined Colleges had been formed by the amalgamation or federation of about 67 Colleges (mostly of Education or Further Education) though not all bear the title 'Institute'. No special provisions will apply to their governance but staff conditions of service will be agreed separately by the LEA in association with the NATFHE. Where courses lead to a teaching qualification, the instrument as well as the articles of government will probably require approval by the DES.

their relationships. Indeed it is the most charitable explanation of the aggressive, overcompensating publicity attendant on the creation of the "new" Universities, the upgrading of the CATs into Technological Universities, and on the emergence of the Polytechnics. None of the new, upgraded or newly emergent institutions is uniquely determined or characterised, whatever its protagonists have claimed'* – which is really more advantageous for the students and the body politic. Selection with absolute accuracy is impossible, individual changes of interests and motivations are not predictable, and occupational changes and choices are not strictly determinable. Planned changes in the educational system take years to become fully effective, and by that time the circumstances for which they were designed may have altered substantially.

Nevertheless, by the early 1970s a pattern could be discerned between the three groups in relation to types of provision and enrolments which in the case of the two most recent ones – Technological Universities and Polytechnics – have, despite controversy based on hindsight, followed fairly closely the ideas of their originators. With the present pattern as a model for the future, allowing for some additions and modifications, and making some assumptions, a comprehensive system of higher education can be envisaged which could cater for all would-be learners beyond school and Further Education College. Within such a system each institution can be autonomous provided that they all appreciate their mutual interdependence. In this way the notion of a batting order could be ignored and overlapping functions seen to be not only inevitable but also desirable.[5] If hierarchical ideas persist then non-degree work, local recruitment and part-time courses will be viewed as inferior and institutions working in these areas will undervalue them and concentrate their energies on recruiting undergraduates aiming for traditional honours degrees.

Dr Suddaby (then Chairman-Elect of the CDP) in his evidence to the Select Committee[6] made the point that the proportions of research 'at the moment are very disparate – in the Universities they

* This passage appears in *Patterns and Policies in Higher Education*,[4] chapter 'Expansion and Overlap of Functions' by the present author – I wryly admitted to having done my bit at the time (of emergence of the CATs), and commented that the gentle art of overstatement is a curious fact of public advocacy and exposition (especially when resources are scarce): this is a particular hazard of the mass media.

have twenty-five times as much as we have, whereas [their] under-graduate teaching is only two and a half times as much'. It would have been surprising if the ratio of grants received had been other-wise at this early stage of the development of the Polytechnics. The important question remains, however, as to whether they should seek to compare with the Universities as regards research. The CDP evidence was that the volume in 1975 was insufficient for the support and stimulus of teaching, and especially for postgraduate and post-experience courses. Nevertheless they recognised 'that it would be absolutely wrong to claim that research should be in the same proportion with respect to undergraduate teaching as it is in the Universities',[7] thus accepting the White Paper's indication that Polytechnics should be mainly teaching institutions.

Sir Alex Smith has commented that this is rather a negative characterisation of function. More positively and constructively, he argues for a dual stimulation and intellectual refreshment through research and '. . . through participation in those wider aspects of society for which we educate people' – in the practice of social work or teaching and its improvement. The refreshment of teachers can come from participating in such practical activities 'rather than in doing narrow academic research'.[8] According to Sir Norman Lindop* this 'rapidly becomes a very enthusiastically adopted philosophy' among new teaching staff recruited from Universities,[9] and could clearly be of great importance in ensuring acceptable goals for staff and students. In sum, Polytechnics will have a research commitment, possibly three to five times their present scale, though not comparable in scale with that of the Universities, together with a strong com-mitment to professional training.†

In contrast, the teaching function to first degree level is shared be-tween Polytechnics and Universities, but there is no significant over-lap in courses of non-degree level; these do and should increasingly constitute a distinctive feature of the Polytechnics, though it is one which they share with the Institutes of Higher Education, the Technical Colleges and other Further Education establishments. 'Advanced work is not the exclusive prerogative of the Polytech-

* Past Chairman of the CDP.

† SRC Report, *Support of Research and Postgraduate Training in the Polytechnics* (HMSO, October 1977). The Council agree with the recommendation that 'emphasis should be placed on vocational and applied aspects in postgraduate training in the Polytechnics'.

nics . . .' and 'some 30 per cent of the full-time and sandwich field and over 50 per cent in the part-time field is at present and will continue to be carried out in Colleges which were not designated'.[10] The respective academic staff are not totally different groups but come to a varying extent from similar backgrounds, for example with experience of industry, commerce and various professions which, as with the Technological Universities, are reflected in their qualifications. Despite certain expectations, students in the various sectors come largely from similar backgrounds, and there is a range of ability throughout with no sharp demarcations. However, there is in general a concentration of superior ability (as judged by A-levels) in long-established Universities.

This is emphatically not to suggest that the Polytechnics are not *'distinctive'* (as opposed to *'unique'*) in their contributions to higher education. On the contrary, their particular blend – of course levels (advanced non-degree and first and higher degree) combined with a variety of modes of operation (in full-time and sandwich, part-time day and evening, and intensive short courses) and their close links with industry and commerce in the locality and the region – makes them notably distinctive. They need no apology, least of all as a defensive reaction against the Universities.[11] The time is overdue for Polytechnic advocates to realise that if they protest too loudly about status all that happens is that others are convinced that the Polytechnics are convinced they have not got it. The same is true of protests about Polytechnics lacking friends: such reactions are apt to be self-fulfilling – a very regrettable sequel with so large and important an educational opportunity to be seized.

Characterisation of the Technological Universities

All Universities are now in varying degrees involved in the application of knowledge, and for the Technological Universities this is a special commitment from the past. This important fact of continuity must not be overlooked, as the view has frequently been taken that the CATs should not have become Universities, because this was bound to lead them to modify, even to abandon, some of their major functions and characteristics. Put another way, it was rather assumed that on transition they would simply and inevitably succumb to conforming influences on joining 'the University club'. In the event the objects specified for the Technological Universities would have been equally appropriate for Charters of the Royal Colleges, as suggested by the Principals' Committee.* The difference lies only in the name.

In coming to their decision to recommend that the CATs become Technological Universities, the Robbins Committee presumably felt that it was quite possible to accommodate a specialised group of Universities within the existing system, a speculation compatible with their note of caution against attempting to combine CATs with existing Universities.[12]

Two questions remain: what if anything would have been gained by having Royal Colleges? and secondly, has the fact of being under the UGC seriously hampered the development and degree of innovation, or changed the characters of the former CATs? The first question raises a host of others: would the RCTs have remained under the Local Authorities (as chartered institutions?), or have been direct grant institutions of the DES – as the Open University and Cranfield Institute of Technology have become: or would some new Technology Grants Committee have been appropriate, or even indispensable: in which case what would have been the relationships with Government and in turn with the UGC and the Universities? There would be the need to relate grant support and investment in similar areas elsewhere, e.g. science and technology in traditional Universities. Besides the policy and administrative questions, other aspects are also significant – a Committee of Rectors of RCTs would presumably have been excluded from membership of the Vice-Chancellors' Committee (CVCP); and from the Association of Commonwealth Universities (the admittance of the unorthodox Open *University* cannot serve as a guide). These latter questions concern particular derivative aspects of the status and functioning of higher education institutions in the workaday academic world; but the basic question is quite other – have the characteristics, functions and relationships of the former Colleges of Advanced Technology been seriously neglected, impaired or become atrophied in their first decade as Technological Universities?

The first main characteristic to be considered is that of the academic spectrum of work, i.e. the high concentration of effort and resources in science and technology. The Principals' Committee recommendation (1962), that the proportion should be reduced by the inclusion of relevant social sciences, is now regarded as a self-

* See Chapter 1.

294

evident proposition. Table 12.2[13] compares their proposals in 1962 with the position in 1974.

The position is quite clear: engineering and the natural and applied sciences still account for two thirds of their work and the rest is made up of social, administrative, business and management studies (the provision for which has almost doubled) together with studies in language and education.

Thus, as a group, the Technological Universities have so far remained faithful to their initial intentions. The UGC has recorded

Table 12.2 Proportions of subject groups: recommended and actual percentages 1962 and 1974

Subject group*	As recommended to the Robbins Committee by the Committee of Principals of the CATs†		8 Technological Universities 1974‡		All UK Universities 1974‡	
Technology	65	80	43·0	67·6	15·8	39·6
Science	15		24·6		23·8	
Social Science	10		19·6		24·4	
Other§	10		12·8		36·0	

Notes: * As in Table 8.11.   † See Table 1.2.   ‡ Condensed from Table 10.3.
   § 'Others' include:
   for ex-CATs: education, languages and paramedical studies (e.g. pharmacy, ophthalmic optics);
   for Universities: education, medicine and dentistry, humanities.

that they have received convincing evidence of the determination of the Universities to respond to the needs of industry. At their visits to the Universities based on the former Colleges of Advanced Technology, there was unanimous affirmation of continuing industrial commitment, and resolution to maintain, often against difficulties of placement, the sandwich course principle.[14]

These Universities have recognised the importance of the social sciences, not only as ends in themselves but also as disciplines relevant to the study of the human and social consequences of scientific and technological developments. They have become an integral part of professional studies and stand in the same relationship to administrative and management studies as do the basic sciences to technology. 'Other studies' are around 13 per cent and there has been no general attempt to establish traditional Arts Faculties.

One pair of statements (7 and 25) in the Academic Staff Enquiry related to the desirability of Technological Universities establishing Arts Faculties, and a second pair was framed in the context of the Universal coverage of subjects by a University, i.e. whether it would be complete without a Faculty of Technology (No. 5) or of Arts (No. 19).

The first pair produced results inconsistent with the other items of the attitude inventory and were not included in the 'CAT man' score. The spread of results is shown in detail in Table AIV9 and, far from providing a clear picture of eight similar institutions set on a steady course towards a common goal, they indicate – particularly in relation to this question of Arts Faculties – considerable disagreement among staff both within institutions and between them.

There is still a strong commitment to technology and the natural sciences but staffing changes could bring about a shift in the balance of Faculties, judging by the responses to statements 5 and 19. Table AIV10 shows that 70 per cent of all respondents considered a Faculty of Technology essential for all Universities and 66 per cent felt the same about Arts Faculties. In the latter case the figure was 53 per cent among the 'old stagers' and 80 per cent among the latest appointees.* Differences by date of appointment were less in the case of the technology statement, varying only between 74 and 69 per cent.

In recorded discussions, when such issues arose, the question was put – 'Do you think that by the mid-1980's the former CATs will still be an identifiable group of institutions, or do you think they will simply be "neo-civic"?' (that is closely resembling the Civic Universities, with traditional Arts Faculties, but with strong commitment to science and technology). The response was very varied, often pragmatic and consistent with the questionnaire responses: from *'We will see how we go'*, to *'We will add subjects if need be to our main commitment in science and technology as we have done in the social sciences'*. Certainly there was no marked inclination towards the traditional in the matter of Arts Faculties. It would no doubt be surprising if Senates with strongly entrenched Faculties of Science and Technology were to vote considerable resources for these purposes in a period of economic stringency.

* This group contained most of the social scientists and 'others'.

The second characteristic to be considered in relation to the change of status is the commitment to sandwich courses, pioneered as they were by the Colleges of Advanced Technology. Enrolments in these courses have continued to increase in absolute numbers but recently they have declined as a proportion of total enrolments (Diagram 5.2). This is due in the main to two external causes – the diminishing applications nationally for science and technology courses, and the difficulty of arranging training places in industry, commerce and professional work generally, difficulties which have been exacerbated by the serious economic crisis. The whole problem is trans-binary, and is too large to be left to the unrelated efforts of individual institutions and departments. However, something much more is needed than the limited recommendations of the Report of the Universities, Polytechnics and Industry Committee (UPIC).[15]* Government action, and the active involvement of the Training Resources Agency and the industrial training boards in seeking out and approving basic training places in industry, are essential. This, however, implies the will to continue. Although there is no sign of diminishing intent at present the will could be weakened if the proportion of staff with no prior commitment to sandwich courses increases since the difficulties in arranging them are, admittedly, greater than for full-time courses. Such a change would be deplored by many of the present staff in the Technological Universities since they see the primary commitment to sandwich courses, and the close contact with industry and commerce which these entail, as a touchstone of their institutional well-being. In the absence of a national body appointed by the Secretary of State,† UPIC will need to be more imaginative, vigorous and sustained in its efforts to ensure that sandwich courses increase and prosper.

Over the last decade the lack of sufficient students of ability coming forward for first degree courses in engineering and other technologies has been a seemingly intractable problem.[16] The time has long been overdue for concerted action and innovation to remedy this serious situation,[17] and it is a relief to note some signs of official action at last (1977). Various proposals under discussion at national level can only be briefly noted here: an initiative by the

* Discussed at the *National Conference on Degree Sandwich Courses*, organised by UPIC, 15th–17th April 1975.
† Representations on this matter failed, giving UPIC the opportunity and responsibility to become really effective.

UGC to establish a comparatively small number of honours level first degree courses of very high quality with a pronounced orientation towards manufacturing industry; and also the possibility, preferably jointly with industry, of organising a scholarship scheme for outstanding students of engineering.[18] The Secretary of State has the intention to amend the Award Regulations so that students may receive payments of up to £500 a year from sponsoring bodies or through scholarships, in addition to the normal £185, without prejudice to the award of mandatory grants by Local Authorities.[19]

Table 12.3 Proportions of postgraduate students 31st October 1976

| University | Full-time students | | | Postgraduates as % of total |
	Under-graduates	Post-graduates	TOTAL	
Aston	4,127	1,000	5,127	*19·5*
Bath	3,018	482	3,500	*13·8*
Bradford	3,713	689	4,402	*15·7*
Brunel	1,991	473	2,464	*19·2*
City	2,123	358	2,481	*14·4*
Loughborough	3,350	572	3,862	*13·3*
Salford	3,726	497	4,223	*11·8*
Surrey	2,546	496	3,042	*16·3*
TOTALS	24,594	4,507	29,101	*15·5*
All Universities Great Britain	222,892	49,595	272,487	*18·2*

Welcome though these schemes will be, they should not distract attention and support from assisting the flow of ability up through the existing structure of courses – from part-time to full-time, from diploma to degree courses, and, on graduation from first degree general/inter-disciplinary courses to one year pre-industry orientation courses. Establishment of the proposed new courses must not engender the notion that all high ability will in future go only by that route – social conditions and differing maturing rates will prevent that (however perfect the selection of those who present themselves). In this respect the plea of the TUC that the Universities should open their gates to more mature students is most pertinent.[20]

Meeting the needs of industry and commerce in terms of professional training, postgraduate teaching, management studies and applied research were the other basic commitments envisaged for the Technological Universities, and these intentions have been fairly faithfully fulfilled in all eight institutions. Table 12.3[21] shows the proportion of postgraduate students towards the end of the second decade.

As with other Universities, the technological ones receive financial support for research from a variety of external sources. Their expenditure for the year 1st August 1975 to 31st July 1976 was as follows:* Research Councils £1,721,000 (38·7 per cent); Government departments £1,196,000 (26·9 per cent); industry and commerce £874,000 (19·7 per cent); other bodies £652,00 (14·7 per cent); total £4,443,000 (100 per cent). The figures do not include expenditure from the universities' own funds on staff salaries, wages or equipment, etc. provided for research.

A basic tenet of British Universities is that teaching and research are interrelated activities, and in consequence they are not costed separately in terms of salaries in the official statistics of income and expenditure. In 1973, at the end of their first decade, expenditure under 'Teaching and Research' in the Technological Universities was £21,802,000 – 60 per cent of the total expenditure of £36,048,000. The figures for all Universities was £281·9m, which was 64 per cent of the total.

In one area the intentions of at least some of the ex-CATs have not been fulfilled, i.e. in the scale of provision for part-time degree courses. Part-time non-degree courses were transferred to other Technical Colleges, but part-time degree courses, previously provided for external students of London University, dwindled. For example, consideration was given to the idea of developing Aston as 'a Midlands Birkbeck', but it came to nothing: partly because of decreasing demand and partly because of other preoccupations. Most of the part-time students in the Technological Universities now are on M Sc. or post-experience courses.† It is, however, likely that there will be a resurgence of part-time degree courses in all Universities.

* Figures for *expenditure* on research from external sources of income supplied by the particular universities.

† The UGC *Annual Survey* 1974–75[22] stated that there were in the Universities 'very large numbers of part-time and post-experience students. The Committee are arranging for the collection of more comprehensive statistics in this important area'.

The pressures to maximise opportunities for all types of student, sparked off partly by the success of the Open University and endorsed by the economic need to make full use of expensive facilities, are likely to grow and the changing ideas about continuing or life-long education add to such pressures.[23]

Social class differences are one aspect of the problem of increasing University enrolments and some criticise educational institutions, such as the Open University, the Technological Universities and most recently the Polytechnics, for failing to attract so-called 'working-class' students. The argument is circular and sterile since one of the main components for determining social class ratings is educational level, e.g. age of leaving school, attendance at FE and HE institutions. The child of a father rated social class V who goes to a University immediately jumps two or three points up the rating scale. As a hierarchical scale its usefulness is limited: the sociologists find farmers, artists, musicians and many other indispensable citizens – all of whom may or may not be well-read – difficult to fit into a scale of social class.

Improving the system

In considering future trends it is useless to produce a blueprint requiring creation *ab initio*; we must start with things as they are. The total investment in sites, building plant and equipment, in academic and administrative staff is too great, and the inherent inertial effect too compelling, to permit wholesale conversion. Thus our starting point is the loosely related system of diverse institutions that we have, providing education post-18, and the question is whether the policy should be to move towards a system of comprehensive institutions or towards a comprehensive system of diversified institutions. The facts of institutional history and geographical location make the former alternative very difficult to achieve, and the inadequacy of resources to provide qualified staff and the lack of material resources to teach all subjects equally everywhere make it impossible.[24] Moreover, some specialisation of function and concentration of effort within an institution is beneficial.

The existing system of diversified institutions could be improved in two closely related ways: by spelling out their functions and their distinctive roles more explicitly and by improving their interrelationships to facilitate movement between them. As things are, students can find themselves stuck in some predestined groove from which escape is difficult. Commenting on this problem in a House of Lords debate* on the Universities, Lord Robbins said in relation to his own Report that 'the Committee on Higher Education . . . recommended expansion . . . explicitly on a specific condition: namely that there should be less specialisation in first degrees. I quote – we should not recommend so large an expansion as we do unless we were confident it would be accompanied by a big increase in the number of students taking broader degrees. In my judgement, in this respect at any rate, the Universities have not done as much as was expected. The impression I still receive is of an undue preponderance of honours specialisation . . . This is splendid for producing dons to produce dons to produce dons, or high experts in a particularly narrow line but, in my judgement, is not necessarily so splendid for those who are to do the main work of the world, a world which demands as much versatility as it does high expertise.'[25] Now that we have a wider range of institutions offering degree courses, the provision of a wider spectrum – from very broad to highly specialised – should be facilitated. The creation of the Polytechnics and most recently of the Institutes of Higher Education should also increase the national commitment to diploma and similar advanced courses such as, for example, the National Diplomas for technicians and designers and the Diploma of Higher Education.

Perhaps the worst feature of the present system of separate and often unrelated institutions is its rigidity. We need a number of focal points of flexibility to ensure sufficient degrees of freedom to meet the varying needs of students and any changing aspirations during periods of study. Such increased flexibility could come through a greater diversity of routes coupled with improved design of preparatory courses and the use of the skills of the educational technologists. Instead of regarding each year of a course as a preordained step function of the succeeding one (i.e. critical barriers to further progress) each year's results could be used diagnostically to decide which next step is the most appropriate. Such a suggestion is a complete reversal of the attitude within Further Education Colleges in the past, where high failure rates were common and were generally regarded as a proof of high standards.† The maintenance of high

---

* Debate initiated by Lord Fulton.

† This recalls the story, possibly apocryphal, of the visit of an H M I to a college whose pass results were consistently high above the national average, to

standards is of course essential, but in the old Further Education examinations it was the rigidities of the system which were a major cause of failure and consequent discouragement.

The flow of students each way between part-time, sandwich and full-time courses must become an established feature of the educational scene if we are to begin to move towards recurrent or lifelong educational provision. Movement between institutions must also be made easier to cope with occupational mobility and the difficulties of such transfers could be greatly eased by the supply of texts, tapes and other aids to learning. The setting up of 'resource centres', perhaps by or in collaboration with the Open University,[26] could help to bridge educational gaps however caused; but the most important requirement is increased collaboration between institutions to allow open access to a wide variety of students. There is no need for further institutional changes such as an Open College or Open School to repeat the work of the Open University in other fields. Collaboration and an adequate resource centre could meet the need, given the will. Several European countries already operate schemes for paid educational leave[27] in order to foot the bill for continuing education and Gösta Rehn's social insurance plan is feasible and also flexible, since it provides for leave from work for a variety of purposes.[28]

Increasing the number of places in higher education does not necessarily widen the *social* catchment of 18-year-olds, and there is no guarantee that greater flexibility would be any more effective. It is likely that once again it would be students from the well-informed, literate, middle-class families who would benefit most. This problem cannot be solved by institutional action alone: the causes are deeply embedded in the family and its economic and occupational history. Publicity campaigns reach only a small fraction of the people in the large sector of society categorised as social classes IV and V, as the experience of the Open University has shown.* If widely based re-

enquire what was wrong, how it could have happened, and how it could be rectified.

* The illiterate are, manifestly, very difficult to reach but progress has been made with the BBC's special campaign programmes 'On the Move' and 'Your Move Now', together with the back-up of the Adult Literacy Resource Agency established by the National Institute of Adult Education (NI A E) in April 1975 with a Government grant of £1m, renewed in 1976 for two further years. Becoming literate is only the first step, as they then need to become politically literate and acquire the know-how to use the educational system.

cruitment to Further and higher education and involvement in life-long learning are to obtain, the necessary basis – less socially divisive than heretofore – must be laid in the comprehensive schools. Thereafter interest will have to be kept alive by employers and trades unionists, in close co-operation with institutions of further and higher education.

A similar communication/educational problem, vitally important to our national prosperity, is concerned with the attitudes on the one hand of the population – students in particular – to science and technology and on the other of employers in industry and commerce. 'The unacceptable face of capitalism' is deeply offensive to idealistic youth, and convincing them that a career in industry or commerce can be a human and creative enterprise can hardly be done by schools and Colleges alone. Arguments for awarding larger grants to entice students to become technologists are seen simply as a cynical extension of exploitation for commercial gain. Management courses on 'personal relationships' and 'understanding people' can too readily appear manipulative unless the employees and the existing managers join in as equals and discuss their own motives. Their success will depend upon the match between the ethos of such courses and the day-to-day relationships between the two groups.

This is also true of the trades unions but they are showing an increasing educational commitment which is most timely in view of their growing responsibilities in industry.

Universities, Polytechnics and Colleges have the important job of widening the education of their science and technology students and dealing with the problems in a socio-economic and conservationist context. Even so this will not be enough. Adult education has so far been mainly literary in character and there is a great need to increase scientific awareness throughout industry, and among parents, teachers, and indeed adults generally. This would be an appropriate task for Adult Education Departments in Technological Universities and Polytechnics in close co-operation with their departments of Science and Technology.

Professionalism

The long-standing relationship between Technical Colleges and the professional engineering institutions was a vital part of their commitment to vocational education and training. Such relationships concerned with professional responsibilities and codes of practice exist within all professions – medicine, the law, teaching – to cite but three examples, but in the light of recent unexpected events serious re-appraisal is now necessary. The taboo on strike action by teachers and doctors has been broken, and vulnerability to corruption is too frequently headline news.[29] Other important though less dramatic problems have also surfaced: for professional workers employed, for example, in local and national Government service; innumerable hazards and serious issues arising directly from the very rapid growth of scientific knowledge: genetic engineering, abortion, tranquillising the unquiet (and difficult) and prolonging unduly the mere physical continuance of the body. The engineers and scientists, as distinct from the medical profession, have to concern themselves with all the environmental hazards – safety in building, transport and industrial processes; pollution; the exploitation of fossil fuels and other natural resources – against the claims of future generations. However, if the present leaders of the professions are seen to be tackling them in open debate, young people will be more readily prepared to accept such challenges in professional work.

Interdependence, autonomy and responsibilities

This book deals with various aspects of the growth in size and complexity of institutions of higher and Further Education in the last two decades. In all such institutions the centre of gravity is in the classroom, workshop or laboratory – in the relationships between teacher and student – and the need to devolve more of the responsibility away from the administrative centres has recently become more widely recognised, even if too seldom put into practice. Similarly in the political sphere, there is public debate about devolution of Government from Whitehall which turns no longer upon the necessity for change but on the form and extent of the changes needed.

Within education the onset of the steady state and the increasing competition for resources have sharpened the issues, and the danger is that there will be less not more self-government and that new national bodies, set up ostensibly to co-ordinate, will in fact impose further controls. The operation of Occam's Razor – that the number of entities should not be unduly multiplied – still needs to be maintained together with the principle of (academic) Benthamism – to establish the greatest degree of academic autonomy for the greatest number of institutions. Absolute autonomy is of course impossible: a network of relationships with both national and local Government to determine how the needs of society and individual citizens should be met is inescapable. There can be no final set of answers, only an ever-changing balance of interests within which the maximum degrees of freedom must be strenuously maintained. In the changes during the last two decades which led from College of Technology to CAT to Technological University, the enhanced degree of academic and institutional autonomy was the major gain. From this study the evidence is clear that throughout the various succeeding changes these institutions have substantially and responsibly held to their original purposes.

Institutions, such as the Polytechnics, on the other side of the binary line do not enjoy a comparable degree of academic autonomy; for example, in their relationship with the CNAA; or institutional freedom, in relation to the Local Authorities. Their emergence is more recent and the thirty designated institutions do not form a homogeneous group, but on the basis of these two principles some modifications leading to a greater degree of autonomy are inevitable in the foreseeable future.

In 1975 the CNAA initiated discussion[30] on greater delegation to the individual Polytechnic within a new quinquennial system of visitations. The ultimate effect of such a change is likely to be the accreditation of an institution as a whole as distinct from separate assessment of undergraduate courses. This will allow for different rates of growth and attainment within the system without endangering the system itself.

In comparison with the Universities the Polytechnics are likely to increase their student numbers considerably, particularly if, as they should, they make a wide variety of diploma courses a major part of their commitment. Since money and personnel are limited quantities the Universities (while overlapping with other institutions at undergraduate level) are likely to maintain their supremacy in research and postgraduate courses. They must collectively be vigilant to secure and maintain the conditions and resources which enable them to do so.

If the Polytechnics do divide into two groups as a result of CNAA policy, those given greater responsibility for the management of their own academic affairs are unlikely to settle for this halfway house indefinitely. Chartered status under the Privy Council gives the final seal to independence. By adopting a title other than 'University' and becoming – say – Royal Polytechnics they could be encouraged to retain their distinctive functions, their local and regional relationships and their wider spectrum of students, and be seen as a separate group of institutions.

At present there appears little corporate enthusiasm for such independence. The CNAA is regarded by Polytechnic staff as a powerful ally in their negotiations with the Local Authorities for increased facilities, and it may be that in a highly competitive world the balance of advantage presently lies with the status quo. Certainly the Directors and other staff have voiced complaints about the reluctance of the Local Authorities to increase their administrative autonomy. The Authorities show a regrettable lack of trust in delegation within their own local institution while at the same time pressing similar claims for themselves from the national Government. According to Sir David Eccles,[31] the CATs became independent of the Local Authorities because their needs had grown beyond them. If in the present situation the Local Authorities refuse to offer Polytechnic staff greater responsibility for the management of their institutions[32] then the chances are high, *pace* Occam's Razor, that another national body, comparable with the UGC, would be set up for the Polytechnics.*

There is of course no inherent reason (though inertia is widespread) why the two principles we have been discussing should not apply also throughout the higher educational system, i.e. in Institutes of Higher Education and Colleges of Further Education as well, using the Weaver Report as a guide.

The Universities face other problems. The UGC is not without its critics, some of whom maintain that it is now a sub-department of

---

* Growing dissatisfaction has at length resulted in the setting up of a Working Group (Chairman, Mr Gordon Oakes MP, Minister of State DES), with the following terms of reference: 'To consider measures to improve the system of management and control of higher education in the maintained sector in England and Wales and its better co-ordination with higher education in the Universities and, in the light of developments in relation to devolution and local authority finance, what regional and national machinery might be established for these purposes.'[33] Many of Mrs Williams's thirteen points will be inescapable agenda items for the Oakes Working Group, and the Universities will have to be very worldly-wise not to find themselves outflanked by a separate and prior reconsideration of them, indeed commitment to them in ways disadvantageous to their role in higher education.

State – an arm of the DES – a post-bag – transmitting Governmental directions without adequate consultation.[34] There appears however no widespread desire to terminate it. In the next decade the main task will be to remedy the severe consequences of inflation. The re-instatement of an appropriately modified quinquennial system is a vital first target. No University is 'an island entire unto itself', however autonomous, and the impact of inflation and some public in-difference verging on hostility has made not only the need for greater interdependence more evident but also the necessity for improving relationships with the general public. Anti-intellectualism may be a product of ignorance on the one side but it is fed by arrogance on the other. It will be of great interest to see how the Association of University Teachers, a professional body acting now also as a trades union, will contribute to the promotion of public goodwill towards the Universities and a greater understanding of their functions.

As we saw in Chapter 1, education is both the basis of a technological society and a defence against its abuses, a duality not generally acknowledged hitherto. To be uneducated is to be severely deprived in any advanced civilised society, and the accelerating rate of change within such societies makes it necessary for all of us, however well educated initially, to continue throughout our adult life.

There have been substantial developments, particularly in higher education, in the last two decades, but the proportion of the populace involved is still much too small for the well-being of the community. The long-term problem is how to move from minority to mass education – how to secure effective educational opportunity for the majority of adults[35] as the penultimate stage towards universal adult education. There is widespread apathy towards such a major change of scale not unconnected with the word 'education' itself, which for far too many citizens reactivates unpleasant associations. The 1944 (Butler) Education Act was passed during the Second World War at a time of international disruption and devastation, but without it the social, scientific and technological advances of later years could not have been achieved.

Today, at a time of great economic stress and of uncertainty in international relationships, we need another comparable step forward for our democracy which will maximise the potential of its greatest resource – the ability, will and imagination of its people. We need to ensure a massive development of opportunities for the education of adult citizens using existing and traditional channels and

307

initiating new partnerships between them, employing the latest methods of self-instruction and all the resources of modern technology. In this development, professional and vocational education must play an indispensable part, for otherwise industry and commerce will not be able to produce the resources to maintain existing educational and social benefits, let alone increase them to meet the needs of the decades ahead. The DES/SED discussion document *Higher Education into the 1990s* (February 1978) presents the challenging effects of birthrate changes. Student numbers are likely to rise from 520,000 in full-time and sandwich courses to about 600,000 in 1984–85, stabilise for about six years, and decline to about 530,000 by 1995–95. The document sets out five possible expansion models, involving various choices of courses and arrangements with differing effects on students' opportunities for higher education, and requiring substantially increased flexibility of institutions.

Chapter 12: Sources

1. Figures for Universities from UGC Communication April 1977. Figures for FE from DES press release, 29th March 1976.
2. Evidence submitted to the Select Committee on Science and Technology (Science Sub-Committee) Scientific Research in British Universities, *Minutes of Evidence*, 10th June 1975, p. 185 (HMSO).
3. *Ibid.*, para. 345.
4. (Penguin Education Special, 1971.)
5. See Charles Carter, 'The Advantages of Freedom and Diversity' in *Patterns and Policies in Higher Education (as 4)*; also p. 185, *ibid.*
6. *As 2*, p. 188, para. 358.
7. *As 2*, p. 188.
8. *As 2*, p. 187.
9. *As 2*, p. 193.
10. Working Party Report of the Standing Conference of Regional Advisory Councils (SCRAC), quoted by J. H. Taylor, *The Impact of Local Government Reorganisation on Further Education*, paper to ACFHE, June 1972.
11. Noel Annan, 'What are Universities for, anyway?'. First Richard Dimbleby Lecture, BBC, reprinted *Listener*, 2nd November 1972.
   Patrick Nuttgens, 'What is Lord Annan for anyway?', *THES*, 9th February 1973.
   George Tolley, 'Time to arm against a sea of troubles', *THES*, 12th March 1976.

12. Robbins Report, Cmnd. 2154 (HMSO 1963), para. 392.

13. Halsey & Trow figures from *The British Academics* (Faber & Faber, London 1971), Table A.2., p. 471.

14. UGC *Annual Survey* 1975–76, para. 19 (HMSO).

15. Report of the Conference published by the University of Bath Press, 1976.

16. See for example *Shortages of qualified engineers:* Report, National Economic Development Office (HMSO, October 1975).

17. Select Committee on Science and Technology (Session 1975–76): Third Report: *University–Industry Relations* (HMSO).

Two important subsequent publications are to be noted: a White Paper on University-Industry Relations (13th September 1977, Cmnd. 6928, HMSO) which stated the Government's reply to the Third Report of the Select Committee; and the Report of an Enquiry, supported by Government and industry, organised by the British Association for the Advancement of Science, and based at Aston University. Entitled 'Education, Engineers and Manufacturing Industry' the Report (Director of Investigating Team Dr J. A. Pope) was published on 25th August 1977 and was discussed at the ensuing meeting of the Association at the University.

The Secretary of State for Industry, Rt. Hon. Mr Varley MP, announced a Committee of Enquiry into the Engineering Profession, with Sir Montague Finniston FRS, as Chairman (membership, *Hansard*, 14th December 1977, cols. 283–84), and Terms of Reference: 'To review for manufacturing industry, and in the light of national economic needs –

i. the requirements of British industry for professional and technician engineers, the extent to which those needs are being met, and the use made of engineers by industry;

ii. the role of the engineering institutions in relation to the education and qualification of engineers at professional and technician level;

iii. the advantages and disadvantages of statutory registration and licensing of engineers in the United Kingdom;

iv. the arrangements in other major industrial countries, particularly in the EEC, for handling these problems, having regard to relevant comparative studies, and to make recommendations' (*Hansard*, 5th July 1977, cols. 483–84, HMSO).

18. Letter from Chairman, UGC, to the Universities, 10th February 1977.

19. Rt. Hon. Mrs Shirley Williams MP, *Hansard* (House of Commons), 3rd February 1977, col. 1267 (HMSO).

20. Mr Len Murray, General Secretary, TUC, reported *THES*, 4th June 1976.

Note also Dr George Tolley, Principal, Sheffield Polytechnic: 'Give places to shop-floor workers', *THES*, 3rd December 1976.

21. Figures from *Hansard* (House of Commons), Written Answer, 31st October 1976. Reported *THES*, 28th January 1977.

22. UGC *Annual Survey* 1974–75, Cmnd. 6435 (HMSO).

23. See the Report of the Open University Committee (Chairman, Sir Peter Venables), *On Continuing Education* (Open University Press, 1976); and cf. Tyrell Burgess, *Education after School* (Penguin, 1977).

24. But see Robin Pedley, *Towards the Comprehensive University* (Macmillan 1977).

25. Lord Robbins' speech: *Hansard* (House of Lords), 31st March 1976, cols. 116–117.

26. *As 26*, paras. 93–98.

27. Alan Charnley, *Paid Educational Leave*: a report of practice in France, Germany and Sweden (Hart-Davis Educational, London 1975).

28. Gösta Rehn, 'Towards Flexibility in Working Life', part of an Anglo-US Conference on Education and the World of Work, *Universities Quarterly*, Summer 1974.

29. See Report of the Royal Commission on *Standards of Conduct in Public Life* (Chairman, Lord Salmon) (HMSO, 1976), also reported *The Times*, 16th August 1976.

30. CNAA Discussion Paper, *Partnership in Validation*, July 1975.

31. Speech to Annual Conference of the Association of Education Committees, reported *Education*, 30th June 1961, p. 1450.

32. But note Tyrrell Burgess, 'Responsibility should be given back to Local Authorities', *THES*, 18th June 1976.

33. *The Times*, 8th February 1977; see also editorial, *THES*, 25th February 1977.

34. The critics have lately been joined by Lord Crowther-Hunt with an article, 'The UGC and the Universities', *THES*, 28th May 1976, the main contentions of which were denied by Sir Frederick Dainton FRS, Chairman of the UGC, *THES*, 11th June 1976.

35. *As 26*, sections 1 & 2.

Appendices

Index

Appendix I:
Glossary of Abbreviations

A AC	Academic Advisory Committee
ACFHE	Association of Colleges for Further and Higher Education (*formerly* ATI)
ACU	Association of Commonwealth Universities
APC	Association of Principals of Colleges (*formerly* APTI)
APT	Association of Polytechnic Teachers
APTI	Association of Principals of Technical Institutions (APC *since February 1975*)
ASEE	American Society for Engineering Education
ATCDE	Association of Teachers in Colleges and Departments of Education (NATFHE *since January 1976*)
ATI	Association of Technical Institutions (ACFHE *since February 1970*)
ATTI	Association of Teachers in Technical Institutions (NATFHE *since January 1976*)
AUT	Association of University Teachers
BACIE	British Association for Commercial and Industrial Education
BEC	Business Education Council
BEd.	Bachelor of Education
CAPS	Co-operative Awards in Pure Science
CASE	Co-operative Awards in Science and Engineering
CAT	College of Advanced Technology
CBI	Confederation of British Industry
CDP	Committee of Directors of Polytechnics
CEI	Council of Engineering Institutions
CGLI	City and Guilds of London Institute

313

CLEA	Committee of Local Education Authorities
CMI	University Council Member engaged in Industry or Commerce
CNAA	Council for National Academic Awards
CRAC	Careers Research and Advisory Centre
CSU	Central Services Unit of the CVCP
CTC	Central Training Council
CVCP	Committee of Vice-Chancellors and Principals of the Universities of the United Kingdom
DES	Department of Education and Science
DHSS	Department of Health and Social Security
Dip.HE	Diploma of Higher Education
Dip.Tech.	Diploma in Technology
FE	Further Education
FTE	Full-time equivalent
GCE	General Certificate of Education – O: Ordinary level A: Advanced level
GEC	General Electric Company
GEE	General Education in Engineering
HMI	Her Majesty's Inspector
HMSO	Her Majesty's Stationery Office
HNC	Higher National Certificate
HND	Higher National Diploma
IHD	Interdisciplinary Higher Degree
ITB	Industrial Training Board
ITC	Industrial Training Council
LEA	Local Education Authority
MCT	Member of the College of Technologists
NACEIC	National Advisory Council on Education for Industry and Commerce
NATFHE	National Association of Teachers in Further and Higher Education (*formerly* ATTI *and* ATCDE)
NCTA	National Council for Technological Awards
NFER	National Foundation for Educational Research
NICEC	National Institute for Careers Education and Counselling
NUS	National Union of Students
OECD	Organisation for Economic Co-operation and Development

ONC	Ordinary National Certificate
OND	Ordinary National Diploma
RAC	Regional Advisory Council
SCRAC	Standing Conference of Regional Advisory Councils
SED	Scottish Education Department
SISCON	Science in a Social Context
SISTER	Special Institution for Scientific and Technological Education and Research
SRC	Science Research Council
SRHE	Society for Research into Higher Education
SSRC	Social Science Research Council
TEC	Technician Education Council
TES	Times Educational Supplement
THES	Times Higher Education Supplement
TUC	Trades Union Congress
UCCA	Universities Central Council on Admissions
UGC	University Grants Committee
UMIST	University of Manchester Institute of Science and Technology
UPIC	Universities, Polytechnics and Industry Committee
UWIST	University of Wales Institute of Science and Technology

Appendix II: Brief Histories

The University of Aston in Birmingham

THE Birmingham and Midland Institute was founded in 1854 to promote the 'diffusion and advancement of science, literature and art among all classes of persons resident in Birmingham and the Midland Counties'. In line with this commitment, the Institute in 1891 accepted an invitation from the Council of the City of Birmingham to organise suitable classes in technical education. They were conducted in two buildings in different parts of the City as the Birmingham Municipal Technical School, with classes in the evenings only, including Saturdays. The two original Departments of Chemistry and Physics, and of Metallurgy and Engineering were subdivided into Chemistry, Physics and Electrical Engineering, Mathematics, Engineering, Drawing and Handicraft. There were also some classes in botany and in typography, and bakery chemistry.

Accommodation became a serious problem, and so remained for many decades. The first of many extensions was opened in 1892–93 but the major event was the opening of the Suffolk Street building in 1895 by the Lord President of the Council as the Minister then responsible for education. In his address to the students, he stressed the need for an efficient and scientific form of education if the country were to withstand foreign industrial competition. Proposals for extensions at Suffolk Street were registered in 1914, made again in 1926 and abandoned in 1927 when it was decided to seek a new site. In July 1933 the City Council approved the acquisition of the Gosta Green site to accommodate the Technical College, a new Commercial College and the School of Arts and Crafts. Work began on the site in 1938–39 but was almost immediately suspended. It began again in 1948, the first section of the buildings for the three Colleges being 'inaugurated' by Her Majesty the Queen in November 1955. At that time College work was conducted in ten different buildings scattered around the centre of the City.

316

After an initial setback, work increased greatly during and after the Second World War: in 1941–42 enrolments, very largely part-time, were 4,000; they increased by nearly 25 per cent the following session, and in 1947–48 a peak total of 9,808 individual students was reached. Work increased not only in volume but in standard, and the Central Technical School became successively the Central Technical College in 1927, the College of Technology in 1951 and on 24th September 1956 it became the first designated College of Advanced Technology. In 1951 the first Governing Body was established, and the process of transferring part-time courses below Intermediate Science and S.3 level to Local Colleges, begun in 1948, was accelerated. This was facilitated by the opening of two new Technical Colleges, Garretts Green and Brooklyn Farm, in 1953. This process was further increased after designation, with the transfer of courses to form the College of Food and Domestic Arts in 1957, and also of technician craft courses to form the Matthew Boulton Technical College in 1958.

After much debate the firm decision was made in 1963 to remain at Gosta Green, where subsequently through the generous co-operation of the City Council the existing site of 1·82 hectares was increased by a further 12·2 hectares. Since 1969 the site has been rapidly developed, with new academic buildings provided for Electrical Engineering, Chemical Engineering, the Computer Centre, and in 1975 the new University Library with about 950 seating places. Residence for 1,500 students has been provided on the Gosta Green site, and a 'student village' site of 6·5 hectares and 950 residential places has been acquired and developed at Handsworth. In addition a sports ground of 36·4 hectares was acquired at Shustoke Farm, Walsall. In 1976 work began on building Phase I of a new Management Centre at Gosta Green, at a total cost of £1·36m.

During the period as a CAT, from 1956 to 1966, the College Officers were:
Chairman of the Governing Body:
1956–58 J. J. Gracie, CBE, HON.ACT (Birm.), MIEE, FIIA.
1958–66 Sir Joseph Hunt, MBE, HON.ACT (Birm.), FBIM.
Principal: Sir Peter Venables, PH.D, FRIC.

The Charter received Royal Assent on 10th March 1966, passed under the Great Seal on 22nd April 1966, and the first Officers of the University, named in the Charter, were:

Chancellor: Henry George Baron Nelson of Stafford, MA, MICE, MIMech.E, MIEE, FRAe.S.
Pro-Chancellor: Sir Joseph Anthony Hunt, Knight, MBE, HON.ACT (BIRM.).
Vice-Chancellor: Sir Peter Venables, Knight, PH.D, FRIC.
Pro-Vice-Chancellor: Kingsley Lewis Stretch, Esquire, MA, LLB, MICE, MIMech.E, MIEE.
Chairman of the Academic Advisory Committee: John Gildas Collingwood, Esquire.

The *Pro-Chancellor and Chairman of Council* since 1970 has been: N. I. Bond-Williams, BSC., HON.DSC.; and Joseph A. Pope, PH.D, DSC., wh.sch., CEng., FIMech.E became *Vice-Chancellor* in August 1969.

The University of Bath

When a Diocesan School in Bristol was closed in 1852, the Trustees asked Canon Moseley to advise on the use of the premises. Under the stimulus of the Great Exhibition of 1851, he submitted a scheme for 'a school of Applied Science, similar to institutions of the same kind then highly successful in Germany and other countries . . . where youths of limited means could be provided with suitable training for an industrial career'.[1]

The school premises were opened in 1856 as the Trade School, the first of its kind in England. This had four main parts: a primary or preparatory department for basic education; a secondary department, with classes in commercial subjects, mathematics and applied science; day classes for adults in chemistry, mining and engineering; and evening classes. In 1875 a new Governing Body of the Colston Trust was established and prolonged negotiations for the site of the Bristol Grammar School in Unity Street were fruitless, until in 1880 the wealthy and influential Bristol Society of Merchant Venturers offered to buy the site and erect a new building for the Trade School. In 1885 the Society took over full responsibility for the School, which moved that year to the new building in Unity Street and became the Merchant Venturers' School, with the published objects of providing 'a complete, continuous, and thoroughly sound preparation for an industrial career'. Evening classes were made 'open to all persons whatsoever, above sixteen years of age, without distinction of sex', and this delimitation became a distinctive feature of the whole institution.

Following the Technical Instruction Act of 1889, and the 'Whiskey Money' Act of 1890, Bristol Corporation established a Technical Instruction Committee to administer funds amounting to £5,700 per annum under the latter Act. A period of rapid expansion and consequent reorganisation followed with division into four parts: a Boys' School; the Technical School with eight departments; an Evening School; and the Government School of Art (but this was closed in 1900 by agreement with the Bristol School of Art). In 1894, with increasing growth of post-school studies, the School was re-named the Merchant Venturers' Technical College. Enrolments rose to 2,768 in 1903, and further additional premises were provided out of the first capital grant received from the Bristol Local Education Authority. In 1906 a fire destroyed most of the main building, but the reconstructed building embodied many improvements.

Founded in 1876, the University College of Bristol later established courses and departments in science and engineering, and the delineation of the spheres of influence and activity between the two Colleges became important. Negotiations took place intermittently in the 1890s upon a possible federation under the title 'The West of England University and Technical College' but came to nothing as the University College insisted on retaining their own engineering classes. The first of the magnificent gifts of the Wills family facilitated the transition of the Bristol College to University status, and one result was that the Merchant Venturers' College provided the Faculty of Engineering of the University; this arrangement obtained from 1909 to 1949.

Among many changes with the growth of advanced work, the College shed the preparatory school in 1908 and the secondary school in 1920, and the Bath and West School of Pharmacy became part of the College in 1929. Other non-faculty Departments which grew in strength were those of Navigation, Printing, Building and Commerce. Enrolments rose to 3,978 in 1936–37, and the Society of Merchant Venturers realised that the costs of the greater development required would prove beyond their means and opened discussions with the Bristol LEA accordingly. Wartime damage and still further growth, plus mounting costs, compelled the Society to relinquish their responsibility for the governance of the College after more than sixty years. The transfer of non-faculty work to the

Bristol LEA became fully effective in 1949. The University gave notice of its intention to terminate the dependence of its Engineering Faculty on the College, once its own engineering laboratories were completed in 1954.

The need for additional buildings and a new site was made more urgent by two things: the potential development of Dip.Tech. sandwich courses from 1955, and the College becoming a College of Advanced Technology in 1960. The story of successive plans and sites is a complicated and unhappy one – from Unity Street to Ashley Down, to the Kings Weston House site in 1960 on the western edge of the city, only again for this site to prove inadequate. An alternative was offered by the city but was regarded as inadequate with the prospect of University status. Early in 1964, Bath City Council offered a site of 60·7 hectares at the Norwood Playing Fields on Claverton Down, and this was promptly accepted by the College Governors. The first building on the new site was occupied by the School of Biological Sciences and the sociology section of the School of Humanities and Social Sciences in September 1965, and the final transference – of the School of Management – from Bristol took place in 1975.

During the period as a CAT, from 1960 to 1966, the College Officers were:
Chairman of the Governing Body:
1960–62 Councillor N. G. Reece.
1962–66 F. S. Tinnion, BSc.(Tech.).
Principal: G. H. Moore, MSC., FRIC.

The Royal Charter was granted on 25th October 1966 as Bath University of Technology, but the name was changed in 1971. The first Officers of the University, named in the Charter, were:
Chancellor: Lord Hinton of Bankside, KBE, FRS.
Pro-Chancellor: Sir Isaac James Pitman, KBE, MA.
Vice-Chancellor: George Herbert Moore, Esquire, MSC., FRIC.
Treasurer: Sir Sydney Barratt, Knight, BA.
Pro-Vice-Chancellor: Doctor Alexander Merrie Hardie, MA, BSC. (ENg.), Ph.D, MIEE.
Chairman of the Academic Advisory Committee: Professor S. C. Redshaw, DSC., Ph.D, MICE, MIStruct.E, FRAe.S.

The *Chairmen of Council* have been:
1966–70 The Chancellor, Lord Hinton of Bankside, KBE, FRS.
1970–73 Sir Sydney Barratt, BA.
1973–75 E. le Q. Herbert, DSC., FRIC, MIChem.E, MInst.F, FH-WC
1975–   Sir Kenneth Selby, FCMA, FCCA, FBIM, MIQ.
   Vice-Chancellor and Principal:
1969–76 L. Rotherham, CBE, DSC., HON. LLD, FRS.
1976–   P.T. Matthews, CBE, MA, Ph.D, FRS.

The University of Bradford

'In Bradford, Yorkshire, religious opinion as a whole was so hostile to the proposal to establish a mechanics' institution, the promoters of the movement being known as men of pronounced sceptical opinions, that no progress was made for several years.'[2] An attempt to establish one in 1825 failed, but a fresh start was made in 1831, and succeeded in 1832 after pacification of certain religious interests. Despite many vicissitudes, including recurrent trade depressions, the Institute was successful, and later housed the School of Design founded in 1848 by a group of textile manufacturers, a School of Building started by the Master Masons in 1867, and a Weaving School – the Bradford Technical School – founded in 1878 by a Joint Committee of the Mechanics' Institute and the Chamber of Commerce. Four years later the Bradford Technical College was opened in Great Horton Road.

The purpose of the School was that of 'imparting to youths, artisans and others, technical, scientific, artistic and general instruction in the various processes involved in the production of worsted, woollen, silk and cotton fabrics and other manufactured articles, and involved in the carrying on or conducting of any profession, trade or industry which now is or may for the time being be practised or followed in Bradford aforesaid or its neighbourhood, or in any matter connected with the aforesaid processes, professions, trades or industries, or any of them'.[3] In the College, Departments of Textiles, Art and Design, Engineering, Dyeing and Chemistry were established, with both day and evening classes, and courses were developed to professional levels and later for London University external degrees. It also had a day school for boys aged 11 to 15 years.

For seventeen difficult years the College remained under private control, harassed by debt and lack of local support. By 1899 the deficit was £14,000 and the College was then taken over by the municipal authority under the Technical Instruction Act of 1891. The changes which followed were not all beneficial, because of a too narrow concept of what was 'technical'. The Boys' School was closed, commerce, languages and general educational subjects were returned to the Mechanics' Institute and the Art Department became a separate entity. Nevertheless, the work grew, though mainly in evening classes, and by 1901 the Horton Road buildings were inadequate. Extensions followed in 1911, but the response from local industry was disappointing, especially for day-time classes. Schemes for the complete rebuilding of the College on the outskirts of the city were bruited in the 1930s, as were proposals for gaining University status, but were abandoned, largely due to the economic stringencies of the time.

During the post-war period, courses for London University external degrees increased, and full-time diploma courses in textiles and other technologies were maintained, but the greater part of the work remained in part-time courses in professional and other studies. Following the 1956 White Paper the Bradford Institute of Technology was established in 1957, with the status of a designated College of Advanced Technology, to take over and develop the advanced work of the Bradford Technical College, the other work remaining with the institution of that name re-created as a Local Technical College. Plans for new buildings were finished by 1959 and the first main building came into use in 1963.

During the period as a CAT, the College Officers were:
Chairman of the Governing Body:

1956–57 – 1961–62	Alderman Revis Barber.
1962–63 – 1963–64	Dennis Bellamy.
1964–January 1965	W. Cule Davies.
January–September 1965	Alderman Revis Barber.
1965–66	Sir Charles R. Morris, KCMG, MA, HON. LLD, HON.DLitt.

Principal: E. G. Edwards, BSC., PH.D, FRIC.

The Charter of Incorporation as the University of Bradford was received on 18th October 1966 and the first Officers of the University, named in the Charter, were:

322

Chancellor: The Right Honourable James Harold Wilson, OBE.
Pro-Chancellor: Sir Charles Richard Morris, KCMG, MA, HON.LLD, HON.DLitt.
Vice-Chancellor and Principal: Edward George Edwards, Esquire, BSC., Ph.D, FRIC.
Pro-Vice-Chancellor and Vice-Principal: Robert Allan McKinlay, Esquire, MA, BCom.
The *Chairman of the Academic Advisory Committee was:* Professor C. E. H. Bawn, CBE, BSC., Ph.D, HON.DSC., FRS.

Pro-Chancellor and Chairman of Council since 1969–70: A. J. Thayre, MBE, BCom., FSS.

Brunel University

Chiswick Polytechnic was one of five technical colleges founded to-wards the end of the nineteenth century, and later it became known as the Acton and Chiswick Polytechnic. In 1928 new buildings were opened, and the Middlesex County Council established Acton Technical College in them, with evening classes in engineering and the Junior Technical School transferred from Chiswick. The College quickly developed, for though it was built to cater for the needs of students up to ONC in engineering in 1930, the following session saw the start of evening classes for HNC and London external degrees. Part-time day release courses were established, almost entirely in engineering.

Acton was one of seven Technical Colleges to be established in Middlesex, the others being Ealing, Enfield, Hendon, Southall, Twickenham and Willesden, and for many it remained a puzzle as to why Brunel suddenly emerged from Acton, ahead of all the others, to become a designated College of Advanced Technology. Two main factors became effective – one a matter of policy, the other the availability of a site and a new building. The first was the effective way in which Acton College seized the opportunity afforded by Dip.Tech. courses under the NCTA. These became the sole pattern of courses over the period 1955–60, London external degree courses being terminated 'as an emancipation', and it thus became one of the leading colleges on Dip.Tech. courses. Secondly, a new science building (started in 1950) became available in 1957, and the ad-vanced work was transferred to it as the nucleus of a new institution,

323

Brunel College of Technology. By leaving the technician and craft courses at Acton Technical College, Brunel was free and able to devote itself to advanced work which included sandwich courses for Dip.Tech. and HND and post-experience courses, to expand research, and to appoint suitably qualified staff.

But the new science building alone would not have sufficed for adequate development. It was the availability of a large site to the west of Acton, at Uxbridge, acquired years earlier with great foresight by the Middlesex County Council, that clinched the matter of the designation of Brunel as a CAT in 1962: in agreeing to it the DES required that the new College be built there and that building at Acton should cease. By the time construction had started, the Robbins Report recommendations about the CATs had been accepted by the Government, in time to affect the designs for a Technological University. Building began in 1965 but was seriously delayed by industrial disputes. Even in 1975 some of the planned buildings had not been started.

The name of the University commemorates the great Victorian engineer and designer I. K. Brunel (1806–59), whose Great Western Railway was built through Acton, and with whom there are local associations.

The Officers of the College from 1956 were:
Chairman of the Governing Body:
1956–57 Wilfred Brown, MBE.
1957–59 Sir Miles Thomas, DFC, MIMech.E, MSAE.
1959–62 Sir John Paget, Bt., MA, CEng., FIMech.E, FIProd.E.
1962–65 Lord Brown, MBE.
1965–66 Arthur L. Stuchbery, OBE, CEng., FIProd.E, FIMech.E.
Principal: James Topping, MSc., PhD, DIC.

The University received its Charter on 6th July 1966 and the first Officers, named in the Charter, were:
Chancellor: John Anthony Hardinge, Earl of Halsbury.
Pro-Chancellor: Wilfred Banks Duncan, Baron Brown, MBE.
Vice-Chancellor and Principal: James Topping, Esquire, MSc., Ph.D, DIC.
Vice-Principal: George Charles Shipp, Esquire, MA, Ph.D, DIC.
Secretary-General: Brian Hope Winstanley, Esquire, BA.
The Chairman of the Academic Advisory Committee was: G. Templeman, MA, Ph.D, FSA.

Chairmen of Council have been:
1966–72 Arthur L. Stuchbery, OBE, CEng., FIProd.E, FIMech.E.
1973–   Peter E. Trier, MA, FIEE, FIERE, FIMA.

Vice-Chancellor and Principal since 1971: Stephen L. Bragg, MA, MSc., CEng., FIMech.E, FRAC.S.

The City University, London

The first formal evidence of origin lies in the Act of 1883 which earmarked funds for the erection of premises and for the endowment of Institutes, Polytechnics and of similar institutions in this and other parts of the metropolis. In 1891 a scheme of the Charity Commissioners provided for the government of 'the City Polytechnic', as an organisation to link the Northampton Institute with two other institutions already in existence – the Birkbeck Institution and the City of London College. The University of London had established its external degree system in 1858, and this factor strongly oriented the development of the Birkbeck Institution, which became known as Birkbeck College from 1903 onwards, and was eventually incorporated as such as a School of the University of London in 1920. The City of London College became a separate institution again on the dissolution of the City Polytechnic in 1907, as a centre for advanced commercial education and, eventually became in 1970, a constituent institution of the City of London Polytechnic.

The site was given by the Second Marquess of Northampton (hence the name of the Institute), the foundation stone was laid on 9th July 1894, and the building was occupied progressively for classes from 19th October 1896. A full programme was begun in the 1897–98 session and covered six main sections of evening classes: mechanical engineering and metal trades; artistic crafts; applied physics and electrical engineering; horology; electrochemistry; domestic economy and women's trades. A wide range of courses was offered 'specifically for the benefit of artisans, apprentices and others engaged in the Clerkenwell trades'. Day work consisted only of a twenty-week full-time course in domestic economy. At an early stage, the Telegraphists' School of Science, conducted by the General Post Office, was transferred to the Institute. A full-time course in horological engineering for boys over 14 years was offered in 1899, and this was the modest origin of a separate National College of

Horology established by Government policy in 1947. In 1904 a separate Department of Technical Optics was formed, which eventually became a Department of Ophthalmic Optics.

The London Education Act of 1903 marked a profound change in the status and future potential of the Institute, as with other kindred institutions. While it continued to be administered by a Governing Body constituted as before, it became an aided institution, supported financially by and within the general policy requirements of the London County Council, and introduced the word 'Polytechnic' into its title in 1907. Over a period around 1915 the Polytechnic Institute ceased to hold classes in building subjects, the Department of Artistic Crafts was transferred to the London County Council Central School of Arts and Crafts and the day school of domestic economy was closed down.

When the University of London was reconstituted in 1900, the Northampton, with certain other Polytechnics, became associated with it as an 'Institution having Recognised Teachers', and matriculated students were thus enabled to enter for internal degrees of the University. This contributed greatly to the success of the full-time engineering degree course started in 1900 and of the part-time courses started at a later date. At the time of the jubilee year in 1945, nearly 1,000 such students were preparing for the London University BSC. internal degree in engineering. Indeed, in 1952–53 in all Polytechnics, such students were over 54 per cent of the University faculty of engineering enrolments. Many Polytechnic students also qualified for the degrees of MSc. and Ph.D in engineering.

Extensions were made in 1902, 1909 and 1932, but each quickly became inadequate, a predictable aspect of growth which—as in other institutions—was never adequately allowed for in advance.

The name Northampton Polytechnic was in use from 1935 and on 1st January 1957 the Polytechnic was designated as the Northampton College of Advanced Technology.

The Officers during the period as a CAT were:
Chairman of the Governing Body: O. F. Thompson, OBE.
Principal: J. S. Tait, Ph.D, BSC. (Eng.), ARTC, MIEE, MIMech.E.

The Royal Charter for the City University was sealed on 23rd May 1966. As the name indicates, it has a special relationship with the City of London: each Lord Mayor in succession is Chancellor of the University, and the Court of Aldermen, the Court of Common Council, the City Livery Companies and the City Parochial Foundation are represented on the University Court.

The first Officers of the University, named in the Charter, were:

Chancellor: Sir Lionel Percy Denny, Knight, MC, The Lord Mayor of London.

Pro-Chancellor and Chairman of the Council: Oliver Frederic Thompson, Esquire, OBE.

Deputy Pro-Chancellor and Vice-Chairman of the Council: Sir Michael William Turner, Knight, CBE, MA.

Vice-Chancellor and Principal: James Sharp Tait, Esquire, PH.D, BSC. (Eng.), ARTC, MIEE, MImech.E.

Treasurer: Ralph George Edward Jarvis, Esquire, BA.

Chairman of the Academic Advisory Committee: Sir David Watherston, KBE, KCMG.

In November 1972 The Rt. Hon. Lord Alport, PC, TD, succeeded Dr Thompson as *Pro-Chancellor and Chairman of Council*, and in October 1974 Edward Parkes, SC.D, FIMech.E, MICE, succeeded Sir James Tait as *Vice Chancellor*.

Pro-Chancellor and Chairman of Council:

November 1972–   The Rt. Hon. Lord Alport, PC, TD.

Vice-Chancellor and Principal:

October 1974–   Edward Parkes, SC.D. FIMech.E. MICE.

Loughborough University of Technology

Early this century the Leicestershire County Council began to establish a series of Farm and Technical Institutes, the latter particularly at Loughborough (1905), and later added Coalville (1924), Hinckley (1931) and Melton Mowbray (1937). The last three made modest effective progress as local institutions over the years, but Loughborough emerged quite unpredictably as a national institution.

The first stage at Loughborough was a Technical Institute and Pupil Teachers' Centre and active growth began with new buildings in 1909, and the appointment of a Principal (Dr S. C. Laws, who later became principal of the Northampton Polytechnic). A vigorous campaign to develop outside classes as feeders to the Institute raised the number of enrolments from 481 in 1909 to 1,900 in 1911–12. Further steady development took place up to the First World

327

War, but the appointment of Herbert Schofield as Principal marked a sharp change of scale and tempo. He persuaded the Education Committee to undertake practical training for industrial war purposes on a large scale, financed by the Government, and requiring many additional buildings and a great deal of equipment. After the war these were not dispersed but converted to the peacetime use of 'training students on production' and to form the nucleus of a major institution.

Work developed on a broad front, and the College grew substantially until 1951–52, when it was agreed by the Ministry of Education and the Local Authority that reorganisation had become essential. From 1st January 1951 the Teacher Training College and the College of Arts and Crafts each became separate institutions with their own Board of Governors responsible to the LEA, and the Department of Continuative Education became the College of Further Education, likewise under the LEA. The several Departments of Engineering and Science became the Loughborough College of Technology, established as an autonomous institution under a Trust Deed, with a chairman appointed by the Minister, and with Dr H. L. Haslegrave as principal (Dr Schofield retired in 1950). It was financed by direct grant from the Ministry of Education, and the College thus anticipated by ten years the first major step taken by the Colleges of Advanced Technology in 1962.

Courses continued to be developed and the practice of in-college training on production was maintained. With the introduction of the Dip.Tech., most courses included professional and practical training externally in industry on the sandwich course principle.[4]

At the time of separation from the Local Authority there were sixteen residential halls, over 53 hectares of playing fields and a students' union, and the continued joint usage of these and other facilities undoubtedly presented difficulties which increased somewhat in later years. In 1971–72 moves were begun by the Council of the University, the Governing Bodies of the College of Education and of the College of Art and Design, and the LEA to re-unite the three institutions.[4] In 1977 the College of Education was incorporated in the University.

The College of Technology was designated a College of Advanced Technology in 1957 and its Officers were:

Chairman of the Governing Body:
1957–63 Sir Edward Herbert, OBE, MA.
1963–66 Sir Herbert Manzoni, CBE, MICE.
Principal: H. L. Haslegrave, wh.sc., MA, Ph.D, MSC. (Eng.), MIMech.E, MIEE, MIProd.E.

The College received its Charter as the Loughborough University of Technology on 19th April 1966 and the first Officers, named in the Charter, were:
Chancellor: Sir Harry Pilkington, Knight.
Vice-Chancellor: Herbert Leslie Haslegrave, Esquire, wh.sc., MA, Ph.D, MSC.(Eng.), MIMech.E, MIEE, MIProd. E.
The *Chairman of the Academic Advisory Committee* was: E. S. Sellers, OBE, MSC., MA, MIChem. E.

The *Pro-Chancellor and Chairman of Council* since 1966 has been David Collett.
Succeeding *Vice-Chancellors:*
1967–75 E. J. Richards, OBE, DSC., MA, FRAe.S, FIMech.E.
1975–   Clifford Butler, BSC., Ph.D, FRS.

The University of Salford

The Manchester Mechanics' Institution was founded in 1824, but in the late 1830s there developed another type of institution in Manchester and district, namely, the Lyceums. These were intended for 'a lower grade of society than that from which the members of Mechanics' Institutions were generally drawn'.[5] The Lyceums were praised by George Birkbeck in 1840 when he said: 'The Lyceums have done precisely what we intended in the formation of Mechanics' Institutions ... I hail the formation of these Lyceums with the greatest delight.'[6] In the literature the relation if any of the Salford Mechanics' Institute to the Salford Lyceum is by no means clear: however that may be, changes took place whereby the Salford Working Men's College became their successor in 1858.

The Working Men's College was governed by a Council of fifty-five members, including twenty students, and published reports annually until 1875, and instruction continued until the 1890s. In 1889 the Salford Borough Council appointed a Technical Instruction Committee to report on 'the necessity of providing technical instruction for the artisan class of the borough', and was soon being urged to accept the offer of the Working Men's College to transfer its property in Great George Street for use as a technical school. In the event the gift was accepted as such, the buildings sold, and the proceeds put towards the erection of an entirely new building financed substantially by the Borough Council with grants received under the 'Whiskey Money' Act. The new building in Peel Park was opened in the 1895–96 session, and served as the main building until 1960. In 1896 Her Majesty Queen Victoria commanded that the Institute be called the Royal Salford Technical Institute: in the flux of time, with custom and use, this became the Royal Technical College, Salford, and this name was confirmed by Ministerial designation as its title as a College of Advanced Technology on 2nd November 1956.

The pressures for technical education in the post-war period became, with Manchester's unresponsiveness, Salford's opportunity, and especially with the introduction of sandwich courses from 1949 onwards. Growth was rapid, particularly in such courses, and about a dozen scattered buildings were rented or acquired, unsuitable in most respects and adapted as may be. After some seven years of persistent effort a new main building was started in April 1954 and opened in 1960.

From 1941 the College had a Governing Body representative of Salford Borough Council and Lancashire County Council. This functioned as a Joint Education Committee, having a considerable degree of autonomy within the annual estimate approved by the sponsoring Councils. The change in 1962 to independent direct grant status was therefore not as marked as it would have been had the College been governed (like Birmingham, for example) directly under a single LEA. At this point the name was changed to the Royal College of Advanced Technology, Salford.

With the co-operation of Salford Corporation, expansion of the College site in Peel Park became possible to a total of 58·7 hectares and substantial academic and other buildings were erected, e.g. the Chapman Building for conference facilities, fine arts and complementary studies and the Newton Building for aeronautics and mechanical engineering. Nearly 1000 residential places have been provided at Castle Irwell in the form of student houses, in addition to the 600 places in halls of residence at Kersal.

The Officers of the College were:
Chairman of the Governing Body:
1956–62 Sir Willis Jackson, FRS.
1962–67 D. W. Hill, CBE, DSc., Ph.D, FRIC, FTI.
Principal: C. Whitworth, MSc., Ph.D, FRIC, FInst.F.

The University received its Royal Charter on 4th April 1967, and the first Officers, named in the Charter, were:
Chancellor: His Royal Highness The Prince Philip, Duke of Edinburgh, KG, KT, GBE, FRS.
Pro-Chancellor: Douglas William Hill, Esquire, CBE, DSc., Ph.D, FRIC, FTI.
Vice-Chancellor: Clifford Whitworth, Esquire, MSc., Ph.D, FRIC, FInst.F.
The *Chairman of the Academic Advisory Committee* was: F. S. Spring, DSc., FRIC, FRS.

The *Chairmen of Council* have been:
1967–75 D. W. Hill, CBE, DSc., Ph.D, FRIC, FTI.
1975– The Rt. Rev. E. R. Wickham, BD, HON. DLitt., Bishop of Middleton.
Since April 1974 the Office of *Vice-Chancellor* has been held by:
J. H. Horlock, MA, Ph.D, SC.D, CEng., FIMech. E, FRAe.S, FRS.

The University of Surrey

The City of London Parochial Charities Act of 1883 empowered the Charity Commissioners to collect the accumulated funds of the old City charities and to apply them through the trustees of a newly established City Parochial Foundation 'to promote the education of the poorer inhabitants of the Metropolis by technical instruction, secondary education, art education, evening lectures, or otherwise, and generally to improve their physical, social and moral conditions'. The Commissioners proposed the establishment of Polytechnic Institutes throughout the metropolitan area and £150,000 was set aside accordingly.

A representative committee, appointed at a public meeting on 2nd December 1887 in Newington Vestry Hall, subsequently submitted proposals for three Polytechnics south of the Thames. The proposals were approved, and the South London Polytechnics Committee was formed. The Goldsmiths' Company most generously undertook to provide for the cost of erecting and endowing an institute at New Cross, and the Committee thereupon proceeded with an institute in Southwark which was opened as the Borough Poly-technic in 1892. The way was then open for concentrated efforts at Battersea.[7]

The Scheme for the administration of the Institute was approved by Her Majesty Queen Victoria in Council on 23rd June 1891, the Governing Body first met on 22 October 1891, and the building was formally opened in 1894. The work was organised in six main Departments: Mechanical Engineering and Building Trades; Electrical Engineering and Physics; Chemistry; Women's Subjects; Art and Music. Classes in commercial and literary subjects, and in physical training were also offered. As regards student activities, facilities for recreation were provided but, as in similar Polytechnics, smoking and the introduction of intoxicating liquors into the build-ing, as well as dancing and drama, were forbidden by the Scheme of Administration. Dramatic performances were allowed in 1911, smoking and dancing were formally allowed in 1932, but the ban on drinking lapsed only in June 1957 when, following its designation as a College of Advanced Technology in October 1956, the Poly-technic changed its name to Battersea College of Technology. The Scheme also prohibited the use of the premises for political, de-nominational and sectarian activities but, despite many protests by the students, this was withdrawn only as late as 1961.

Courses were well established by 1900, but were largely part-time. The scheme of having teachers recognised by the University of London stimulated the growth of full-time degree courses and thus of a corporate spirit in the Polytechnic. Besides advancing its own work, the first principal, S. H. Wells, foresaw that the London Poly-technics would become central and higher technical institutions, and so for Battersea promoted the establishment of 'feeder' in-stitutes, in Tooting and elsewhere, from 1901 onwards. These became maintained institutes of the London County Council following the Acts of 1902 and 1904, but the close association remained.

Because of the academic success of courses, the Governing Body made application to the University of London in 1911 for the Poly-technic to be recognised as a School of the University. Though this had no effect, it was the first sign of a continuing preoccupation of the Polytechnic. With the growth of advanced work, the City Parochial Foundation became very uneasy and made investigations from time to time, but the Polytechnic was able to prove that the majority of its advanced students came from the poorer classes, and so the endowment was continued. However, it was later again in jeopardy because the Governing Body had established hostels for students.

The period 1927–39 was one of consolidation with increasing emphasis on science and engineering; and most significantly metallurgy was added, but the closure of the Art Department in 1936 was regretted at the Polytechnic. As with other Polytechnics, 1945–57 was a period of raising the standard of as well as expanding the work: some space was gained with the early separation of the Domestic College in 1950; but both aspects underlined the need for new and suitably equipped buildings. No progress was ever made on the Battersea site however, even as a College of Advanced Technology, and the apparently insoluble problem led to the decision of the University to move to a site of 131 hectares close by the cathedral at Guildford. The move to entirely new buildings on this site began in 1968 and ended in 1970.

The Officers of the College from 1956 were:
Chairman of the Governing Body: S. F. Rich, OBE, JP, LLB.
Principal:
1956–60 R. W. West, CBE, DSC., FRIC, FIRI, ARCS.
1960–66 D. M. A. Leggett, MA, DSC., FRAe.S.

The College was granted a Royal Charter on 9th September 1966 and the first Officers of the University, named in the Charter, were:
Chancellor: The Right Honourable Alfred Baron Robens of Woldingham.
Pro-Chancellor: Sir George Robert Edwards, Knight, CBE, DSC., HON. FRAe.S.
Vice-Chancellor: Douglas Malcolm Aufrere Leggett, Esquire, MA, Ph.D, DSC., FRAe.S.
Treasurer: Lieutenant-Colonel Sir William John Herbert de Wette Mullens, Knight, DSO, TD.
The *Chairman of the Academic Advisory Committee* was: Professor M. J. Lighthill, DSC., FRS, FRAe.S, FIMA.

Chairmen of Council have been:
1966–67 S. F. Rich, OBE, JP, LLB.
1968–71 J. E. Bolton, DSC., MA, MBA, FBIM.

1971–75 B. J. Mason, CB, DSC., FRS.
1975– T. Irvine Smith OBE.

Vice-Chancellor:
1975– Anthony Kelly, BSC., PhD, DSC., FRS, FIP, FIM.

Chelsea College, University of London

The quickening of the movement for working-class education in the 1880s led the Commissioners for the Chelsea Public Library to start a campaign for a Polytechnic Institute for South-West London. With others they applied to the Charity Commissioners in 1888, who made an offer of 50,000 for the endowment of the Institute provided that an equal sum was raised in the district. It was a condition also that the Institute would provide for the needs of the areas of Chelsea, South Kensington, Fulham, St George's Hanover Square and Westminster. The proposed Polytechnic Institute was to be modelled on the lines of Quintin Hogg's Regent Street Polytechnic, and was to provide technical and commercial schools and science and art classes and recreational facilities for 5,000 young men and women above 15 years old. Day schools and evening classes were also provided for boys and girls between 13 and 15 on leaving the elementary schools.

Though £20,00 was quickly raised by public subscription, the rate of support was not maintained, and the tenders received exceeded the architects' estimates of costs by nearly 50 per cent. The foundation stone was laid on 23rd July 1891, and the buildings opened in 1895–96, though all sections were not opened until October 1896. Day work included an Organised Science School for Boys and Girls, a Domestic Economy School for Girls, art classes and miscellaneous classes, and there was a wide range of evening classes. University Extension Lectures were held from the very first year.

The Polytechnic Institute became known as the Chelsea Polytechnic in 1922, and was administered on behalf of the Charity Commissioners by a Governing Body appointed and acting in accordance with schemes made under the City of London Parochial Charities Act of 1883. Financially it was aided by the London County Council, the City Parochial Foundation and by private donations.

The standard of work increased over the years, especially after courses leading to London University degrees were started. In 1900 the University introduced its scheme of Recognised Teachers, and by 1952–53 some seventy staff were so recognised, and of the internal students in the Faculty of Science of London University, 37·1 per cent were registered under this arrangement. The London County Council used its influence to rationalise the work of the then Polytechnics to some extent, and while Battersea Polytechnic concentrated more on engineering and metallurgy, Chelsea almost entirely on science and had no engineering. This made its selection as a College of Advanced *Technology* rather a surprise, not to say an anomaly except in the high standard of its work, but it was duly designated in January 1957 as the Chelsea College of Science and Technology.

Developments between the wars included forming the Departments of Biology and Geology from the original Department of Natural Sciences; later the Biology Department was split into three— Botany and Zoology, Physiology and Pharmacology, and Chiropody, and the School of Pharmacy was formed from classes within the Department of Chemistry. After designation, the school of Chiropody was transferred to the Paddington Technical College, and the School of Art combined with the Art Department of The Polytechnic, Regent Street, to form a new independent School of Art in Chelsea.

Following the Robbins Committee Report the College had high expectations of becoming a separate University, but the definitive outcome of a long, unhappy period of uncertainty and conflicting policies was that it was eventually granted a Charter in 1971 as Chelsea College, with the status of a constituent School of the University of London.

The site problem remained acute. It was alleviated to a small degree by the acquisition of four factories and warehouses in Hammersmith and Fulham during the period 1962 to 1968, permitting the establishment of new developments in Science Education, Electronics and Applied Biology. In 1969 the UGC approved proposals for the total removal of Chelsea College to a new site at Springfield in Wandsworth, and the site was acquired in 1975. The foundation stone of the first building, a hall of residence, was laid by Her Majesty the Queen Mother, Chancellor of the University of London, on 11th November 1975. Following the recommendations of the Royal Commission on Medical Education, acquiring the new site will enable the College to develop as a multi-faculty institution in association with the St. George's Hospital Medical School and the Royal Hospital of London School of Dental Surgery.[8]

335

Ap. II *Brief Histories*

Officers of the Chelsea College of Science and Technology were:
Chairman of the Governing Body:
1956–57 Professor G. Bullough, MA, FRSL.
1958–70 J. H. Townsend, BA.
1970–72 M. Weatherall, MA, DM, DSC. FInst.Biol.

Principal:
1956–62 N. M. H. Lightfoot, MA, FRSE.
1962–65 C. C. Hentschel, MSC., FLS, FES.
1965–72 M. R. Gavin, CBE, MA, DSC., FInst.P, FIEE, MIERE.

The *Chairman of the Academic Advisory Committee* was: Professor
D. H. Hey, Ph.D, DSC., FRIC, FRS.

The Royal Charter was granted on 22 December 1971 and the first
Principal of Chelsea College, named in the Charter, was: Malcolm
Ross Gavin, Esquire, CBE, MA, DSC., FInst.P, FIEE, MIERE.

The *Chairman of the Council* since 1972 has been: M. Weatherall,
MA, DM, DSC., FInst.Biol.

Principal:
1973– David J. E. Ingram, MA, DPhil., DSC., HON.DSC., FInst.P.

The University of Wales Institute of Science and Technology

A Mechanics' Institute existed in Cardiff from 1841 to 1856, but no
link has been traced between it and the classes held in 1862 in the
Free Library, or the Science and Art Schools started there in 1865–
66. Subjects catered for in these Schools were geometry, machine
drawing, building construction, mathematics and art, and the classes
were moved to rooms in the Royal Arcade in July 1870 and remained there till July 1882.[9] The next move was to the present
Library building in the Hayes, opened in 1882, and the work was
continued under the Library Committee still under the Libraries Act
of 1855, until after responsibility was taken over by the new University College in 1890. The Technical Instruction Act of 1889 and
the 'Whiskey Money' Local Taxation Act of 1890 led to the appointment by Cardiff County Borough of a Technical Instruction Committee, which took over from the Library Committee.

The title 'Cardiff Technical School' soon came into use. The
University College provided accommodation for the expanding

336

evening classes and the School finally left the Library premises in 1892 – in effect, the Borough farmed out this work to the College for a fixed annual payment. From 1890 to 1908 the first Principal of the University College acted as Principal of the Technical School. In these circumstances, and widely scattered as it was in many unsuitable buildings, the Technical School had no identity and was reported on adversely by Sir Philip Magnus in 1907. A Superintendent of Technical Education was accordingly appointed, and the Local Authority decided in 1911 on a new building which was opened in 1916. The site allowed further extensions, which were provided in 1918, 1927 and 1936.

The work was organised into the following Departments: Architecture, Art, Bakery, Chemistry, Commerce, Engineering, Mathematics, Navigation, Pharmacy and Physics. The Smith Nautical School was housed in the Technical College (so called in 1919) as was also a Junior Technical Commercial School, but this moved out in 1931. The foregoing pattern remained largely unchanged for twenty years, but full-time courses (started after World War I) developed steadily. Following the Report of the Royal Commission on the University of Wales (1917) the University established a Faculty of Technology and the Technical College was granted affiliation to the University under this scheme in 1923. Besides this affiliation, many students took London University external degrees. From 1937 students of pharmacy could prepare for an internal degree of the University of Wales, pursuing a course provided jointly with the University College and the Welsh National School of Medicine. Similar arrangements were made for architecture in 1939 but degrees were not awarded until 1948.

Acute accommodation problems in the post-war period were temporarily eased, but not solved by the transference elsewhere of the building classes, the Bakery Department, the Art School and the junior schools, and the Llandaff Technical College was opened in 1954 as a contributory college.

The College was designated a College of Advanced Technology on 15th March 1957, the only one in the Principality, with the title of Coleg Technoleg Uwchradd Cymru or the Welsh College of Advanced Technology. Work continued to expand, including sandwich courses, greatly hampered by the site problem, still basically unchanged until 1975. The College became financed by direct grant from the DES in 1962 and after the Robbins Report in 1963 it was quite widely supposed that it would become a University in its own right. However, other, strongly national, views prevailed against having a second University in Wales.

The major and severely frustrating problem of obtaining an adequate site, perforce away from Cathays Park, Cardiff (after an abortive attempt to establish a higher education precinct in combination with University College) showed welcome signs of resolution in 1975. Gwent County Council invited the Institute to move to a prospective site of 72·8 hectares at Llantarnam. Most of the site had been acquired by Gwent by December 1975, but the whole plan came to naught in 1976 because of Government refusal to provide the finance.

The Officers of the CAT were:
Chairman of the Governing Body:
1956–59 Councillor Llewelyn Jenkins.
1959–60 T. H. Huxley Turner, CBE, BSC., FIOB.
1960–61 Councillor Llewelyn Jenkins.
1961–62 Councillor H. Ferguson Jones, JP.
1962–67 W. F. Cartwright, DL, JP, MIMech.E.
Principal:
1956–68 A. Harvey, BSC., Ph.D, FInst.P.
The *Chairman of the Academic Advisory Committee* was: A. G. Ramsay, LLD, BSC., ARIC.

On 11th December 1967 the Royal Charter was granted incorporating the College as a constituent institution of the University of Wales as 'The University of Wales Institute of Science and Technology' (Athrofa Gwyddoniaeth a Technoleg Prifysgol Cymru). Officers since then have been:
Chairman of Council:
1967–68 W. F. Cartwright, OSt.J, DL, JP, MIMech.E.
1968–74 A. G. Ramsay, LLD, BSC., ARIC.
1974–76 G. Forbes Hayes, CSt.J, MA, MIMech. E.
Principal:
1967–68 A. Harvey, BSC., PhD, FInst.P.
1968– A. F. Trotman-Dickenson, MA, BSC., Ph.D, DSC.

Heriot-Watt University

On the initiative of Mr Leonard Horner FRS, now regarded as the founder, a group of well-known Edinburgh townspeople formed a committee and issued a prospectus for a 'School of Arts of Edinburgh for the Education of Mechanics in such Branches of Physical Science as are of Practical Application to their Several Trades'. It met with an enthusiastic response and the School was opened at the Freemasons' Hall, Niddry Street, on 16th October 1821. From 1837, the School rented premises in Adam Square, and these were purchased in 1852. This afforded a belated opportunity to take up a proposal made by Lord Cockburn in 1824 of a memorial to James Watt, who had then recently died, and the name of the School was changed to 'The Watt Institution and School of Arts'. In 1871 the building was pulled down, and the move was made to new buildings in Chambers Street in 1873–74. The debt then incurred, and the subsequent growth of work entailed financial difficulties such that in 1879 the Directors approached the Governors of the George Heriot Hospital Trust for assistance. As a result a Scheme was obtained in 1885 from the Educational Endowments (Scotland) Commission whereby the endowments of the two bodies were amalgamated, and the Institution was named the Heriot-Watt College.

The new Governors developed evening classes in art, trade, technical and commercial subjects, and started a Day Technical College for students wishing to obtain a sound technical training on University lines. They extended the building, provided suitable laboratories, classrooms and workshops and appointed a Principal and Professors. New Departments were added for mining, printing and allied trades and technical mycology. In 1902 a scheme of co-ordination was agreed between the governors and the School Board of Edinburgh whereby elementary classes were transferred to the Board and became a contributory to courses at the College for students qualifying from them. In 1908 the Edinburgh College of Art was formed by the combination of the Art School of the Royal Institution and Art department of the Heriot-Watt College.

Under the Heriot-Watt College and George Heriot's Trust Order Confirmation Act of 1927, a new Governing Body was established and met first in 1928. A plan of extensions was approved in 1931; the first section opened in 1935, and the second in 1938. The Governors entered into negotiations with the University of Edinburgh to

339

revise the existing Agreements, with the result that the College became an affiliated College of the University of Edinburgh. In 1935 the School of Pharmacy of the Royal Public Dispensary was incorporated with the Pharmacy Department of the College. In 1952 a new building in the Grassmarket for the Pharmacy Department was opened, and in 1953 another for the Mine Rescue Station. In 1958 the third section of the College main extension was opened by HRH The Duke of Edinburgh.

The proposals of the 1956 White Paper on Technical Education for establishing Colleges of Advanced Technology did not apply to Scotland, which already had Central Institutions (paras 113–14) and Heriot-Watt was therefore not designated as a College of Advanced Technology. It was, however, so considered in the Robbins Committee Report (p. 133) and its future University status assumed. The Scheme of Affiliation with the University of Edinburgh, already mentioned, did not prove congenial or fruitful and, after the Robbins Committee Report, any suggestion of possible incorporation within the University on the lines of UMIST stood no chance of success.

With the University status opportunity came to move to a new site of 31·5 hectares at Riccarton outwith the City of Edinburgh, which is well developed, but the central city site of 0·85 hectares is still used.

The Officers of the Heriot-Watt College from 1956 were:
Chairman of the Board of Governors: Lord Provost of the City of Edinburgh *ex officio.*
Vice-Chairman: Herbert A. Brechin, CBE, FH-WC, FRICS.
Principal: Hugh Bryan Nisbet, CBE, Ph.D, DSC., FH-WC, FRIC, FInst.F, FInst.Pet., FRSE.

The College became Heriot-Watt University on the grant of the Royal Charter on 4th March 1966 and the first Officers, named in the Charter, were:
Chancellor: The Rt. Hon. Sir Alexander Frederick Douglas-Home, KT, MA, DSC., DCL, LLD, FRSE, MP.
Principal and Vice-Chancellor: Hugh Bryan Nisbet, Esquire, CBE, Ph.D, DSC., DLitt., FH-WC, FRIC, FInst.F, FInst. Pet., FRSE.
The *Chairman of the Academic Advisory Committee* was: Sir Edmund Hudson, MA, DSC., FBIM, FRSE.

The *Chairmen of Court* have been:
1966–72 The Rt. Hon. the Lord Balerno of Currie, CBE, TD, DL, JP, MA, MSA, DSC., FRSE.
1972–   Sir Herbert Brechin, KBE, DL, JP, DLitt., FH-WC, FRICS, FRSE.
Principal and Vice-Chancellor:
1967–68 Professor Raymond A. Smart, MA, FIMA (Acting Principal).
1968–74 Robert Allan Smith, CBE, MA, Ph.D, FRSA, FRSE, FRS.
1974–   George Murray Burnett, Ph.D, DSC., FRIC, FRSE.

Appendix II Sources

1. J. Latimer, *The History of the Society of Merchant Venturers of the City of Bristol* (J. W. Arrowsmith, Bristol 1903) quoted by R. A. Buchanan in *A Technological University: an experiment in Bath*, ed. Gerald Walters, (Bath University Press, 1966).
2. Mabel Tylecote, *The Mechanics' Institutes of Lancashire and Yorkshire before 1851* (Manchester University Press, 1957), p. 51.
3. Indenture of foundation of Bradford Technical School, 3rd May 1871, cited in *Endowed charities, administrative county of the West Riding of York; and the County Borough of Bradford*, Vol. 2 (HMSO, 1897), p. 168.
4. Leonard M. Cantor and Geoffrey F. Matthews, *Loughborough: from College to University* (Loughborough University of Technology, 1977).
5. As 2, p. 78.
6. *Ibid.*, p. 80.
7. H. Arrowsmith, *Pioneering in Education for the Technologies: The Story of Battersea College of Technology* (The University of Surrey, 1966), p. 2.
8. Harold Silver and S. J. Teague (eds), *Chelsea College – a History* (Chelsea College, 1977).
9. A. Harvey, *1866–1966, One Hundred Years of Technical Education* (Welsh College of Advanced Technology, 1966).

Appendix III: Some Statistics

Table A111a Quinquennium 1967–72: numbers of students and size of recurrent grant per student place*

Institutions	1967–68		1968–69		1969–70		1970–71		1971–72		% increase	
	(a)	(b)	(a)	(b)	(a)	(b)	(a)	(b)	(a)	(b)	(a)	(b)
8 Technological Universities	17,717	£969†	19,103	£890	20,371	£931	21,334	£1,008	22,261	£1,114‡	26	15
All UK Universities	199,672	£754	211,485	£752	219,506	£830	228,131	£933	234,985	£1,061	18	41
Technological Universities as % of the whole	8·9		9·0		9·3		9·4		9·5			
Ratio of grant Technological Universities/Total	1·3:1		1·2:1		1·1:1		1·1:1		1·05:1			

Sources: UGC Report on *University Development 1967–72*, Cmnd. 5728 (HMSO, 1974) and UGC *Statistics of Education*, Vol. 6 (HMSO). Five volumes, covering 1967–72.
Key: (a) Number of full-time students. (b) Amount of grant per student place. (a × b) = Total recurrent grant.
Notes: * For the eight Technological Universities in this quinquennium the total recurrent grant was approximately £100 million. Of this, £4m was allocated between Aston, Bradford and Salford to meet the loan charges for capital expenditure on buildings incurred by their former governing bodies.
    † Six of the eight Technological Universities were within ± 10 per cent of the mean figure of £969. Aston was 15 per cent higher and City 26 per cent lower.
    ‡ Five of the eight fell within ± 10 per cent of £1,114. Brunel was 12 per cent higher; Bath and Loughborough were 20 and 16 per cent lower respectively.

Table AIIIb   Conferment of Diplomas in Technology (NCTA) 1958–64

Colleges of Advanced Technology	Years*						TOTAL
	1958–59	1959–60	1960–61	1961–62	1962–63	1963–64	
Battersea	—	8	12	82	78	87	268
Birmingham	34	89	125	154	171	184	757
Bradford	—	—	—	—	9	72	81
Bristol	—	—	—	6	54	49	109
Brunel	—	4	54	44	61	91	254
Chelsea	—	—	—	—	11	4	15
Loughborough	—	—	24	47	96	116	283
Northampton	—	5	42	121	195	151	514
Salford	—	—	—	60	84	119	263
Welsh CAT	—	—	11	12	16	26	65
TOTAL CATs	34	106	268	526	776	899	2,609
TOTAL all Colleges	34	129	309	620	927	1,073	3,092
CATs as % of Total	*100*	*82·2*	*86·7*	*84·8*	*83·7*	*83·8*	*84·4*

Note: * Years run from 1st April to 31st March.
Source: NCTA Annual Reports.

*Table A*III*c* Details of Imperial College of Science and Technology, University of Manchester Institute of Science and Technology (UMIST) and the University of Strathclyde

In relation to the Robbins Committee proposal of Special Institutions for Scientific and Technological Education and Research (SISTERS) (Chapter I), brief summary details are given below of three institutions proposed as such, to indicate their range of work (figures supplied by the institutions).

(i) *Full-time registered students at 31st October 1976*

	Under-graduate	Post-graduate	TOTAL	Per cent postgraduates
Imperial College	2,711	1,509	4,220	*35·8*
UMIST	2,692	1,111	3,803	*29·2*
University of Strathclyde	5,204	1,104	6,308	*17·5*

(ii) *Expenditure from external grants/contracts for research*

Income from external grants/contracts: expenditure in year 1975–76

	Research Councils	Government departments	Industry & commerce	Other bodies	TOTAL £000
Imperial College	2,262	596	593	338	3,789
UMIST	449·6	164·4	173·9	56·8	844·7
University of Strathclyde	434·8	574·6	119·5	323·2	1,452

Note: Total values of SRC Awards (only) as at 31st March 1976 are given in the 1975–76 Annual Report, Table 2 (HMSO): Imperial College £4,381,000, UMIST £1,375,000, Strathclyde £1,004,000: 3 University institutions had total awards of £4m and over, 6 of £2–3·9m, 12 of £1–1·99m, and 47 less than £1m. The last group included the eight Technological Universities, with a range from £208,000 to £889,000, and total value of £3,675,000.

Table A11d Enrolments in full-time higher education (England and Wales) in relation to projections 000s

Year	Universities (including former CATs)		Colleges of Education (including Technical)		Further Education		All full-time higher education		% students in Universities	
	(a)	(b)	(a)	(b)	(a)	(b)	(a)	(b)	(a)	(b)
A										
Robbins Report projections										
1962–63		109		48		28		185		59
1963–64	119	116	53	55	33	33	205	204	58	57
1964–65	130	127	59	63	36	40	225	230	58	55
1965–66	144	141	66	73	38	47	248	261	58	54
1966–67	155	155	71	85	40	55	267	295	58	53
1967–68	163	168	75	96	43	66	281	331	58	51
% growth 1962–68	50	54	56	100	54	136	52	79		
B										
EPP projections										
1968–69	179	178	108	104	76	76	363	359	49	50
1969–70	189	184	114	107	85	83	388	374	49	49
1970–71	202	192	117	109	94	88	413	386	49	50
1971–72	216	197	118	111	103	94	437	403	49	49
1972–73	229	201	119	113	112	96	460	410	50	49
% growth 1968–73	28	13	10	9	47	26	27	14		

C	1973–74	240	205	119	111	119	100	479	416	*50*	*49*
EPP projections	1974–75	254	210	120	104	127	106	502	421	*51*	*50*
	1975–76	269	221	122	88	136	127	527	436	*51*	*48*
	1976–77‡	287	231	124	(*)	146	(†)	557	439	*52*	*53*
	1977–78	307		127		156		590		*52*	
% growth	1973–78	*28*		*7*		*31*		*23*			

Key: (a) = projected (b) = actual

Sources: The general form of this table is based on Table A9 (omitting Scotland) in Richard Layard, John King, Claus Moser, *The Impact of Robbins* (Penguin Education Special, Harmondsworth, 1969). This book gives an excellent appraisal as of 1969. The Robbins Report projections appear in Appendix One, Part IV, Table 51, p. 167 (HMSO).

The projected figures for Parts B and C (1968 onwards) are the number of places given in Table C, p. 45 of Education Planning Paper (EPP) No. 2, *Student Numbers in Higher Education in England and Wales* (HMSO. London. 1970). Sources for actual figures are *Statistics of Education*, Vol. 3, *Further Education*; Vol. 4, *Teachers* and Vol. 6 *Universities*; figures for 1975/76 and 1976/77 were supplied by the Department of Education and Science.

Notes: * + † = 208.

‡ Provisional on estimated figures.

Table AIIIe Technological Universities: Size of campus December 1975

University	Total area in hectares	Additional area in process of acquisition
Aston	60·7	—
Bath	70·5	6·1
Bradford	38·0	6·1
Brunel	66·4	—
City	17·9	
Loughborough	81·0	—
Salford	59·0	—
Surrey	131·0	—
Chelsea College	6·9	
UWIST	7·9	
Heriot-Watt		
– at Riccarton	77·9	
– in Central Edinburgh	2·1	

* See Brief History for planned development on new site.

Table AIIIf Polytechnics and constituent institutions (April 1977)

	Constituent institutions*
CITY OF BIRMINGHAM *Designated January 1971*	North B. Technical College South B. Technical College B. College of Commerce B. College of Art and Design B. School of Music Anstey College of Physical Education City of B. College of Education Bordesley College of Education
BRIGHTON *Designated April 1970*	B. College of Technology* B. College of Art
BRISTOL *Designated September 1969*	B. Technical College B. College of Commerce West of England College of Art Redland College College of St Matthias

Note: * Indicates institutions listed as a Regional College in 1956–57.

Constituent institutions*

HATFIELD *Designated January 1969*	H. College of Technology*
HUDDERSFIELD *Designated June 1970*	H. College of Technology* Oastler College of Education H. College of Education (Technical)
KINGSTON *Designated January 1970*	K. College of Technology* K. College of Art
LANCHESTER *Designated January 1970*	L. College of Technology* Coventry College of Art Rugby College of Engineering Technology*
LEEDS *Designated January 1970*	L. College of Technology* L. College of Commerce L. College of Art Yorkshire College of Education and Home Economics City of L. and Carnegie College of Education James Graham College
CITY OF LEICESTER *Designated April 1969*	L. Regional College of Technology* L. College of Art and Design City of L. College of Education
LIVERPOOL *Designated April 1970*	L. College of Technology* L. College of Building* L. College of Commerce L. College of Art
THE POLYTECHNIC OF CENTRAL LONDON *Designated May 1970*	The Polytechnic, Regent Street Holborn College of Law, Languages, Com- merce Sidney Webb College
CITY OF LONDON *Designated May 1970*	C. of L. College Sir John Cass College King Edward VII Nautical College (part)
NORTH LONDON *Designated May 1971*	Northern Polytechnic* North-Western Polytechnic
NORTH EAST LONDON *Designated September 1970*	Waltham Forest Technical College and School of Art

349

Ap. III *Some Statistics*

	Constituent institutions*
	West Ham College of Technology*
	Barking Regional College of Technology*

POLYTECHNIC OF THE SOUTH BANK *Designated September 1970*	Borough Polytechnic* Brixton School of Building (advanced work only) City of Westminster College National College for Heating, Ventilating, Refrigeration and Fan Engineering

THAMES *Designated September 1970*	Woolwich Polytechnic* Hammersmith College of Art and Building (Departments of Architecture and Surveying only)

MANCHESTER *Designated January 1970*	M. College of Commerce M. College of Art and Design John Dalton College of Technology

MIDDLESEX *Designated January 1973*	Enfield College of Technology Hendon College of Technology Hornsey College of Art Trent Park College of Education New College of Speech and Drama

NEWCASTLE UPON TYNE *Designated September 1969*	Rutherford College of Technology* Municipal College of Commerce N. u. T. College of Art and Industrial Design City of N. College of Education

NORTH STAFFORDSHIRE *Designated January 1970*	S. College of Technology North S. College of Technology* Stoke-on-Trent College of Art

OXFORD *Designated April 1970*	O. College of Technology Lady Spencer Churchill College of Education

PLYMOUTH *Designated January 1970*	P. College of Technology*

PORTSMOUTH *Designated September 1969*	P. College of Technology* P. College of Art and Design (Department of Fine Art)

*Constituent institutions**

Bournemouth College of Technology (Department of Surveying)

P. College of Education

PRESTON *Designated September 1973*	Harris College of Further Education Chorley College of Education Poulton-Le-Fylde College
SHEFFIELD *Designated January 1969*	S. College of Technology S. College of Art S. City College of Education Totly-Thornbridge College of Education
SUNDERLAND *Designated January 1969*	S. Technical College* S. College of Art S. College of Education
TEESSIDE *Designated April 1970*	Constantine College of Technology
TRENT *Designated June 1970*	Nottingham Regional College of Technology* Nottingham College of Art and Design Nottingham College of Education
WOLVERHAMPTON *Designated September 1969*	W. College of Technology W. College of Art
THE POLYTECHNIC OF WALES *Designated April 1970*	Glamorgan College of Technology* Glamorgan College of Education

Source: List supplied by DES, 14th April 1977.

Appendix IV: Enquiries using Questionnaires

THESE were addressed to various groups of people involved with the CATs from 1956 onwards, and the methods used included requests by letter for factual information, 3–5 day visits to the institutions for semi-structured interviews and a 14-page questionnaire incorporating an attitude survey addressed to a stratified random sample of staff in the eight Technological Universities and the two University Colleges, Chelsea and UWIST.

The functions and work of the Academic Advisory Committees: Questionnaire 1

This questionnaire was sent to all Members (N = 63) appointed by the UGC to the eight Colleges designated to become Technological Universities. 57 – over 90 per cent – replied. Results are reported in Table 7.3.

Questionnaire 1

[In this and subsequent questionnaires an ellipsis . . . indicates that in the original a suitable space was left for the response. To give as compact a view of the content as possible no attempt has been made to reproduce the actual amount of space.]

STRICTLY CONFIDENTIAL

1. Name of University . . .
2. (Optional question) Name . . .
3. Post held at time of appointment to the Committee . . .
4. Do you consider that the terms of reference of the Committee were reasonably adequate for its work?
   Yes | Doubtful | No (Tick)

[On the actual questionnaires boxes were provided for items requiring ticking or ringing.]

Comment on any changes which, in your opinion, would have enabled the Committee to be more helpful to the University.

5. In your opinion was the number of Members on the Committee *Too large | Satisfactory | Too small* (Tick)
   Comment . . .

6. Did you feel that the balance of the membership was generally satisfactory? *Yes | Doubtful | No* (Tick)
   Comment . . .

7. Among all the matters that your Committee had to deal with please list the three that you found most difficult.
   (1) . . . (2) . . . (3) . . .
   Comment . . .

8. From your experience would you consider the appointment of an Academic Advisory Committee to be
   Unnecessary | Desirable | Indispensable (Tick)
   Comment . . .

9. Did you find that the total period allowed for the Committee to complete its work was *Too long | About right | Too short* (Tick)
   If too long or too short, indicate by how much . . .
   Comment . . .

10. In the general debate on the increase in the number of Universities in the 1960s, one frequent question was whether it was better to establish entirely new Universities or to convert existing institutions. This may arise again with the doubling of the University population in the 1970s, and it would be very helpful to have your comments on this issue.

11. One of the purposes of this study is to discover how far, if at all, the change from College of Advanced Technology to University has affected the work of these institutions.

    Listed below is a set of statements indicating possible changes in the direction of the traditional Civic Universities. Please indicate appropriately with a tick in Columns A and B your own preferences and your impressions about the direction of change in your institution.

M   353

Column A	Column B				
My attitude to this change is one of: (*Tick*)	It is my opinion that my institution has changed in the traditional direction: (*Tick*)				
	1	2	3	4	5
Un- Dis- Approval certainty approval	Very much	Consider- ably	Not certain	Hardly at all	Not at all

[The options for ticking given above were repeated, with appropriate space for comments as well, against each of the following *Possible changes of emphasis*:]

(a) Fewer part-time courses

(b) Fewer sandwich courses

(c) An increase in Social Sciences and Arts courses with a consequent decrease in the proportion of science and technology

(d) A greater emphasis on research

(e) The addition of an Arts Faculty

(f) Reduced interest in applied courses designed to meet the needs of industry and/or commerce

12. There is at present no general agreement:
    (a) about whether or not it is desirable to have a group of Universities especially designated as technological institutions
    (b) if such a group *is* desirable, what their characteristics should be.
    Please comment ...

13. Please add comments on the future of the Technological Universities, bearing in mind particularly (a) the emergence of the Polytechnics and (b) the creation of 'centres of excellence' by a policy of Research Councils in concentrating grants for research and major equipment.

Relationships with industry and commerce: Questionnaire 2

This form was sent to 100 Council Members of the eight institutions who were believed to have associations with some branch of industry or commerce. 64 returned completed forms and many of the remaining 36 wrote, making some comments but disclaiming competence to deal with all the questions. The results are reported in Table 7.4.

Questionnaire 2

[As noted at the beginning of Questionnaire 1 an ellipsis . . . indicates that
a suitable space was left in the original for the response.]

STRICTLY CONFIDENTIAL

1. Name of University . . .   Name (Optional) . . .
2. (a) Period(s) of membership of Council . . .
   (b) Period(s) of membership of Governing Body of the former
   College of Advanced Technology . . .
3. Please indicate (a) the nature of your own employment . . .
   (b) what body, if any, nominated you to the Council . . .
4. One of the purposes of this study is to discover how far, if at all,
   the change from College of Advanced Technology to University
   has affected the work of these institutions.

   Listed below is a set of statements indicating possible changes
   in the direction of the traditional Civic Universities. Please indicate appropriately with a tick in Columns A and B your own
   preferences and your impressions about the direction of change
   in your institution.

Column A

My attitude to this change
is one of:
(*Tick*)

Un-	Dis-
Approval	certainty	approval

Column B

It is my opinion that my institution has
changed in the traditional direction:
(*Tick*)

1	2	3	4	5
Very	Consider-	Not	Hardly	Not
much	ably	certain	at all	at all

[The options for ticking given above were repeated, with appropriate space
for comments as well, against each of the following *Possible changes of
emphasis*:]

(a) Fewer part-time courses
(b) Fewer sandwich courses
(c) An increase in Social Sciences and Arts courses with a consequent
    decrease in the proportion of science and technology
(d) A greater emphasis on research
(e) The addition of an Arts Faculty
(f) Reduced interest in applied courses designed to meet the needs
    of industry and/or commerce

---

5. Assuming that some groups might exert an influence favouring change towards more traditional patterns and others might resist such changes, please indicate what, in your opinion, was the degree and direction of influence of the following:

	Your opinion of the degree and direction of influence for and against traditional university patterns (*Tick*)				
Group	Strongly in favour	Moderately in favour	Not certain	Moderately against	Strongly against
Council	...	...	...	...	...
Senate	...	...	...	...	...
Academic Advisory Committee	...	...	...	...	...
Academic staff	...	...	...	...	...
Students	...	...	...	...	...
Representatives of industry and commerce	...	...	...	...	...
Professional bodies	...	...	...	...	...

6. There is at present no general agreement:
   (a) about whether or not it is desirable to have a group of Universities especially designated as technological institutions
   (b) if such a group *is* desirable, what their characteristics should be.
   Please comment ...

7. In the general debate on the increase in the number of Universities in the 1960s one frequent question was whether it was better to establish entirely new Universities or to convert existing institutions. This may arise again with the doubling of the University population in the 1970s, and it would be very helpful to have your comments on this issue.

8. Please add comments on the future of the Technological Universities, bearing in mind particularly (a) the emergence of the Polytechnics and (b) the creation of 'centres of excellence' by a policy of Research Councils in concentrating grants for research and major equipment.

Visits to Universities, University Colleges and Polytechnics

Twenty-one institutions were visited for discussions with groups of staff and students as well as individuals. These were tape-recorded and the typescripts analysed by institution under thirteen subject headings.* In the case of the ten ex-CATs and Heriot-Watt there was a preliminary exploratory visit after which the programme for the second occasion, which spanned 3–5 days, was planned.

Ten Polytechnics – chosen from the thirty to be representative in terms of size and range of studies – were each visited for a day of recorded discussions with the Director and senior staff. The detailed records of all these discussions were the source material for comments and judgements and verbatim quotations throughout the text.

Other enquiries by letter

There has naturally been considerable correspondence during the study seeking information on a wide range of topics including statistics.

The Academic Staff: Questionnaire 3

The final version of the questionnaire used in this study is reproduced at the end of this section. It was intended to be anonymous but a few respondents did in fact sign their comments at the end.

Item 1 is a code number indicating the University or College of origin followed by an integer determined by the order of receipt, thus monitoring the number of respondents from each institution without identifying them.

Part I

(a) Items 2–12 deal with biographical data: age; sex; rank; date of first appointment to the College/University; previous experience, e.g. industrial/non-industrial; schooling and qualifications.

(b) Items 13–31 were taken, with the permission of the authors,

* Transition problems; Charters; sandwich courses; general studies; curricula and teaching; academic staff; students; research and postgraduate work; industry, commerce and the professions; attitudes to Polytechnics and part-time courses; finance; administration; future plans.

357

from the Halsey and Trow survey* to provide comparative data. They explore the experiences of teachers and research workers; what resources were available to them, including study leave; and their academic publications and outside activities. Items 27–31 relate to the educational and occupational status of the respondents' parents and to qualifications of the spouse and education of children where applicable. Results on Part I are reported in the following Tables: 8.4 to 8.10 and 8.12 to 8.23.

Part II

This consists of 20 pairs of categorical statements to which the respondent is invited to agree or disagree on a 4-point scale. Every pair deals with a different aspect of higher education using two statements polarised towards opposite extremes. There are two groups of statements (X and Y) and responses were recorded separately, but in constructing the questionnaire their order was randomised and they were presented as an entity.

Group X: the Attitude Inventory

This consists of 6 pairs (12 statements) dealing with the ethos of the CATs, a shorthand phrase which is explained later. Together they form a scale constructed in the manner devised by Likert,† which allows scores on each statement to be summed to give – in this particular case – a 'CAT' score. Results are discussed in Chapter 8 and presented statistically in Tables 8.29 to 8.32 and Tables AIV4 to AIV11. The numbers of the 12 statements in the questionnaire are: 1, 2, 6, 7, 13, 18, 21, 25, 32, 34, 35 and 38.

Group Y

This comprises the 28 remaining statements, some of which are taken from the Halsey and Trow study. They deal either with the respondent's own situation, e.g. time spent on research/teaching, or with his opinions on various aspects of Universities, e.g. size, promotion policies, general and professional studies, etc. These are

* A. H. Halsey and Martin Trow, *The British Academics* (Faber and Faber, London 1971).

† R. Likert, 'A technique for the measurement of attitudes', *Arch. Psychol.*, No. 140, 1932.

See also, A. L. Edwards, *Techniques of Attitude Scale Construction* (Appleton-Century-Crofts Inc., New York 1957).

reported in terms of the percentage of respondents *agreeing* with each statement. Results are incorporated into the appropriate chapters: 2, 4, 5, 7, 8, 10, 11 and 12.

Rationale

As is discussed in Chapter 1 the change from Local Technical College to University took place in three stages. When the Advanced Colleges were designated difficult decisions had to be taken about who should transfer to other Colleges and who should stay. Some members of staff made the decision for themselves, opting perhaps for senior posts in other Local Colleges in preference to an unpredictable future in the emerging independent institutions. However, an enquiry in 1972 showed that 12 per cent of the staff in post in the ten institutions had been appointed before 1956.*

In studying the changing status of these institutions the point of departure was to monitor the changing nature of incoming staff at each of three nodal points: 1956, 1962 and 1966–67. Changes could be expected in the academic standing of applicants and in the final stage candidates already occupying University posts would be in the running, which was a rarity in the College days.

The plan was to divide respondents into four groups according to period of appointment and to record inter-group differences in attitude scores, academic attainment, previous experience, etc.

Group O consisted of those appointed before August 1956, i.e. in the Technical College days.

Group I were those appointed from August 1956 (when the Colleges of Advanced Technology were designated) up to:

Group II July 1962, when they became independent direct grant institutions under a Trust Deed, and

Group III those joining the staff during and after 1966–67, when Charters were granted.

It was postulated that the attitudes of the stereo-typical 'CAT man' as distinct from the 'traditional' university man would be linked to:

1. a commitment to sandwich courses with their organised and supervised training on the job alternating with academic study.

* A further 26 per cent were in Group I, i.e. 38 per cent had been appointed before 1962. Variations among the institutions were from 31 per cent at Bath to 43 per cent at Surrey and 44 per cent at Chelsea. See Table 8.5.

2. the idea of specialised technological institutions (with no Arts Faculties) retaining their special identity alongside some of the other new Universities with little or no technology and a strong commitment to the arts.
3. a greater emphasis on the teaching function.
4. introductory professional studies in, for example, management and economics, during the undergraduate years.

General or complementary studies were also a feature of the Diploma in Technology course, but how far staff and students had remained committed to this idea was uncertain. Statements in this area were included in the inventory, but no prediction was made as to the outcome.

The concept plan of 20 items for Part II is set out below. Using this plan, 80 statements were devised (four per item) and were incorporated into the first draft of the questionnaire, which was presented to a pilot sample of staff drawn from the University of Aston of whom 30 (83·3 per cent) responded. The consistency of their responses was measured by calculating phi coefficients* for each group of four statements. As indicated in the plan, high scores (3 or 4) were given to those responses favouring the opinions and attitudes expressed in the SE segment of each of the 20 areas.

Questionnaire Part II: Concept Plan

Areas to be monitored and topics within each area to be converted to statements

SE segment scores high in all cases. [In the actual document the topics were set out in rectangles divided diagonally, with the first in each of the paired statements below placed in the NW, and the second in the SE corner.]

H & T refers to Halsey and Trow, *The British Academics*, Questionnaire, Appendix B, pp. 497–507.

A. *The ethos of the CATs and the Diploma in Technology*

1. Sandwich courses and relationships with industry and commerce
   (a) *Sandwich courses*
   Not essential : Indispensable

* J. P. Guildford, *Fundamental Statistics in Psychology and Education* (McGraw Hill, New York 1950), pp. 340–345.

(b) *Real-life experiences*
Experience outside University not necessary : Highly desirable
(c) *Value for staff*
A distraction – separate personnel needed : Keeps them up to date
(d) *Relations with industry and commerce*
No different from other Universities : Should aim to be different from the technological departments of other Universities

2. Specialisation within Universities
(a) *Universal coverage*
Essential for any institution calling itself a University : Would interfere with the specific nature of a Technological University
(b) *Arts Faculties*
Need to counteract the influence of scientists and technologists : Would add to the traditional pressures
(c) *The future – special identity*
Merge with the rest : Keep their identity

3. Teaching/research
(a) *H & T 49(i), p. 505*
Research first loyalty : Greater recognition of the teaching function
(b) *H & T 49(vi), p. 505*
Emphasise research : Emphasise teaching
(c) *H & T 49(vii), p. 505*
Promotion; Published works : Teaching

4. Professional studies
(a) Deferred to postgraduate : At undergraduate stage

5. General studies
(a) *Not germane to Universities*
Only needed for lower level students : Ex-CATs should retain them
(b) *Universal need*
Implicit in the structure of a University : Need to be explicit for all students – Arts as well as Science

B. *University education generally*

1. Specialisation / broad cultural education
(a) *H & T 49(ii), p. 505*
Widely cultural : Train experts

361

(b) *H & T 49 (iii), p. 505*
General degrees : Single subject honours

2. Professorships
   (a) *H & T 49 (iv), p. 505*
   Elite (Britain) : Normal expectation (USA)
   (b) *H & T 49 (viii, ix), p. 505*
   Professors too powerful : Rotating Chairmen of Departments

3. Size of Universities : expansionist/elitist
   (a) *cf. H & T Q.6, p. 499*
   More means worse : Expansion

4. Transfer of numbers to other forms of higher education
   (a) *H & T 49 (xii), p. 505*
   Preserve quality : Expand other forms of higher education
   (b) *Polytechnics*
   Unwelcome : Welcome

The results from the Attitude Inventory (Group X statements) were expected to indicate how far, if at all, 'CAT' attitudes had persisted and whether the new status and the appointment of new staff had begun to press these institutions into a more traditional mould. With the Group Y statements there was no assumption that attitudes would necessarily be dichotomised on the CAT/traditional continuum. However, for the sake of clarity, the direction of scoring was broadly away from traditional attitudes, reserving the high scores for responses favouring changes of status towards the American pattern; expansion; greater co-operation between institutions of higher education and some specialisation of function within Universities.

The 80 statements devised to cover this plan are set out below. They were presented to the pilot sample in random order together with a four-column answer form labelled *Agree firmly*; *Agree on the whole; Disagree on the whole; Disagree firmly*. In surveys of this kind a five-column answer form is frequently used, allowing a central, *neutral/don't know* column. This is less irritating to the respondents who object to being confronted with black/white situations, but a forced choice using only four categories is advantageous to the research worker. Judging by the co-operation we received, our explanation/apology at the head of Part II on the final form was fairly generally accepted. It read: 'There is no column for "not certain"; this is deliberate. In practical situations, choices are forced upon us and you are asked to say where you would stand in the last resort.' Understandably enough some respondents protested, a few vigorously, and some statements were ignored.

The 80 statements based on the Concept Plan used in the pilot run

		Q. Serial No.	Random No.

A. The ethos of the CATs and the Diploma in Technology

1. Sandwich courses and relationships with industry and commerce

(a) *Sandwich courses*

		Serial No.	Random No.
	(i) In the Technological Universities sandwich courses should comprise at least two-thirds of all courses.	1	39
	(ii) The organisation of scientific and technological courses in the Technological Universities should not aim to be specifically different from those in the traditional Universities.	2	80
1c*	(iii) The advantages of sandwich courses do not justify the extra difficulties involved in arranging them.	3	1
35c	(iv) The Technological Universities would be losing their greatest asset if they abandoned sandwich courses.	4	68

(b) *Real-life experiences*

	(i) Some supervised training in the practical application of a subject outside the University should be obligatory for students of a Technological University.	5	27
38c	(ii) There is no overriding argument for the provision of supervised practical training during the period of a degree course.	6	76
18c* †	(iii) The argument that professional training and undergraduate study can be closely related is untenable.	7	28

* Numbers are those used in the final version of the questionnaire q.v. The letter C indicates that the statement was used to determine the 'CAT' score.

† Indicates that the form of the statement was reversed in the final questionnaire. Applies also to statements numbered 37 and 8.

363

		Serial No.	Q. Random No.
	(iv) A student's learning of his academic subject is advanced by a sandwich course programme.	8	44
(c) Value for staff			
21c	(i) Sandwich courses enable staff to keep in touch with industrial and commercial developments.	9	33
34c	(ii) The supervision of industrial periods on sandwich courses needs a special establishment of non-academics.	10	63
	(iii) Supervisory visits to organisations employing sandwich course students are too great a burden for academic staff.	11	20
21c	(iv) Supervisory visits by academic staff to sandwich course students in training are advantageous in improving curricula and teaching, and/or in stimulating research projects.	12	3
(d) Relations with industry and commerce			
	(i) Technological Universities should maintain special relationships with industry and commerce different from those obtaining with other Universities.	13	69
	(ii) A close identification with industry and commerce is inappropriate for a University institution.	14	24
32c	(iii) Industry and commerce have a great need for graduates who have had a sandwich type of training.	15	61
2c	(iv) After a year in a job the three-year trained engineering graduate is indistinguishable from a four-year sandwich course graduate.	16	2

2. Specialisation within Universities

(a) Universal coverage

19	(i) A University is not complete without a Faculty of Arts.	17	29
5	(ii) A University is not complete without a Faculty of Technology.	18	8

			Q.
		Serial	Random
		No.	No.

| | (iii) Nowadays no University can claim to cover every academic subject. | 19 | 49 |
| | (iv) There are advantages in different Universities concentrating their efforts on different parts of the spectrum of knowledge. | 20 | 25 |

(b) Art Faculties in ex-CATs

	(i) The introduction of Arts Faculties into the Technological Universities would very soon make them indistinguishable from the traditional Universities.	21	40
	(ii) It would be to the mutual benefit of engineering and Arts students if all Technological Universities had an Arts Faculty.	22	37
7c	(iii) My University should not establish an Arts Faculty.	23	10
25c	(iv) My University would benefit by having an Arts Faculty.	24	46

(c) The future – special identity for ex-CATs

	(i) The sooner the Technological Universities become indistinguishable from the rest of the University world, the better.	25	53
6c	(ii) It would be bad for technological education in this country if the ex-CATs lost their special identity.	26	9
13c	(iii) The ex-CATs should not aim to preserve a distinctive role for themselves in the University world.	27	18
	(iv) It is advantageous to have an identifiable group of Universities specially committed to the application of knowledge.	28	60

3. Teaching/research

(a) cf. H&T 49 (i) p. 505†

| 14 | (i) An academic man's first loyalty should be to research in his discipline. | 29 | 19 |
| 33 | (ii) There should be more academics in Universities whose main commitment is to teaching. | 30 | 62 |

† H&T refers to statements used in the Halsey and Trow study.

		Serial No.	Q. Random No.

(iii) The teaching of students and the running of one's University are secondary considerations in an academic career. — 31 — 15

(iv) The first loyalty of members of a University staff should be to the teaching of students. — 32 — 72

(*b*) cf. *H&T* 49 (*vi*) p. 505

(i) Most teachers of my subject put too much emphasis on teaching compared with research. — 33 — 6

(ii) Most teachers of my subject spend too much time on research compared with teaching. — 34 — 32

15 (iii) Successful research in my subject requires teams of full-time research workers. — 35 — 21

24 (iv) In my subject I have no problem in combining good teaching with effective research. — 36 — 42

(*c*) cf. *H&T* 49 (*vii*) p. 505

9 (i) Promotion in academic life is too dependent on published work. — 37 — 12

(ii) The devoted teacher should be promoted more often than he is. — 38 — 22

(iii) Promotion within the University should be reserved for those who have shown themselves capable of fundamental research. — 39 — 45

31 (iv) The distinguishing feature of the University don is his ability as a research worker. — 40 — 59

4. Professional studies

(i) The engineering undergraduate course should contain some introductory professional studies. — 41 — 30

23 (ii) Professional studies in, for example, management and economics, should be introduced at the undergraduate stage. — 42 — 38

29 (iii) Management education and/or similar professional studies should be delayed until after graduation. — 43 — 57

366

		Q.
	Serial	Random
	No.	No.

(iv) Professional studies should not be introduced at the undergraduate stage.   44   74

5. General Studies

(a) Not germane to Universities

37*   (i) The Technological Universities should continue to include General Studies in their degree courses.   45   73

    (ii) General Studies Departments are not germane to a University institution.   46   48

    (iii) The introduction of General Studies is only necessary for students on elementary courses.   47   34

40   (iv) The education of a technologist is incomplete if he is not given the opportunity of disciplined study in the Arts or social sciences during his undergraduate years.   48   78

(b) Universal need

    (i) It is just as important for Arts students to be numerate as it is for science and technology students to have some appreciation of literature.   49   43

27   (ii) University teachers should concentrate on teaching their speciality and leave students to look after the wider aspects of their education themselves.   50   54

    (iii) All undergraduates, whatever their speciality, should be obliged to spend part of their time on non-specialist studies.   51   64

8*   (iv) With respect to the wider education of their students, Universities should restrict their efforts to the provision of voluntary courses and seminars on non-professional subjects.   52   11

B. University education generally

1. Specialisation/broad cultural education

    (a) cf. H&T 49 (ii) p. 505

       (i) University education in England puts too

		Serial No.	Q. Random No.
	little emphasis on the training of experts.	53	52
	(ii) University education should concentrate on the education of widely cultivated men.	54	79
3	(iii) The three or four undergraduate years should be mainly devoted to becoming thoroughly competent in one subject.	55	4
11	(iv) Undergraduates should not specialise in one subject only.	56	14

(b) cf. *H&T 49 (iii) p. 505*

	(i) In English Universities the single-subject honours degree is over-emphasised.	57	7
	(ii) There are too few general degrees in English Universities.	58	66
22	(iii) The single-subject honours degree is ideal for the student with a vocational commitment.	59	36
20	(iv) The student committed to a particular career should not be expected to do a general degree.	60	31

2. Professorships

(a) cf. *H&T 49 (iv) p. 505*

	(i) A Professorship ought to be the normal expectation of an academic career.	61	67
	(ii) The British Universities should retain the title of Professor for only the most outstanding academics.	62	41
4	(iii) The status differences in Britain between Professors, lecturers and teachers are outmoded.	63	5
17	(iv) The use in Britain of the title 'Professor' for most University teachers, as is done in America, would be a retrograde step.	64	26

(b) cf. *H&T 49 (viii) (ix) p. 505*

26	(i) A serious disadvantage of Redbrick Universities is that they are all too often run by a professorial oligarchy.	65	26
16	(ii) Most British University departments		

		Q. Serial No.	Q. Random No.

would be better run by the method of circulating Chairmanship than by a permanent Head of Department. — 66 — 23

(iii) The Charter of my University gives too little representation on Council and Senate to non-professorial staff and should be revised. — 67 — 47

(iv) At my University the influence of Professors has been seriously weakened by a reduction in their representation on Council and Senate. — 68 — 16

3. Size of universities: expansionist/élitist

(a) cf. H&T Q.6 p. 499

39   (i) In relation to University expansion 'more' *does* mean 'worse'. — 69 — 77

10   (ii) We have by no means reached the limit of able young people who could benefit by a University education. — 70 — 13

(iii) The numbers of students in British Universities should be at least doubled by 1980. — 71 — 50

(iv) Student numbers in the Universities of Britain should remain at their present level for many years to come. — 72 — 75

4. Transfer of numbers to other forms of higher education

(a) H&T 49 (xii) p. 505

(i) A halt to further expansion is necessary to preserve the essential quality of British University life. — 73 — 71

12   (ii) Non-University forms of higher education should be expanded, leaving the Universities as they are. — 74 — 17

28   (iii) Local or regional mergers between all forms of higher education would be advantageous. — 75 — 56

(iv) Colleges of Education and Polytechnics should become part of the University system. — 76 — 35

369

		Serial No.	Q. Random No.
	(b) Polytechnics		
30	(i) The establishment of 30 Polytechnics is a great mistake.	77	58
	(ii) The growth of the Polytechnics will threaten the expansion of the Technological Universities.	78	65
	(iii) Technician education will not suffer by the upgrading of the Polytechnics.	79	55
36	(iv) The creation of the Polytechnics is a good answer to the problems of expansion in higher education.	80	70

Among the questions in Part ɪb borrowed from Halsey and Trow's study were some dealing with political and religious affiliations. Some respondents on the pilot run objected to these on the grounds that anonymity was not completely assured. This was true: the Halsey and Trow survey was large and conducted by post; this one was smaller and more intimate as it included interviews – free-ranging and unstructured – as well as the postal questionnaire. Moreover, worker and subjects were in many cases well known to each other. Within a small Department with – say – only one Professor and one senior lecturer anyone wishing to identify such a respondent could have done so. The question did not in fact arise because the recording and coding of the responses was done by the research assistant who had little, if any, personal contact with respondents. Nevertheless the objection was respected and the questions omitted.

However, the most important reason for the pilot run was to test the first draft of the Attitude Inventory. By means of the phi coefficients the 80 statements were reduced to 40 by choosing the two out of each group of four statements which produced the most consistent responses. Two statements may appear to the research worker to oppose each other but be perceived by the respondents as ambiguous and so produce inconsistent answers. Valid conclusions on any of the separate topics can only be drawn if the paired statements confirm each other and where a group of statements is to be summed it is clearly essential that the responses be consistent. In the event 61 out of the 80 statements (75 per cent) produced a highly consistent result with a probability that it was due to chance of 0·01 or less. Six others had probabilities of the order of 0·02 and the remaining 13 were unsuitable for use in a summed score, the probabilities being 0·05 or higher. In the final questionnaire all but one of the 12 statements (No.6 p = 0·05) in the Attitude Inventory had probabilities of 0·01 or less. Of the other 28, 23 had a value of 0·01; three (14, 19 and 21) rated 0·02 and the remaining two (5 and 33) had probabilities of 0·5 and 0·3 respectively. Results in such cases are only of value if treated as opinion ratings.

The statements chosen were numbered 1 to 40 in random order and this number is indicated at the left on pp 363–70.* Those included in the summed 'CAT' score have the letter C added. In three cases (indicated with an asterisk) alterations were made from the *form* of the statement used in the pilot survey. This ensured that there was a negative and a positive statement under each item in cases where the two out of the four statements with the best phi coefficients were polarised in the same direction. In another case (under 1c, Value for staff) the two positive statements (serial Nos 9 and 12) were combined to produce statement No. 21.

Sampling and response rates

Of the ten ex-CATs eight became Technological Universities, and their calendars for 1970–71 showed a total of 2,652 staff in post. The two others (Chelsea and Cardiff) became constituent Colleges of the Universities of London and Wales, with staff numbering 210 and 249 respectively.

Since the influence of senior staff on Senate and Council is likely to be disproportionate in relation to their numerical strength, it was argued that the sample receiving the questionnaire should be weighted in order to make the absolute numbers of responses from all ranks of staff reasonably comparable. Thus a structured sample to give approximately 1 in 5 overall (20 per cent) was drawn from the alphabetical lists of each institution (in 1971) by taking approximately 1 in 2 of the Professors (50 per cent), 1 in 4 Readers, senior lecturers and research staff (25 per cent) and 1 in 7 lecturers (14 per cent). Table AIV1 sets out the numbers at risk by institution and rank; the numbers included in the stratified random sample and the response rates. The middle column under each rank indicates how faithfully the sampling followed this pattern. The overall response

* cf. the final questionnaire.

Table AIV1 Sampling and response rates by institution and rank

Institution	Professors			Readers and senior lecturers			Lecturers			Research staff			Totals		
	Nt	Ns	Nr	Nt	Ns	Nr	Nt	Ns	Nr	Nt	Ns	Nr	Nt	Ns	Nr
ASTON	36	18	16	97	22	12	268	40	27	33	8	5	434	88	60
$\frac{Ns \times 100}{Nt}$ $\frac{Nr \times 100}{Ns}$	50	89		22	57		15	68		24	63		20	70	
$\frac{Nr \times 100}{Nt}$	44			12			10			15			14		
BATH	21	11	9	50	12	4	175	29	16	11	3	1	257	55	30
$\frac{Ns \times 100}{Nt}$ $\frac{Nr \times 100}{Ns}$	52	82		24	33		17	55		27	33		21	55	
$\frac{Nr \times 100}{Nt}$	43			8			9			9			12		
BRADFORD	35	19	11	82	17	14	275	41	17	19	5	2	411	82	44
$\frac{Ns \times 100}{Nt}$ $\frac{Nr \times 100}{Ns}$	54	58		21	82		15	42		26	40		20	54	
$\frac{Nr \times 100}{Nt}$	31			17			6			11			11		
BRUNEL	20	10	7	37	9	8	140	20	14	8	2	2	205	41	31
$\frac{Ns \times 100}{Nt}$ $\frac{Nr \times 100}{Ns}$	50	70		24	89		14	70		25	100		20	76	
$\frac{Nr \times 100}{Nt}$	35			22			10			25			15		
Institution	Nt	Ns	Nr	Nt	Ns	Nr	Nt	Ns	Nr	Nt	Ns	Nr	Nt	Ns	Nr
CITY	19	11	9	80	17	9	206	31	15	4	1	1	309	60	34
$\frac{Ns \times 100}{Nt}$ $\frac{Nr \times 100}{Ns}$	58	82		21	53		15	48		25	100		19	57	
$\frac{Nr \times 100}{Nt}$	47			11			7			25			11		
LOUGHBOROUGH	36	18	7	53	12	8	181	26	14	22	6	2	292	62	31
$\frac{Ns \times 100}{Nt}$ $\frac{Nr \times 100}{Ns}$	50	39		23	67		14	54		27	33		21	50	
$\frac{Nr \times 100}{Nt}$	19			15			8			9			11		
SALFORD	24	12	8	74	17	12	317	48	25	36	9	nil	451	86	45
$\frac{Ns \times 100}{Nt}$ $\frac{Nr \times 100}{Ns}$	50	67		23	71		15	52		25	nil		19	52	
$\frac{Nr \times 100}{Nt}$	33			16			8			nil			10		
SURREY	25	13	11	71	16	9	189	27	17	8	2	1	293	58	38
$\frac{Ns \times 100}{Nt}$ $\frac{Nr \times 100}{Ns}$	52	85		23	56		14	63		25	50		20	66	
$\frac{Nr \times 100}{Nt}$	44			13			9			12·5			13		
SUB-TOTAL	216	112	78	544	122	76	1,751	262	145	141	36	14	2,652	532	313
$\frac{Ns \times 100}{Nt}$ $\frac{Nr \times 100}{Ns}$	52	70		22	63		15	55		26	39		20	59	
$\frac{Nr \times 100}{Nt}$	36			14			8			10			12		

	Professors			Readers and senior lecturers			Lecturers			Research staff			Totals		
CHELSEA	18	9	6	33	9	4	140	20	12	13	4	nil	210	42	22
$\frac{Ns \times 100}{Nt}$ $\frac{Nr \times 100}{Ns}$		50	67		23	44		14	60		31	nil		20	52
$\frac{Nr \times 100}{Nt}$			33			10			9			nil			11
UWIST	19	10	9	45	10	5	181	27	19	4	1	1	249	48	34
$\frac{Ns \times 100}{Nt}$ $\frac{Nr \times 100}{Ns}$		53	90		22	50		15	70		25	100		19	71
$\frac{Nr \times 100}{Nt}$			47			11			11			25			14
GRAND TOTAL	253	131	93	628	141	85	2,072	309	176	158	41	15	3,111	622	369
$\frac{Ns \times 100}{Nt}$ $\frac{Nr \times 100}{Ns}$		52	71		21	61		15	57		26	37		20	60
$\frac{Nr \times 100}{Nt}$			37			14			8			9			12

Key: Nt = Total number of staff included in the sampling ('T' sample).
Ns = Number in stratified random sampling ('S' sample).
Nr = Number responding ('R' sample).

	6 institutions	4 institutions
Respondents	206	163
Non-respondents	181	70

Chi Sq. = 16·43.   p < 0·00001.

was 60 per cent* which provided a respondent sample of 12 per cent of the total at risk.

In relation to response rates the institutions readily divide into two groups – above average and below. Four taken together give an average response of 70 per cent distributed between figures of 66 and 76 per cent, and rates for the other six ranged from 50 to 59 with an average of 53 per cent. Such an order of difference is very unlikely to have arisen by chance.

Differential response rates by rank can also be read off from Table AIv1 in the third column under each rank. Thus for Professors it ranged from 90 per cent to 39 per cent with 71 per cent on average; senior staff 65 per cent (range 89 to 33) and lecturers 57 per cent (range 70 to 42).

Sampling according to the four 'period of appointment' groups was impossible in an anonymous enquiry but we were able to check

* Response rate for the Halsey and Trow study was 51 per cent (see p. 509).

Table AIV2 Staff percentages by institution in 1971 and 1972*

Institution	1971 percentages	1972 percentages
Aston	*13·9*	*12·6*
Bath	*8·3*	*8·2*
Bradford	*13·2*	*13·5*
Brunel	*6·6*	*7·1*
City	*9·9*	*10·3*
Loughborough	*9·4*	*8·8*
Salford	*14·5*	*14·9*
Surrey	*9·4*	*9·5*
SUB-TOTAL	*85·2*	*84·9*
Chelsea	*6·8*	*6·8*
UWIST	*8·0*	*8·3*
GRAND TOTAL	*100*	*100*
N	3,111	3,037

Note: * cf. Table 8.3.

Table AIV3 Response by period of appointment in relation to staff in post in 1972

		Period of appointment					
		O	I	II	III	TOTALS	TOTALS (1971)
Staff in post 1972 Nt 1972	N	370	773	740	1,167	3,037	3,111 (Nt 1971)
Nr 1971	N	40	92	83	154	369	(369)
$\frac{Nr \times 100}{Nt\ 1972}$	Col. %	*11*	*12*	*11*	*13*	*12*	$\left(\frac{369 \times 100}{3,111}\right)$ $=12$

the respondent sample (Nr) against the numbers in the ten institutions a year later, i.e. in 1972.* Table AIV2 shows the distribution of staff by institution in 1971 (the date of the enquiry) and 1972.

The total figures for each year are very similar, so the respondent sample (Nr = 369) is 12 per cent of the 1972 figures also. In Table AIV3 Nr for each period group is compared with the total numbers

* See Chapter 8 for details.

in these groups in 1972 (Nt 1972) and the inter-group variation is no more than one integer either side of the average – a highly satis-factory outcome confirming that the respondent sample was ade-quately representative of the four groups.

Among the 369* questionnaires returned the response to Part II – the 40 statements – was not total and 11 scripts were excluded altogether from the analysis for this reason. The remaining 358* re-spondents omitted to respond to an occasional item in the Group Y statements, so that the 14 tables embodying these results show minor variations for the value of N. Responses to the Group X state-ments – the Attitude Inventory – had to be summed to give a total score, a constraint which reduced the total of usable scripts to 350.*

Presentation of results

Most of the results derived from the questionnaire are presented in the appropriate chapters in the main text. Those relating to the Attitude Inventory are divided between this Appendix and Chapter 8† where high-scoring responses, i.e. 'CAT' scores, are analysed in detail for 10 of the 12 attitude statements. The two relating to arts faculties are dealt with below.‡ Tables AIV4 to 7 record overall differences in mean 'CAT' scores according to: period of appoint-ment; institution; rank and subject group for the eight University institutions only. Results from Chelsea and UWIST are recorded separately.

The analysis by period of appointment (Table AIV4) shows the expected reduction in mean level of 'CAT' score with recency of appointment. The differences are small, however, and all are above the median score of 25.

The rank order shown in Table AIV5, compiled from average scores, differs only marginally from that given in Table 8.28 which is derived from the results on individual statements. The relative positions of Aston, Bath and Salford are slightly rearranged. The following four-point division is the best summary of the result:

1. Brunel. 2. Aston, Bath, Loughborough and Salford.
3. Bradford and Surrey. 4. City.

City and Surrey are the new names for two London Polytechnics of

* For the eight Universities only the figures were 313, 303 and 296 respectively.
† Tables 8.24 to 8.27 inclusive.
‡ Table AIV9.

long standing (Northampton and Battersea respectively) which have been considered almost as part of the University of London for many years. At Brunel all courses are run as sandwich courses.

The detailed results reported in Chapter 8 bear out the overall impression from the four tables included here that in 1971 there was still a considerable body of staff continuing to support the four

Table AIV4   Attitude Inventory: Mean 'CAT' scores by period of appointment: 8 Universities only. Range of scores possible: 10–40

Period of appointment	N	%	Mean	Standard deviation	Range of individual scores
O Before August 1956	34	*11·5*	31·7	4·6	19–40
I August 1956–July 1962	72	*24·3*	32·1	4·6	17–40
O + I	106	*35·8*	32·0	4·6	17–40
II August 1962–July 1966	65	*22·0*	28·0	6·3	14–40
III August 1966 onwards	125	*42·2*	27·2	5·8	12–39
II + III	190	*64·2*	27·5	5·8	12–40
TOTAL	296	*100·0*	29·0	5·8	12–40

Notes: Differences between means of not more than 4·6 are not high enough to be statistically significant with such a wide range of scores giving standard deviations of over 4.

All means are however above the median of 25·0, i.e. there are more high scores than low scores on the ten statements and significantly more in the first period compared with the last.

Period O   (N = 34): proportion of high scores 274/340 = 80%
Period III (N = 125): proportion of high scores 706/1,250 = 62%

Chi Sq. = 41·7.   p < 0·00001.   cf. Table 8.29.

concepts linked to sandwich courses and professional training at undergraduate level. On the subject of the Technological Universities retaining a special identity, institutional differences were marked (Table 8.25) and the responses under this head (statements 2 and 13) are the main source of the – quite small – institutional differences evident in Table AIV5 and summarised in the four-point division. Between 60 and 55 per cent of respondents at Surrey and City rejected the idea and at Brunel over 80 per cent supported it.

It can be seen from the final columns of each of the four tables of

Table Aiv5 Attitude Inventory: Mean 'CAT' scores by institution:
8 Universities only

Institution	N	%	Mean	Rank order	Standard deviation	Range of individual scores
Aston	60	*20·3*	29·2	3 =	5·9	12–40
Bath	30	*10·1*	28·7	5	5·4	17–38
Bradford	40	*13·5*	28·3	7	5·4	18–37
Brunel	27	*9·1*	31·4	1	4·1	20–40
City	33	*11·1*	27·8	8	6·9	16–40
Loughborough	29	*9·8*	29·6	2	6·0	15–40
Salford	41	*13·9*	29·2	3 =	6·3	14–38
Surrey	36	*12·2*	28·4	6	4·9	17–38
TOTALS	296	*100·0*	29·0		5·8	12–40

Notes: Mean differences are not statistically significant.

Brunel (N = 29): proportion of high scores 235/290 = 81 %
City   (N = 33): proportion of high scores 204/330 = 62 %

Chi Sq. = 28·19.   p < 0·00001.   cf. Table 8.30.

Table Aiv6 Attitude Inventory: Mean 'CAT' scores by rank:
8 Universities only

Rank	N	%	Mean	Standard deviation	Range of individual scores
Professors	76	*25·7*	29·5	6·4	14–40
Readers and senior lecturers	71	*24·0*	29·9	5·6	12–39
Lecturers	135	*45·6*	28·5	5·7	15–40
Research staff	14	*4·7*	27·6	3·0	22–31
TOTALS	296	*100·0*	29·0	5·8	12–40

Note: There are no significant differences whether calculated on mean scores or
on number of high scores.   cf. Table 8.31.

mean scores that the spread of scores between individuals was large
in every row. More detailed analysis shows that 25 individuals (8·4

Table AIv7 Attitude Inventory: Mean 'CAT' scores by subject group: 8 Universities only

Subject group	N	%	Range of percentages between institutions	Mean	Standard deviation	Range of individual scores
Technology	110	37·2	25 (Bradford)–46 (Salford)	30·7	5·6	15–40
Natural sciences	110	37·2	24 (Loughborough)–47 (Surrey)	29·3	5·5	17–39
Social sciences	56	18·9	7 (Brunel)–23 (Bath)	25·1	5·4	12–40
Others	20	6·7	5 (Aston)–17 (Bath)	29·0	4·2	21–38
TOTALS	296	100·0		29·0	5·8	12–40

Notes: Mean differences are not statistically significant.
Note Social sciences group mean is at the median (25·0), i.e.
Technology (N=110): proportion of high scores 842/1100 =76·5%
Social sciences (N=56): proportion of high scores 301/560 =54·0%

Chi Sq.>90.   p<0.00001.   cf. Table 8.27.

per cent) had very high total scores of 37 to 40 and 24 others (8·1 per cent) had very low ones of 20 and under, which means on the one hand total agreement with the ethos of the CATs and on the other almost total disagreement. As shown in Table AIV8 they fall into the expected pattern: *decreasing* numbers of extreme high scores by recency of appointment and *increasing* numbers of extremely low scores.

No consistent pattern was discernible in relation to rank or subject group. Professors, senior lecturers, technologists, natural scientists and social scientists were to be found in each of the eight cells and lecturers in all but one.

Three Universities – Bath, City and Salford – had considerably more extreme scores at both ends than the other five, suggesting interesting divisions on the campus. The other five – Aston, Bradford, Brunel, Loughborough and Surrey – had fewer extreme scores and a higher proportion of moderate scores of around 30. On one of the

Table AIV8 Proportions of extreme scorers by period of appointment

Period of appointment	N at risk	High scorers 37 upwards		Low scorers 20 downwards	
		N	%	N	%
O	34	5	*15*	1	*3*
I	72	11	*15*	2	*3*
II	65	5	*8*	8	*12*
III	125	4	*3*	13	*10*
TOTALS	296	25	*8·4*	24	*8·1*

'divided' campuses it was possible to find a Department in which two Professors scored below 20 and two lecturers had scores of 37 and 38 respectively. The second had a senior lecturer among the high scorers and a lecturer in the same subject below 20. On the third campus in yet another Department a similar situation obtained this time with the senior member in the low group.

Responses to statements 7 and 25 relating to arts faculties are shown in Table AIV9. The assumption that the staff of the Technological Universities would not favour the establishment of Arts

Table A$_{\text{IV}}$9   Arts Faculties – statements 7 and 25: percentages agreeing with each statement

Groups	N	7. My University should not establish an Arts Faculty %	25. My University would benefit by having an Arts Faculty %
Period of			
appointment O	34	*44*	*54*
I	72	*37*	*62*
II	65	*35*	*68*
III	125	*22*	*77*
Universities			
Aston	60	*45*	*52*
Bath	30	*17*	*87*
Bradford	40	*35*	*65*
Brunel	27	*44*	*56*
City	33	*30*	*73*
Loughborough	29	*31*	*69*
Salford	41	*17*	*83*
Surrey	36	*25*	*64*
Rank			
Professors	76	*41*	*54*
Readers and senior lecturers	71	*37*	*66*
Lecturers	134	*25*	*74*
Research staff	14	*14*	*79*
Subject			
Technology	110	*31*	*66*
Natural sciences	110	*42*	*59*
Social sciences	56	*16*	*82*
Others	20	*20*	*75*
TOTALS	296	*31*	*67*

Faculties was not confirmed. The statements proved to be ambiguous, as none of the institutions has established a traditional Arts Faculty including the classics.

Two other statements (5 and 19) in the staff questionnaire relate

380

to the idea of universal coverage within Universities. Responses to these are presented in Table Aɪv10. Again the assumption that staff would favour specialisation of function within the University system was not confirmed. The differences between the four groups are marked: those in group O saw technology as a more important component to ensure the completeness of a University than arts: those most recently appointed (which included most of the social scientists and 'others') voted firmly for both.

Table Aɪv10 Universal coverage – statements 5 and 19; percentages agreeing with each statement, by period of appointment

	Period of appointment								All respondents	
	O		I		II		III			
	%	N	%	N	%	N	%	N	%	N
5. A University is not complete without a Faculty of Technology.	74	34	72	74	67	67	69	127	70	302
19. A University is not complete without a Faculty of Arts.	53	34	51	73	61	67	80	128	66	302

Chelsea and UWIST

These two institutions differ from the other eight ex-CATs in that they were each incorporated (following Robbins) as constituent Colleges in an existing University – London and Wales respectively. There the similarity ends: in most other respects they were very different. The difference in the spectrum of studies is shown in Table Aɪv11.

Chelsea was misnamed as a College of Advanced Technology – its strength always lay in its Science Faculty, which has now been split into two by the creation of a faculty of medicine with a BPharm. degree at pass and honours levels and including basic medical sciences, i.e. biochemistry, biophysics, human biology, pharmacology and physiology.

The University of Wales Institute of Science and Technology at Cardiff is not so atypical as Chelsea, but it also has its own particular mix of subjects as indicated in Table Aɪv11.

The responses from these two Colleges to the Attitude Inventory are shown in Table Aɪv12.

| Subject areas | Chelsea | | | | UWIST | | | | | |
| | TOTALS[1] | | Respondent sample | | TOTALS[1] | | Respondent sample | | 8 Technological Universities[9] | |
	N	%	N	%	N	%	N	%	N	%
Technology	12[2]	5	1[2]	5	78[5]	31	12	35	110	37
Natural sciences	165[3]	74	16	80	77[6]	30	12	35	110	37
Social sciences	3	1	nil	nil	33[7]	13	3	9	56	19
Others	45[4]	20	3	15	66[8]	26	7	21	20	7
TOTALS	225	100	20	100	254	100	34	100	296	100

Notes: 1. Staff listed in 1972–73 prospectuses.
2. Electronics only.
3. Including 44 in Pharmaceutical Studies.
4. 'Others' (Chelsea) comprise Science Education Centre 33, History and Philosophy of Science 3, Humanities 9.
5. Including 16 in Maritime Studies.
6. Including 28 in Pharmaceutical Studies.
7. Including 13 in Applied Economics.
8. 'Others' (UWIST) comprise Architecture 19, Town Planning 10, Ophthalmic Optics 10, Humanities 17, Law 10.
9. cf. Table AIv7.

The Academic Staff questionnaire

This is the form in which the questionnaire was distributed.

A Study of the Technological Universities

Information for Respondents

This study of the transition of the former Colleges of Advanced Technology to University status also includes an examination of their present state of development, problems and opportunities, and their plans and hopes for the future.

In order to gain an adequate inwardness to the study, I have made two visits totalling 4–6 days at each institution and recorded many

382

	Chelsea			UWIST			8 Universities		
Period of appointment	N	Mean	Range	N	Mean	Range	N	Mean	Range
O	3	29·2	28·5–30*	2	32·0	—	34	31·7	19–40
I	4	24·5	19–30	11	31·9	26–38	72	32·1	17–40
II	4	24·9	23–27	8	29·4	15·5–38	65	28·0	14–40
III	9	27·9	22–35	13	29·5	22–39	125	27·2	12–39
Rank									
Professors	6	24·7	22–29	9	29·3	15·5–37	76	29·5	14–40
Readers and senior lecturers	4	27·9	24·5–30	5	30·6	23–38	71	29·9	12–39
Lecturers	10	27·6	19–35	19	30·7	22–38	135	28·5	15–40
Research staff	—	—	—	1	34·0	—	14	27·6	22–31
Subject group									
Technology	1	35·0	—	12	31·75	15·5–39	110	30·7	15–40
Natural sciences	16	26·0	19–30	12	29·0	22–34	110	29·3	17–39
Social sciences	—	—	—	3	29·3	23–38	56	25·1	12–40
Others	3	28·3	28–29	7	30·9	23·5–38	20	29·0	21–38
TOTALS	20	26·8	19–35	34	30·4	15·5–39	296	29·0	12–40

Note: * In the few cases where an item was ignored, a mark of 2·5 (midway between 1 and 4) was recorded. The reason given was usually lack of experience of sandwich courses.

discussions. In addition, I wish to gather all shades of opinion and variety of background through a random sample of the academic staff in the ten institutions, and I hope that you will kindly co-operate in completing this questionnaire.

The enquiry is on the basis of strict confidentiality; and you are not expected to give your name. The analysis of results will not be in terms of individuals but in broad categories such as age, date of appointment, status, subject taught, etc. I therefore hope that you will feel able to be frank and forthright in your replies. There is a plain final page to the form for any additional comments you may care to make.

The scope of the enquiry goes somewhat beyond the issues raised in the discussions during my visits, and some of the questions in

Part I are taken by permission from the survey of 'The British Academics' by A. H. Halsey and Martin Trow (Faber & Faber, 1971). This is in order to monitor changes since 1965 when the survey was carried out.

A franked addressed envelope is enclosed for your reply, which it would be most helpful to have as soon as possible, and in any case within fourteen days of receiving the enquiry.

With thanks,
(signed) Peter Venables.

Part I

[As noted for Questionnaire 1 and Questionnaire 2 an ellipsis . . . indicates that an appropriate space was left in the original for the response.]

Code nos.

1. Serial number . . .   (1) (2) (3) (4)

2. Date of first appointment to your institution . . .   (5)

3. What was your initial rank? . . . (L, SL, etc.)   (6)

4. What is your present rank? . . .   (7)

5. Present department (the one in which you primarily work) . . .   (8)

6. Date of birth . . .   (9)

7. Sex *Male* / *Female* (Tick)   (10)

8. Marital status
   Single / *Married* / *Widowed* : *Divorced* (Tick) (11)

9. Previous appointments.
   Please list in chronological order in the manner shown below the sectors in which you have held full-time appointments. In the University sector please give the grade of each full-time post, and the name of the University. For posts in the other sectors the name of the post need not be given, and successive posts should be aggregated.

   List of sectors: Indicate by letter in column one below.
   A. *University: full-time research posts*; B. *University: other posts*; C. *College of Education*; D. *Further Education College*; E. *School teaching*; F. *Nationalised industry*, (i) *Research and develop-*

ment, (ii) *Other*; G. *Private industry and commerce*, (i) *Research and development*, (ii) *Other*; H. *Civil Service*, (i) *Research and development*, (ii) *Other*; I. *Local Authority*; J. *Professional institution – full-time staff*; K. *H.M. Forces*; L. *Other – specify*

---

*Sector   Dates   Name of institution Grade (of any
letter   from – to and country   teaching post)*   (12)
[Then followed eight lines of ruled boxes for entering details.]

---

10. Secondary education
    Type of school *Direct grant* 1 | *Grammar* 2 | *Technical* 3 | *Modern* 4 | *Public* 5 | *Other – specify* 6
    (Ring)   (13)

11. Age of leaving school . . .

12. Qualifications; state the year when obtained and whether study was A. *full-time*; B. *sandwich type*; C. *block release*; D. *part-time*   (14)

---

*Qualifi-   Subjects   Year   Type of study
cations   obtained   A B C D (Tick)*   (15) (16) (17)

[The thirteen subdivisions that follow were set out in tabular form under the headings given above.]

    (i) *O-levels or equivalent*; (ii) *A-levels or equivalent*; (iii) *O N C*; (iv) *O N D*; (v) *H N C*; (vi) *H N D*; (vii) *Other certificates or diplomas: specify*; (viii) *First degree(s)*; (ix) *Higher degree(s)*; (x) *Associateship(s)*; (xi) *Fellowship(s)*; (xii) *Other higher awards*; (xiii) *Post-experience courses (e.g. management, etc.)*

Comment here if you wish . . .

13. Do your own interests lie primarily in teaching or in research?   (18)
    Very heavily in research   (Ring) 1
    In both, but with a leaning towards research 2
    In both, but with a leaning towards teaching 3
    Very heavily in teaching   4

N   385

14. What are the major handicaps that you experience
    in carrying on research?   (19)

	(Ring)
I experience no major handicaps	1
Insufficient time because of teaching commitments	2
Insufficient time because of commitments other than teaching	3
Insufficient financial resources	4
Slowness of machinery for obtaining equipment and/or books, etc.	5
Insufficient contact with other workers in your field	6
Insufficiencies in your library	7
Unresponsiveness of your departmental or College administration to your needs	8
Other: specify . . .	9

    Comment . . .

15. Do you feel under pressure to do more research
    than you would actually like to do? *Yes, a lot* 1 /
    Yes, a little 2 / *No* 3 (Ring)   (20)

16. Apart from time, are the resources available to
    you (library space, technical assistance, etc.) ade-
    quate for the kind of scholarly or scientific research
    you are doing? *Excellent* 1 / *Adequate* 2 / *Some-
    what inadequate* 3 / *Highly inadequate* 4 (Ring) (21)

17. Are you able to carry on research during term?
    A substantial part of it 1 / *Only a little of it* 2 /
    Almost none 3 (Ring)   (22)

18. Did you have leave of absence while on the staff
    of a CAT? *Yes/No* (Tick)   (23)
    If yes, for how long? *One term or less / Between
    one and three terms / Three terms or more* (Tick)
    Where did you spend it? . . .
    What did you do during your leave? . . .
    Who paid? . . .

19. Have you had leave of absence since 1966 at this
    or any other Technological University (i.e. ex-

CAT)? *Yes | No* (Tick)   (24)
If yes, for how long? *One term or less | Between
one and three terms | Three terms or more* (Tick)
Where did you spend it? ...
What did you do during your leave? ...
Who paid? ...

20. Since gaining your first academic appointment,
    have you ever considered leaving academic life
    permanently? *No | Yes, have given it serious con-
    sideration | Yes, considered it, but not seriously |
    Would consider an industrial post* (Tick)   (25)
    Comment ...

21. Have you ever held office in a national or inter-
    national academic, learned or professional
    society? *Yes | No* (Tick)   (26)

22. How many academic articles have you published?
    None 0 | *1–4* 1 | *5–10* 2 | *10–20* 3 | *More than 20* 4
    (Ring)   (27)
    Year latest article was published ...

23. Have you written a book which was published?
    Yes | No (Tick)   (28)
    If so, how many? ...

24. Are you preparing a book for publication?
    Yes | No (Tick)   (29)

25. Have you been abroad for primarily professional
    and scholarly reasons during the past twelve
    months, e.g. lecturing, conferences, etc.? *Yes |
    No* (Tick)   (30)
    If yes, how many times? ...

26. Are there any public activities outside your
    University that take up an appreciable amount of
    your time? *Yes | No* (Tick)   (31)
    If yes, would you care to state what they are? ...

27. (i) What is (was) your father's occupation? Please
    be as specific as possible: e.g., if a teacher, at what
    level of education? ...   (32)
    (ii) Is (was) he self-employed or an employee?
    Self-employed | Employee (Tick)   (33)

28. What was the age at which your parents left
    school? Ring as follows: (34)

	13 or younger	14	15	16	17	18 or older	Don't know
Mother	1	2	3	4	5	6	7
Father	1	2	3	4	5	6	7

29. Did either have any higher education? *Yes | No*
    (Tick)   (35)

	Mother	Father
University (where)	...	...
Other higher education (kind)	...	...

30. (For married men) Is your wife a University
    graduate? *Yes | No* (Tick)   (36)
    Other qualifications ...

31. Do you have any children of secondary school age
    or older? *Yes | No* (Tick)   (37)
    If yes, indicate type of education:

Age	Sex	Type of secondary education	Type of further education (if University, which?)	(38)

[Then followed seven lines of ruled boxes for entering details.]

[Fifteen extra code nos.
(39–53) were allowed for on
the actual form at this
point.]

Part II

This section consists of a list of statements with which you are asked
to agree or disagree on a four-point scale, viz:
AA, *Agree firmly*; A, *Agree on the whole*; D, *Disagree on the whole*;
DD, *Disagree firmly*.
There is no column for 'not certain'; this is deliberate. In practical
situations, choices are forced upon us and you are asked to say where
you would stand in the last resort.
[On the actual form four columns, headed AA to DD were provided at the
right-hand side for showing responses by ticks.]

Statements

1. The advantages of sandwich courses do not justify the extra difficulties involved in arranging them.

2. After a year in a job the three-year trained engineering graduate is indistinguishable from a four-year sandwich course graduate.

3. The three or four undergraduate years should be mainly devoted to becoming thoroughly competent in one subject.

4. The status differences in Britain between Professors, lecturers and teachers are outmoded.

5. A University is not complete without a Faculty of Technology.

6. It would be bad for technological education in this country if the ex-CATs lost their special identity.

7. My University should not establish an Arts Faculty.

8. With respect to the wider education of University students, some courses and/or seminars on non-professional subjects should be compulsory.

9. Promotion in academic life is too dependent on published work.

10. We have by no means reached the limit of able young people who could benefit by a University education.

11. Undergraduates should not specialise in one subject only.

12. Non-University forms of higher education should be expanded, leaving the Universities as they are.

13. The ex-CATs should not aim to preserve a distinctive role for themselves in the university world.

14. An academic man's first loyalty should be to research in his discipline.

15. Successful research in my subject requires teams of full-time research workers.

16. Most British University departments would be better run by the method of circulating chairmanship than by a permanent Head of Department.

17. The use in Britain of the title 'Professor' for most university teachers, as is done in America, would be a retrograde step.

18. The argument that professional training should be provided within the overall period of undergraduate study is a sound one.

N*

19. A University is not complete without a Faculty of Arts.

20. The student committed to a particular career should not be expected to do a general degree.

21. Supervisory visits to sandwich course students in training are advantageous to staff in their academic work.

22. The single-subject honours degree is ideal for the student with a vocational commitment.

23. Professional studies in, for example, management and economics should be introduced at the undergraduate stage.

24. In my subject I have no problem in combining good teaching with effective research.

25. My University would benefit by having an Arts Faculty.

26. A serious disadvantage of Redbrick Universities is that they are all too often run by a professorial oligarchy.

27. University teachers should concentrate on teaching their speciality and leave students to look after the wider aspects of their education themselves.

28. Local or regional mergers between all forms of higher education would be advantageous.

29. Management education and/or similar professional studies should be delayed until after graduation.

30. The establishment of the Polytechnics is a great mistake.

31. The distinguishing feature of the University don is his ability as a research worker.

32. Industry and commerce have a great need for graduates who have had a sandwich course type of training.

33. There should be more academics in Universities whose main commitment is to teaching.

34. The supervision of industrial periods on sandwich courses is a waste of academic staff time and needs a special establishment of non-academics.

35. The Technological Universities would be losing their greatest asset if they abandoned sandwich courses.

36. The creation of the Polytechnics is a good answer to the problems of expansion in higher education.

37. The Technological Universities should not continue to include General Studies in their degree courses.

38. There is no overriding argument for the provision of supervised practical training during the period of a degree course.

39. In relation to University expansion 'more' *does* mean 'worse'.

40. The education of a technologist is incomplete if he is not given the opportunity of disciplined study in the Arts or Social Sciences during his undergraduate years.

[A final, blank, page was provided headed as follows:]

Your views on the present state of development of the Technological Universities, their problems and opportunities and their plans for the future will be very welcome.

List of Tables, Diagrams and Graphs

List of Tables, Diagrams and Graphs

List of diagrams and graphs

Name Index

Abercrombie, M. L. J., 152
Acton, Lord, 12
Adamson, Colin, 250, 252
Alexander, Sir William/Lord, 223
Allen, D. A., 153
Alport, Lord, 327
Annan, Noel/Lord, 219, 223, 224, 283, 308
Archer, Margaret S., 224
Argles, Michael, 33
Armitage, Sir Arthur, 270
Armitage, Peter, 281
Armytage, W. H. G., 16, 33, 61, 90
Arrowsmith, H., 341
Ashby, Eric/Lord, 14, 33, 73, 81, 90, 153, 155, 196, 224, 276, 277, 285
Astle, D., 250
Atkinson, Richard, 76

Bailey, F. G., 60
Baldridge, J. V., 60
Balerno, Lord, 340
Ball, R. J., 251
Banfield, Tom, 92
Barber, Revis, 322
Barratt, Sir Sydney, 320, 321
Barzun, Jacques, 196
Bawn, C. E. H., 323
Beard, Ruth M., 152
Bearden, Colin, 224
Bellamy, Dennis, 322
Berdahl, R. O., 60, 126, 196, 281
Berrill, Sir Kenneth, 284
Billing, D. F., 251
Bills, Sarah, 253
Binyon, M., 90
Birkbeck, George, 329
Black, A. N., 254
Blackburn, R., 225

Blackstone, Tessa, 196, 197, 224
Blain, Mr Justice, 224
Blaug, M., 155, 281
Bleakley, Lesley, 250
Bligh, Donald A., 151
Bloom, B. S., 152
Bolton, J. E., 122, 333
Bond-Williams, N. I., 318
Bottomley, J. A., 285
Bowden, B. V./Lord, 91, 221
Box, S., 126
Boyle, Edward/Lord, 249, 250
Bragg, S. L., 222, 325
Brancher, David, 88
Braun, F., 90
Brechin, Sir Herbert, 340
Brentnall, John, 10
Briault, Eric, 255
Briggs, Asa/Lord, 90, 283
Broady, Maurice, 152
Brooks, Glenn E., 284
Brosan, George, 255, 256
Brothers, Joan, 223
Brown, A. J., 267
Brown, Wilfred B. D./Lord, 324
Brunel, I. K., 324
Bruner, J. S., 152
Buchanan, R. A., 341
Bullock, Sir Alan/Lord, 155, 285
Bullough, G., 336
Burgess, Tyrell, 33, 126, 249, 253, 256, 282, 310
Burgliarello, George, 92
Burlin, T., 252
Burnett, George Murray, 341
Butcher, H. J., 151, 152, 196
Butler, Clifford, 329
Butler, R. A./Lord, 91, 307
Butterworth, B., 153

397

Subject Index